JOURNEY TO BROTHERHOOD

Awakening, Healing, and Connecting Men's Hearts

FRANK D. CARDELLE, Ph.D.

With a Foreword by
YEVRAH ORNSTEIN

GARDNER PRESS

New York • Sydney • London

Foreign orders except Canada, South America, Australia, and New Zealand to:
  Afterhurst Limited
  27 Palmeira Mansions
  Church Road, Hove,
  East Sussex BN3 2FA, England

Orders for Australia and New Zealand to:
  Astam Books
  27B, Llewellyn Street
  Balmain, N.S.W., Australia

LIBRARY OF CONGRESS
Library of Congress Cataloging-in-Publication Data

Cardelle, Frank D.
  Journey to Brotherhood:
  Awakening, Healing and Connecting Mens Hearts
  and brotherhood / Frank D. Cardelle
      p.   cm.
  Bibliography: p.
  ISBN 0-89876-153-0
  1. Men — United States — Psychology. 2. Sex role — United States.
  3. Masculinity (Psychology)   I. Title.
  HQ1090.3.C37 1989
  305.3'1 — dc19   88-11701 CIP

"It is hard to grow up when existing facts are treated as though they do not exist. For there is no dialogue; it is impossible to be taken seriously, to understand, **to make a bridge between oneself and society.**"

Paul Goodman, **Growing Up Absurd**

"A great man is he who has not lost the heart of a child."

Mencius

Dedication

This book is dedicated to the young male and female children throughout the world. The young seeds of creation who have a chance to learn to live in this world as a global human family, in co-existence, co-operation and co-creation as beset by nature's will; not man's.

I further dedicate this book to my father, my step-father and my two brothers. Each of you has been a very important link in my recycling. Though much of our contact was painful and harsh, today I can see how this is the fertilizer for my growth.

Acknowledgements

It is hard to write a book without the support, influence and assistance from so many others. In my travels I have met many people, befriended many more and carry their shared expressions with me. While I can't remember all of these I would like to thank the following people who have been my friends, colleagues and teachers, who have supported my growth and have been part of the culmination of this book either personally or professionally. Those I don't mention are still close to my heart with much thanks.

These people were: Dr. Tony Stickel, Virginia Satir, Al Bauman, Phil Lane Jr., John Eagle Day, Dr. Terry Burrows, Dr. Ed Elkin, Christina Fowler, Michael Tacon, Dr. Ghram Moore, Hal Milton, Grey Wolf and Jeannie Eagle Swinney, Peter Smith, Darrell Butler, Renn Butler, Maggi Dywer, Roger Paine,- Jaelene Jaffe, Barbara Jacoletti, Janet Telford, Denis Hamel, Andre Lord, Kim Chemerika, Rose Davis, Jeannie Harris, Pat Johnson, Peter Hagn, Donna Fazan, Kathleen Peshala, Wim Rasing, Lucia Mouktar, Dr. Lazslo and Margot Honti, Dr. Josef Paradi, Dr. Josef Telkes, Ilona Ban, Bruce Meyers, Dr. Patricia Veleminska, Drs. Mirek and Eva Hoferik, Dr. Octavio Geraldo Neira, Dr. Graceila Aldana, Nancy Otero, Dr. Maria Franco, Zsuzsa Csoscar, Michele and Afra Harlacker, Dieter Smidth, Otto and Sabina Richter, Dr. John Rafael Staude, Helgarde Dillion, Sibylle Sulser, Claudia and Guiedo and Stephan Presselmyer.

Thanks to my publisher Gardner Spungin and his staff who worked along with me in editing, proofing and bringing this book to its birth. Also thanks to the readers who have consented to have their names and comments on the cover of the book.

Lastly, a special and warm appreciation to my good friend George Neufeld who offered his support, energy and home to me during my extensive traveling. A true gesture of Brotherhood.

Foreword

Frank and I met, so to speak, several years ago while I was publisher of *The Men's Journal*, a quarterly publication where men speak from their hearts about being a man today. I say "so to speak" because I met Frank through the written word in the form of letters. We became "pen pals," an old fashioned phrase, perhaps a bit corny, but then again there's something quaint and appropriate about it.

A year had come and gone since the first men's gathering I had attended and *The Men's Journal* was about to put out its first anniversary issue. I felt aflame with the desire to share the passionate movement I was experiencing in the company and companionship of other men — fellowship of brothers exploring, questioning, attempting to redefine this most peculiar, at times troublesome, and precious thing we call masculinity. I was and am a fellow traveller in this journey to brotherhood.

One day a letter arrived from Canada with warm words that went something like, "Hello out there! I too am a searcher and a seeker!" Frank also wrote to tell me of his excitement over having seen *The Men's Journal*, and to be that kind of friend, that kind of kindred spirit that says YES to expressions of positive change.

So began our friendship, one that crossed a national border, unhampered by physical distance and unencumbered by politics. Frank submitted an article that I ran in the early days entitled, "Face To Face." Perhaps one of the most complimentary rewards I could pass along to him was the response from a woman who wept as she read it.

"Face To Face" speaks from the heart, graphically and vividly. It's the story of a boy's painful introduction and indoctrination into "being a man." The boy was Frank Cardelle. This modern day rite of pseudo-passage set the stage for the rules of today's game and grants the reader insights into the sadness and tragedy of our elder's notion of manhood as passed along from father to son, as they too were the recipients of this flawed and damaged legacy.

That reader's tears possess the seeds, the potential, to begin the healing so many of us are in need of today.

I was glad to see this same story in the beginning of *Journey To Brotherhood*.

Within a year I received another article from Frank along with intermittent letters that have since kept our friendship alive and well. What I noticed more than anything else in Frank's writing was his emphasis and valuation of men supporting men concomitant with his eye upon a deeper healing between men and women. He had taken that extra step that we all need to take, the one that awaits us and will eventually blossom into a global flowering of true humanity unlimited by conventional delineations of sexual roles and definitions.

In his letters to me, Frank usually closed with "In brotherhood," which brought back memories of something Richard Bach wrote in his book *Illusions*, something quite wonderful —

The bond that links your true family
is not one of blood,
but of respect and joy
in each other's life.

Rarely do members of one family
grow up under the same roof.

I loved that aphorism when I first read it and I still do. Frank is indeed family on the journey to brotherhood and a person who actively champions love and respect and joy for all.

I finished his book in the morning, reading the last pages in a light drizzle while walking with my dog-friends to the post office to pick up the mail.

I am honored to be asked to write this foreword and a bit unsure of what to highlight.

As I was reading, it occurred to me that among the most prevalent words in this work — human, soul, heart, and feelings — appear often throughout the chapters.

There's good reason why these words appear as often as they do for this book is an expression of spirit, of spirituality that transcends notions of limited identity and reveals the author's deep desire for healing and alliance.

I like the overview and historical context this book provides. It puts today's gender-related symptoms, maladies and manifestations into a recognizable landscape that has the potential to stimulate the reader into understanding, empathy and action. *Journey To Brotherhood* is indeed a call to action for this is very much of who Frank is. In his own words;

People who want change
must be the agents of that desire.

Desire and change come together as one in this book. I feel a sympatico here with Frank because it is one of my own biases; the enacting and translation of dreams into action, the need and proclivity to implement ideas and values into the everyday world of here and now.

Journey To Brotherhood is a road map of sorts. In this time of rapid change and widespread confusion road maps, suggestions for change and guidelines into comprehension are much needed and appreciated. This work is a journey in and of itself. It is an exploration into the past where the roots of cultural definitions of gender emerged, and is today's imbalances within society. Guidelines for change are provided and a vision of a more fulfilling tomorrow are elucidated. No easy task, by any means.

In thinking back upon its many pages I wondered what I could say about *Journey To Brotherhood* without writing a mini-novel of my own, that would be of value to its readers.

I have been actively involved with the men's movement since 1983 and in that time I have been privileged to touch and be touched by many men. More often than not our healing involves allowing a great deal of suppressed pain, and at times anger, to surface. I have known my share and have felt changed for the freedom to be authentic in the company of other men. The need to give voice to anguish, at times frustration or joy, can be transformative.

When men are free to explore and give voice to their feelings without shame and guilt, the stage is set for movement. Rigidity is all too often a consequence of our collective dilemma. We men drop dead from illnesses of the *heart*. Heart attacks (hardened arteries that choke off the very breath of life, oxygen), kill men more than any other disease today. Is it simply a coincidence that we die of a disease of the heart more than any other illness? Our hearts are indeed hardened, constricted into non-feeling. Herein lies a major aspect of the problem.

Frank's contribution is his focus upon the heart and his sincere desire for a deeper union, in all ways. There is good reason this book's sub-titled, for the emphasis IS upon *Awakening and Healing Men's Hearts*.

I was stretched and prodded and nudged in reading this book. I know that readers of *Journey To Brotherhood* will find those passages that speak to them personally and profoundly. No matter how large or small, I believe there's something of worth here for everyone.

In my time as publisher of the Journal, I very much welcomed women into its readership because as we get to know more about one another, we amplify the potential towards reconciliation and enhance a progression towards deeper value fulfillment. I hope this book finds its way into the hands and hearts of many men and women.

In closing, I exerpt from Frank's own summation:

Separately and together, men and women need to create new and re-defined ways to contact one another and deepen their communication and understanding. Men still need to know more about the world of women on a much deeper level and women need to expand their understanding about men's processes.

A unified effort to explore similarities and differences and tap the sub-stance of this combination of talents and energy will benefit both who go beyond the separatists' fragmented ideas of male and female and move closer to a recognition of the human being. Once we recognize the human element first, the male or female qualities and differences will spring from this in a more healthy integrated way.

I thank Frank for going beyond the urgency and rewards of men support-ing men. The fullness and beauty of this book lies in its broader sense of humanity.

Yevrah Ornstein
The Men's Journal
P.O. Box 545
Woodacre, CA 94973

PREFACE

Re-newal   Re-construction   Re-creation

This book is my contribution to the beginning of the new male journey. It is a blueprint , a map, that can help point the way for men to discover and deepen the purpose and meaning of their own journeys as men. It shows how to plot a new course through the winding rivers and clogged pathways of our male psyche so that we can begin to shape our lives and identities from the totality of our male energy pools.

Today, the spirit of our brotherhood is awakening within us, challenging us to listen to the message. For many men who lack the necessary guide-posts, this awakening is frightening and threatening. For others, these stirrings herald a long-awaited celebration and the birth of a new way which will free us from centuries of conditioning that have imprisoned us. They can anticipate the movement toward a greater and fuller existence as men.

As the author, I serve as the navigator on this journey, guiding us through the threatening and rough waters of our male inheritance, offering some alternatives that can assist in broadening our focus and redefining our skills and wisdom as we relearn how to sail through the stormy seas of our present intense, penetrating changes.

In writing this book, I have served in a dual capacity. While acting as navigator, I am also a participant on this journey. I share many of my own experiences of growing into manhood, many of which were painful and frightening. I believe, however, that by being vulnerable I am modeling a way that other men can identify with and use. More men need to know how to become vulnerable in healthy and positive ways without using typical male patterns of protection to prevent domination or control from other men, or being fearful that other males will view our vulnerability as being "sissy" or weak. I am risking being seen and heard from a much deeper, more trans-parent level and by doing so, I am assisting my own healing and renewal. Drawing from my own journey and those of others experienced during my personal and professional career, I present ideas, offer suggestions and tools that men can use to further their own journeys and to help others who are beginning to look at their own. I also believe that this will be of help to women who are attempting to more fully understand the male journey. Both sexes have inherited scripts that make us enemies of each other. We need to work together to help heal the wounds we have received.

This book is presented in three parts, the first of which deals with familiar learnings and roles that comprise the outdated 'Old Male Image.' Here I explore the origins of our male identities, travelling back to when we first entered this physical world and focusing on the crisis of these times. In this chapter I bring to light the terrible cost of our 'masculine warrior training' showing how it has become the greatest, most destructive aspect of our cultural child rearing practices. Men are primed from infancy to fight the conflicts of the military-industrial complex and our education is governed by the accepted economic foreign policies of our nation.

I believe that the present danger of the arms race with the Soviets is a mere play-back of all the old tapes and rituals that are part of a battlefront consciousness with which men have been involved for centuries. Thus, our present world crisis is an extension of the deadly, overly used style of handling human conflicts and ideological difference reflected in the old attitude that might is right!

Chapters two and three explore the extent of our masculine training, depicting false inherited images and showing how many of these learnings contribute to the decay and demise of males in our society. It is through this learning that we begin to lose the deep connections to our true male energy and power, thus losing the balance, integrity and purpose of our lives as men. I believe that if we are able to see the whole picture of our life journey we will need to view the destructive, unhealthy messages heard during our beginnings and only then can we filter through those messages of destruction that continue to harness and limit us.

The second section of the book focuses more directly on the transition phase so many are experiencing today. Here I have outlined some alternative directions and strategies we can use in turning our defensive postures into more open, healthy ways of improving our relationships with other men. I offer suggestions that can be employed in learning how to regain our strength and intelligence as whole functioning human beings. I address some social, economic and political issues and provide a prescription for becoming a vital male who possesses passion, a depth of spirit and a commitment to humanity.

My vision of what **we** can become and are evolving towards is discussed in the third and final part of the book. Here I offer solutions that can aid growth and change through stronger organization, purpose, vision and the creation of support systems for men. Survival of the transition in which we are currently engaged cannot be accomplished alone. It is time to develop a strong unified spirit of Brotherhood and be an active participant in the blossoming of this emerging spirit. We must also join with women as our allies and place the survival of our planet as the number one priority. The vision of what our society can and will be, will be determined by actions we choose today, together and separately.

This book has been painful for me to write, however, much of what I have learned about myself as a male and my journey has been profound. I sincerely hope that in a small way, my efforts and commitment in writing this book and travelling this path, will be beneficial to those of you who read it and make the journey.

A Fellow Traveller
Frank Cardelle

I would suggest that the reader move through this book in a way that suits your interest and readiness. It is not necessary to read it from cover to cover. If you desire to read portions or chapters that catch your eye first, please do so. Trust this urge as it will guide you through portions of the book that will enable you to become connected to the areas that match your desires and openess. Make the reading a personal project and begin where you are ready to begin.

I have found that completing some of the exercises in Chapter Eight makes the reading more relevant and personal. You can choose this as one way to get into the book and complete the journey. Do not treat the book as a textbook, but more as a creative process that in some way is common to your own.

JOURNEY TO BROTHERHOOD: AWAKENING, HEALING, AND CONNECTING MEN'S HEARTS

OLD MALE IMAGE

TRANSITION AND TRANSFORMATION

Brotherhood. . .
I sought my soul, but
my soul I could not see
I sought my God but
My God eluded me,
I sought my brother
and found all three. . .

FACE TO FACE

Introduction

I had just arrived home from the diamond, after pitching two grueling hours in the Pee Wee Championship game. Despite our best playing of the season, our overwhelming enthusiasm and playing an extra tie-breaker inning, we lost by one point. I had longed for this day and this victory. We had trained hard and played hard. The thought of losing, after gaining a substantial lead in the series, never entered our minds. The coach told us to get out there and play our best. The parents and others in the community who came out to support our winning streak, were who we were really playing for. We wanted victory because they wanted us to win. I felt particularly important as the pitcher and leader of the team to those who were counting on me. Each time I sent the ball across the plate and the umpire called out "Steeeer-ike," the tension in my shoulders lessened. I was the 'shoulders' of the team, I was carrying them. Of course, it takes the combined effort of all players to play and win at pee-wee ball, but to a youngster in the responsible position of pitcher it was like being the manager of a company, who in his silent and lonely way, carries the burdens of all his employees. I was acting out what I would be doing later in my life when I became an adult 'man'. I was now being primed for my future slot in the male marketplace. So this was an opportunity to learn how to "compete" and "win."

As I entered the house, my hand seemed to be welded to the door knob, my shoulders were sore, my head hung down and my cement-entombed feet seemed to barely move through the door. The kitchen smelled familiarly of hamburgers and fried potatoes, the usual Friday night fare. My stomach felt empty and I felt lifeless as I dragged my defeated body through the door. An eternity seemed to pass before I reached the living room where my stepfather was sipping a beer in his rocking chair glued to the six o'clock news. Time had stopped. I was stuck in this moment with an eternal "wave of loss" swimming through me. This moment was going to last forever.

Leaving the baseball field had marked the end of the season. To me, an eleven year old boy, this was the end of the world. I was exhausted and heartbroken. This felt like the longest night in my life, tomorrow would never happen and this nightmare was my life's destiny. I had let my team, my parents and my community down. I had done my best and it was not good enough; we had lost. To me and my team mates it was a lot more than just a game, it was a contest, a ritual of manhood. We had been taught the importance of winning and we had failed to measure up to this masculine edict.

We had lost the big one, the championship. The winners could celebrate, but losers do not celebrate defeat. This was what we had been taught by our adult male mentors.

I attempted to get by my stepfather and head for the seclusion of my room where I could hide my disgrace and failure. I wanted to retreat, to hide. I could not face him. "Well?", I froze, my feet nailed to floor and my heart beat faster; my head was ready to explode. "How did it go?" shouted my stepfather, "Did you win?" I could not move; his thundering voice coming from his six foot frame, made my whole body tremble. I turned and his penetrating eyes met mine. He was looking right through me. Caught within his steel-like stare, I felt numb, motionless. My throat was parched, trickles of urine ran down my leg. I felt dizzy in the presence of this master of interrogation. My legs became rubbery. I wanted to run but was immobilized. He waited, then his voice rolled out again, "What is the matter? The cat got your tongue?" This sent a chill down my spine; my gut was tied in knots and I finally I could not hold back. My body began to shake and the urine burst from my groin streaming down my legs. My chest heaved, my voice cracked, the ache inside exploded and my emotions rushed through my body like jolts of electricity. My eyes welled with tears and I began to sob uncontrollably. The urine streamed down my leg forming a pool at my feet and I stood completely vulnerable, broken, the hardness of my body armour dissolved. The emotions oozing from my heart's cavity were the accumulation of the many times I had been hurt and had tried to hide it for fear of being called a "cry baby." Now I was my real self; scared, confused and open to the deep hungering pain of needing to be supported and held most of all by my father. I was hurt and needed to be comforted and protected. I wanted to reach out to him and be held.

"Stop that crying!" he bellowed, "You're a big boy now!" Another chance for father and son to touch was destroyed by the destructive messages that are passed down through the masculine fraternity. Another chance, an opening, a new beginning, was turned into another wound and barrier to a natural, healthy connection between father and son. Close your heart's door, this is not how men touch. It is neither masculine or accepted. "Men do not touch and that is how it is, so live with it."

I have always remembered that time when my stepfather told me to stop crying. I do not believe that I cried again until I was in an encounter group in the sixties where we were frightened into expressing tears. Even then, crying was one of the most frightening experiences of my life. I could get angry easily and this was a powerful expression pattern in my life but to show my vulnerability and lose control was next to impossible. Like other men, I had succumbed to overpowering masculine "shoulds" and despite their negative effects upon my life, I held on to these as if my life depended upon it. I remember my father that day watching my every move. He was more afraid of my exploding emotions than I was. He was terrified of his own need to release and resigned long ago to keep his feelings locked inside. This encounter between us models the saga of most males wherein a man and his son are together yet lack the bridge to bring them together in sharing, commoness and connection. This inability to connect continues to harness and hinder relationships among males regardless of their age, position or role. That which occurs between fathers and sons, brothers, mentor and student, boss and employee constitutes the 'gap' in men's relationships. We fail to connect with the father part of ourselves which is externally represented by our fathers and by other males around us. Underneath these defensive layers, lie the wounding events and the pain of disconnection which creates distance, competition and intimidation.

I believe that within this territory of disconnection, this vacuum, this place of limbo, lies the keys to discovering our true selves. Therein can be found those parts of ourselves that we surrendered to the dominant messages we began to receive upon the onset of our physical births. These masculine, human seeds still lie within us, waiting for us to reclaim and replant them so we can open ourselves to the vastness of our human capacities.

We have been led astray down a path that is laden with half truths and dangerous, unhealthy outcomes not only for ourselves as men but for all those we desire to connect with in more intimate and human ways. The masculinity we have inherited and accepted as our true birthright is half empty and false. We have learned to fill this emptiness with hollow promises, "over-doing," and becoming overly masculine.

To discover ways to break the hold that our masculine inheritance has imposed upon us, we must begin a deep inner journey. We have been taught to externalize our world and so we lose touch with the strength and true power or our inner domains. We have our sights set on conquering "outer space" while fearing the unknown paths of our inner space which contains rich gifts that are part of our male legacy. Within ourselves is where we touch our deeper relationship with all of life's aspects and are connected with our inherited creatureness. Within the core of our being we touch the essence of the masculine spirit. We find as well in this inner space the true connection with women and our natural alliance with them. This domain contains the blueprint for human wholeness and the means to experience our natural affinity to the human family as well as ourselves.

We live in a perilous time, a time when technology man has created could serve to enslave us and ultimately wipe us from the face of the planet. Do we want a machine society regardless of how sophisticated this may be, or do we want a human society? Where has our faith in the human spirit gone, that we are substituting the domination of the 'faultless machine' to man-

XIX

age our society? Perhaps the weakening of the human spirit is at fault. We have to accept the responsibility for what we have created. As men, we must begin to use our intelligence more wisely and find better and healthier ways of relating to ourselves, the world and all species. We must break the shackles of centuries of destructive patterns that keep us locked into the "warrior stance," even during times of peace. We must find the strength and courage to come face to face with our learned and adopted fears and know that beneath these learnings are fresh seeds of new alternatives that offer us saner choices and direction for our life's journey and planetary survival.

We have much to discover and much to do. It is time to become the pioneers of a new kind of male journey. We will learn to construct bridges across the wide gaps within ourselves and in our relationships with others. Most importantly we must share the responsibility of learning to co-exist with one another. Co-operatively we will close the gaps of distance and fear revealing the hopes, dreams and possibilities for the expression of the human heart which beats within every one of us.

As men we **now have a choice** to not only create history, but to change it, to remake it. Good luck to **US.**

The journey begins. . .

XX

OLD MALE IMAGE

"The shackled male can free himself only if he allows himself to be somewhat imaginative. Men lacking imagination cannot conceive of a life better than the one they know. When discomforts overwhelm them, they will realize they are suffering bondage — but most men born in cultural captivity walk their cells weighted by invisible chains."

Jack Nichols
Men's Liberation

CHAPTER **I**

World War III: "The Final Cockfight"

"Each year, the number of bombs has grown, until now there are some fifty
thousand warheads in the world, possessing the explosive yield of roughly
twenty billion tons of TNT. These bombs were built as "weapons" for "war" but
their significance greatly transcends war and all its causes and outcomes.
They grew out of history, yet they threaten to end history. They were made by
man, yet they threaten to annihilate man!"

Jonathan Schell
The Fate of the Earth

'WARRIORS IN ACTION':
This is how it is.

Captain Johnathan Peters and Lt. Jeffrey Arnold, U.S. Air Force, sit
calmly in the launch centre nestled deep within the caverns of the Colorado
Rocky Mountains. Arnold sips coffee while Peters chews gum. It is 3:55 a.m.,
Monday, October 3, 1986. Citizens of Colorado, other parts of the U.S. and
Canada are asleep except for those within other time zones who are awakening and preparing themselves for another day. The two have been repeating
this routine for the past year. They are responsible for launching intercon-
tinental ballistic missiles upon the flashing of the red warning light. From
this moment, both have been trained, they know the procedure by heart.
Simultaneously they turn the keys that will launch the missiles from their
silos which are aimed at strategic targets and major Soviet cities. Both have
revolvers at their sides and orders to "shoot to kill" if one of them fails to
carry out his mission. The Air Force knows that despite their rigorous
training and careful screening, one of them could freeze in the final moment.
Capt. Peters pauses for just a moment as images of his two sons, Theodore,
age 6 and Johnathan Jr., age 8, pass through his mind, "God, I sure love my
two boys," he thinks to himself. Arnold views the radar screen and its
multitude of circles wondering if he will will ever turn the key. Soon his shift
will be over and after he is relieved, he will go home, get cleaned up and pick
up his fiance from the University. This routine is repeated over and over, day
after day, shift after shift. Arnold and Peters could do it blindfolded, they just
sit and wait!

1

. . .On the other side of the world, in the Soviet Union, tucked away, underground within the Ural Mountains, Capt. Uri Androvich and Lt. Leonard Zakarov, sit calmly in the launch centre, eyes fixed on the radar screen, prepared upon command to turn the keys which will launch the Soviet SS 20's from their silos, aimed at the U.S. and other strategic targets. Zakarov glances at the photo of his recently born son while still watching the blips on his radar screen. He wonders if he will live long enough to see his son grow up. Capt. Androvich sits thinking about his eleven year old daughter who got sick from eating too much ice cream at her birthday party last week and he had to sit with her stroking her head until she fell asleep. They have been trained like their U.S. counterparts for their mission and they know it well. They are soldiers and will do their duty and like Arnold and Peters have orders to "shoot to kill" if one of them fails in his duty. Time passes, the radar screen is clear and they sit and wait!

"When will the red lights flash and the keys turn, and why?" Who is to say how this intense critical situation has evolved. Some believe that it began when the U.S. dropped the bombs on Nagasaki and Hiroshima while others believe it began with Sputnik's launching. Ronald Reagan would have us believe that we are dealing with an evil empire while our intentions are honourable. Both sides would like to convince us that the other is to blame. Whomever we choose to blame, the nuclear clock continues to tick.

One might be surprised that I would begin a book about and for men by focusing upon the present nuclear threat. I believe that the crisis of today is very much a part of the masculine journey and if we are to grasp the deeper meanings of this journey, we must examine aggressive characteristics that have been repeated since the dawn of civilization. Masculine stereotypes are part of our evolution and these patterns cut deeply into our psyche. I also believe that the nuclear threat exemplifies the seeds of destruction that are part of the manner in which men have dealt with human conflicts and interactions with other species. What we have today, as we stand on the edge of potential annihilation, is a repeated historical evolutionary pattern adapted to respond to life's past challenges.

As for war, men have been fighting and destroying one another since they first learned the use of weapons. They have fought for survival from warring tribes, for territory, over religious beliefs, over women and for the sake of fighting. They have been fighting for centuries and still are. Men have been violent towards themselves, one another, other species and the planet for too long.

We are now forced to ask ourselves whether this old way of handling conflicts and aggressive urges is still effective in a technological era or whether it will destroy us.

I believe that through tracing the depths, events and meaning of male conditioning, we can bring to light some very important considerations. Since I am not a historian and have no formal schooling in this area, many of my ideas and conclusions will come from my personal life and what I have learned growing up, relating to males in the education arena, the workplace and the military. I do not wish, in any way, to speak as an authority on this subject. The traditional academic approach is short- sighted at best as this deeper pulse of the male journey is beginning to be experienced. To understand the complexity of masculinity we have to view it from common as well as personal perspectives and allow ourselves to be affected beyond our conditioned responses in all areas of our lives.

In this chapter, I want to view the pervasiveness of our learnings about being male and reveal how this has contributed to the nuclear crisis presently facing us. How we learn to express ourselves, inherited images passed on through generations, our ways of perceiving the world, our attitudes towards nature, and our interactions with others are interwoven and do affect our present stance on a national and global scale. Also, the rigidity of our beliefs, images and thinking has fragmented our potential for creative, sexual and human expression leading to further conflicts in all aspects of our living; ie) social, spiritual, home, work environment and finally politically. As we create an incredible technocracy, we have also evolved more sophisticated ways of fighting wars and killing people. This situation is primarily an expression of the aggressive force of masculine energy which has also changed men's roles, alienating them from one another and every relationship whether on the battlefield, playing field or in the marketplace. Aggression affects every facet of men's lives they have with another human being. With the birth of machines and technology, the humanity that once existed on the battlefield is no more. There was a time when men honored their enemies for gallantry and heroism. In a sense, despite opposition, a spirit of brotherhood did exist.

Consider the effects of technology on the military and how through computerization and highly sophisticated weaponry, the human element is disappearing, further affecting the relationships among men. Through technology in warfare, people have become mere objects, printouts from a computer program. Machines do not facilitate human contact and do not have heroes. Men have become obedient, carrying out the commands of other machines — the ultimate dehumanization.

How we grew up as males and how we learn to integrate technology into our lives is a powerful influence in shaping our human interactions. The "warrior seed," inherited from our warrior forefathers, has sprouted and grown far beyond hand-to-hand human combat that was once warfare. It is no accident that our cocky attitude and obsession with winning have become trademarks and styles of our masculine defensive postures. The attitudes inherited from thousands of years ago are still being expressed today and we still pass these on to our male offspring. What begins in our infancy and is nurtured in childhood and adolescence comes from the unconscious intentions that form our civilization. I hope that through my sharing of these perspectives, I can offer a blueprint with which other men can identify.

CHILDHOOD TRAINING FOR WAR

Every fifteen to twenty years the U.S. has been involved in some type of wartime activity. The U.S. has also been involved in the cold war with the Soviet Union since the end of World War II. Some believe this cold war was in a freeze following the Russian Revolution in 1917 and that certain events were required to thaw it. The U.S., since that time, has believed that a communist world takeover was imminent unless prevented by force. Young men have been raised to believe that the Soviets are a threat to our way of life and free enterprise system. There is no doubt that young Soviets are similarly schooled as to the dangers of capitalist ideology and that the U.S. is a threat to their civilization and culture. Whether we choose to believe the stance of either, both systems and nations have fueled the flames of fear and indoctrinated their young. Both believe that their "superior" system requires defense and protection in the traditional male way — through overwhelming force.

I remember that first time my father took me jackrabbit hunting. This was a special time. Learning to shoot and acquiring other skills of my avid hunter father, was one of my initiation rites into manhood. As I held the single shot .22 and pulled the trigger, I felt a surge of power in my young body. I was ecstatic when my bullet found its mark and the swift moving jackrabbit tumbled into the sagebrush. As I approached the bloodied, dying rabbit flopping on the ground, even though I was proud, for a moment I felt haunted. The rabbit's eyes seemed to ask me why I had shot it and I felt guilty. My stomach churned, yet I knew I could not let this imagined interaction between the rabbit and me "get" to me. Men are hunters and animals have to die and this is part of the drama that occurs between the two. The men must be the winners and the animals are the losers.

Until the age of twelve, I always asked for guns and holsters for Christmas and spent hours learning the fast draw techniques of Wyatt Earp on T.V. I was thrilled when I could duplicate these and even cut notches in the handles following gun duels with neighborhood friends. Occasionally I was defeated but then I would practice even harder to ensure victory in the next duel. By the time I was in high school, even though I had given up guns, I was an excellent shot. One of my favorite activities was playing "stretch," a game in which two boys would attempt to throw a knife between the out-stretched feet of one another. The one who could throw the knife closest to the feet of the other was the winner. I continued to play this game until I accidently stuck a knife into the foot of one of my classmates. I will never forget the look on his face as blood poured from his foot. I knew that I had lost as sticking another meant disqualification however, I did feel lucky to be the "sticker" and not the "stickee". This game is another young man's ritual which is part of the initiation into manhood. Taking dangerous risks, knowing that there had to be a winner and a loser, was all part of the male tradition. My father taught me how to box and wrestle so I could 'defend' myself against the aggression of other males.

These rights and rituals have been experienced by most men as part of their preparation for living and surviving in the male world. We were taught that without these skills we were in danger of "taking a licking" or worse, of being labelled a sissy, chicken, or faggot. These rituals have been practiced by fathers with their sons for centuries and are seen as necessary not only for personal, but for tribal and national defense. The 'warrior' training begins as soon as our mother proclaims the news of pregnancy and that she hopes for a son.

The nation's sons have been going off to war since prehistoric times. Worthy sons must, if necessary, fight and die for their country. If, for some reason a young man does not agree with this tradition, then he is not really a man, his masculinity is suspect. "Warrior" trained fathers of such sons feel ashamed, that they have failed as fathers.

In the twilight of the twentieth century, while we have witnessed some changes in the traditional warring function of men, we still find numerous situations where this male warrior image persists. The violence experienced throughout the world reflects the repeated patterns of male socialization since the dawn of time. George Bernard Shaw once wrote: "North America is the only society that went from barbarism to decadence without going through a phase of civilization." We believe that we have become civilized humans and that we have made tremendous progress in all fields of endeavor. The spirit that guides us, however, is still polluted with the decayed remains of our barbaric ancestors. We have not changed the genetic coding that makes us from birth warriors first and humans second. Until we change this archaic view of ourselves and the world, we will always find the enemy, for **he** lives in the hearts, minds and souls of all of us and, like a shadow, follows us wherever we go. Once we acknowlege that "he" is within us, we will cease to view him as being "out there" which necessitates our perpetually rigid defense postures. Until we accept that we are still being programmed by old manhood training scripts, we will never find our true spirit of brotherhood or be able to teach our sons the same. If changes are not made, decayed vestiges of our 'warrior' ancestral psyche will be given the devasting power of today's technology, our destruction.

FROM THE LOCKER ROOM TO THE BATTLEFIELD

"Atten-hut!" our junior high gym teacher would shout each morning, signalling us to fall in for roll call. As we stood at attention, he would walk the line, inspecting our gym clothes ensuring that we were properly attired, sneering like a drill sergeant if anyone had forgotten to tie his shoes or had a dirty t-shirt. Following the routine inspection, he would then call "At ease," and proceed with roll call. We answered with "Here, Sir". This routine was repeated every day for three years during my junior high school. Mr. Bethel, or Coach, as we called him, had been a professional baseball player before the war, in which he was an Army Ranger wounded on a secret mission behind enemy lines. He often told us about various campaigns he had been in and of the heroism of his Ranger unit, which he believed was the best in the U.S. Army. He would have us spellbound with the dare-devil feats of the men in his outfit and make us laugh when he told tales of those who "couldn't cut it." Soldiers who wet the bed, couldn't climb rope or cried when the sergeant gave them a tongue-lashing were not Ranger material and not impressive specimens of manhood. Mr. Bethel had a way of turning the most bizarre situation into a comedy and would have made a good stand-up comic or sports announcer. He was tough, aggressive and gave all of himself into his work as coach and gym teacher. He organized a contest once to see who was the most physically fit and he set up a challenge in which some of us particpated. I did over six hundred situps and scored high on several of the activities. I was sore for days and had an open wound where my jock strap had rubbed against the crack in my ass. About one third of the class scored within my range. A handful scored even higher; one boy did close to a thousand situps. The unspoken message of this contest was "no pain, no gain" and it seemed to ring true when members of the class bragged about their accomplishments. This contest separated the "mice from men" and those of us who were trying so hard to be men, were willing to hurt ourselves to prove it.

The method behind the discipline, drive, and push the coach used in his phys-ed classes was exemplified by a sign in his office which read, in large letters, "A quitter never wins and a winner never quits!" He wanted to teach us to become winners in life, excelling at whatever we did and to be the best we could be. This motto had worked for him. He had grown up in poverty and through hard work and determination made it to the big time in profes- sional baseball. The coach was our mentor, our guide, and had taken it upon himself to ensure that these young boys would grow to manhood, prepared to conquer life. He was the kind of father that many of us wished we had. He took an active interest in us and regardless of his military teaching style, we listened to him and modelled ourselves after him. He taught us to do battle, if necessary, on the sports field and in the community. He, like other coaches of young males, was teaching us the best way he knew how, out of love, in the hope that we would survive.

Male school teachers, phys-ed instructors and other adult males have a tremendous influence in shaping the minds, emotions and bodies of young males. Junior high is a time of puberty accompanied by its physical manifestations — such as pubic hair, facial hair, deepening voices and other changes that drastically alter a young man's self-image. During this time, young men begin to question, doubt and compare themselves with other males their age and older. The locker room influences much of our understanding and acceptance of ourselves and our bodies. Here we learn how we fit and 'measure up' to other young males. How we survive this experience determines how we compete, survive and live on the 'battlefield' of the male world.

During the period of locker room education, young males experiencing puberty create unique rituals and contests to test and challenge their maleness. Some of these are cruel and bizarre but are usually accepted as inevitable. To complain would be to fall into the ranks of cry baby or sissy and any struggling young male trying to find himself and his masculinity simply would not take the risk of such labels. If he revealed his fear or confusion it might force others to do the unacceptable in a man's world, that is, to acknowledge their own insecurities.

I am wondering how many who are reading this book are remembering their own locker room education; the contests and cruelty, and the fears that had to be kept hidden. Remember how fixated we were upon the size of our penis and the amount of genital hair we had. Those who were well-endowed were the envy of the rest and those who were less fortunate suffered constant harassment. Young boys are good at creating contests and rituals for penis functioning and usage, such as peeing contests and towel snapping.

Within the locker room, young males engage in experiences that harden them, teaching them to endure pain. They do battle with one another, competing in every imaginable way through contests often centering on their genital energies, the source and symbol of their manhood. So much of the self-image is focused on the penis. The size and function of it will influence their relationships, social interactions, and even their policies. For example, Rough Rider and hero of San Juan Hill, Teddy Roosevelt and his slogan: "Speak softly and carry a big stick" personifies the macho warrior image of men in battle. He represents the archetype of the hard-driving, hard-playing, hard-winning man of adventure, seeing risk-taking as not only a part of being male, but the very essence of manhood. He was the 1900's version of John Wayne or Clint Eastwood's "Dirty Harry." He was hard, daring, disciplined, fearless, a weapon of destruction by himself. If alive today and in the position of President, he would probably be at war with Latin America. Teddy was a wild game hunter, a war hero and the kind of guy who, "...wouldn't take shit from nobody!"

The male phallus and its symbolism have evolved throughout civilization. As technology adances, its phallic imagery is manifested on the world's battlefields as steel erections that are harder, bigger and more powerful than guns, spears and other weapons of destruction. They shoot farther with more accuracy and continue to become bigger and more sophisticated than in the past. The I.C.B.M., the cruise and the submarine-launched missiles are the dream children, now grown up, of phallus worshippers.

As the arms race escalates, the two macho-warrior super powers attempt to outdo one another in the perfection of the the most effective and sophisticated phallus. Each envies the other and each steals the other's blueprints to determine what they can add to their own designs to compete successfully. Both act out locker room rituals, as they compare, compete and duel.

Perhaps if men could learn at a younger age to respect and accept themselves and one another, they might invent manhood testing rituals that do not involve bloodshed, violence and destruction.

As long as men assimilate and lock inside the message that our phallus is the essential symbol of our masculinity, we will be stuck forever in the puberty stage of the male journey.

CREATIVE USE OF AGGRESSION:
"Throwing the Meg-a-tantrum."

How often we hear the reference to men's tendency toward aggression. There is a suggestion that this tendency is the cause of much of the violence and other problems within the world.

Usually when this aggression is referenced, it is expressed in a negative light which is directed to the whole masculinity package of competition, violence and other unhealthy aspects for men. I can see how people have come to reject men's aggressive traits and their application. However, I do not believe what we comprehend to be male aggressiveness has anything to do with the true aggressive spirit of males or of other life forms. I submit the idea that men are not aggressive enough and further suggest that it is not aggression that is unhealthy or negative; rather it is the lack of response to the deeper aspects of our aggressive natures that has become the problem. At the core of these aggressive traits lies our 'potent' creative force and when human beings are blocked from drinking from this life pool, their aggressiveness becomes unhealthy. When an infant is unable to be fulfilled through feeding from the mothers breast, it becomes frustrated and unsatisfied. As all parents know, a hungry baby is discontented and difficult to deal with. However, if it is fulfilled, the baby's interaction with others will be healthy and rewarding.

Basic failure in comprehension of the true nature of male aggression has led to rejection and repression. Now, I wish to bring to the surface some misunderstandings of aggression and to distinguish unhealthy from healthy expression of this trait. I further wish to focus on how the unhealthy expression of aggression has contributed to the arms race. I hope this discussion will clear the way to reveal other hidden, false beliefs and practices regarding men's natures. Society in general, and men in particular are due to create a new definition of masculinity.

Basically, men, women, animals and plants have aggressive natures without which there would be no evolution, no movement of life. It makes us strive, grow and fulfill our needs for expansion and complete functioning. Aggression can be viewed as the cornerstone of the structures that animate and regulate life. Secondly, aggression is an inner flow of life energy that moves throughout our body-mind system like blood flows throughout our physical systems. Thirdly, aggression is the bridge to our 'creatureness,' our animal nature that joins us to all other life kingdoms. Without this trait we would still be existing in caves or be exinct like the dinosaurs. Unfortunately, due to a distortion of Darwin's theory of evolution, this natural, healthy aggressiveness has been turned into a justification for social predatoriness. If we draw from the creative pool where aggression resides, then perhaps we would have a more humane civilization.

Aggressive energy can be explained with an analogy to a bathtub. If you place a plug in the drain, the incoming water will not only fill the tub, it will overflow, eventually flooding the room. The only way to stop this flood is to pull the plug or turn off the tap. By applying this concept to aggression we can see how important it is to let it flow unimpeded. As soon as we block any phase of the process, we are in danger of having the life force flood out of control. Learning to control this energy and focus it through a natural outlet will enable us to enjoy a warm, comfortable bath. The problem is based upon the premise that nature has to be controlled, that we must have dominion over nature. Overcontrol of any aspect of nature will eventually spell disaster. Nature's dam builder, the beaver, always leaves an opening in the structure to ensure that the waters can still flow through. Instinctively, the beaver respects the natural flow of the water, so it and the river engage in a natural relationship of give and take. Man always wants to be in complete control of the river, the dam and the land surrounding the structure.

Frederick Perls, the father of Gestalt therapy, wrote in the '50's that repression of aggression and not sexual repression as Freud and others believed, is at the core of our personal and social conflicts. When we dam the opening of our instincts and true aggressive urges, we are setting the pattern for development of social neurosis and eventual psychosis. This repressed urge simmers in our unconscious and if the lid is held on long enough, it will boil over. A society that is repressed and passes this training on to its youth is a walking time bomb. An inbred hostile pattern develops and the people continue to be increasingly frustrated. The most devastating result of the extreme misuse of aggression is war.

There is a possibility that war is the male substitute for giving birth. In an issue of **Esquire**, William Broyles Jr. wrote an article entitled,"Why Men Love War," He states very convincingly that,"War may be the only way in which most men touch the mythic domains in our soul. It is, for men, at some terrible level the closest thing to what childbirth is for women: the initiation into the power of life and death. It is like lifting off the corner of the universe and looking at what's underneath. To see war is to see into the dark heart of things, that no man's land between life and death, or even beyond." After reading that paragraph, I initially thought that if we men have only war to put us in touch with the miracles of life's unknown, then we do not have a chance to survive on this planet. Surely there must be an alternative to put us in touch with our essence, the mystery of creation. Perhaps our true nature is calling us to destroy the patterns and scripts that suffocate us, preventing us from reaching the depths of our creative soul. Not war, but self-exploration is the key to our survival. Men and women are "childbirthers." Men are also a part of that process in another natural and complementary way. I do not believe that war is a substitute for birthing. The wars fought on the battlefield are an externalization of the war occuring within. It takes a willingness and courage to transcend the archaic patterns that blind us to our greater depths and wisdom which remain hidden under piles of decay guarded by ghost warriors of the destructive past.

I will now approach the issues of war and aggression from a historical perspective which will remind us of the patterns we have inherited and lived through time. To do this I will draw on the expertise of a woman who offers some enlightening perspectives from the feminine side. Most of our history has been written by men and yet everyone suffers during times of conflict and war.

Sue Mansfield, in an interview with **Psychology Today**, talked about her book **The Gestalt of War.** She discussed how repression of aggression ultimately leads to war.

> 'We have to begin by distinguishing aggression from war-making. There is no way that life could be sustained or reproduced without some degree of aggression. But war is a particular type of "institutionalized aggression" in which social pressure is used to force individuals to kill other people they may not even hate or fear."

How many American, Canadian and English men work with and are friends with German, Japanese and Italians? During World War II, these men or their fathers were enemies on the battlefields of Europe and in the

South Pacific. What they have in common today never had the chance to be realized because they fought one another as enemies. How many potential friendships were never experienced because of this war? Would it ever be possible for Capt. Peters and Lt. Arnold to befriend Cpt. Androvich and Lt. Zakorov?

Governments have been recruiting men to fight and die because they cannot go beyond their own egos, internal fears and shadows. If politicians could experience more family sharing without the veils of political "power images" leaving "political stuff" aside until after they got to know one another, I believe that political negotiation would have lasting results. However, politicians still make war declarations and when a young man is ordered to fight, he willingly obliges. Mothers weep, never knowing if their sons will return alive or in a box draped with the country's flag but fathers bid them farewell, and wish them luck, willing to give their sons to fight for the country. Another war, more sons lost, the saga continues. The boy is facing a great unknown; he is aware that if he is to come back alive, he will have to kill the enemy.

Broyles states in his **Esquire** article that though he was very fortunate not to have experienced the horror of battle, he still saw enough to teach him about the agony. The nightmare of war and its tragedy is vividly portrayed in the classic book and film **All Quiet on the Western Front.** It is a story of a young Frenchman called to fight in the trenches of southern France. It deals with the phases he experiences each time he is called into battle and returns home. The camaraderie he has with his fellows and the relationship he develops with his sergeant are expressed. He watches the new recruits and as many of them fall, he becomes accustomed to the living and dying of the new soldiers. He learns not to become too close for he may have to hold them in his arms while they die. In one scene portrays the death of his friend, the sergeant, dies during a German attack and he assumes command. This scene opens with him running for cover during an artillery attack and him sliding for cover at the same time as a young German soldier. They fight, the Frenchman overpowers the other and believing the German to be dead, rolls over exhausted from the duel. Hours pass and he is forced to listen to the groans of the soldier he thought was dead. He tries to ignore the suffering but, cannot. He hopes the German will die but he continues to agonize and scream. The Frenchman cannot leave the shelter because of incoming artillery. He begins to question the meaning of war, of killing. His mind pounds within his skull, coupled with the artillery's thunder and the moans of the dying soldier. Finally, he rushes to the German's side and begins to doctor his wounds. The Frenchman shouts to the wounded man, "Please don't die! I'm sorry, I'm sorry!" Minutes later the soldier gasps, blood trickles from the corner of his mouth, and he is still and silent. This story not only points out the agonizing dilemma that every soldier endures with regard to killing another human, it portrays the madness of the battlefield that each soldier confronts; the edge of insanity, where the soldier fights, always doubting, strangled by his own fear yet never letting it show. Soldiers are expected to experience this existential ripping, keeping it together until the time comes to pull the trigger and kill the faceless enemy who is but a shadow of themselves.

As long as war is the outlet for pent-up, frustrated, and blocked aggressive urges, history will repeat itself complete with all the agony and insanity. If we believe that due to men's aggressive natures, war is inevitable, we are perpetuating a terrible falsehood, a deadly myth and a self-fulfilling prophecy. We must realize that war is acceptable if we believe it to be so. If we change our beliefs and our thoughts, we can create fresh and healthy ways to vent our aggression. As Mansfield states, war is created by our social institutions, contrary to our beliefs. Men began using weapons for war 13,000 years ago before that time, implements were constructed primarily for farming and hunting. Those who greedily took more than their share of resources found themselves in the position of having to defend their territories and themselves. Before such greed became apparent, war was merely a ritual in which a few lost their lives as symbolic sacrifice. This was not the complete slaughter that we have come to associate with Vietnam or Sherman's march to the sea during which everything living was annihilated.

The battlefront consciousness has permeated the marketplace of free enterprise, academia, as well as other fields of men's endeavors. Men have ruined the lives and careers of their competitors .The rule is to outflank and destroy the opponent keeping in mind that, "All's fair in love and war." If the society teaches men to express their aggressivenes creatively then we can regain the harmony and balance with nature upon which our survival depends.

Aggression which is dammed up, blocked or hidden creates a backup, which when released, expresses itself in a destructive manner. This destructiveness affects our functioning on all levels; intellectually, physically and emotionally. We become "dis-eased" which further hinders our creative development. One effect of this unexpressed aggression can be witnessed as children absorb the distortions and unnatural teachings of their nuclear parents and their social parents,(school, church, community, political system.) Children can become carbon copies of their parent's repressed natures and learn to view people and the world in similar distorted ways. Men growing up after World War II modelled the beliefs of their fathers who fought in Germany and Japan. When I was in the third grade, a Japanese family moved to our town. I remember trying to pick a fight with their son the first time I met him. I recalled my father talking about the "Japs" that had killed his buddies when they were stationed in the South Pacific. This boy was my enemy because he represented an enemy to my father. It took quite a while to befriend this boy and I do not believe that I ever totally accepted him. As a male, aged eight years, I was already learning how to block my emotions. Many of my friends have since been from various races, heritages and backgrounds yet, I still feel an occasional tinge within me when I meet a Japanese man. When I am able to fully explore this deep-rooted attitude locked within the psyche of that eight-year-old boy, I will be able to put to rest this prejudice. Still when I close my eyes, I can see a little boy with a toy gun, surrounded by a bunker while across from him is a little Japanese boy in a similar situation, both believing the war is still on. This battle scene still exists within me. There are reports of Japanese soldiers living in the jungles for over twenty years following the end of the war, who still believe they are fighting American marines. Within us, as men, we have these children still fighting a war we were told about by our fathers or their friends. In a society that has turned its aggressiveness to military energy, our son's grow up fighting long before they hit the beaches or crawl into a fox hole. The powerful imprinting is deep despite the subtle way these tendencies become apparent in our growing personalities. As long as we prohibit the expression of our aggressive energy and discourage the natural creativity of our young people, we have the makings of armies. The messages that the child absorbs are not necessarily verbal but can be the result of unconscious communication from the adult world. All males can become mentor-representatives of a warring style. As Mansfield states, the young male becomes a student of "institutionalized aggression." He is further shielded from his potential resources and begins to carry a defense shield that he has learned will protect him from the inevitable enemy. Hidden behind this shield, his natural tendencies are bubbling, churning and pushing for expression. His anger grows and resentment festers from being locked within. He desires self-expression but has learned of its consequences when he threw a tantrum at the age of three. If he learns to wait to express this energy and if he is lucky, perhaps he will release it positively through exercise, sports, art or dance. If not, he will let it simmer until the rage melts the shielded walls of entrapment. If someone pushes the button, or turns the key, the walls may collapse and he will come charging out of his prison angry, wounded and daring anyone to stand in his way or attempt to put him back in his cage. Later, when he goes into battle, the depth of his rage and hatred is focused upon his trigger finger and legal killing allows the expression at long last. Freedom and release.

Repression of aggression creates an alienation within men to their deeper impulses. The more controlled and corraled this energy is, the more machine-like we become. Eventually we adopt this pattern as part of our character and become resigned to it. We conform and are obedient to other representatives of this repression, the old male guard. We mistrust our natural inner senses and turn to external sources for meaning and security. When told to go to war, we do so out of duty, not questioning the necessity or morality of destroying other human beings. We become cowards, mere shadows of what we are or could be. We are able to stand by and watch others express aggression, greed or contempt for life because deep within us we secretly believe we are nothing.

In one of the launch centres, a key is turned by Cpt. Peters or maybe by Cpt. Androvich, perhaps by miscalculation or miscommunication. Whatever the reason, man's most powerful invention explodes into final freedom. The aggressive child born by man, bursts out of its prison shell to become, once again, a part of creation.

This deadly child, this persona shadow of man's denial of his potential, unleashes devastating destruction. The creative possibility of healthy aggression is lost to history. Man's creative urge, still entrapped and pulsating to be expressed now, knows the feeling of being free of its body prison. No more body, no more prison, no more society, no more anything. . . No more, period! Man's last tantrum in megatons.

It is our decision whether or not to do our part in preventing this holocaust.

CHAPTER II

'Supra' Man — False Image Male

"Self-indulgence means satisfying the smallest part of you... that's only temporary...

Newmann, Berkowitz
How To Be Your Own Best Friend

"A person who lives in his images, who denies his body's feelings and needs, or tries rigidly to control them in such a way that he rises above them, acts destructively in relationship to himself... which can mean anything from flagellation to asceticism to over-indulgence."

Stanley Kellemen
The Human Ground

Rousseau stated, "Man is born free but everywhere he is in chains." Since the dawn of civilization, man has attempted to comprehend his mission and purpose on this planet. He has used his basic aggressive nature to create societies that were once only dreams. He has attempted to satisfy his unquenchable thirst for knowledge by constructing institutions of learning and education. He has invented incredible machines that hasten the production of goods and make our lives more efficient. He has even found the cure for some diseases and antidotes for others. He has successfully manned a spacecraft and landed on the moon. Yet, he is more alienated from himself and the world than ever before. It is as if his drive for progress has moved him farther away from himself and others. Estranged and lonely, he is removed, cut off from the very source of himself that he has invested his life's work into preserving and honoring. It is no surprise that his urge for progress and space pioneering has become an obsession, causing his relationship with Mother Earth to be distant, antagonistic and out of harmony with the order of the universe.

Man does not know how to live in harmony with himself. He lives according to the image of his existence, a false picture that constitutes a system of thinking and living designed to control nature and obscure its harsh realities. He attacks the world, its creatures, its earth, and other humans. He is unaware that by such action he is further isolating himself from his true home, his connection with life and with himself.

15

In this chapter I will present a graphic picture of man's enslavement of himself to false gods, beliefs and systems for living; and how men, generation after generation, have inherited and passed on these false 'gods' in a most dominating and punishing manner. This heritage influencing the development of persons has a dramatic and traumatic impact. It has limited the potential of individuals; physically, emotionally, mentally, spiritually, and socially. It has affected the fabric of our educational milieu as well as having fostered corruption, power plays, injustice and exploitation in the highest of government bastions. This denial and greed now threaten to destroy the reality we have created.

Each young male is stifled as his freshness and perfection become perverted by the ghost spirit of preceding generations. This false, half-real predatory spirit sucks vitality, depleting the zest for life as soon as the child enters the physical world. Studies indicate that the fetus is dramatically affected by the emotional and social environment before birth. The conditioning begins before the child can even speak or confront the world. By the time the child is speaking or walking, he has absorbed many false beliefs which will continue to deny his true potential for a healthy, full-functioning life experience.

People have a tremendous capacity for greatness, creativity, intelligence and love; a truly healthy life journey. They must learn to dissolve the crusted walls of socially "institutionalized aggression." This compartmentalizing process influences the musculature of our bodies, the clouded areas of our minds and the constricted areas of our false belief systems. We have to remove the cloaks of self-deception and self-negation to allow our true, vital and free selves to emerge. Those 'self' seeds, our essence, became lost within a society that is itself, disconnected and hidden.

I'M A LITTLE MAN:
The Masculine Fraternity

Mother lies on the birthing table, the pain is coming in regular intervals, sweat trickles down her face. The nurse encourages her with "Push! Push!" and finally the announcement "It's a boy!" Father paces, smoking his tenth cigarette in an hour. Grandmother sits and waits. Grandfather paces too until he has to rest. The nurse announces the news, everyone is ecstatic. Father passes out cigars, his smile reaching from ear to ear. "It's a boy!" He passed the test, not only can he reproduce, he can create a son, the seed of the family bloodline! Everyone is pleased. The reception committee receives another offering from nature. These rituals mark the beginning of the male's process in learning how to separate himself from others. He is weighed, measured and wrapped in a blue blanket and for many years he will wear blue to distinguish him from the feminine pink. As a baby he is treated as though he were a "little man" or as a source of interest and amusement for other children and adults. The paradox is that his environment is composed primarily of the unfulfilled needs of the adults who are supposed to provide for his needs.

I recall my mother angrily telling a story of how my father and his brothers got my two-year-old brother drunk. They continue to laugh at this episode. Infant sons are challenged and teased to prepare them to be tough and masculine. To ensure they can "take it" they are treated in a rough manner. This process, part of unconscious societal learnings, receives daily reinforcement. The male infant is gradually prepared for his position in the masculine fraternity. What he should do in his life has already been decided and the task of his parents and other 'molders' of his destiny is to shape him towards this preordained role.

LEARNING TO BE FALSE

The parents of the new infant watch as he grows through stages of crawling, walking and then running. They are hopeful that they do not repeat those mistakes that their parents made with them. They often keep these unsettling thoughts to themselves, particularly the new father, who feels he should be ready for fatherhood simply because that is what he is facing. He feels free to give a lot of physical affection to his son. Later he will become distant, physically aloof just as his father was with him. Mother cuddles and caresses her new son. For some, within their arms lie their major hopes and dreams. She desires to shape this young being into the gentle, compassionate man her father was not. Often the infant male can represent her idealized father and there may be tendencies to want to duplicate her father through her new son. The parents are already communicating in subtle, often unconscious ways, how the infant needs to be for them. Their hidden, remaining needs and unexpressed fantasies become apparent with this new life spirit, their son.

Parents make up only a portion of the message committee the young boy will encounter. He will experience other messages on the street, at school, in the church, through neighbours and the actions of his playmates. The social environment will convince him that he must trust its messengers even if what they represent is contradictory to what he truly believes in himself.

The first time I saw my father cry was when my parents got a divorce. I recall being puzzled as I saw the tears roll down his cheeks. I remember feeling glad that he was crying, aware that I always felt better after I had a cry. I was confused, too, for I had never seen a man cry before, especially not my father. Somehow, I felt that it wasn't right, that my father was not supposed to be crying. "Men don't cry," that is what I had been taught. I could remember my father expressing other emotions like joy and anger, but now he was exploding my image of him. I was seeing a side that contradicted my masculine training. I had already swallowed the training and was now experiencing an emotional aspect of myself that was almost foreign to me. I wondered if it was real.

When most men describe their fathers, they are usually portrayed as distant, aloof, detached and/or angry, mean dictators. Their fathers did not touch or hold them. These negative descriptions carry an uncomfortable feeling with them. Usually they say, "he wasn't such a bad guy," even though they were unable to reach him, they still loved him. I have heard others talk about experiencing their father's tears and as they speak their faces express a puzzled, little boy look. They too, had found it difficult to understand such tears since they had been socialized not to shed their own.

The young boy continues with his education learning the unsettling truth about the difference between what he feels and what he sees. Asking his parents does not shed much light. If his parents were aware and in touch with their own depths, they would be able to answer the searching questions. They have, more often than not, closed the doors to their own memories of incidents out of their young lives that created their own deep concerns. Unless the boy can find a source from which to satisfy his need for deeper understanding, he will close the door on his emotions and the quest for important feelings in his life. Over time, he will move continually away from these emotionalized depths while developing a ritualized pattern of self-denial. The more he is taught to deny himself, the more he will construct a false sense of self. This 'self' is exemplified in many of the young men who have been initiated into the masculine fraternity. As Fromm states in **Escape From Freedom:**

> "Denial is a way of life. More accurately it is a way of diminishing life, of making it seems more manageable. Denial is the alternative to transformation."

The young male learns how to deny his wholeness, his vitality; he learns he must take his place with all the others, he must conform. Little boys have to learn at an early age to work out their problems on their own. They are taught not to discuss emotional issues, just to "get on with it." Hard physical work and occupying one's time will make the feelings go away. Men still carry a multitude of unanswered questions about their actions and those of the adults around them. These men learned early in life to suppress questions because attempts to get answers were unsatisfactory. When attempts were made to discuss these emotional issues with their playmates, they received blank stares or ridicule. Discussion of such issues is what mommies and girls do, not what "little men" talk about. Thus, "little men" continue to develop false images.

THE PLAYGROUND: THE FIRST BATTLEFIELD

Herb Goldberg, author of **The New Male,** cites an example of a typical masculine battlefield scene:

"It happened on Highway 126 in Fillmore, California, on April 26, 1976. A car with four young men passed another containing three male occupants. The young men in those two cars had never seen each other before. One of those in the passing car made an obscene gesture at the guys in the passed car. If one is even slightly familiar with hair-trigger defensiveness of the masculine psyche and the stereotyped, predictable quality of its reactions, the next scene in this freeway drama could be easily predicted."

He explains that both cars halted, the occupants jumped out and fought with one another. As the cars were leaving, a shot was fired, which killed one of the fifteen-year-old boys.

Goldberg introduces a new term that describes such behavior, "macho-psychotic behavior." This term refers to the uncontrollable reflex action or "temporary insanity" of males trying to prove their masculinity. A raised middle finger results in the death of a boy. How did it all begin?

R.D. Laing, London psychiatrist and author, provides a good example of the origin of this behavior when he talks about the development of the false self. One part separates, seeming alien to the other, as if exists alone, possessing own autonomous function; yet both influence the total function and well-being of the person.

"His false sense of self does not serve as a vehicle for the fulfillment or gratification of the self. The self may remain hungry and starved in a most primitive sense while the false self may be apparently genetically adapted. The actions of the false self do not, however, gratify the inner self."

"The false self arises in compliance with the intentions or expectations of the other, or with what are imagined to be the other intentions or expectations."

As previously stated, the male's false self develops early in life. The subtle needs and wishes of the parents are absorbed into the young male infant's psyche, which is vulnerable and open. As children, we are like sponges, absorbing every tidbit of information, negative and positive, conscious and unconscious, real and imagined. We struggle for survival as the environment crowds us; we cannot take in all stimuli at once and distinguish between our needs and "theirs." As Laing suggests:

> "All his actions were ruled not by his own will, but by an alien will,
> which had formed itself within his own being."

This "alien will" is inherited from the unfulfilled needs of those parents and of the adult-children the male child encounters. These unmet needs are hidden within the unconscious and are passed from one generation to the next. The bloodline, the family name, is the vehicle for this continuous cycle of unmet needs. The unconscious impact of history is apparent in every moment of our lives.

When "little men" act out their frustration and disappointments on the playground, they are re-enacting history. They become gladiators, crusaders, World War I flying aces, submarine pilots and Wyatt Earps, ready to finish off the enemy. Their keen, creative imaginations allow them to satisfy unmet needs for more love, touching and acknowledgment. They substitute aggressive hero roles that dull the pain they have learned to deny so early in their upbringing. They substitute power for love. They can become giants, kings, and heroes inventing weapons more powerful and accurate than the razor straps, willow branches or hands that strike them. They can act out their hurt by inflicting pain on the other boys, thereby releasing tensions. Through fantasy, they can purge themselves of the lies, the unanswered questions; no longer afraid of the goblin (father) or witch (mother) that may lie in wait under the bed ready to take them away to nothingness.

Bullies are created from the genetic anger that quickly becomes part of the psyche of the newborn son. Various ethnic groups have maintained their particular code of honor that is passed down through the ages. "You are an Irishman, you have a temper and can drink anyone under the table." How many Irishmen, Germans, Chicanos, and Indians do not match the stereotype of their fathers and forefathers, but have incorporated that image of self expression as if it were a part of their own nature?

The playground is not necessarily a literal interpretation but can be considered any territory designed for children for physical activity, mental stimulation, meditation, problem-solving and experimentation. The playgound is the private refuge, the fortress of the child. It is here the male child learns to act out the aggression which he learns to endorse for fear of punishment. Often he will test his limits to see how far he can push. This exempflies the need to have space to move, grow and express.

Many family disagreements between father and mother are acted out by children in the playground environment. As a boy I enjoyed making swords from wood and, like Robin Hood, would search through back alleys, looking for just the right piece. Sometimes I would carve the handles of the swords just like those of the Knights of the Round Table. My favorite fantasy was acting out the Three Muskateers with friends. We would engage in battle, duels, and search and destroy missions. "You're dead! I got you in the heart!" we shouted. "No, I'm not, you missed!" The debate would go on as we competed to win and kill. Sometimes it would turn into a real fight with stick swords becoming real weapons and stones and fists would fly. "Darren hit me with a sword!" Rick would shout through tear-filled eyes to his mother, looking for solace and nurturing. The ceremonial sword fights were only symbolic enactments resulting in defeats we would have liked to cause the powerful adults who bullied and intimidated us.

A young boy acts out the conscious and unconscious anger that parents direct toward one another and toward him. When he can trip another boy, his self-esteem is momentarily heightened. By belittling a girl playmate, he is repeating his father's, grandfather's, teacher's, or uncle's attitude toward women and he may also be getting his revenge upon his mother, sister, or female babysitter. He constantly experiments with ways to release the burden of frustration which interrupts his fun and his play.

I met a friend for coffee in a shopping mall and while I stood in line waiting to get our coffees, I witnessed a struggle between a father and his son. I have to admit that being a professional therapist was what kept me from giving the father a tongue lashing or worse. It seemed that the whole family was tired of shopping and was ready to leave. Everyone's patience seemed to be wearing thin. The cranky little boy was giving his dad a rough time and dad was losing his cool. "Don't you dare raise your voice to me!" As the boy flinched and tried to duck, the father's hand slammed across his face. I thought about grabbing the man, who was twice my size, and throwing him up against the counter saying, "I don't care if he is your son, you have no right to hit someone so small!" With great difficulty, I restrained myself and headed back to my table. I told my friend of the event and she identified fully with the situation. She had two boys who had both been physically abused by their father, her ex-husband.

I do understand the father's reasons for his loss of control but it hurts me to see the continued violence cycle among men. I can empathize with the pains of such a situation as I come from a similar background. This treatment often will erupt in another form of violence. This father's father probably used his physical strength to intimidate and control him, keeping in line his physical aggression. The damage of three generations or more continues to influence the spirit of this young boy. News stories include that of a teenage son blowing his father's head off and then committing suicide. Grandfather's bullwhips can be transformed into bullets three generations later.

THE WILD STALLION: CORRALED BUT NOT BEATEN

Donahue, one of my favorite controversial talk show hosts, had several women who had been battered by their husbands as guests on his show. He also had a battering husband as a guest. The audience was made up of people who had battered or had been battered. The tension was evident in the audience. Members expressed anger and disgust everytime the husband-batterer spoke. Other women rushed to the microphone to ask, "Why did you beat your wife?" He recounted his childhood which affirmed the premise that most children who have been battered become batterers. He spoke of feelings of guilt and remorse and never wishing to hit his wife, "She knows how to push my buttons, and like a reflex action, my fists were clenched and I was on her." Often, after the event, he could not remember what had triggered the outburst. Smugness was evident on the faces of some of those who took the microphone, they seemed to be projecting their own violent potential upon the man on stage. He became the scapegoat for their hidden fears and hatreds. By examining themselves, they would see these feelings of anger and helplessness originated in their earlier years. Some of the audience had learned to work through their blocks, to see, to understand, and therefore, to forgive. Others still held the pain within their psyche which necessitated the persecution and condemnation of someone who had the courage to step out on national television and say, "I'm a product of battering, please help me so I don't repeat the cycle!"

The U.S. is one of the most violent countries in the world. This violence is even more deadly due to a projected image that we are not violent and have everything under control. This deception promotes violence. It is quite understandable that men grow up learning to be violent. We are brought into the world often through the use of "force-ceps," We learn violence in our homes, in school, we see it on T.V. and we live it in our lives; teaching males and females to fall short of their potential. This, in itself, is a violent act against nature and as we continue the process we will be haunted by the restless ghosts of generations.

Fritz Perls helps us to further understand the negative effects of damming up our natural aggressive energy;

> "I now consider that neurosis is not a sickness but one of several symptoms of growth stagnation. Other symptoms of growth stagnation are, the need to manipulate the world and control madness, character distortion, reduction of human potential, and lack of "response ability." And most of all, the production of holes in a personality."

While in Marine boot camp, I recall a recruit who had been taken onto a ditch bank by his father and beaten until he was unconscious. The man's intention was to beat the boy's 'stubborn will' out of him. He talked about the experience without any show of emotion. His face was expressionless and he spoke in a flat, monotone voice. His eyes were icy cold and vacant. I felt uncomfortable in his presence as he talked. I could sense the locked-in hate and deeply buried hurt that possessed his body. He remembered the sting of the belt that brought him to consciousness on that day. As I got to know him better, I noticed that during physical exercise, he would do the minimum and then fall back in quiet apathy. Yet during bayonet practice, and hand-to-hand combat, he became ferocious, a wild beast. His eyes would roll and he would shout, "Kill! Kill!"

It was obvious why he joined the Marines out of high school and was heading off to Vietnam. He was unconsciously being guided by the wild animal inside of him that had been beaten. He was trying to find a way to reclaim his lost will. His father's ghost had been living with him since the event and his going to Vietnam would give him the release he was looking for. There he could express the pent-up pain and release it upon the "enemy." Through the institution of war, he could legally exorcise his father's demon from within. Carl Jung would say:

"The face of the enemy is only a 'Shadow' of ourselves which we deny and don't believe is akin to us. When we kill, we are killing part of ourselves. This is perhaps one of the reasons for the commandment, "Thou shalt not murder."

The wild stallion, aggressive creature within us, lies in wait for a chance to escape its imprisonment. Though society may be able to hold it down, to cage it, society usually cannot destroy it. If held down long enough, aggression will rise to kill us or some other enemy shadow of the person or event that imprisoned it.

Men today are searching, albeit in the secret way they have learned, to solve their inner problems and imbalances. They want solutions to the perplexing situation in which they find themselves. They are becoming more willing to open themselves to discover what created the monsters within. When we try to comprehend the training process in depth, we may not like what we find, but this pain is better than wallowing in our hate. We need to see the ancestral and societal patterns that have tainted our souls.

The wild animal part of ourselves is not to be feared or repressed. It is pure life energy that is limitless, without boundaries or territories. It is of the universe and lives within it. This energy requires blending with the nurturing, feminine qualities of life to be calmed, but not suppressed. Both male and female energies operate through an inner control and answer to an inner authority that respects both and yet guides each in union. The aggressive male spirit cannot be corraled or caged for if it is, it will find another more destructive way to express itself. Whether it is creative or destructive, aggressive energy will emerge.

III

Men's Death Script

"But the making of merer 'IT' that is imagined, postulated, and propagated by such a man has nothing in common with living mankind where thous may truly be spoken."

Martin Buber

"When we use our willpower to achieve goals that do not spring out of us, but which we set for the sake of pleasing others or to fulfill a fantasy about who we are, we create a kind of monster, a mechanical man in which our living self is trapped."

Neumann and Berkowitz

SCRIPTS:
They are born before us and live on after us.

The late founding father of transactional analysis, Eric Berne, introduced the idea of scripts. Scripting is making decisions early in childhood regarding our relationship to our purpose in life. These decisions become the directing force in our lives, giving us a false role to play as if it were our true purpose and character. Many scripts are negative, hindering our growth and development. They can completely control our lives causing a great deal of unhappiness. We receive these scripts during circumstances and stressful times when dealing with parents and other adults. They affect and control our very existence as persons — friends, parents and contributing citizens. The society which we were socialized into applies pressure for us to conform to these intended roles. Masculine and feminine elements sometimes in concert, more often in conflict, contribute to the already hefty burden left by original scripts. Berne's definition is as follows:

"A script is a complex set of transactions, by nature recurrent, but not necessarily recurring since a complete performance may require a whole lifetime."

In this way, scripts become our burdens. keeping us bound to a certain way of seeing life. The painful, sometimes nightmarish quality of childhood interaction with parents or other adults becomes like a haunting ghost, intruding upon our lives.

An example of scripting exists with one of my earlier clients who remembers telling herself in early childhood that because of her hellish, tortuous upbringing, when she became a mother she would only stay alive long enough for her child to reach his or her teens. After being married for seventeen years, her daughter approached her teens, and this woman's entire life began to fall apart. She was fearful of everyone and everything and began to have suicidal thoughts. By the time she came to me, after delaying the search for almost two years, she was a basket case. She had another script which said she was strong and proud and did not need anyone else's help. Over time she was able to see the depth of her script "death wish" and the reasons for her choice of such a drastic course in her life. She had become totally exhausted by her family environment, even to the extent of losing her will to live. Her desires for motherhood became entangled with hopeless, despairing feelings. She had set her course in life drawing from the twisted pieces of her life as a young girl.

Similarly, little boys create powerful scripts that limit their relationships with women. If a boy decides, for instance, to take care of his mommy for the rest of his life, then it is not surprising that his wife, or other women in his life will not be able to reach him deeply or emotionally since they cannot replace his mother. He has vowed to sacrifice his life for his mother.

Scripts come in many forms; they can be intellectual, or involve emotions or the lack thereof, or they can occur around power issues. They can be created out of any situation involving low self-esteem, high-stress childhood events. My purpose in discussing scripts is to clarify the destructive, long lasting effects of the masculinity script. This ancient drama of death and destruction is approaching its climax. Our "death wish," as Freud called it, is likely to be granted unless we radically alter our present course.

The destructive seed lies deep within us and we have been listening to its message as surely as if the 'devil himself' were guiding us. I believe that societies and civilizations have scripts just as individuals do. The repetitious pattern of self-abuse and destruction is one very influential historical script. The pattern continues to recycle its message of annihilation and disharmony which negatively influences our growth, the development of our young, dashing our hopes for a better world as it draws us back into the script whirlpool.

The masculine ego has declared itself superior to God and nature and we have become islands unto ourselves. The ego has a purpose, but when it is unconnected with the cycles and purpose of nature, it becomes self-limiting. This self-will eventually becomes self-indulgence and narcissistic worship. It feeds upon our desires to own life's kingdoms; land, material things and people. The life force running amuck promotes the exploitation and manipulation of other living creatures. We attempt to buy time, love and other people.

Each time a chemical company produces another potentially dangerous product it contributes to the reality of the death script. Each time a politician lies for money, power and postion, he too contributes to the death script. Each time we sit, with our heads in the sand, while our country involves us in another war to "protect" us, we contribute to the death script. When we worship apathy, denial and deception of self and life we are furthering the reality of this death script.

If we sit idly by and watch our world move toward nuclear destruction while fearing to look at the alternatives, we might as well push the button ourselves, for by our inactions we are perpetrating the death script. Like zombies, under a voodoo spell, men wander blindly failing to smell the flowers or appreciate the uniqueness of their sons and daughters. Freud stated in the thirties in **Civilization and Its Discontents:**

> "It is impossible to escape the impressions that people commonly use false standards of measurement — that they seek power, success, and wealth for themselves and admire them in others, and that they underestimate what is of true value in life."

Perhaps the only way we learn to appreciate something that we take for granted is to lose it. I worked with a handicapped counsellor who enjoyed a full, happy life until a serious car accident shortly after his nineteenth birthday paralyzed him from the waist down. Doctors said he would never walk again. Up to the time of the accident he was captain of the volleyball team, an excellent skier and tennis player, and loved to go backpacking. He said that after the accident he endured a deep, almost catatonic, six-month depression. He was angry and bitter until he began to realize the source of his depression was the feeling of being ripped off, in being dealt a blow so early in his life. He remarked that he was beginning to understand how he had taken life and others around him for granted. He had thought he was God's gift to women and went through relationships the way a cross-country walker goes through shoes. He had been disrespectful of his parents, spoiled and inconsiderate of others, and had never considered the possibility of having to cope with a handicap. Despite his handicap, or possibly due to it, he became one of the best rehabilitation counsellors in the agency.

How many of us live each day through the grinding routine the renders us dull, losing interest in the joys and finer things offered by life? How many continue to be only half-living, pretending the hole of emptiness and fear within us is an inevitable part of responsibility in life — their script? How many of us wake up, only to find that it is too late? For example, a man has a cancer checkup, exploratory surgery is recommended, and during this operation the doctors discover that the cancer has spread throughout his body and they close him up again. He waited too long. Consider the oil executive, used to working fourteen hours a day, who smokes cigars, eats a lot of red meat and does not exercise. He has a heart attack and after the surgery, the doctor recommends that he take it easy and stop smoking. Then after his release, he goes back to the same routine, completely ignoring the doctor's advice. Three months later after eating a steak dinner, during his after dinner-smoke, this man dies of a massive coronary.

These males all have in common a playing out of some type of scripting and the belief that he could defy the odds. My counsellor friend suffered more following the accident than during the actual crash. The cancer victim probably held the script that he was invulnerable; hence his fatal bad timing. The oil executive, similar to my counsellor friend, was basically a very unhappy man addicted to his work the way an alcoholic is addicted to booze. He could not handle the silence, because if he slowed down long enough, he might have had to hear the voices inside him crying with loneliness and fear. His actions were strong indications of his desire to die as his life was full of destructive, self-abusive, and negative patterns. In accordance with his controlling script, he worked himself to death.

I count myself lucky, at my age, not to have an ulcer. As a kid I believed that I had a "cast-iron stomach" that could handle anything. I know about men who believe they can drink or eat whatever they desire. The "Duke," John Wayne, was noted for his capacity to drink and his Hollywood life-style, coupled with a macho attitude that probably contributed to stomach cancer, heart disease and his eventual demise. Being the "Duke" could not save him from himself.

Man's script of destruction is being thrown back in his face. Polluted air and water, poisoned land, weather pattern changes, exploding volcanoes, flood and disease, are nature's response to abuse.

Man has reached his crisis point and will continue to "reap what he sows." As stated by Karl Bednarik:

"The crisis under consideration is undoubtedly being experienced by the human race in general but it is the human male who has brought it upon mankind, beginning with himself. Women share the blame, but they are not directly responsible. Both the bomb and the pill were invented by men."

He continues: "The male is obviously in retreat, though not from the onslaught of emancipated women or any 'coming matriarchy.'' He is in retreat from what he himself has wrought; from a world of overautomatized, over centralized controls that make him feel superflous as a man."

Man has fallen from grace and has created havoc in Eden. His denied self, "Brother Lucifer," has come into his own. The script was written centuries ago and man is now ready to bring the curtain down — on his own head.

Goldberg points out that men try to live the "tough guy" image even into death. Men who choose suicide as a way out of life's misery, select instruments that allow no turning back. Women choose pills but men choose guns, ropes, or stepping in front of trains and jumping from buildings and bridges. Even in death , the "cardboard Golliath" has to die like a macho man.

MIND OVER BODY —
A Decay of Imbalance

Ever since scientists split the atom, man has sought to dominate his body with his mind. Descartes' rationalism and its affect on societal values was mentioned earlier. Reason and logic have replaced intuition and emotion, resulting in distorted modern technocratic values. Today, we enjoy a very high standard of living, but our children have become addicted to TV and more recently, video games. These technological "toys" challenge the mental process while numbing the feeling process. Man's mind has served him well and yet, these mental creations have moved him farther away from the softer, more humane parts of himself. Overemphasis upon mental activity has perpetuated a split of mind and heart that continues to alienate man from the feminine aspect of his nature. Through distorted logic and reason, void of the softening, tempering influence of feminine emotion, our society accepts the possibility of nuclear war and its potential devastation. This is indicative of imbalanced, sick minds and also "death script" thinking.

Bednarik states that both the U.S. and the Soviet Union have analysts who attempt to determine whether or not they could fight and win a nuclear war. The American physicist, Herman Kahn, who authored the controversial book on thermonuclear war, **On Escalation,** concludes that a nuclear war would not destroy the world. He hypothesizes that:

> "...at the very worst, one tenth of the present American population would survive, that this would be increased to two-thirds by providing some protection against radiation, and that large scale protection by all available means would raise the proportion to over three-quarters."

His theory has been examined by the military and has had profound influence on it. During World War II, Kahn shocked military officials by scoring 181 out of 182 on intelligence tests. He was also famous for his total rejection of emotions and for focusing upon the future and "thinking the unthinkable." Labelled as the "Dr. Strangelove" of the nuclear age, he analyzed the consequences of a nuclear war between the Soviet Union and the U.S. with cool, calculating, rational detachment. His only expressed fear was the possible destruction of the ozone layer which protects the earth from solar rays. Although he admitted that he would not like the planet to be turned into a "virtual Sahara," he went on to say, "I don't wear a hat. However, that wouldn't be a problem, just uncomfortable."

The Reagan Administration's insistence that limited nuclear war is possible stems partially from this "boy wonder" genius, the physicist who maintains that hundreds of millions of people are expendable. This dangerous, short-sighted thinking is coming from a Model X100 computer within the brain of a "human" scientist. Does too much brain power lessen the connection with heart power?

In the U.S.S.R. Marshall Soholoresky's book **Military Strategy,** published in 1962, has had a dramatic influence upon the Soviet military command. This book, completed by Soholoresky and other military officials, acknowledges nuclear war as imminent:

"A war of the future will be decided not by a series of battles but by annihilating strikes at enemy centres. All that is left for conventional forces to do is occupy enemy territory and mop up pockets of resistance."

Both countries depend upon scientific calculations to determine the outcome of our world. In the words of the American mathematician James R. Newman:

"Wars are now planned scientifically with cold logic and the most up-to-date mathematical techniques — a procedure which is not only incapable of preventing war but may even prepare the way for it."

He is a strong critic of Kahn's work, which he states is "a moral treatise on mass murder: how to plan it, how to commit it, how to get away with it and how to justify it." Man and his machines can rationalize anything, even genocide. This type of thinking was endemic in the policies of the Nazi regime through which liquidating millions of human beings in the most effective way possible was treated as a business-like, scientific procedure. What makes this rationale so patently dangerous is that many men, especially those in positions of power, have been thinking this way for a long time. If we consider that this shallow, insensitive psychopathic outlook is leading us closer to a confrontation, let us consider how it begins. How is it that open, vulnerable, sensitive, fully alive male infants become such machine-like creatures, plotting the death of the world in such a desensit-ized manner?

We are born into this world with unlimited potential to grow and feel. Our bodies and minds are integrated, flexible and functioning as one living process, as is a seedling of a giant Redwood tree. Babies' movements, sounds and functions are in total balance with the rhythm of life's expression. As they begin to open themselves to the shock and reality of an imbalanced world, they gradually become estranged from their very life support systems. Although the effects of gradual strangulation are subtle, they are permanent and limiting. Each new generation passes through this deadening process as if it were a necessary part of the ritual of being born into the world. This handicap is the split that occurs between the two parts of self - the mascu-line (mind) and the feminine (body). This split creates a neurotic process, whereby one part (the mind) dominates the other (the body) which results in a type of internal war game. This imbalance can and will eventually become 'the' accepted status quo as the organism endures the rigid tensions of perpetual conflict.

> "And instead of the wholeness of the expansive tree, we have only the twisted and stunted bush."
>
> Eric Fromm

Strangulation, though a harsh word, does aptly describe what happens to those who have been stifled in their life process and have experienced the anxiety and pain of the mind-body split. Strangulation is a gradual process; life is slowly choked out of you and your eyeballs bulge from their sockets, distorting your image of the external world.

Janov, the founder of primal therapy, helps us to understand the neu-rotic process which evolves from this stangulation of our young. He states:

> "We are all creatures of need. We are born needing, and the vast majority of us die after a lifetime of struggle with many of our needs unfulfilled. These primal needs are the central reality of the infant. The neurotic process begins when these needs go unmet for any length of time, but when the child's needs go unattended, he hurts."

Janov shows us the pain of having our needs unfulfilled and how over time, this causes strangulation and the eventual decay of our wholeness and vitality. He also states that neurotic processes are substitute ways of satisfy-ing our unmet needs.

> "Neurosis is symbolic behavior in defence against excessive psy-chobiologic pain."

Hence, neurosis results when the natural processes are interfered with and cannot function in harmony with our being. The organism's desire to live is strong; therefore the child will go on living, but with shut-down needs as attempts to have them met are unsuccessful. Simultaneously, these repressed, locked away needs render an individual numb to his feelings and his experiences. How many men are dead from the shoulders down even though their rational, "computer" heads are active and functioning? They have substituted thinking for feeling, as it is less anxiety-provoking and less painful. The further they can remove themselves from feelings and stored memories, the less they have to fully experience their reality.

Men have difficulty in the presence of women who are crying. They are unsure as to whether they should comfort or retreat. This stress "flight or fight" syndrome is an example of the perpetual split between their minds and their bodies. It is less stressful to "think through" than feel an emotional situation. Men can be "calm and cool" as long as they do not feel those emotions that are desperate for expression beyond their limited, rational cage. By shutting down their bodies from the pain of unmet needs, they automatically train themselves to live without emotional release. A supervisor shouts at his workers, "Put a lid on it and let's get back to work." So, men numb and deaden their bodies by holding in their tensions.

Another way in which men deaden their feelings is to build protective physical armor around their bodies. The looks of determination on the faces of body builders suggest the extreme conditioning to which they are willing to subject themselves to build a protective wall.

Overdevelopment of the mind is another way that man continues to strangle himself. In my first undergraduate psychology course, the textbook defined psychology as "the scientific study of human behavior." My courses were primarily in learning theory. I spent more time with laboratory rats and pigeons than anything else, reinforcing their "positive" behavior and punishing or extinguishing their "negative" behavior. We learned how to modify people's behavior. Until recently, most graduate schools were Behavioristic in orientation. I have a bias against Behaviorism yet, in the right hands and with proper application, I have seen it be effective in bringing about change and healing. One of my instructors used a bell to condition us to signify the end of class. The first few times it rang, we responded by taking books in hand and preparing to go. He then scolded us for being inconsiderate and selfish in not allowing him to complete his lecture. From then on when the bell rang, we remained locked in our seats and waited until he waved that it was time to leave. He had, over time, conditioned us as though we were rats in a maze. I have heard of other Behaviorists who condition their children to eat, sleep and do certain chores. One even charted the resultant behavior changes in his children. This type of practice surely indicates a severely imbalanced ego in those who substitute modification for love and affection, thereby strangling the human needs of those under his influence.

One similarity between the United States and the Soviet Union is in their scientific pursuits. Behaviorists were greatly influenced by the Russian psychologist Pavlov, who trained dogs to salivate at the sound of a bell. Such power and control! Behaviorism lacks the compassion necessary to see and experience humans as creatures who are fully alive and unique. The U.S. chose to adopt more ways to further control and dominate.

Man's scientific rigidity is another way of hiding from his dammed-up emotions. His striving for scientific utopia is an unreal quest which keeps him from thinking and feeling simultaneously with fullness and passion. Man, as a thinking machine, is out of touch with his center, his connection to his feminine side and his vitality, his passion. He attempts to project externally to himself that which controls him within. It is no wonder that the Behaviorists are uninterested in the external process, believing that it does not exist as a necessary element of human behavior. This may explain why men feel empty inside but control this "fact" with rational justification. Men basically are ruled by their external environment while women are ruled by their internal. Feelings govern both, keeping us aware of and in tune with reality. The mind can render possibilities and the heart/body softens and makes us human.

Rational justification keeps the male, lost in the false image of himself. If this image persists over time he learns, often too late, that part of himself is still "needy." The body in action is no longer an expression of the self rather, it is a mirror reflection of the false image he projects. This is a "self" separate from "him" and "never the twain shall meet". He does his best to live in his mental process to the exclusion of his feeling self and try as he might, he cannot convince his deluded rational self that his unfeeling body is real, he cannot avoid the sense of haunting fragmentation which further splits his psyche. If left unaided, the male typically becomes a mass of bits and pieces which leave him sleepless, pervert his rational process and render his body tense and anxious. His rational self loses its hold as his feelings threaten to break through.

> "Why did the peacock scream in order to hear himself?
> Why did the peacock scream?
> Because he couldn't see himself"
>
> R.D. Laing

A colleague of mine is a professor in a medical school in research chemistry. He battled the university administration for years as it became more like a business. Once a researcher was praised for completing a few experiments, now he is required to publish numerous studies or collect his 'walking papers.' This creates an incredibly competitive atmosphere with the stress level in the labs becoming almost intolerable. These researchers are the "cream of the crop" in brain power, and yet their contributions to humanity are met with "gimme more." I saw a documentary on the pressures within the fields of research and was apalled. The "thinking machine" attitude is replacing the initial scientific heart of those who experimented for cures for diseases and ways to help human beings lead healthier lives. Now, researchers steal ideas and proposals from one another to make names for themselves or merely to hold onto their jobs.

If the "love starved" scientific community has become like a pack of wolves acting like sheep, hiding behind their degrees and titles, then we are in trouble. Our society has given power to these intellectuals and if they are becoming as "dis-eased" as the rest of us, who is going to steer the ship?

Since Sputnik was launched, both East and West have intensified the "brain power" competition. In the West,

> We define ourselves as people by what we do, what we have, and
> what we believe — not what we know or are.

We train our young men in this "doing" and grant them titles as reward.

I met a lawyer who was disappointed that his son had gone to M.I.T. and received a medal from the President for achievement, had dropped out and ended up living in Greenwhich Village making candles. He rejected his father's life-style of luxury and status and desired to become an actor. He was later accepted by a New York playhouse. His father spent thousands of dollars on his son's education. His son had been interested in helping humanity and he wanted to become a scientist. At M.I.T. he discovered others were more interested in experimenting with dreams of space travel than in working to solve the crucial problems of our time. The "top dogs" were more committed to the future than to the present.

While attending an international training conference, I participated in a cultural evening organized by three professionals from the Philippines. A recent Ph.D. in psychology stated that she had to learn to use the rational side of her brain to complete her studies. The Fillipino culture is more intuitively and feeling based than ours. As a Gestalt therapist, exploring the feeling process came easily to her. Compartimentalized, rational thinking was more difficult. She said that she began to experience more tension and anxiety as she explored the masculine side of learning. She also lost her love of playing guitar as her learning process became dominated by the strict, rigid quality of the rational process. In her second semester, she took a dance and yoga class and shortly began to "feel" once more. Her body had become foreign to her as her head assumed control. Now, again, her studying became more enjoyable. Most post-graduate programs are dominated by rational masculine values wherein the head rules, the scientific is the "bible" and the body is merely something to be studied.

Since man has learned to control his emotions through the rational processes of his mind, this rationalism is like an addiction to drugs. He lives in the "inbetween" world of the split between his mind and body. This vacuum sucks his vitality and enthusiasm for living as he becomes used to being dead, numb. Like sensations created by novocaine, his bodily processes are irregular, out of balance and disguised. His blood pressure is either too high or too low and his heart pumps too quickly. His mind races daily a hundred miles a minute and finally collapses into exhaustion and apathy. His mind is a kind of ruler within his skull while the needy, hungry child within his body is tense, ready to throw a tantrum and "tear the fucking place apart" and hurt those around him who are provoking, pushing his vulnerable buttons. Rather than explode, he implodes, strangling himself with the self-destructive internal control that he learned from his father and his father's father and all history's fathers. This effect, this imbalance, becomes the 'way it is' and defines the way 'he' is. This is the way of imbalanced rationalism; the way of the masculine script and it means to kill. From the **Hazards of Being Male:**

> "What emotions, impulses and needs is the male blocking? The answer, I believe, seems to be more or less all of them. Almost from infancy on, he is taught to control the expression of feelings and needs that interfere with the masculine style of goal-directed, task oriented, self-assertive behavior. That is, in the emotional area his socialization experience was 'Thou Shalt Not,' systematically, in direct or subtle ways, feelings and impulses were constantly being surpressed."

NUMB FEELING: But Not Dead

Men in our culture learn to fear their feelings as if they mean harm, render men helpless and remove their control. Unlike women who can experience the healing release of having a good cry, men through masculinity training are supposed to be strong, cool and detached; to "have their shit together." This training influences their whole lives and often numbs their awareness of other parts of themselves, which eventually become totally foreign through lack of expression.

When women comment, "I wish I knew what he was feeling," too often so does he! The average male does not know how to feel as feelings are within the domain of the feminine aspect.

Recently, I trained alcoholism counsellors in northern Alberta. After some intense therapy work, one trainee commented, "I realize now that I did feel hate inside of me." He had been working with his inability to feel intensely for anyone or anything. His emotions were numb but his thinking process was active. When I train counsellors, I always encourage them to unblock their own feeling process as I believe that counsellors are more successful when they know themselves. They are unable to help others if this element is missing from their perspective.

This training session lasted for over a month with much time spent delving into our personal lives beginning with childhood. The trainees, through this time, came to remember situations they had denied as part of their experience. They risked by removing their social masks and revealing more of their inner selves. Some of the men were astounded by the discovery of feelings thought long forgotten, seeing that beneath their protective barriers those feelings were alive and operative. They were able to see beyond the usual 'anger response' to the hidden hurt and pain. Once they could feel the place where the tears are stored, they were able to release them, transcending the rational response.

The trainee referred to earlier, learned denial of his feelings through his religious upbringing, which taught him that his parents were always correct and were to be respected. He began to break out of his "nice guy" image, which was a confusing, frightening process since anger or hatred toward his parents did not fit his learned image. He began to drink in his twenties to numb the fear and chaos he felt under stress. He became dependent upon booze and within a ten-year period he lost his job, his wife left him and he attempted suicide. During this time, he was denying the terrifying feeling that he really wanted to kill his parents. If the judge had not ordered him to the treatment centre after being charged with his fifth violation, he would probably be dead today. After his initial treatment, he joined A.A. and after six years of being sober, decided to help others with their drinking problems. He learned, as we all do, that if we hold onto pain, our false images, and our denial we eventually destroy ourselves and our loved ones. Suppressing these painful events also stops our memory of the joyous and positive times.

Other therapists can empathize when I speak of the difficulty men have sharing their feelings during counselling. Even when a marriage is at stake, it is common for a man to say, "I don't know what I feel," or to objectify his feelings with "I think" statements. When they do get close to true feelings during therapy, men often do not return with such excuses as they don't have time or they were not getting anything from the therapy. Its easier to "put a lid on it," keeping their feeings within, than to find healthy and creative ways to express them. Men would rather talk about sports, politics, business; anything that is not on an emotional level. When conversations, particularly with other men, become focused on a feeling area, they often change the subject or sabotage the conversation with platitudes or inane statements. Theodore Rubin, author of **Compassion and Self-Hate,** sheds some light on male inability to contact and know their feelings:

> "As children, we have little ability or experience to dilute or fend off what we learn. Therefore, we are extremely sensitive, vulnerable and impressionable. That which is during childhood — our period of maximum flexibility and development — becomes part and parcel of our very substance and is never forgotten. Our 'feelings' about the incidents and attitudes and moods grow out of those feelings."

The male child, like the female, is dependent upon parents and the social milieu for guidelines and directions he must follow to adulthood. Society, critical of the "cry baby," teaches young males to contain and control their emotions and be "tough." A young boy goes to his father with a cut knee, while the father applies the bandaid he says, "Come on, there is no reason to cry, it's not that bad." This message, whether implied or overt, received by the son each time he is hurt is a message of negation which is eventually absorbed as there is "no reason to cry." When his mother sees the hurt and attempts to comfort him, he says, "It's okay, it's not that bad." The human organism is designed to discharge pain through emotional release and when this natural process is interrupted by social expectations and pressure, the expression becomes difficult, if not impossible. When men are physically hurt, as in an accident, they tend to "grin and bear it" rather than express the severity of their pain.

When riding my bicycle home, I was struck by a motorcycle. I took my bloodied self home and said calmly to my mother, "A motorcycle hit me." She almost fainted at the sight of me. Men are encouraged to believe that the more pain they can withstand, the more manly they are. It is common to take incredible risks just to prove this manhood. Fraternity initiations are notorious for tests of masculine endurance, humiliation and ridicule. The Marine Corp's slogan is "The Marine Corp Builds Men!" and they will go to great lengths, to teach young recruits to endure physical and emotional pain. Their task is to push to the limit, then push one step beyond. Those who do not make the grade are sent to the "fat farm," which is a program designed to make overweight, sissies, into Marines. As this is a situation I experienced I can attest to the military approach to conditioning a man. The military image bombards a child early in his life; shoot a cap gun, watch war movies and cops and robbers on TV, and play "Star Wars" with playmates. He must be the protector, provider, be capable of withstanding pain, and be strong. Such responsibility necessitates rigorous training.

When a father is told by his son's principal that the boy was in a fight in school, he is secretly proud even though he has to discipline the boy. The father is glad that his boy stood his ground and fought "like a man" when another child called him "sissy" or "chicken."

A woman might say that fighting was silly if the fight was over a girl, but if one of her suitors backed down, she might be unimpressed and she might even lose respect for him. The liberation movement has not hit the silent majority with such an impact and this is an ancient form of chivalry that has existed from the beginning of time. When women are in danger, unless they are knowledgeable in some form of self-defense, they tend to rely upon the strength and courage of the male.

So the young male gets his conditioning from both genders. Often if he attempts to break free of his 'macho' role he is viewed as less of a man, so usually, he takes his pain and conceals his feelings. Either way he is trapped and loses. When he numbs his feelings, he is less than a fully functioning human being and this can contribute eventually to diseases of the heart and other bodily and mental functions.

One result of emotional repression is the generation of self-hate. If we are taught to be false people and this falseness becomes a dominant living feature, how can we live with ourselves? Disapproval from adults feeds this self-hating process as too many 'put downs' plant the seed that what we are "is not enough." That suppressed part of ourselves continues to live within us as the "outcast," "criminal," or "ugly duckling." As this part emerges occasionally, this "other side," displeases us as much as it does others. One way of coping with suppressed emotions is the male attachment to mechanical toys. Because we live in a material society, there is some comfort gained through the solace of a symbolic relationship with something. Because his relationship with other humans is unhealthy, the man can spend hours working on his car, motorcycle, boat or camper. These mechanical toys ask nothing and give him complete control over their function. The toys often are tangible examples of speed, power and of man's technological achievements. They are his, just as he belongs to the society that owns him and dictates his behavior. Everyone demands a part of him his boss, family, community and nation. Within each context, he is expected to measure up. He does not have much which is solely his own.

The boy begins with mechanical toys like train sets, bicycles, motor scooters and skateboards. As an adult, he may continue to play engineer or anything else that allows him to be in control. The typical stereotype of a military commander is one who has collections of toy soldiers which permit him to control, command and play 'war games.'

The ultimate test of manhood occurs upon completion of the driver's test and the subsequent heavy foot on the gas pedal of a powerful machine. The bigger the engine, the more powerful the 'horses', the stronger is the tendency to press the accelerator even further. "Lets see what this machine can do!" becomes the challenge from his peers. It is no wonder most traffic fatalities involve young people usually under the influence of alcohol and exceeding the speed limit. The "machine" has such power, the kind of power with which the young male is unfamiliar. He is unaware of his true personal power and confuses power of his car with his personal power. The thunder of the motor, screeching of tires, and burning of rubber are the ritual of displacement of one's inner strength through externalization. Owning a "machine" gives one title to status, prestige and position, adding to the false sense of being a man. The machine also provides a direct means of getting in touch with his feelings. When not competing with male rivals in proving his masculinity, he is indulging in "backseat boogie." Society sanctions this as an acceptable means to express his masculinity and his feelings through his genitals. If he impregnates a girl as a result, he receives the blessings of the masculine fraternity. He can choose to take responsibility for the event or he can leave town for college or the military. The message is to "do it" because it makes the man, but do not get harnessed with the consequence.

Our feelings are never dead even though that may seem to be the case. They keep us in contact with our vitality, our experience of living and our passion. Many men have lost their passion so it is no wonder that 'hear-throbs' like Tom Jones and Elvis Presley send women into swoons of passion. These men are the expression of vitality and sexuality. They move, they feel deeply with conviction and passion, and women sense this. Women desire such feelings because they know how to experience them. They wish for such feelings in their husbands and boyfriends and are continually disappointed when they find their men unresponsive emotionally.

Our feelings keep us connected to our authenticity and the more willing we are to experience our vulnerability, the more our feelings will bring us into the light. Without emotional expression we remain huddled in the dark corners of our minds, secretly desiring to expand our ideas into something creative, meaningful and wholesome. We sense that:

> "...The best and most beautiful things in the world cannot be seen or even touched. They must be felt with the heart..."
>
> Helen Keller

A JOURNEY INWARD:
Reclaiming Our Denied Selves

While browsing through the comics in the newspaper, I discovered a couple of strips that illustrate the dilemma men face in the attempt to know and express their inner selves. In the first one, a man and woman greet each other; she asks, "How are you today?" "Fine," he replies. She says, "Fine... that is what all men say when asked how they are feeling." The startled man decides to reveal how he is really feeling. He tells her about fears, inadequacies, confusion, etc. and goes on at great length. The woman then says, "Oh, I'm glad you're feeling fine." This exemplifies the confusion felt when men do finally open themselves to allow feelings, thoughts and memories to pour. There is a backlog of powerful emotions; that may overwhelm the listener. Often, the man is regretful that he took the risk. In the second strip, a dog is dragging himself along, ears drooped to the ground, eyes vacant, seemingly carrying the weight of the world on his shoulders. The caption reads, "You know how it is some days... queasy... out-of-sorts... no go! I must pull myself together and snap out of it!" The next column shows him with changed body stance and the caption reads, "Head up... shoulders back... chest out... tail erect... that's more like it!" The dog struts, holding himself like a proud peacock, enjoying his momentary release from the doldrums. It is only momentary. The last column shows him back to his original state and the caption reads, "Waste of time, I still feel terrible."

This script reveals the typical male's attempts at masking his emotions while beneath the facade he feels lousy and empty. Over time, these stored emotional fragments coupled with depleted self-esteem overwhelm him. They will eventually become the bars of a tormenting inner prison with the unexpressed parts of self becoming the prisoners. Emotional release is one way to freedom though most men have forgotten the method. It takes a man a long time to find his feelings' source as he is well indoctrinated not to display emotion. Women comment on him not revealing his feelngs while males block and sabotage his attempts to do so. He is caught in a double bind which holds him prisoner. This conflict is often expressed in body posture; with his head sitting high above the rest of his tense, rigid body. Men's unhealthy physical bodies are expressions of repressed emotionality.

As a therapist, I have watched men struggle in attempting to disclose their feelings and inner processes. Often the therapy group, particularly the women, eagerly anticipate the man's "spilling of his guts." These men become symbols of many men in a woman's life who did not express their feelings except perhaps in anger, whimpering or violence. The men often envy those who can express, sitting back hoping their brother will give them some hints or direction as to how to break free from their emotional prison. Often, those with the best intentions of sharing their inner selves get side tracked along the way, intellectualizing and becoming defensive for no apparent reason. Before he knows it he has lost his path, the map for getting to the source of his pain. I have seen groups cruelly attack the man who leads them on a 'wild goose chase.' He often talks trivia, dipping only briefly into deeper expression and then darting out once again. Groups can become impatient, critical and judgemental of those who won't 'shit or get off the pot.' He wants their attention and compassion, but as much as he wants to express himself he does not know how. As a child he was in touch with this world, as an adult he has lost the way and maybe even the faith that it does exist. Entering this world again is more terrifying than pleasurable and who needs more pain added to this life?

I remember times when I wanted to express my inner, tearing feelings but I could not find the words. I felt as though I was caught in a whirlpool and it took all my strength to prevent myself from being sucked into it. In conflict I wondered to whom I should listen? Which voice was correct? The listener sits and waits, puzzled, needing some sign to be able to express his thoughts in a clear, comprehensible manner. The tormenting conflict lives within us and we are aware of the desperation of the deprived parts of ourselves that demand expression. During stressful situations the prison doors fly open and these other selves ravage us, making us feel fearful, anxious and suffocated. We are uncertain as to whether we should accept the feelings or withdraw from them. As Hugh Prather says:

> "Feeling a certain way is one feeling, not wanting to feel that way is another feeling, and it does not cause the first feelng to stop. When I disown a feeling I do not destroy it, I only forfeit my capacity to act it out as I wish. Fear is often an indication I am avoiding myself. Fear is static, that prevents me from hearing my intuition. Anxiety, fear, panic, etc. . . . is a fleeing from something. There is something over there in the corner of my mind, some thought, some image that I don't want to look at, that I want to run away from."

The problem is not so much that men have difficulty in expressing their feelings, rather they have difficulty discovering feelings that fit their thoughts, images and actions. Often men's feelings are fragments of sadness, loss and rejection hidden within anger and rage.

Through lack of expression, men eventually lose the ability to recognize feelings and the bridges to others they represent. Most of the time men recognize the mental highways they have travelled so thoroughly during their lives. This paved, concrete pathway crumbles during times of stress or emotional crisis. When a man expresses anger or violence he rambles on about many different issues simultaneously, babbling and often incoherent as his conscious becomes flooded with forgotton psychic debris.

This inability to tap his emotional nature renders him helpless and isolated, surrounded by many internal fears which drive his imagination into an uncontrollable frenzy. Franklin D. Roosevelt once said, "The only thing to fear is fear itself." For a man thus trapped, it is impossible to know fear "itself" when the very fear of knowing fear stops him in his tracks. Men live with this gnawing sensation that ties them into knots, usually shortening their lives. Fear of his inner self drives him to destroy his environment, others and mostly, himself.

How can a man distinguish fear from the images and memories which intensifies, magnifies, exaggerates, and distorts those very images and memories? Many a man has asked himself, "What is happening, I do not understand." Attempts at understanding are thwarted and use of the imagination does not help as it becomes the master and he its slave. Imagination brings this horror show from its dressing room with the denied parts of self becoming the actresses and actors giving repeat performances of situations that brought us pain, fear and abandonment.

It is one thing to encourage the expression of this inner self and quite another to provide men with a process for doing so. Men have learned all too well how to survive within their prisons and have few references to healthy ways to escape or even accept that they are in a prison. They may search for the key to their emotional cell blocks, but most do not know where to begin to search. Men have been sentenced to spend their lives half in and half out of prison. They have been charged, put on trial then judged and found guilty. This sentence has been passed before birth. They have been judged before even committing a crime. The lives they face are full of crimes committed before their time. Each generation lives out its sentence for these crimes. They can be put on probation if they are "good little boys," and conform to their elders' and masters' wants. These authorities do have the power to pass further sentence and throw the disrespectful and rebellious back into prison. They too were born 'sinful' into this world and became so good at serving their sentence, they are now rewarded with authority positions. They are caretaker-prisoners watching over other prisoners; "the blind leading the blind."

In the classic story, **The Count of Monte Cristo**, we see this tragic situation enacted. A French naval officer, Edmund Dante, is charged with conspiracy by four power-thirsty noblemen who wish to prevent Dante from obtaining a captain's commission. One of them also wants Dante's fiance. Dante goes before the prosecutor who vindicates him, but indicates that he is required to spend one night in jail. He finds himself being taken to a horrid prison in the middle of the Mediterranean to serve a life sentence for a crime he did not commit. For the next ten years, Dante lives in solitary confinement speaking only to the jailor who brings him his meals. The cockroaches, coupled with his despair and dim shadow of hope, wear thin his will to survive. He has bursts of excitement in his dreams but when he awakens and finds he is still surrounded by thick walls and prison bars, his hopes are dashed once again. Finally, in utter despair, he stands in the middle of his cell and screams from the very pit of his belly - the nesting place of the soul. Screams are common in the prison and only fellow inmates hear them. These screams of anguish were once part of his hope, his faith which are now foreign to him. He befriends a cockroach and a rat who share his cell; he is aware they are there by choice and he is not, hence they are free.

One day he hears a different noise, he listens for days and finally in desperation he calls, "Are you a prisoner like me?" To his amazement, he hears a faint voice on the other side of the wall. Dante begins to dig around one of the bricks in his cell wall and after finally removing one, discovers a little man with a dirty face and mud-caked hair. The little man climbs into Dante's cell and he steps back in fear. Is this real or are his eyes playing tricks on him? This is a real human being, a man like himself who understands the agony, the terror. They stare at each other, sniffing at the foul stench they both carry due to years of confinement. Each yearns for physical contact. This is similar to the handshake which, for modern men is the symbol of a bridge of connection and communication, and is often a holding stance, one of interrogation as potential human brothers are strangers; enemies not to be trusted.

Dante sees the wooden cross around the other's neck and feels more at ease, he is with a man of God. They cautiously approach each other, eager to touch and as they come nearer, they burst into simultaneous laughter. They each sensed the absurdity of their cautious, masculine meeting ceremony. They are in prison. There is no etiquette. They embrace, holding each other tightly. Dante is sobbing. He has a brother in the flesh, a symbolic image of himself. The holy man is a symbolic father figure. He also portrays the nurturing feminine aspect which brings Dante closer to his essence, his humanness. This meeting is the symbol of lost selves being found. Through the emotional embrace they help each other to reconnect the denied parts of selves locked within prison walls.

Abbey Furrier, an Italian priest, was framed like Dante for a crime he did not commit because others perceived him as a threat. However, Abbey felt no sense of revenge and still desired to serve his fellow man. He had been digging his way out of prison with crude tools made from fish bones and parts of his bed and armored with strong faith. Dante, aware the priest was older and wiser asks him to teach everything he knows. The priest is well versed in philosophy, economics, theology and other subjects and his desire to pass this knowledge to Dante is keen. He does wish for someone who can teach him beyond his level of knowledge. In spite of the years spent digging his way to freedom, he is not free:

"...five years spent digging on a tunnel to freedom only to find that it is only another man's cell."

This statement symbolizes the dilemma which faces men today and has for centuries. Mankind has spent centuries seeking answers to the riddles of the universe. He has built civilizations and toppled them, and from ruins constructed a vast technology. He has conquered space travel, milked the earth's natural resources and developed communications networks and world satellites. Tremendous sacrifices have been made to pursue such quests. The journey's end finds him back where he began. Despite his numerous technological accomplishments, he is quite primitive in the understanding of himself and his relationship to life and others, particularly to men. He remains trapped in the prison of his own construction and though he has repeatedly attempted to dig his way to freedom using sophisicated tools, he realizes he is miles away from the cell's exit. He sees the futility of the energy expended yet is helpless to change the destructive pattern as exemplified by the priest's statement. This predicament is obvious when males meet, each looking for an escape only to find his reflection in the presence of another male 'prisoner' which reminds him of his life 'sentence'.

Dante and the priest continue to tunnel their way to freedom. The priest helps Dante understand why he had been framed and this realization makes Dante even more determined and angry for revenge. He begins to exercise daily to build his strength for his escape and listens intently to the other's wisdom. The priest advises him to release the revenge from his soul. Dante assures him that the four men require punishment and this would be an act of God and he will be the one to carry out the mission. They continue their labors until the priest takes ill and can not continue. He tells Dante he is dying and gives him a map hidden within his wooden cross to a treasure hidden within an ocean island cave. The treasure is the priest's but as he can no longer use it, he tells Dante to do so for "God's work." With his dying breath he bids Dante "Godspeed" and falls into the sleep of death. Dante mourns the priest for many days as though a part of himself died with him. The jailer upon discovering the body of the old man, wraps it in a body bag. Dante sneaks into the cell, deposits the fellow's body in the tunnel and sews himself into the body bag. The bag is thrown from the cliff's edge and plunges to the ocean below. Dante frees himself with a concealed knife and he drifts for days until he is picked up by some smugglers who nurse him back to health. The only way Dante's escape was possible was to pretend to be dead. This could easily relate to the rising death rate for men. If they are unable to escape the 'masculine' prison cast into at birth, then their only release is through death. Is this a conscious choice? Some choose gradual death through addictions and self abuse, while most do live out their life sentence in a responsible fashion, "guilty as charged".

Dante, upon recovering his strength, finds the treasure and returns to carry out his revenge. He uses his riches and prominence to destroy the four men; two are sent to prison, one to an asylum and the other commits suicide. Dante realizes he is still empty upon completion of his mission. All his wealth, power and manipulative ability still leaves him hopelessly disconnected from himself. His desire for revenge carried him through years of imprisonment but is not enough to give him happiness or peace of mind.

This drama is acted out in the world of free enterprise where many a man has climbed to the top by stepping on those beneath him for personal gain. Men use one another to find the security and 'heaven on earth' through power, control and manipulation. Men who have been manipulated and controlled as children will repeat destructive patterns with their sons unless they free themselves. Others revenge themselves for their own imprisonment by making others their slaves.

The market crash of the '30's revealed that men were willing to cut the throats of others before someone did the same to them. The losers of this master-slave game ceremoniously committed suicide by jumping from bridges, putting guns to their heads and leaping from tall buildings. The option available to the 'loser' was life in disgrace and failure as a man, or death.

The need for revenge which ruled Dante and the lives of many modern men is more than the result of losing a battle in the industrial marketplace. It is a deeper conflict that resides in men today as it has for generations and it has become an acceptable part of the male's experience in life. The conflict is between his spirit and socialized role, his external and internal self. This conflict is deeper than any wound and cannot be touched with the rational process which, in fact, keeps it sealed even tighter within. This is man's insatiable thirst to become united with his spiritual self, his essence. Instead of this essence, man has trapped himself within his false ego; his false sense of "I-ness," which is separate from "Thou." He lacks the feminine principle expression in relation to this balance.

Dante carried out his revenge believing he had been chosen by God to punish those who framed him. How many crusaders believe their mission of destroying the Moslems was ordained by God, marching into the holy lands with symbols of crosses upon their chests?

Do those calculating, cold aspects of men keep the revenge cycle alive? Do we seek revenge for being weaned so soon from our mothers; for being led down the accepted path of 'manhood' only to find we had been used, punishing others who made us play a game of "please me, . . . or no love?"

We were taught to mistrust our inner selves, the guiding authority which seeks to help one become a fully-functioning human being with balanced qualities of masculine and feminine. These prisoner selves are fragments of the psyche denied and destined to survival within the confines of the prison. These selves see each other daily but address one another as separate "cell mates." Each is a prisoner within himself and to one another. What they see is fear, caution and need for revenge. With incomplete feelings they are unable to be the hope and faith aspects of themselves.

For generations our fathers, have secretly desired that their sons be able

to break free of the destructive chains that prevent the reclamation of those
parts of self and liberate the confined soul. Men have externalized their
wrath about their life sentences by expressing it in their environment,
towards other people and themselves. Like zombies, their vitality and
strength are wasted in living out their sentence only half-aware. They mask
their feelings so others do not see the deception, the fraud. Most of their life's
role models lived as frauds too. They modelled a mode of behavior which
made them prisoners having no information on how to change the condition. We all know a model prisoner may 'get off for good behavior,' however,
those in positions of authority are imprisoned as well.

Men learn to externally conform but at the cost of internal essence. A
male becomes controlled by this external authority; it becomes his accepted
lifestyle. When a man goes within and risks viewing what is really there, he
can free himself from the clutches of externalization. He has to reach beyond
the socialized scripts and be willing to challenge the pseudo explanations of
what is 'right'. We have been outwardly dictated to for too long, controlled by
our minds and isolated from our feelings. Within our inner world live the
remnants of our past, the memories of our history, goals and dreams intertwined in the living expression of the present. Each is connected and serves
to move us toward integration and wholeness. We need to connect with the
many male mentors of our lives who taught and guided us, sometimes
incorrectly; who praised or hurt us and taught us about being 'male.' We also
need to meet with the many women who nurtured, supported, loved and
confused us.

It is time for men to face what we truly are, what we have become and if
necessary, pull our heads from the sand. We have been trapped and conditioned no more or less than women. Both require liberation and transformation to break our chains.

We are at a turning point in history. We cannot rely on past value systems
and the future is unpredictable. We are in transition from the stage of our
psyche's development that leads to imminent destruction and to an exciting
new stage of potential possibilities and alternatives. We must make the
choice — being free or dying as prisoners; being guided by inner, innate
forces of human truth and love or be controlled by external authoritarian
forces. Many people caught within the prisoner drama are half aware or too
busy "searching and doing" to stop, look inside, listen and feel. Those willing
to go within and remodel are planting green grass where cement once was
and are building meditation spaces and discovering new directions and
alternatives to the present course of inaction.

The old self must die to allow the emergence of the lost and hidden self.
Our totalness is our birthright which has been sacrificed to the false,
"masculinity" god, trapping both sexes. We are both aspects; neither mascu-

line nor feminine.

As we leave this chapter, we are removing the confining strait-jacket and clearing ourselves for fresh possibilities and healthier, connected directions. When we chart new courses, creating maps for inner discovery, we will become architects for a new kind of male personality. If we can pilot our time machines through space as did H.G. Wells, then we can find the courage to reconnect our feelings and can then travel through Dante's inferno and return again.

The creative feminine process can teach us a great deal. It is a part of us awaiting expression. We can be free spirits, men without cages, stallions with no corral boundaries. We do not have to withdraw from the very thing we pursue. The feminine creature that we seek outside ourselves is a symbol of need that is not fulfilled within.

It is time to be responsible, sensible internal navigators and explorers. Once we clean out past residue, we can begin to heal. We can trust again and be open and challenge those actions which confine us from our script learning. By travelling within our unconscious, we can increase the connections between it and our waking world by applying the messages from this place of soul. Success depends upon how far we are willing to go. We can view our childhoood training with fresh perspective and begin to soothe and heal the self-hate wounds with forgiveness and love. We owe it to ourselves to free ourselves and will be happier for it. We can build bridges to others while exploring ourselves, being truly brothers and appreciating the desired love and support from other men in our lives.

> "Adulthood arrives when one stops thinking he can walk on water and starts building himself a bridge."

MOM & DAD: Molders of Society's Sons

"She treats me like a little boy and I'm over thirty years old!" Phil explained. His frustration was obvious as he talked about the relationship with his mother. I had just picked him up from the Calgary Airport. He was returning for his annual parental visit. Though Phil and I knew each other only briefly, we had discovered several areas of mutual interest. Our awareness of men's issues and the desire to explore new ways to relate to men made us comfortable with each other. His expressed frustration was not new to me. We had spoken before, comparing our childhoods, and had both been addressing these similar issues when we met. I was glad to know him and valued his willingness to be open which made it easier for me to share.

Phil related that his mother had always been overprotective as a result of almost losing him in the birth process. Later, he was striken with a physical disease and was skinny and pale in appearance as a result. Phil was an only child. His mother, because of his sickly condition, forbade Phil to play football, street hockey and other sports with neighborhood boys as they were too "rough." She was afraid he would be injured. As a result he spent most of his time in his room. His collection of comic books would rival Spielberg's. He often fantasized about being one of the super- heroes, fighting crime, defending against evil and possessing super-powers. He subconsciously desired the strength to "break out" of his in-home cell. He really desired to be out playing with the other boys. He felt like a prisoner, isolated, like a fragile piece of breakable china. He said he loved his mother and knew she loved him, but her constant attention and worry smothered him.

His relationship with his father was the opposite. Like many of us, it was distant, almost non-existent. His father was the youngest of nine siblings, which may have similarities to being raised as an only child. He was quiet, solemn and often unapproachable. He had worked for twenty years as a mechanic in an industrial machine shop. He was hard worker and had been a good provider for his family, fulfilling his 'father' role as best he could. He attended church services regularly and disciplined Phil when asked to do so by Phil's mother. Phil felt that he did not know his father, that he was a stranger in the house who carried the title, "Father." Phil could remember it having been different when he was a child and used to crawl onto his father's lap when he was watching TV. He can recalls wrestling with his dad, but his mother stopping it with the caution of ". . .don't hurt little Phil!" Eventually these rare moments of physical contact faded and Phil missed those times. He attempted to contact his father in other ways, but could not penetrate the wall of reserve. Phil began to develop a similar wall around himself which further increased the distance between the two. When he was going through puberty, he recalls having tried to talk with his father about the changes his body was experiencing. Phil's father became very uncomfortable and told Phil to ask his mother. He really needed feedback from a male who had been through the changes he was now experiencing. Many men have found this to be a typical father's response to such sexual inquiry.

Phil's mother was a model housewife-homemaker. Meals were always on time and she constantly cooked Phil and his father's favorite foods. Apple Strudel, his father's favorite, was a family tradition. She had always tried to be a 'good 'wife and mother and was told by her mother on her wedding day that, " the way to a man's heart is through his stomach." Phil felt she was often more of a 'mother' to his father than she was to him as she constantly doted on his father. She picked out his clothes, brought him his slippers and his beer when he was watching T.V. She spoiled both of them and Phil was aware of his dependance on her and that he took her for granted. She cleaned his room, did his laundry and bought his clothes until he was a teenager. Today, she still chooses his father's wardrobe and sends socks and underwear to Phil in Toronto on a regular basis.

Phil was a scholastic success as a result of being an avid reader. He was always at the top of his class academically, a member of the honor society and active in many clubs and organizations. He seemed to be a model student and his mother was obviously proud of him. He did not smoke, drink, get into trouble or go out with girls. He was a loner and a bookworm He was afraid of girls and probably modelled his father's aloofness and lack of involvement.

In his senior high school year, he began to break out of his shell trying marijuana at a party and liking the way he felt when he smoked it. He began to smoke cigarettes and drink, though his indulgences were mild compared to his classmates. His parents were unaware of the changes in his behavior. One night, before graduation, this situation changed. He and several others had been at a party that had been busted for pot and his parents had to come down to the police station to get him. His mother was in hysterics all the way home crying, "Where have we failed?" His father was quiet as usual as his mother continued her interogation about pot. Phil felt that his father may have been angry, disappointed or surprised but he never expressed it. The charges were later dropped against Phil when the police could not prove that he had been smoking. He was grounded for two months, having to stay home every night. This form of punishment was a replay of his boyhood days. He began to realize that he had to break his dependency pattern and make a life for himself or he was going to suffocate. He decided to attend a University in the East. He was scared but he knew he had to push himself from the nest because his parents would never encourage it. His mother wanted him to attend University in Calgary and live at home.

The day came when Phil won a scholarship to the University of Toronto. He immediately accepted as it was his chance to be free. His mother tried to dissuade him and his father seemed indifferent. The next three years passed quickly and Phil studied zealously and was tops in his faculty. He lived in the student dorms and disciplined himself to the task of scholarly achievement, out to prove himself in the manner which he was accustomed. Upon gradua- tion, he was immmediately accepted into the graduate faculty of Sociology. He decided to continue with his schooling and got an apartment nearby.

He discovered that living on his own was not an easy undertaking and while he was enjoying his freedom, he found that he missed his mother's attentive pampering and home-cooked meals. He was growing tired of the routine of eating in restaurants and faculty lounges so he tried cooking, quickly discovering that he did not know the first thing about preparing a meal. He resorted to prepackaged foods, like TV dinners and found they tasted like their cardboard containers. He missed having his clothes ironed and when he couldn't get the ladies from down the hall to do them, he wore them wrinkled. Occasionally, he would have his clothes cleaned and pressed professionally, but his meager teacher's assistant salary made this prohibitive. He tried to iron his own clothes, giving up after burning holes in them. Academically, he was outstanding but his personal self-care habits and well-being were hopeless. At the age of 26, Phil was a little boy in an adult's body.

Phil began to date during his undergraduate years. This was a novel experience for him and he felt out of his league. Over time he became more comfortable but found most women he liked were either too independent or overly nurturing. The independent ones intimidated him and the others reminded him of his mother. He tried living with one of his girlfriends, but the arrangement ended dramatically. He began to think that he lacked what was required in relationships and withdrew. He was successful as a student but he continuously felt vulnerable and intimidated by the assertive, out-spoken female faculty members. He increasingly became aware that his dependency on his mother and his lack of communication with his father was affecting his self image. As a scholar, he was a professor's dream, an intellectual giant, but as a male and a person, he was a dwarf. He felt anxious, lacked confidence and did not know how to survive on his own.

Phil was about to give up on his relationships with people when he met Cathy. She was different from most women he had known. She was inde-pendent, ambitious and was from a closely knit family which encouraged her to be what she wanted to be. Her brothers and sister had their conflicts but their parents always taught them to see and respect each other, not only as family, but as persons. Phil envied the relationship that she had with her family. Cathy was also caring and compassionate. She didn't need Phil the way other women had. She was not down on men either. Cathy was her own person and had a keen interest in people and in life. She possessed a balance of head and heart which frightened and attracted Phil simultaneously. They became very good friends able to talk with one another about everything from politics and parenting to relationships and sex. She helped him under-stand more clearly the conflicts he was experiencing with women. Cathy worked in a children's home and had a way with children which was not surprising considering her warm openly loving nature. She was in her last year of social work. Phil credited Cathy with helping him know himself better and develop a new way of being with women — friendship. Cathy, upon graduation, took a position in a native community in Northern Onta-rio. They kept in touch by mail but eventually Cathy faded from Phil's life. She had been his greatest ally, helping him to know the deeper aspects of himself and to use his head and heart together. He was on his way even though he had a long journey ahead of him.

Phil continued to visit his parents during Christmas and for two weeks each summer. He was gaining a perspective on his dependency on his mother but he was still confused. During one visit he noticed his mother was acting strangely. She became obsessed with housework, she was either scrubbing floors, vacuuming or carrying a dust rag about the house ever ready to catch a particle of dust that dared to appear on a table or window pane. When not cleaning, she would sit on the porch and flip through family photo albums or Phil's high school year books. Upon his departure, she embraced him so tightly, he had to break her hold. Her eyes, full of sadness and fear, were brimming with tears. During his flight, Phil thought of her holding onto him as though she would never release him. He was concerned that she was in such pain and began to realize there was another side to the dependency issue between them. She, too, was dependant upon him. This was a new insight. Perhaps, she needed Phil to be dependent upon her. Phil sensed the conflict of his dependency with his mother was beginning to turn around, he now had a new perspective which could free him from the cycle.

Upon completion of his course work for his masters degree, Phil again graduated with distinction. He was offered a teaching position with the faculty but he declined, choosing instead a position with a small community college which he felt would be a fresh beginning for him. Within a few months he had made the adjustment and was enjoying the small campus atmosphere.

In his second year he noticed an announcement for a men's support group. He had heard of such groups and was curious as to what an all male group was like. Several women he knew were involved in similar women's groups. He signed up. Initially, he was uncomfortable, guarded and uncommunicative. He listened to others talk of their thoughts and feelings of growing up male and found his interest being sparked. He began to feel more at ease and realized, as others talked of their relationship with their parents, that his situation was not unique. It was a new experience to have other men share themselves. He felt for the first time in his life, supported and not isolated.

Phil attended the sessions for two years and he thrived on the experience, actually becoming somewhat outspoken. He discovered that he had something to offer the others. Many had been married and shared the pain of loneliness after their divorces. They shared lessons learned in marriage and that the dependency issue was part of their marriage conflict. Most had been raised traditionally and, like Phil's father, were dependent upon their wives as they had been on their mothers. They were basically comfortable with this arrangement.

Phil knew the support group was helping him further understand his relationship with his mother as well as with men and women. Some of the discovery was painful. Seeing himself locked into his mother's dependency needs still confused him and frustrated him, though these feelings were less apparent. He was aware he needed to be separated from his parents now that his mother was increasing her dependency need for him. He was determined to continue with new perspectives as he was finally getting some answers which he had sought since childhood.

We turned onto the street where Phil's parents lived. I observed Phil's silence during our trip in from the airport, he looked pensive and apprehensive. I turned off the ignition and mentally debated whether I should comment on what I had noticed. "What is going on? You're as pale as a ghost." Phil, silent, stared through the windshield. "I feel like vomiting," he uttered, "and I have a headache." I listened as Phil shared with me that in the last few visits home, he would feel sick to his stomach before arriving. He did not know the cause but felt it had something to do with his mother. Lately, he had been experiencing an overwhelming fear when he was around women whether they were friends, colleagues or strangers. He felt as though there was a whole inside of him which was sucking him in regardless of his trying to escape the overwhelming feeling. It took all his concentration to combat this powerful feeling. I could identify with this situation as I had had a similar experience when living in California. I shared my experience with him and he seemed to relax slightly. I told him to take some deep, slow breaths and as he did the colour returned to his cheeks. Looking less strained, he said, "Thanks, I'll be all right now." His voice was broken as he stared into space, unmoving, absorbed by his thoughts. We sat in silence. Finally, Phil's hand edged towards the door handle, shaking, trying to open it. He succeeded on the third try. He grabbed his suitcases and dropped them between his feet turning to look at the house, then back to me, then again to the house. I got out and we stood looking at each other, smiling. Words were unnecessary. He looked at me again, his head half down, and I knew he needed something. I paused and said, "How about a hug?" He nodded and we embraced. I felt more like a brother than anything else. I empathized with him as I had experienced similar feelings with my own mother and am still working with those feelings. With eyes closed, I held him. Initially, he held onto me then, there was a shift and he was holding me. I could feel the tears welling in my eyes asking myself why people have to experience so much pain in order to become healthier human beings? Why did Phil and his mother have to suffer so much? What do we human beings fail to understand in raising our children? Hopefully, all the pain and suffering reaps its just reward.

My mind began to be flooded with thoughts and images of Phil and his mother. I was unsure as to whether I was 'reading' his mind or not. Maybe I was seeing an image, a metaphor, that has been enacted countless times between parent and child. The images became more vivid. I saw Phil, suitcases beneath each arm, approach the back porch of his parents' home. The door opens and Phil's mother teary eyed with anticipation is standing in the doorway. His father stands behind her, silently, his large hands cupping the doorframe. Phil and his mother's eyes meet, she moves toward him with open arms. Phil stops, unable to move. His insides are churning, confused he looks again. Who is this woman? HIs mind races back in time, searching out events and people who have been part of the drama. Is this Jody who wanted to be married and take care of him? Is this Helen who frightened him with her aggressiveness? Is this Cathy who taught him of love and friendship? Again his eyes connect with hers; is this the one who brought him into the world; took care of him when he was ill; treated him as though he was special, spoiling him? The images rock his mind. "Phillip! Phillip!". . . someone calls his name, who is it ? His mind is flooded with memories. He turns to the direction of the soft, warm feminine voice and the images begin to fade bringing him to the 'present' once more. The voice is not that of Helen, Cathy or Jody, but his mother, the first woman he knew in his life, closer and as much a part of him as his own soul. She was duplicated in other women he had known. His mother leaves him ambivalent, loving and hating simultaneously. He knows he must free himself to become a whole human being, to continue his male journey in life. He must see, accept and love his mother for her humaness and being, like him, a "society's child."

Phil's story describes the dilemma of men who have grown up in industrial, modern society and what many of us experience in learning to break dependency patterns with our parents. This journey must be undertaken by all men, sooner or later, to be their own persons, in charge of their own lives. Phil's situation may be a slightly unique one in that he was an only child and stricken with physical disease early in his life. I believe, however, his situation magnifies the dependency. He had to struggle even more because he was an only child and received excessive attention. An only child learns to be alone in the world and this was accentuated by his mother's overprotection and his father's lack of involvement. There is something of value in Phil's story for all men. We can find our own dependencies which took root early in our lives and learn how this came to shape our images of being male.

We are aware of the lasting effects that our childhood upbringing has upon our lives and how our parents fit into the scheme. Whether vague or clearly outlined, we can see how many of our traits, attitudes, beliefs and behaviors about life and raising our own children have come from our parents. Some of these we are able to acknowledge and adopt while others we try to deny or reject. Our parents had a tremendous influence on us and for some, they still do. Our parents are our first primary teachers and models. Whether their teachings were life enhancing or otherwise, the lives we lead today have been chosen as a result of our parental relationships. These could have been a blessing, a curse, or a combination.

Though my focus is parent-son relationships and how this produces unhealthy male images, it is in no way an attack against parents. Parents today, receive more than enough criticism and blame for numerous social ills. My intention is not to bring parents to trial. During my years as a therapist, I have heard many stories and witnessed episodes of the parent-child issue. From situations stemming from both sides, I conclude that parents have been given a 'bum rap' and have been expected to do the impossible. They lack the necessary tools and skills to fulfill the requirements an ever-changing society has bestowed upon them. They have been similarly socialized through assembly line education and then pressured to perform in more loving, compassionate and human ways. Times change, people change and society's blueprint for living changes. Unless people are prepared for such changes, chaos can result. This may be especially true in child-rearing practice. In order to gain a perspective on the effects parents have on their son's self-image and whether this is negative or positive in the long run, it is necessary to look beyond the parental role. To comprehend the the whole picture, we must include the social, economic, and spiritual factors that form the foundation of all aspects of parenting. Parents have indeed been molders of the male personality but we must consider how they themselves have been shaped by beliefs, laws, politics and social institutions. Prior to the industrial revolution, parents were the major teachers of the young male. Today this has changed dramatically. We are not merely the sons of our parents nor are they just our parents. We are "society's sons" and behind our parent's molding and influence, our lives are governed by ideology that influences our parents as well. Our parents now answer to a higher parenting body composed of institutions, beliefs, laws and values of society. By tracing the historical development of such influence, we can gain a comprehensive outline.

A mother makes a great contribution to the quality of her son's development as does the presence or absence of a father. What mothering skills a woman has inherited are dependent upon the nature of her own childhood. Similar influences are important for those who had fathers who were distant, abusive or dominant. Obviously, this has impact as far as a man's behavior and attitude toward his own sons. We must understand what made up the "social fabric" of the times to fully discover the answers. Society's patterns have been changed through modernization and these changes have altered the importance of the family and transformed child-rearing practices.

The birth experience, one of life's miracles, takes the energy and love of a man and woman to commence the process. It is important to continue this love energy after the birthing. Birth can mark the start of a fearful, struggling process called life or it can mark the beginning of a journey of love and learning. Life's journey can leave a son fragmented, out of touch with his identity and purpose, spending his time seeking security, acceptance, and love through temporary gratification using "things" and power over others as a means. He can hide aspects of who he is from himself and others. He learns that certain parts of who he is are best left unexpressed, kept under lock and key. He learns he must conform, fit a mold.

So what are the consequences of being born into a post- industrial world that holds technology and scientific achievement as a priority over the health and well-being of people? How does parenting and growing up within this world differ from before the onset of the industrial revolution?

If modern children sat down and spoke with their grandparents, they would discover a world much different than today. Times were harder but families were closer with the roles of parenting more simply defined. The family was the cornerstone of the society. The father physically protected and provided for his family. Sons were apprentices to their fathers, learning at an early age how to tend livestock, plow and harvest, or learn a craft or trade. Mother's role was defined as having children and homemaking. She passed this education on to her daughters as an expectation of wives and mothers. The family was larger and the survival of it depended upon the shared tasks and responsibilities of its members. Children were required to help with housework, farmwork and raising other brothers and sisters. Everyone had to participate. Parents had to be adaptable and flexible, both were authorities and they shared these roles and each held the other with respect. Survival dictated a clearly defined division of labor.

Following industrialization, society and its institutions were altered and the "cornerstone" began to crumble. Families became smaller and fathers' role changed to one of less involvement as they saw their chance to make it big in the cities. Fathers began to stay away from home, working in factories and offices during the day while mothers remained at home. Industrialization and mass production was taking over the world of trades and individual craftsmen were having difficulty surviving. The "powers that be" determined that large numbers of people would be required to keep the new industries alive and that they must be educated in sciences to advance research in higher levels of industry. Horace Mann, a leading industrialist, believed that children could be put through an assembly line type learning process, modelled after factory production. Laws were passed to keep children in school until a certain age. This was the onset of 'schooling' still characteristic in today's world. Industrialization was changing the very fabric of life. Specialization was becoming the trademark for professions and preparatory education.

The family still maintained its connection around the supper table, family outings and church, but the esssence of the family was owned and dictated by the state. Family life and the sharing of resources, teachings, learnings and dreams was becoming a memory.

At the height of industrialization we experienced two world wars. Though wartime was an era of loss, it was also a time of advancement of industrialization through the production of weapons. Many a shrewd business man made his millions from this production.

Following these wars, a great deal of effort and involvement was initiated to rebuild what the wars had destroyed.

Women were encouraged to have many children to replenish the population that was lost to the war and childrearing became a federally supported enterprise. So, those who gave birth to more sons, were fulfilling their patriotic duty. Baby production became as essential as producing goods and services and keeping society's industries afloat. Government and industry had become kissing cousins. What was good for industry, was good for the country and what was good for both, was good for the family. So industry and government were gradually taking over certain parental roles. Government supported schools were assuming responsibility for children's learning, a task once performed by parents. Gradually, parental influence was dwindling as social institutions increased their impact on children's lives.

It is obvious that industrialization has done much to fill our lives with leisure and efficiency and we have a great deal to be thankful for. But let us not fool ourselves. The dream of our industrial fathers has gotten out of hand. It has stripped us of much of our humanity. It dictates our choices, our beliefs, our social policy both national and foreign. It suffocates our potential for bonding with one another. It renders us slaves to our external world while our inner world finds no expression. It has alienated us from ourselves and from one another, turning us into strangers, robots and much like the machines we create and operate. It fragments us and makes people rigid, arrogant and self-indulgent. We exploit Third World countries to enjoy tremendous affluence in our own country.

Parents have been victims of the power of this dream; they are immersed in it. They are helpless to break this influence chain and continue to subject their own children to similar ideology. Fathers, who were 'strangers' to their fathers, or were bullied and controlled by them, become the same role models for their children. Mothers who were taught that their mission in life was to produce children, housekeep, tend to children's and husband's needs are reduced to a function that hardly leaves room for self-actualization. This further creates a woman who becomes trapped and dependent upon the needs of her children. As Ester Harding says in **The Way of All Women,**

> ". . .she has become dependent upon their dependency and she
> will hardly know how to live without them."

This was demonstrated with Phil's story.

Society's images that parents and children are to serve its needs, strips away the most essential ingredients for living; being real and being human. The advertising images created to encourage consumerism, "to keep the wheels of progress turning," move us more certainly into a man-made world of make believe. It is a world that is a reflection of what man would like to be without acknowledgement of what he truly is. This tempting dream world can easily entangle and seduce people into losing themselves. Once they are entwined, their offspring become equally mesmerized.

Parents have a tremendous impact on the development of their offspring. However, it takes the combination of society's traditions, myths, past and future dreams plus present attitudes and practices, to shape a human being.

Thus far, I have used the term 'parent' loosely in describing parental influence. I will now examine each parent's influence, showing how this is over-shadowed by other factors.

Mothers who ensure their sons' over dependency upon them, have themselves been socialized into less than a whole person. As young women, they learned to be dependent and that their ultimate destiny was to be a 'good' wife and mother. They were taught that men were superior in intelligence and ability in every area except motherhood and housekeeping which is left to the domain of the female of the species. They were taught that it was essential to please their husbands by duplication of his mother's tending and care. His mother was often there to ensure that this was carried out. This is the basis of a traditional in-law rift through which wives have been subjected to intensive intimidation. Often these women compensated for any potential failure in the mother-in-law's eyes by being the best mother they could to their husbands and to their children. Mothers-in-law could be a fresh nurturing presence but often cannot get past the role and function expectation. Other talents and needs that a woman has are not permitted to be expressed or experienced within the traditional role set. She becomes dependent upon her mother role and sacrifices much of her other ability and talent. Her entire identity is defined within the nurturing role of the 'happy housewife and homemaker.' Part of her yearns for expression and this yearning is often transferred to her son so that her wishes and desires may be fulfilled through him.

If she had a difficult relationship with her mother and is unable to change the negative patterning, she will find it difficult to meet her son's needs. He will become like a ghost of her unfulfilled needs, a constant reminder. Her frustration with the child will be a carry over from the confusion experienced in her own childhood. She will live through the child in the hope that she will discover some answers about her childhood. Unhealthy exposure to the male world through her relationship with father, grandfather, uncle, playmate or brother will create problems in her ability to distinguish "her" needs from "his" needs. Part of her holding on to her son stems from her unconscious and the memories of incompleted situations with father, brother, etc. This unconscious residue mars the childrearing process. The child's constant need for attention can create stress, serving to remind the woman of her unfulfilled needs for attention and recognition. This could block her connection to the child and its need for love and affection. The "left overs" are expressed through her fears, insecurities, and uncertainties which are absorbed by the child. Many of the deep insecurities with which we struggle are not our own.

The father-son connection, being of the same sex, is as powerful as that of the mother and daughter. Lack of bonding can create a very destructive imbalance in the son's psyche. Our pioneering fathers were better equipped to teach their sons and facilitate a healthier journey for them. As fathers became estranged from their children, leaving the childrearing primarily to women, they have missed a very rich rewarding experience. Men fortunate enough to have a healthy relationship with their fathers can attest to this. Fathers who are removed from this important time in a boy's growth in the world, feel alienated from them. Like mothers who have unfulfilled needs from their childhood, fathers can either force themselves into their son's lives or get caught within a push-pull dance remaining frustrated in their attempts to reach out, but remain distant. This reaching out can be threatening to the father who never had such experiences or who was smothered by affection from his own mother or his surrogate wife-mother. The inability to communicate as a result of his upbringing will create a lack of response to his own son. Like Phil's father, many men remain in the background, quiet and distant. A father-son bond can create psychological chaos or a special kind of nurturing.

The parenting cycle is repeated generation after generation with that which is gained or lost being passed onto the next offspring who, it is hoped, will be more successful in breaking the negative patterns which destroy our capacity for life and love. This is the plight of our search for "easy way, instant cures" and "instant success." This attitude and behavior is that of a spoiled child who views the world as territory that he can and must conquer.

As man creates the kind of world he thinks it should be, he fails to see in his drive forward, how this influences other people. The dream to colonize space and create worlds of leisure and mechanization, further separates him from people. When people turn from each other to embrace things, we alienate ourselves. When the world of things is connected to childrearing there are fewer human attributes which affect the young. Parents who buy their children's love with things are creating superficial bonds to their children. A child treated as an object will grow up — correction — will age, grow taller and develop and will in turn treat children as objects.

Western society depends upon perpetuating images that sell products. Advertising often stretches the truth and fabricates images. People are taught, as consumers, they should mold themselves into these images. To sell a product, people are often "propped up" or "put down." The subliminal messages influence human perceptions and choices as has been proven in research. This form of brainwashing is called "marketing." The images created are often unreal and unattainable. Those who are successful in attaining these status images are often chained to the image-producing process that consumes their lives.

Parenting in an unreal, image-producing society, is a difficult task and chances of rearing totally balanced, healthy children without misfortune, is a near impossibility. People become the casualties. If one's children do not know how to "play the game" and "play it well," then one has failed as a parent. Children can become the convenient scapegoat, the victims whom parents use to camouflage their own mistakes.

In a society that views itself as the Matt Dillon of the world battling against the outlaws of Western free enterprise, parents are responsible for training their deputy-sons to root out 'evil' from the farthest outposts.

A society whose scripts enslave women in rigid, limiting roles of home-maker, mother and continue to estrange fathers from their sons, should not be surprised by the violence it produces.

Society's parenting images create false male images. Mothers unable to explore and experience other dimensions of their potential humanness, often pass resentment on to their children. Resentment can take the expressed form of harsh criticism or can be sickly sweet with the negative qualities hidden. Fathers, who have been locked into the rigid role of protector-provider, lose much of their potential vitality causing a buildup of denial of self and others. The reality of everyday living controls every move and choice. Both parents are victims of social rules that inhibit their whole-ness in living and the potential for being more human. They become separated from their other halves — men unable to express their feminine nature and women unable to acknowledge their assertiveness, their maleness. If one quality is dominant in the human psyche, then an unhealthy imbalance exists. Both feminine and masculine qualities exist within us. Mothers who are unable to understand the male aspect of themselves will be unable to appreciate their son's maleness. If they have not had the opportunity to know the deeper quality of the feminine side through their own mothers or other significant female relationships, they will be unable to bridge the feminine aspect of their sons in a comfortable way. A man denied his connection to his feminine aspect, (ie. being able to cry for healing and release), will experience his masculine aspect controlling his whole nature. By distancing himself from his feminine side, he can build a fortress of defenses that will not acknowledge or rationalize the emotional, nurturing aspects of himself. He learns to adopt a distorted image of himself oversha-dowed by the internalized living and breathing images of his parents. He cannot contact the mother part of his consciousness and will be unsuccessful in helping his son do the same.

Upon reaching adulthood, we carry the depersonalized effects of our socialization through our learnings from parents, teachers, schools, etc. within the fragments of our psyches. Ego structure and basic life attitude and perception is crowded with socially dictated "rights" and "wrongs." Rather than resist, men seek refuge in the social image:

> "When men attempt to escape from the world of what men are not aware of within themselves, the unconscious, they take on attributes of social superficiality so continually falling into the stereotype of the male. The "sexist" male if you wish."

Paul Olsen
Mothers and Sons

Mothers, who are unaware of this knowledge, will enhance this social image as they too are confused about the role they should play in the male's development. Fantasies of what her son is to become are idealistic, a mixture of socially prescribed images coupled with her repressed energy and remaining unmet needs. She becomes part of the sabotaging process unable to see her son wholly; to see his total possibilities through her own fragmented image. She often misinterprets the young male's cues for direction and separation as signals from the denied aspects of her self. She is unaware of how to deal with these messages and often she holds on tightly to her son, hoping that through action she can avoid the pain of her denial and disconnection. Her smothering can further cut her son off from the feminine aspect of himself creating additional anger, confusion and mistrust.

Fathers, having been through the masculinity training, are numb to the isolation and separateness which they accept as an inherited part of their destiny of being a male. They often hold on to their father role hoping to regain some security, some contact with their family. In other ways mothers proclaim the bonds with their sons as unique and eternal. As psychologist and mythologist John Perry explains:

> "...that apparently eternal 'triangle' is probably at heart a two-part interaction: mother and son, with the third leg of the triangle being the image of the father and communicated nonverbally, then verbally by the mother to her son." .

We have witnessed a mother speaking to the son who inquires about his father's behavior, "Your father means well." The father learns to be distant to his son and reinforces this "stranger" relationship. The son learns that to get close to his father, he pulls away from his mother while losing parts of himself that he has internalized as the "stranger" part of his father. He takes this as the real and alive nature of his father's expression as part of himself. Hence, the actions personify, he is a "chip off the old block." He will re-enact this pattern with his own son unless he is able to change these learned patterns. He may eventually come to resent the close bond that his son has with his mother and debate and quarrel over trivial matters which carry an undercurrent of hostility and competition.

The boy experiences this competition early through his father's desire for his mother's nurturing. He learns caution and manipulative techniques when around other males. Typical childhood rivalry is a smokescreen for winning Mommy or Daddy's favor. He learns too, to be cautious around women and attempt to take control before he is controlled or manipulated. He learns to hide his inner-most thoughts and feelings for fear of disclosing his strategy. His energy is invested in his will to survive, to have his needs met, and to gain some recognition and understanding. Thus, he learns to become a game player as his essence is at stake.

The young male attempts to synthesize his early training experiences to gain a foothold for his life's journey. If lucky, he has learned to be as cunning as a fox and as slippery as an eel in the development of his relationships with his two most important teachers in life. He has the messages from both parents of "how it is" and "how it is not." His father teaches him to not let any man get too close, while his mother says, "You must help others as best you can." This dichotomy exists within most men. Which is real and which is false ? If he risks and experiments to discover the answers, he may encounter situations like; reaching out, trusting another man only to get beaten up by him. This serves to strengthen the split and increase the sense of conflict. Until he can find another way to change this fixed belief, he is doomed to have the negative patterns become self-fulfilling prophecy. If he chooses to live his mother's philosophy, he risks losing connection with his already distant father. For example; the Archie Bunker type of man who converts his son to his mode of thinking and behavior requires that the son hide his deep, inner emotions and sensitivities in his father's presence. He has to camouflage these feelings even from himself. If he chooses to challenge his father by the expression of these feelings, he stands the risk of losing what flimsy contact he has with him. Macho, sexist or not, this man is still his father. Living with this perpetual conflict of the aspects of himself that are his mother and his father pulls him apart, straining his ability to keep a balanced perspective. The conflict tears at his dual loyalties to his mother and his father. If he adopts one, he sacrifices the other.

The pressure from the male environment helps him choose his course. "Suck it in," "Get on with it," "Do your part," and "Bury it" all contribute to the male image. The young male accepts the path of conformity, lacking as of yet, the strength to stand unique. He joins the masculine fraternity, hiding his deeper emotions through rational process and pretending all is fine when he is empty within. He accepts society's mold and denial as his destiny. He joins the core of the status quo and is initiated into the half-alive, half-aware fraternity of the disowned. He is now destined to live in the false dreams of image-producing, elitist faction lost within its own self-indulgent, narcissistic and addictive lifestyle. By not joining the status quo, they would have to accept their true reality that they are indeed strangers to themselves and to life. "Super" men only see the false image of themselves.

> "Denial, however human and natural a response, exacts a terrible price. It is as if we settled for living in the anterooms of our lives, and ultimately , it doesn't work. A part of the self keenly feels the the denial pain."
>
> Marilyn Ferguson

TRANSITION AND TRANSFORMATION

"You are lead through your lifetime by the inner learning creature, the playful spirited being that is your inner self.
Don't turn away from the possible futures before you're certain you don't have anything to learn from them.
You're always free to change your mind and choose a different future, or a different past."

Richard Bach
Illusions

CHAPTER IV

Unbecoming the 'Supra' Man:
Dissolving the Gap between
Body Feeling and Mind

"At the meridian of thought the rebel thus rejects divinity in order to share in the struggle and destiny of all men.
"In the first light, the earth remains our first and last love. OUR BROTHERS are breathing under the same sky as we; justice is a living thing.

"NOW is born that strange joy which helps one live and die, and which we shall never again postpone to a later time.

"On the sorrowing earth it is the unresting thorn, the bitter brew, the harsh wind off the sea, the OLD and the NEW DAWN. With this joy through long struggle we shall remake the soul of our time."

Camus

"A sane society will flower when men liberate themselves from continued socially fabricated prohibitions, cultural straight jackets, and mental stereotypes that control and inhibit behavior through arbitrary definition of what it means to be a man."

Jack Nichols

As a consultant, I design and conduct stress management workshops for social service agencies, schools and industry. Recently, I designed a workshop for executives in a Canadian oil company in conjunction with a health program through the company's medical clinic. I worked with the head nurse of the clinic as we attempted to develop a program that was viable, relevant and fit the needs and character of the company's executives.

Many a consultation with her was necessary as she familiarized me with the type of persons who would be attending the workshop. She reminded me that many of the participants would be hard-core resisters, the "old guard." These were engineers, geologists and other executives who had been with the company and/or the industry for most of their lives. She indicated that they would resent someone younger trying to tell them how to work and live better with stress. Also, they primarily felt that stress and other such personal growth programs were a waste of time. They had been dealing with the pressure and anxiety for years in their own way and were resistant to any change now.

These members of the "old guard" made routine visits to the clinic requesting tranquilizers and other drugs to calm their nerves. They also complained of the stressful situations involving department heads and suggested that if they could communicate with their bosses about specific office problems, there would be a release of this anxiety.

The evidence revealed that the employees needed support and communication while the "old guard" faction was locked into the old way of handling matters. One company vice-president supported the idea of the stress workshop but did not have the time to take it himself. He was too busy with the day-to-day operation of the company. He probably needed the workshop more than his employees as he was recovering from a very recent heart attack. Despite doctor's orders for him to slow down, quit smoking and cut back on his drinking, he maintained his usual hectic pace. He once said to the nurse, "I am killing myself, aren't I? " His pace has not altered at all, in fact, it has increased due to current stresses on the oil industry. He will probably be the victim of his prophecy. In his own paternal way, he showed concern and caring for others, but could not extend this to himself. This is the plight of many of the "old guard" faction. Another member of this faction went out of his way to squelch the workshop. He was not interested in the workshop and did not believe that his employees needed it either. I discovered that he was an alcoholic and that his physical and mental health were deteriorating rapidly. His employees complained of his non-flexible tryrannical approach which created a great deal of stress. His motto was "people work better under stress." Several of his employees were constantly "crying the blues" at the medical clinic. One individual resorted going to the cocktail lounge every night after work which of course, affected her work performance. "You can't teach an old dog new tricks" is the saying, but in fact, it is the "old dog" who is tricking himself. The business world has its share of these self-destructive tricksters. They are without essence and cling to outmoded values. They are firmly locked into place, chained to the false and learned image of being a 'man.'
Robert Prisig describes this character as an:

> "...ego climber,...like an instrument that's out of adjustment, he goes on when the sloppiness of his steps shows he's tired. What he is looking for, what he wants, is all around him. Every step an effort, both physically and spiritually, because he imagines his goal to be external and distant."

Like King Midas who revels in being able to turn everything into gold, he doesn't realize his 'riches' are close to him and not outside himself. The external riches that he seeks and the power he desires is in his humanity, of which he is unaware due to being out of touch with himself, others and life's true meaning. The "old guard" image has a pre-determined destiny. Men who remain locked in this 'supra' man identity are doomed to its false goals and intentions. As long as they hold on to this old way they will never be free, but will fall even deeper into confinement from which they can only be released through death.

THE EMERGENCE OF THE NEW MALE

Men are beginning to acknowledge that they need to change. It took the cry and courage of the women's movement to bring this need into focus. Throughout the ages, great thinkers, poets, artists, and other concerned human beings have advocated this need. They could see the eventual destructive course of man in his ceaseless drive for knowledge and power. The women's movement brought this into focus. This movement, though an organized feminine group, is actually a human movement. It has taken the vanguard of this movement some time to remember this. Now, both factions of the human character, male and female, need to commit themselves individually and together to plant the seeds for the birth of a new kind of human being. Women need to continue to grow, to experience and release their anger towards men, while men need to embrace a new way of being. This new being has actually been lying dormant waiting to be expressed. In times of great societal change this is not an easy task. This keeps us in a state of anxiety and uncertainty. The images of who we are as men are changing rapidly as are our identities as human beings. As Toffler states in **The Third Wave,**

> "Instead of being handed a selection of coherent identities to choose among, we are required to piece one together: a configurative or modular "me.""

The late Fritz Perls, founding father of Gestalt therapy, helped remind us that, "to suffer one's death is not easy," and yet this is what we are being called to do as we are being swept into a new renaissance of humanity. All of us are feeling the effects of this encompassing movement. We are being uplifted into a new human consciousness never before possible on such a global scale. Whether we choose to participate or not, it is here and we are having to learn to adapt to its powerful thrust for inner change. A new human being is being born and we are the creators as men and women working together and individually. Toffler adds:

> "Whether we know it or not, more of us are already engaged in either resisting or creating — the new civilization."

For now, I am not interested in validating scientifically or otherwise, whether men need to change their attitudes towards themselves, other men or the natural world. I choose not to fight against the mountains of denial and resistance that, at times, exhaust my attempts to make the ascent. I believe, like Rogers:

> "A new type of person, with values different from those of our
> present culture is emerging in increasing numbers and living
> and being in ways that break with the past."

Tillich, years before, envisioned,

> "A new type of person who would be in harmony with nature, less
> driven, more perceptive, more in touch with his own creative
> energies."

As a man, I choose to align myself with these new emerging people and
offer this book as a bridge to these evolving human beings. The task is upon
us, by sifting through what has been we must bring the seeds, the essence of
our humanity, into the present to be nurtured in new fertile soil that will
bear the fruit of a new society; a new human being.

To those of the "old guard" who choose to remain locked in their outmoded and destructive patterns, I wish you "Godspeed" and I am saddened.
To those who are willing to return to the teachings of life with a willingness
to surrender false egos, I welcome you as brothers. Your seasons of experience coupled with a new spirit of vitality can ensure the harmony and
balance that is required. We can learn from one another with the teaching
being directed from our inner selves and not dominated by external, rigid
authority. As brothers we are linked together by threads of humanity that
transcend age, position and role. Life is our real teacher and our true
communication stems from deep within us. This is the domain of the
brotherhood; of the new emerging male. If we men choose to be a part of this
new evolution, becoming healthier and vital, reclaiming our life's energy, we
need first to accept our situation. We must accept that we have been trapped
before we can move an inch beyond our prisons. Reich says:

> "It is possible to get out of the trap, however in order to break out
> of the prison, one first must confess to being in a prison."

Similarly, an AA member stands and declares to his group, "I am an
alcoholic." This acceptance is a form of change in itself as it is a shift from
denial and resistance. Acknowledgement of our ordeal is an important step.
It will take time, commitment and learning to ride the rocky waves of chaos.
Our goals will have to be those of moving and living with the constancy of
change. The rigidity of the fixed belief and perception will no longer serve
our needs. During our transition, the old images and perceptions will still
attempt to control, interrupt and sabotage our new emerging self. It has
reigned over our lives and will not give up its domination without a struggle.
The old way of dealing with any struggle would be to fight it to the death. The

new way, rather than a constant internal battle and rationalizing its effect, would be to learn to befriend it and see what lies behind its facade. Underneath it all lies the remnants of the genuine before we learned to deny it and lock it in. This genuineness, this richness of life, vitality and well-being, is our seed for transformation and growth. This is our gift from creation and it is intended for sharing.

The shelves are full of self-help books to enable one to become a healthier, happier and better person. The method for becoming healthier in all ways involves to know oneself better. These books offer a variety of methods for achieving self-awareness, self healing and change. The pathways to personal liberation are endless. One important ingredient is essential for any of these paths to offer knowledge and teaching. This is the true desire to heal, change and grow. As Bernard Shaw once wrote:

> "As to the method, what can be said except that where there is a will, there's a way? If there be no will, we are lost. That is the possibility for our crazy little empire, if not for the universe; and as such possibilities are not to be entertained without despair, we must, whilst we survive, proceed on the assumption that we still have energy enough to not only will to live, but to will to live better."

Many people have given up and have lost their will to live. It is written on their faces which show helplessness, despair and waiting. They feel that nuclear war is imminent, our human problems are insurmountable, and some hold to the biblical prophecies making annihilation our self-fulfilling prophecy. Nothing is to be done as our destruction is part of the divine plan so they wait to die to know their salvation. It is an easy cop-out to place the blame on man's sins. The belief that destiny is preordained makes not taking action seem palatable. If this is true, we will need more than faith and promises to evolve into a new kind of human being. To break out of our prisons and not be pulled back by the cynicism of society, we will have to re-unite with the spirit of life within us. This same pioneering spirit existed and was expressed by the people who founded the United States.

What has happened to men of spirit like Jefferson, Nathan Hale, Patrick Henry and Lincoln who were willing to stand up and be counted? These men had intense compassion and a life spirit rich and full of promise and optimism. These men possessed a revolutionary spirit while we are the lifeless ghosts of a stagnant spirit. Back in history, the expressions of Kant, Kierkegaard and Socrates defied the hold of rigidity and conformity. What has become of our pioneering essence that challenges established order? We could use a few Gandhi's in our midst.

To remove the stones from the doorway of the prisoner caves we will need men with courage, vision and passion with principles of life spirit and humanity. I believe that behind the facades and exhausted image cloaks these threads of principles do exist. Those willing to dance to the beat of a different drummer and willing to challenge their own misinformation will be able to step into the fresh spirit of new perspective.

I challenge men of the world to step out of their prison attire, disguised as three piece suits and walk vulnerably beside their similar thinking brothers and sisters who believe in this new age. Let us reconstruct a society, as well as individuals who are human and just. A society that respects nature, its creatures, and is composed of human beings desiring a harmonious evolution which will dissolve the unhealthy intimidation which forced us to become alienated from one another. I ask you to drop your guard, throw away your spears and shields and reach out with openness to embrace one another. Feel free to touch in ways in which you have always needed. Step forward. Take a stand on any human injustice, nuclear war, community and social conflict with hearts full of courage and purpose. The isolation and lack of concern for our fellow man is most destructive and unjust. We need to move towards a commitment of caring for and loving ourselves.

This outlook requires a new perspective, a broadness of imagining ourselves to be more than what we are now. We must know that we do not have to do this alone. Solitary endeavor would follow the old way. "Eventually, anyone concerned with the transformation of the individual must engage in a social act," states Marylin Ferguson, author of **The Aquarian Conspiracy.** We are not meant to be alone; our natures are social and we desire to be united. The '90's is a time of working together, side by side. It is a rebirth of the '60's spirit.

A broadness of consciousness that rises beyond rigid, narrow and rational routines of the masculine ego is required. This consciousness envelops the very essence of life. It touches what Robert Prisig refers to as "quality":

> "Quality is a characteristic of thought and statement that is recognized by a non-thinking process. Because definitions are a product of rigid, formal thinking. . . quality cannot be defined."

Being free will release unexpressed creativity, originality, imagination and facets of ourselves that have been lying dormant since our early childhood socialization. This is a social consciousness, an awareness of what is really happening. As men we need a commitment to becoming unified with society as a whole. It is time to join the human race instead of always attempting to win the race.

In these chaotic times when the world feels as though it is being turned upside down and we are asked to change course, Ferguson writes:

> "We are living in the 'change of change', the time in which we can intentionally align ourselves with nature for remaking ourselves."

Men need to become active participants in this human transformation and new age of this planet. It is not something that a man needs to seek, to find or invent, it is already alive if he chooses to awaken and be a part of its reality. It is a conspiracy towards life moving away from the destructive and negative. It is this death cycle which keeps men enslaved within false masculine images.

The decision is not to prove that this movement towards a new perspective exists, but rather to choose whether or not to be a part of this intense stream of consciousness transformation. Men have to choose where they will give their loyalty and support. One path is that of life, growth and well-being while the other holds destruction, decay and death. There is no third alternative for there is no option in doing nothing and being nothing. Buckminster Fuller believed, "Humanity has the option to make it." Men as individuals and together decide which path to take. This inward soul search will confront us with our denied and false values. We will face our distorted ideologies that lack feelings and the facade we have substituted for our essence. We must ask, "Is the old way valid? Do we need it anymore?"

It is time for men to make a self-proclamation and construct a personal manifesto for human and self-freedom and, like Martin Luther King, place these demands upon the inner prison doors. This proclamation is an act that affects the destiny of humanity. What we decide to do will be an act of creation towards life; healing our destruction towards ourselves and fellow human citizens. The choice is ours.

If we choose transformation and creation, then we have to begin the resurrection of the new male. This new male embodies the spirit of brotherhood, a passion for life and conviction of our pioneering fathers. I call this new male the "Revolutionary Man."

> "I see that revolution is coming not in some great organized movement, not in a gun- carrying army with banners, not in manifestos and declarations, but through the emergence of a new kind of person thrusting up through the dying, yellowing, putrefying leaves and stalks of our fading institutions."

Carl Rogers

THE REBIRTH OF THE REVOLUTIONARY MAN

The wisdom of E.E. Cummings reminds us:

"One's not half of two, it's two are halves of one."

While sitting on a porch waiting for a friend, a young, sandy-haired, blue-eyed boy approached me. He told me his name was Gary, he was four years old and he lived next door. I was awed by the way he handled himself for one so young. I thought back to the time when I was his age. Similarly, I would walk up to strangers and carry on conversations with ease. I could not only talk with older people but there seemed to be a feeling of mutual enjoyment. Gary reminded me of myself at that age. I had the curiosity of ten cats and the keen desire and courage to know what was going on in the world. I enjoyed how Gary was teaching himself to organize and learn about his world. He was an example of what I had been. Gary was being totally himself and allowed me to see who I was potentially, at the age of four and how my growth towards adulthood had resulted in the loss of many fine qualities. I went from being a bold, curious and spontaneous child to a cautious, inhibited and sometimes shy adult male. I compensated for my insecurities by acting strong and confident. I could sense the loss of the little boy inside of me who sometimes appeared as a scared little boy in my psyche. As an adult male, I always kept this feeling to myself and like other men, feared exposure of such would label me weak and insecure.

Gary gave me a gift by just being himself, allowing me to see myself and those aspects that I had denied for years. It was the spontaniety of life within Gary, his essence which was a symbol of the purity and vitality of life. He was being a four-year-old Gary and not trying to be anything other than what he "is." This "life" transcends age, profession and sex. We can learn from all aspects of life if we listen and trust.

By being open to this "life" within Gary, I was able to re-claim part of my denied self by allowing me to see how I really was at the onset of my journey. Many men are afraid to be open to children's openness and honesty which reminds them of their earlier years. Yet men who seek liberation must learn these qualities to be whole again, flexible and trusting enough to allow life's pulse within them expression. The hearts of those around them can guide them to those places within. Much of what a man seeks in external gratification is nothing more than the sum totalness of himself which lies waiting within for his return.

In the few years that I have been shaping the framework for this book, I have seen the painful struggle experienced by men as the force and impact of the women's movement and other social and technological inroads affects their reality.

For centuries men have enjoyed their pedestal of power and control which provided a certain comfort, solace, identity and purpose that lent meaning to their lives. They knew where they stood and basically where they fit in the scheme of things. Their lives contained a connecting link to the social and political climate of their world rendering a sense of security.

In the past 20 to 30 years, this security blanket has been pulled out from underneath them. Mechanization initially took over their jobs and more recently, the computer is revolutionizing the workplace. The unstable current economic situation further antagonizes their role as breadwinners and sabotages their role as protector. The once secure masculine system which controlled society is now unstable and slipping through their fingers.

Some have seen the coming storm and have adapted to these changing conditions. Most men have not and are trapped, unprepared and find the transition overwhelming. Society has a lack of effective training programs to educate men in these rapid changes. This is not surprising as the masculine rational influence is behind the controls of change where people's welfare is secondary to the progress of the technological machine. If men decide to wait until society is ready to address their needs, they may never be acknowledged.

Women who were able to respond to their feelings created a healthy, effective support system. They responded to the needs of other women by including them in the liberation process. This is one reason why the women's movement has been so successful and has had so much impact. When you create and grow from a base of support and unity built upon a deep, feeling purpose, the strength of the movement is apparent.

If men hope to move into transcendence they will, like women, need to create a model that will lift them out of the outmoded, useless fading image of being a "man." They require a model that is humane, growth producing and which instills the full use of their resources in what is to be a truly human being. The "revolutionary man" is a good start. This model is not set up as another goal-directed task which suggests that men become the "revolutionary man." It merely offers some guidelines to help men become aware of their human possibilities. Rather than strive to become a particular kind of man, another image, it initiates a process that helps men to reach a place within their own beings that already exists and to which they can return again and again. When men learn to trust and follow instincts with a passion, then we will lessen the need for control and domination of the energy within us. This will bring us to the center of healing and reconstruction through the acceptance of those once dormant qualities that move throughout our bodies, our minds and our hearts.

CHARACTER AND QUALITIES
OF THE REVOLUTIONARY MAN

The strongest quality of the revolutionary man is that of synthesis. This man sees the integral relationship which exists among people, creatures, plants, the land and the cosmos itself. He is aware of his relationship to the enviroment and to his part in the universe as a whole. He "is," and he is aware of the wholistic aspect of all that he encounters. This man is a constant learner and all of life is his teacher.

He is not an image or a false rendition of a human being. He is a person who is fully, passionately alive both in his waking moments and in his fantasies and dreams. He has an insatiable curiousity regarding all aspects of life, but he proceeds with humbleness and respect; seeking to know and willing to listen to the messages received. He respects nature's gifts and sees himself as a caretaker and the symbolic act of self-care indicates he is a partner with nature and her forces. The Indian people lived with such inner awareness and harmony with wisdom in their relationship to the earth.

The revolutionary man accepts and lives through both his masculine (Yang) and feminine (Yin); his creative and destructive; his assertive and receptive potential, in one encompassing wholeness. He is aware he must acknowledge what he has created and destroyed in order to rebuild, renew and heal. This man is part animal, vegetable, mineral and spiritual in nature. He is the seed of the universal mind which stems from the heart rather than the head. He understands the natural functioning harmony of the universe and that it is the foundation for the organization of the universe of which we and the world are only a part. This man has qualities that Carlos Castenada refers to as "warrior."

> "To achieve the mood of a warrior is not a simple matter. It is a revolution. To regard the lion and the water rats and our fellow men as equals is a magnificent act of the warrior's spirit. It takes power to do that."

I have known a man that spoke with the animals of the forest and they seemed to understand and converse with him. Grizzly Adams may be a family movie, but some men do live in harmony with nature having this gift and respect for living things. They do not hold themselves above the creatures of the land and they embody a quality of energy within their bodies that is resilient. They have a soft flexibility within their minds which provides them with the very power that Castenada describes. Their power is not one of dominion, rather it is connected to the depth of life and its passionate form. Those who experience such a man are transformed by this warrior spirit enveloped within the richness of vitality. He is free of societal inhibitions regarding death and is even freer to experience life. He's released from his need for his ego to create his world, he has transcended society's ego and has merged with the universal oneness. E. Becker in **Denial of Death** suggests that this type of man is:

> "a man strong enough to live and therefore strong enough to die."

Again, the Indian people lived this type of strength and power as do other so-called primitives and uncivilized people. It is clear that men seeking the wrong kind of power desire to destroy those who truly possess the real power. The threatened sector is unaware of the true essence of power.

The revolutionary man possesses a capacity to love. His life is directed towards the compassionate, caring and healthy development of humanity. Ghandi, Buddha, Christ, Albert Schweitzer, Martin Luther King and other great men possessed this quality. Their common trait was their ability to love their fellow man as brothers and not be caught within destructive competitive games. As Fromm states in his classic work The Art of Loving:

> "If I have developed the capacity for love, then I cannot help loving my brother."

When a man loves unselfishly, he is able to love all of life, all of creation. The man who loves is connected with the many treasures that life offers.

Gail Sheely would see the revolutionary man as a "pathfinder:"

> "A man who is just as concerned with his inner achievements as he is with his outer."

The inner and outer perceptions are integrally similar and man is not locked into rigidly defined rules for growth in either sector. He knows when to "kill the buddah," knowing clearly that the true teacher is always within himself. His inner sense and his external actions stem from deeper sources which transcend both. He lives in the now and is able to weave in comfortably the memories and events of past learning as well as projecting himself into the future as a mirror reflection of what existed before and what exists now. He sees the past, present, and future linked together in the fullness and creativity of the moment. He is essentially a man of spirit living practically in the human form with the total awarenesss that being fully human is the highest spiritual attainment. He is what Shostrom calls a man of "mastery."

> "They are intensely human faces and at the same, intensely spiritual, not unlike the polarities, which are human, and the source, which is spiritual. It is the integration of the intensely spiritual and the intensely human which makes for the power of

the mastery."

Again Sheely gives an example of the spiritual man who embodies the qualities of the the revolutionary man:

> "I feel creative for the first time. Every single thing I'm going through now is a preparation. A rehearsal. I am not a reborn Christian. I am a reborn human being. And while I don't have formal religion in my life any longer my spiritual life is many times richer."

The revolutionary man, similarly, is learning or has learned that his uniqueness as a human being is a miracle in itself. He is grateful for being a part of the cosmic evolution and sees his life, actions and growth as part of the divine tapestry of creation in motion. He lives with the "Godhead" rather than worshipping it externally to his inner self. He knows that all life is this "Godhead." He respects the existence of all living creatures, no matter how insignificant, and he views them as equals in the cosmic brotherhood. He is a man of essence and sees this in life everywhere.

When a man is truly loving he is in touch with his feminine nature, his compassion and nurturance. The revolutionary man is androgynous. He embellishes his feminine qualities as much as he does his maleness. He knows each is an essential aspect for his complete integration as a human being. The more he feels and expresses compassion, softness and tenderness, the more balanced and integrated his masculine nature becomes. He supports and encourages this balance in women as well. He realizes that the more he supports women's emancipation, the more he respects his own freedom.

When visiting a former publishing friend in northern California, I was asked what was important in my life and career to be a success. I remarked, without hesitation, "Integrity." Surprised, he said that in these times that was a rare quality as most men wanted power, money, and status. Integrity was often the last thing on the list if it was mentioned at all. Thinking back to that day, I know I would still reply to such an inquiry with the same answer. Men with integrity are rare. Many have sold their souls for the dollar and some would even be willing to go for first and second mortgages for the right price. Many people owe their lives to the bank and spend their lives paying the installments that enable them to have prestige, power, and position in the eyes of society. They have chosen money and its subsequent status to symbolize and substitute for the aspects of their inner selves beyond their reach. They have chosen to give in to the conformist majority of the elite "power mongers" who also use their resources to attain power over others. To challenge the dictates of the status quo would mean a loss of accumulated goods and a risk of non-acceptance.

The revolutionary man possesses integrity. He is, in the words of Jack Nichols:

> "Confident enough to say no when the society around them insists that they should live by antiquated precepts. The choice facing them requires courage. It is a choice between integrity and approval."

In the '60's many young men refused to take part in the Vietnam War. Some went to jail, some left the country, while others went into the service but refused to fight. Some scientists today have left their work once they discovered their contribution to developing weaponry for nuclear war. Workers in chemical plants have left upon realizing that their company was producing harmful goods. There are executives who have left six figure paying positions to raise chickens after recognizing that the pace was killing them. Being true to oneself is a rare gift in this society which uses untold, subliminal pressures to mold people to conform. Conformity is the way of cowards — integrity is the way of the revolutionary man.

This man is in touch with his feelings trusting them over what his rational, analytical mind instructs him to do. Goldberg states that the qualities of the liberated man also co-exist with those of the revolutionary man:

> "The liberated male will simply not want to disguise and numb the pressures of a pained harness. He will reject externally imposed, predefined "masculine" roles, not for ideological reasons, but simply because they are painful and self destructive."

Often men are challenged by their buddies to " have another drink " or by their boss's insistence to work overtime when they would rather be at home their families. A man who believes in himself will follow his inner messages to heal and relax. Most men when confronted with the choice will ignore the inner voice sometimes taking their resentment out on someone else or wallowing in self-pity. A man of integrity however, would listen to his inner voice and adhere to its message. Integrity stems from a deeply human place and a man who permits such direction in his life and actions, lives from a truly centered place. His life is his own and he is not tempted by wealth offered to him through the selling of his true worth. His riches, his wealth spring from his humaness with belief, trust and faith guiding his living. Goethe stated, "When a man trusts, he will know how to live." A man of integrity knows this makes his life richer.

The qualities that compose the revolutionary man are many and yet they are not new for men throughout history have exemplified them. A male infant begins with a potential for greatness and these qualities are always available. Only a few have had the courage to realize these, to risk becoming what they truly are. Their choices are not without pain and hardship, but the struggle is part of what makes them who they are. Men do not spring to this state of being in an instant, it takes time. To be a great man requires the spirit of compassion, the courage of a lion, and a willingness to die many times over and be reborn as an elevated human being. Heaven waits for those who are willing to release their excess baggage of false images, false hopes, and false needs and the courage to be who they uniquely are. In this discovery are all the riches and wealth of a lifetime.

He is not a new man but what he has always had the capacity to be. This includes reclaiming what qualities we have lost or denied and bringing them into our lives with a power that is equally gentle, compassionate, masculine and feminine. It is eloquently expressed in this poem by D. H. Lawrence:

> "Not I, not I, but the wind that blows through me! A fine wind is blowing the new direction of time. If only I let it bear me, carry me, if only it carries me!
> If only I am sensitive, subtle, oh delicate, a winged gift!
> If only, most lovely of all, I yield myself and am borrowed.
> By the fine, fine wind that takes its course through the chaos of the world."

BECOMING THE REVOLUTIONARY MAN

In Chapter two, I talked about the corporate lawyer whose son dropped out of the aerospace industry to live in Greenwich Village. This man's story is significant beyond the portrayal of a conflict of values. When I met the lawyer he had recently walked out of his firm without a second glance. He had become increasingly dissatisfied with his life and at the age of fifty felt something was missing. His father, also a lawyer, had made it possible for him to have the best education money could buy. He had graduated from Yale and later Harvard Law School. One of the most successful lawyers in New York city, he had sixty lawyers working under him and his prestigious accounts brought him an income well over six figures. He drove a Mercedes, belonged to an exclusive country club and lived in an exquisite home. A few years before his walk out, he felt that his world was falling apart. He had become grumpy and impatient. His impatience almost caused a woman's death one morning as he hit her after running a red light. This accident turned his life around. A few weeks later he told a client to, "stick it up his ass," and then hung up. He had been wanting to say just that to this client for over ten years. This client had been very demanding, constantly threatening to drop his account if he did not get the response he wanted. He began another practice in Florida shortly afterwards. When we met his wife had left him and he was heading to Colorado to dig for gold. This man, at fifty, had lived his life according to the rules and had been rewarded lavishly. He represented the pinnacle of success, he "had it made!" And yet, a more appropriate statement could be, "he had been made." He had become all that everyone else wanted him to be, fulfilling society's definition of a man of success. After fifty years of fulfilling scripted expectations, he felt lonely, empty and unhappy. His trip to Colorado to dig for gold symbolized a search for riches of which he was unaware. It stands to reason that he would search for this treasure in an external manner. Although his own son was able to release himself from this external pursuit, he was not.

To illustrate the steps that must be taken to become a revolutionary man, I have used this example. The son was able to get in touch with his own person by experiencing his own direction. Until the father finds his unique, true self and his path becomes his own not one dictated by society, he will be sentenced to searching for his 'wealth' outside himself.

Learning what you can become as a male is a journey that each man is presently on though we may be unaware of it. Most men look everywhere else but to themselves. They see the stress they experience as a form of punishment — they have been singled out in the eyes of their "creator," their wives, parents, bosses and children who send messages that they are failures. Acceptance of this lot in life is regressive.

Those who desire to release themselves from such entrapment, will need to be in charge of their own lives and march to the beat of their own drum. Then they will be connected to their source of self-healing, self growth and self-direction.

We have explored the qualities of the revolutionary man and what makes him who he is. He is not a new type of human male or human being but a resurrection of what already exists within every man.

I will now offer some guidelines that can be utilized to rebuild and express the unique, loving persons that live within us. These tools represent the steps and processes that are available when a man chooses to make this new journey. The application and integration in daily living is vital to their continued use and development. If the genuine desire exists then one can become a man of integrity, courage and love. To release one's false sense of self will include making some sacrifices which may create anxiety and uncertainty. It will open hollow places within us that at first will feel empty and frightening. To stay attached to these hidden anxieties will eventually lead us into deeper isolation, despair and hopelessness. By choosing to learn through doing, we will become "finders" on our own "path" and we will move into the unknown with awareness and commitment.

When we learn to meet and accept the old "me" and say "goodbye" to this limiting aspect of ourselves, we can embark upon the remaking of the new "me." This journey will begin with us ending our self-defeating negative patterns and realizing our own self-healing and renewal.

GUIDELINES FOR BECOMING THE 'REVOLUTIONARY MAN.'

SELF CARE

Teaching men to care for themselves is often like asking a rattlesnake to give warning without it's rattles. Men have been totally ingrained with the idea that they should be taken care of. We are socialized to be on the go constantly, often to the point of burn out. Since we are cut off from our feelings and abuse our bodies, we become disconnected from nature's physical signals to slow down or stop a destructive pattern. We see men being told by their doctors to cut down on sweets, coffee, smoking and alcohol. They will sometimes follow this advice as the physician is an authority figure, a symbolic mother image. Self-care and nurturance stems from the feminine aspect. Most men recall always being cared for by their mothers when they had a fever, cold or flu. Mom was there with kind words, hot soup and a healing touch. Mother also prepared their meals, did their laundry, kept their environment clean and organized and ensured they were up for school or work. When these men married, their wives became substitute mothers fulfilling many of the same needs. Men are like babies when ill. This could be because it is the only time that they slow down long enough to allow themselves to heal as their wives or girlfriends watch over them. Men do not know how to take care of themselves and they resist putting themselves in a position of non-control in which they may be viewed as passive or weak.

Recently, a Canadian surgeon with the University of Calgary dropped dead from a coronary while cross-country skiing with his family. Many of his colleagues were surprised as he exercised regularly, did not smoke or drink and seemed to be the picture of health. He was very active, working up to sixteen hours per day. He loved his work and his family. What caused the fatal blow? I would imagine that the autopsy and his medical history revealed he was prone to heart problems. It is possible that he hastened the process by overwork. It is natural to rest and relax. This man needed a passive activity that fulfilled this need. Ironically, as a heart surgeon, he was accustomed to advising others on how to care for themselves. I have been told by a friend within this profession, that heart surgeons are not known for their long life spans. The statistics prove that problems with alcoholism, drug, and other forms of self-negation are highest in the medical profession with the rigorous training required for recognition contributing to this. Many students become pill poppers and use alcohol to handle the stress of their medical training. If they cannot care for themselves, how can they advise their clients ? The attitude is take a pill, numb the symptoms and continue with your routine. Such messages are delivered regularly through powerful advertising. If men are to follow their destiny of being providers they must work, be strong and healthy. However, when ill, they are like children letting "mommy" care for them. This double-bind message contributes to a man's ill health and self-abuse. The pressure to be strong, in control of the situation while being seen as a weakened child when faced with an illness is incongruent. Neither image is the truth and both contribute to a false image.

Men also lack knowledge of self-care due to their goal orientation and success madness. This drive to win and conquer at any cost, has sent many a man to his early grave. This push and drive becomes a runaway process. For many it takes an accident, a serious illness or a major set-back to bring this push to a halt.

I speak here from experience. While completing my Masters degree, I worked full-time as part of the program. I had the option of working part-time but for me it was "all or nothing." It was demanding as I was counselling young male delinquents and my studies were rigorous and extensive. For a year I was locked into this routine, my world was filled with only work and school. Halfway through the program I began to feel the stress of both .endeavors. I became extremely tired and increasing my sleeping hours did not alleviate the fatigue. I was a candidate for burnout being both emotionally and physically exhausted. I came down with mononucleosis but thought that I was just overtired.

I continued my pace until I was flat on my back with hepatitis in the hospital. Then I was able to stop. During the weeks of convalescense I had to face the situation and myself. I could no longer remain in the graduate program nor could I work. Originally I was determined to get my degree and achieve my goal because this was my ticket for opening career doors. At least, this is what I had been taught. Lying on my back in the hospital made me realize the tremendous price that I had been willing to pay to gain that piece of paper. I had sacrificed my health, my social life and my friends. I had to ask myself if the degree was worth it.

I have witnessed men in my stress workshops who are wound up like rubber bands ready to snap at the slightest provocation. They hold everything in, swallowing their pent-up anger and resentment, creating impatience and irritability in their lives. They are so goal and success driven they are unable to tell their left from their right foot. With eyes focused so far in the distance, their bodies exhibit the strain of being pulled ever onward to the attainment of some fantasy or goal. In the here and now, they have difficulty being present, touching, making real contact and slowing down to experience reality or other people. These driven personalities suffer from ailments such as high blood pressure, heart problems, ulcers and other stress-related diseases. They are unaware of how to take care of themselves nor do they take the time to find out.

I read about a successful construction executive who was viewed by friends and colleagues as being strong, responsible and dependable, a natural born leader. After his wife left him, he realized he did not know the first thing about caring for himself or surviving. He lived on hard boiled eggs and T.V. dinners for months. His clothes, an array of clean and soiled, were strewn about his apartment. He was responsible for paying the bills but his nutritional and nurturing needs were unfulfilled. At work he was envied as an able bodied leader but at home he was a lost little boy. Some men are exceptions, some of the best cooks in the world are men and I have seen men with exceptional house keeping skills. Basically, when it comes to self-care most men without a women's help or influence, are lost. They are not that way by nature but have been socialized to be dependent in these areas.

In order to change this situation men have to learn to re-parent themselves, to mother and nurture themselves. Then they can take back a special power that is theirs but was lost to their parents' control. Psychologist Howard Halpern, in his book Cutting Loose, describes this type of influence:

> "This image of your parent is built partly of your memories, and many of those memories were collected and stored when you were very young. Before being stored away they were filtered and interpreted by your ways of thinking and perceiving as a young child."

As youngsters our parents are the centre of our needs. We depend upon them for direction, recognition, love and nurturing. Emotionally healthy parents will teach self-sufficiency and independence and self-care. Those of us taught to be too dependent on our parents, especially men upon their mothers, are blocked from learning to draw on our own nurturing resources. If our father was the epitome of the "He man," this increased the chances of our being blocked from our self-nurturing and healing resources. To be caring towards ourselves, we must be comfortable with the softer, feminine aspects of ourselves. Obviously, whatever our parents modelled regarding self-healing and self-caring influences our lives.

Much of my work with clients is helping them become fathers and mothers to themselves. Each of us has within us the dependent child, who, during moments of crisis desires our parents. This dependency created in our childhood has lasting effects. To break free of this pattern we must accept the true feelings we hold toward our parents and learn to parent ourselves.

In the '60's activists Abbie Hoffman and Jerry Rubin shocked college audiences by telling them to "kill their parents." Some believed this was meant literally. The message was to cut the umbilical cord and become our own authorities. Only then can we parent ourselves.

In transactional analysis, it is believed that everyone has a parent, an adult and a child ego state. As children we absorb the egos of our parents as our own. Our adult lives are regulated or at least influenced by our parent ego states. We can be the parent, adult or child aspect of our parents as well. Transactional analysis teaches clients to cleanse their own ego states of their parent memories and events. A person reacting from a healthy, cleansed ego state has effective and harmonious interactions with other human beings.

To permit our lives to be dictated by these parental memories will make freedom impossible. I am not suggesting that men go out and cut off all ties with their parents. We need to examine our lives and see if they really are our own and how our actions are dependent upon parental approval, whether they even feel the need to give it. Much of our effort is geared to acting out some deep seated need to please our parents or to get revenge on them for not being all we wanted them to be. When our lives become truly our own our opportunity to experience ourselves, others and life is enhanced. This deep feeling of pleasure and wonder gives us the desire to nurture and be nurtured. Caring for ourselves comes from an attitude of loving and caring for life. The natural parent concept lies within the same place as the child aspect of ourselves. In a healthy person each reaches out and supports the other's growth and development. When we discover our own parenting we will have deeper, more rewarding relationships with the father (support) and the mother (nurturing) portions of our natural make up. We will be able to acknowledge the teaching from both to be given to the child within.

When men nurture themselves, their relationships with women change. Women are moving away from the mother role with their husbands while single women are searching for men who can care for themselves so they will not be put in the position of surrogate mothers. Men will be able to experience women as persons rather than as substitute mothers.

WHAT ARE MY NEEDS?

A man must know his needs before he can know himself as a more fully functioning human being. When working with couples, I am always amazed when I ask them, "What are your needs?" The woman is usually able, after some prodding, to express hers while the man stares blankly and responds, "I don't know" or "I don't understand what you mean." Women can express their needs due to their connection with their feelings and body sense. Men, however, express from their "wants" because they are not in touch with their feelings or their bodies. Figuratively speaking, men express their "wants" from their heads and not their hearts.

In the first section of the book, we examined how men are socialized to respond from their thinking processes and to deny their feelings. Some are encouraged to respond only to their wants and learn manipulation as a means of gaining satisfaction. A man's childhood tantrum can result in wife battering when she does not meet his needs. Having our needs met is high on the survival list regardless of the situation.

As infants we are dependent upon our parents and others to have our needs met. As adults we are still dependent on others to have these fulfilled. All human beings have needs and strive to have them met in the best way they know how. As children we learned certain patterns for this fulfillment and we carry these into our adult lives.

My purpose in this discussion is not to expound on needs. There are countless books and courses available which handle this effectively. I wish to explore the needs issue and how this relates to men learning or re-learning use of the once buried resources they have. Knowing one's needs results when the feelings behind those desires surface. I will deal with the feelings aspect later. Now, I will probe the ways and means that men attempt to have their needs met and whether these methods are healthy and effective in the long run.

It has taken years of growing and learning to distinguish between my needs and wants. As a male I lived my needs as my "wants" and found my world of being cared for, externalized. Needs come from within while wants are "out there." There has been pain in learning the difference. As I write pages of this book, I experience the continuing conflict of "wanting" to say what is required and expressing myself from a place of need. I find consistently I become lost trying to say what I mean in my writing rather than allowing feelings to be expressed on the page. I struggle with saying how I feel and saying what I am supposed to. I find myself having to go within to retrieve thoughts and feelings that stem from my needs. I find my situation is similar to other men as they attempt to understand what they are experiencing below the surface of their thinking processes.

In 1981 while completing an internship for my doctorate degree I was involved in the treatment and rehabilitation of drug abusers. These people taught me a great deal about myself.

I can recall vividly, how these men and women under intense therapy conditions revealed the child as part of themselves. They were living in larger bodies attempting to satisfy their adult needs, but were essentially coming from a child perspective. I witnessed forty-year-old adults becoming children again as the false images of pride and strength were stripped away. The therapy used was based on the synanon method mixed with gestalt, family therapy and transactional analysis. This combination of therapies was very successful in breaking through the barriers carried by the drug abusers. Basically, these people used manipulation to get their needs met and this behavior mode was costly as they spent most of their lives in and out of prisons.

Drug abuse often encouraged their manipulative behavior. For example, they would steal to support their drug habit and this became a way of life. They were not only addicted to the drugs, they were addicted to self-destructive and abusive habits to get their needs met.

Therapy revealed their victimization by parents who were aloof or absent. With men, however, over protective mothers created a sense of being smothered which they rebelled against. They had negative self images, low self esteem, and false identities and lacked a sense of morality. They learned early in life that if they wanted something, they took it. Most were 'bought' with material things disguised as love. Eventually materialism became a substitute for genuineness and love. Their lives became based upon possessions and they became possessed by their drug habits.

These people are a minority example in our society. We can learn a great deal from the study of extremes and deviance for we as "normal" members of society exhibit some of these same behaviors. Just as they learned to get what they desired by taking it, we who live in an affluent society have a spoiled attitude. Like them our real needs for love, recognition and acceptance were substituted with a toy, a game or some other reward.

Some of these prison bound men were the most sensitive people I have met. Some were extremely talented artists and musicians, and underneath their criminal attitude was a compassion deeper than that of the average man. If these men were able to "get it together" combining all aspects within themselves, they were truly unique. Charles Manson remarked, "You made me what I am" during his murder trial.

As long as men are born into a world that attempts to live off his potential, he will never be able to fully be himself unless he breaks free of the maddening destructive cycle. In the book *My Mother, My Self,* the powerful influence a mother has over her daughter's life is examined. I would like to see a book for men entitled, *My Parents, My Self.* It is time for men to rediscover their true needs by feeling what they truly need. The first need, is to feel. Others will fall into place once feeling is accepted. Some women are apprehensive of "needy" men who are attempting to break free of their cycles. Men may avoid such an individual altogether or will stay up all night "nursing" him over a pint of bourbon. When men are able to declare, "I need," they will be set free from the catacombs of their minds and be able to experience what their needs are rather than just imagine them.

How a man responds to the acceptance of his needs, and the rediscovery of them, and not placing "wants" in front of feelings, will depend upon whether he remains trapped in a "needy" unfulfilled place or not.

FEELINGS ARE HEARTFELT

"Feel me, see me, touch me," is a line from the hit song of the rock group The Who which was a favorite of the sixties flower children. It conveys the sentiment of so many young people who sought their identity through the pathways of drugs, music and counter culture. The search was for something real, tangible and with substance that would fill gaps in their empty hearts as a result of growing up in the middle class world of material values. They were searching for authentic human qualities that were void in the modern, dog-eat-dog society. Their search was to soothe the painful, wretching feelings within their hearts which were torn apart by false love promises. They desired a reconnection with real, living and experiencing human beings.

Those false promises resulted from the power-driven masculine society which attempted to fill those gaps with leisure, perfection and the technological utopian dreams of science. As children we remember the bribes of ice cream and candy to soothe our tears. Those "rewards" became substitutes which were better than no recognition at all. What we really needed was a warm embrace or some reassuring words of compassion. We soon learn to settle for second best. Shostrom desribes the results of this non-feeling attitude on the modern world:

> "Modern man is dead, a puppet. This corpse-like behavior is part of every modern man. He is deliberate without emotions — a marionette. He is reliable, but without live intentions, wishes, wants, and desires. His life is very boring, empty and meaningless. He controls and manipulates others and is caught in the web of his own manipulation."

It is obvious that a man of no emotions is the result of such socialization.

In **Zorba the Greek**, Zorba teaches an Englishman how to dance. What the lesson really is, is how to feel. The dance comes on its own when a man can feel. Whenever I see a movie which brings tears to my eyes, I know that my heart has been opened. During "E.T.," I was deeply saddened to witness E.T. hooked up to the life support system. My tears joined with many other patrons in the theatre. I saw tears steaming down the cheeks of men and women alike which brought me joy as I felt that I was part of a living drama where people were displaying their emotions freely. Many men quickly removed the signs of their emotional display while their wives, girlfriends and children continued to experience theirs. By the time I was outside the theatre, not one man was teary-eyed while the others were still experiencing. When I reached my car my eyes were dry and I was back in my thoughts ready to discuss the movie in my usual analytical fashion. I asked my lady companion what she "thought" of the movie. Her reply was, with swollen eyes, "It moved me." She wasn't in the mood to "talk about" the movie.

The world acclaimed heart transplant surgeon Dr. Christian Bernard was a guest of the Johnny Carson show several years ago. As he spoke of the death of a close friend and colleague, tears welled in his eyes and he could not speak. Millions of viewers watched as a prominent man began to weep on national television. I wonder what male viewers were feeling to see such an emotional display. I would bet some were thinking, "C'mon Doc, get it together!" The viewers in a local pub may have looked on long enough to simply shrug their shoulders and have a another drink. Maybe some were secretly envying that a man, a famous man, was able to be so publically vulnerable.

When my stepfather ordered me to stop crying as outlined in the introduction, I had difficulty in doing so. In the past ten years through the experience of various therapies, I have found it easier to share my emotions with others. I have been able to cry in therapy groups when the pain was too much to handle rationally. It has taken a long time to allow this experience to happen. Today, I am still learning how to express my deepest emotions.

Even though I have found it easier to shed my emotional defenses in others' presence, it is more recent that I have been able to cry alone. I envy women who can handle crisis by having a good cry.

I met a woman who appeared in my life when I needed someone. I was depressed, had just completed my Ph.D. and was in the middle of a mid-life crisis. I had no sense of direction and was uncertain, and insecure. I was stuck in the inbetween, or what William Bridges in his book, **Transitions,** calls the "neutral zone." After meeting Nancy, I began to experience some hope and a sense of direction. I was considering a teaching job in South America and Nancy was going to accompany me. I was in seventh heaven. Then, Nancy began to act distant and rejecting towards me. This began to build as I had opened myself and was feeling particularly vulnerable. I began to do immature things like calling her in the middle of the night and when I was unable to hide my hurt, I whimpered like a hurt puppy. This of course, only escalated her aloofness. The hurt was beginning to control me. One night, after midnight, I called her and a male voice answered. I hung up, totally stunned. I did not know whether to call again or scream like a banshee. Numb, I laid on the bed for about an hour and stared at the ceiling. I felt like my body was a mummy's corpse, held tight within its wrappings. I began to roll on the bed, pounding it with my fists and breathing more and more rapidly. Finally, I let go a blood curdling scream that scared even me. I yelled out again, "Fucking bitch! Fucking bitch!" My mind became filled with images of women in my life that had brought me pain. Other women also appeared in my mind's eye. My mind became flooded accompanied by a gut wretching pain and I was not able to breathe. I panicked, feeling that I was on the edge of an abyss from which I would never return. I seemed to dangle on the precipice, hanging on by a very thin thread. My mother's image and Nancy's flashed through my mind simultaneously — then Mary's, another girlfriend, and then Deanna's my first love, appeared. As each appeared, my chest began to throb and my stomach knotted with intense pain. My breathing was rapid and tears began to roll down my cheeks. I began to whimper, my voice cracked and my whole body was in convulsion. At one point I thought I would climax. Then the tears of pain came, releasing thirty five years of control and fear. I did not fall apart, die or go crazy which is what I thought would be the result of such a release, but I felt good all over. I now knew what women experienced when they cried alone. Since the age of eleven I had not known the luxury. The next day I called to tell Nancy the good news; to me it was a spectacular event. I did not feel that she shared my enthusiasm but it did not matter. I was able to find a lost part of myself and she was a catalyst for that transformation. It was painful but that is what was required to shed that script that I had adopted so many years ago with my stepfather. She gave me a gift and the gift was myself. I am grateful to her for that.

I share this experience to reveal that like most men, I have been branded with a particular set of rules about feelings. I have felt the pain and numbness of non-feeling and know how lonely and frightening it can be. I have experienced rejection when I became vunerable. It hurts! To learn of the domain of feelings requires that we enter doors of pain. Women know these doors only too well and men often cause a great deal of this pain. It does no good to punish ourselves for that now, the bottom line is we have done the best we know how. This does not mean we cannot improve our skills and ourselves by learning to be more of what we are. We are feeling persons and we do cry. Tears are releasing, softening and healing.

Men are releasing themselves from the self-destructive habits learned during masculine training. They are realizing they are short changed and need to find their paths back to that which they have forfeited. As brothers, we share our pains, our fears and our confusion as it stems from similar training processes. With this common ground we can assist and help others, they in turn can pass this support on. Destructive competitive feelings harden the heart. We can open our hearts to one another and be part of a new feeling community that cares for their fellow man rather than viewing him as an object to manipulate and dominate. To be a man without feeling is to be a man without a heart, a hollow man, a machine.

THINKING PASSIONATELY

To be "mellow" is to be integrated emotionally, mentally, physically and spiritually. Such men have the gifts of the revolutionary thinkers. A mellow man has great passion which gives him strength in all aspects off his life. This passion, akin to his thinking process, makes him a man of heart and intense compassion for life and for humanity.

We have been blessed with men of this stature — great poets such as Longfellow, Frost, Blake, and artists like Michellangelo, Van Gogh, and Picasso; and humanitarians such as Albert Schweitzer and Buckminster Fuller. Gandhi, an educated man of the justice system, possessed a deep compassion, an intense feeling sense, and had a mind like a steel trap. It would seem that men who feel their thoughts have a powerful impact upon the world. It is the integration of mind and emotion that lends them their strength and compassion.

Only recently, within the past thirty years, have men of Western science and rational thought begun to acknowledge that the combination of mental and emotional processes does bring about healthy results.

The education system still advocates cognitive (mental process) in the training and development of the young. Some systems are becoming aware of the value of a more integrated process, allowing effective learning (feeling, experiential) to be part of the education of our young people. Graduate schools are overladen with the demands of scientifically proven work from students completing their theses and dissertations. Lately, non-traditional approaches have attracted the attention of more creative, individualistic and feeling students who are encouraged to grow as individuals as well as professionals.

The single-minded, narrow world of the rationalistic man is being challenged by a new wave of people, some of whom are developing their feeling natures.

Some academics advocate such integration. Most do not. Many students can attest to the effectiveness of a professor who keeps them inspired in a topic. We are also aware of the teachers who speak in monotone voices and seem half alive. Most classes at the university level are boring, leaving students with years of routine and lack of enthusiasm. D.H. Lawrence sums up this point:

"All our wonderful education and learning is producing a grand sum total of boredom. Modern people are inwardly thoroughly bored. They are bored because they experience nothing, and they experience nothing because the wonder has gone out of them. And when the wonder has gone out of the man, he is dead."

It is no surprise to see graduates of universities lacking zest, passion or the readiness to partake in the riches of living. Those fortunate enough to come through the system having had some inspring mentors, often lose their enthusiasm after a few years of ramming their heads against the walls of apathy, red tape and society's refusal to change. They usually fade into the background or move into another field of endeavor or succumb to the majority's way, joining the ranks of mediocrity. As long as we sit back, believing we can do nothing, the passion that lives in our hearts and minds will die. We become like deadwood, welcoming the next batch that is pushed into the warehouse of life from the assembly line regulated by an institution called a university or college.

Thus ends the negative side of the picture. It is necessary to view both sides of an issue to maintain balance and perspective. I will now discuss the passion of thinking, being mellow, and those men who are an inspiration to the revolutionary man's style of thinking.

Initially, I will speak of author, lecturer and international traveller, Dr. Leo Buscaglia. He has a tremendous following of men and women, lay people and professionals. He is known as the professor of Love. After his lectures, people line up to receive a warm hug and kiss from this powerful and passionate man. I have not had the good fortune to attend one of his lectures, but I did see a video tape. It is obvious why he is one of the most sought after speakers of our time and why his books are bestsellers. As he spoke, he held the audience spellbound, similar to Ram Dass and the late Allan Watts. Buscaglia spoke directly to the audience through the passion of his heart with each word welded with deep feeling and intense expression. The audience listened as he methodically, like a skilled surgeon, cut through the protected layers of self, touching people in those inner places of meaning and significance. He did not speak down to them, as the authority, but directly to them, to their humanness. He spoke from a place where all people experience life; from fear, doubt, pain as well as joy, hope, and transcendence. It was obvious he spoke from experience. He became angry with passion just as easily as his mood changed to sadness or humor. He was able to capture all human emotions and expressively weave them as a fine tailor who has mastered his craft. I saw people in the large audience become overwhelmed with emotion as he struck places deep within their hearts when he spoke of life's trials, tribulations and endless struggle. He painted pictures with his words that all could see. From the video tape, I was shaking inside. His presentation evoked thoughts and feelings within me which had been dormant for years. By his voice tone, his passionate delivery and his choice of words, I was deeply touched. I saw the truth in the rumor of people lining up for a hug after this man speaks. I wish I could have been there too, to hug this gigantic man of great compassion.

It is people like Leo who instill life in the empty places inside of us. These aspects of ourselves yearn for contact with life, with the profound. Men like Dr. Buscaglia give substance to life and put us in touch with our greatness, our humanness. This quality exists in the hearts and minds of men of revolution. By their thoughts, actions and words, people are transformed.- Next I will speak of another man of great passionate thinking, Chief Dan George. He is remembered as the great chief in the movie with Dustin Hoffman called "Little Big Man." By working with native people in Canada, I feel closer to this type of man. Native people have much to teach us about passion for life. I have met wise native men who live by what they say and do. I have met some who know Dan George personally. They have only the very best to say of him. I have read some of his poetry. His writings speak of years of growing up Indian in a white man's society. He uses his years of living as a model for his own people to help them adapt to the unfeeling, greedy ways of the white man and his machines. Well into his eighties, his mind is still rich and crisp because he has the heart of a young man. Indian people by living through their hearts, have managed to survive the purge of the white man's conquest.

I am amazed when in the presence of those native people who have learned to release the bitterness they once harbored towards the white man's destructive influence. Their thinking is soft, fluid and I am able to feel what they are thinking. It is quite unlike the inflexible, rationalistic thinking that I experience with most white businessmen and academics. The native people have passion in their lives despite their hardships. I feel good that their acceptance of me is total, that they know the whole of me; my thoughts, feelings, experiences and humor. They are themselves and allow me to be the same. Chief Dan George is a credit to his people, living his heritage as a native person in a white man's world with passion and integrity. He is an example to all people, not just native.

The T.V. drama "Quincy" became one of the most popular programs. People seemed enthralled by this character, played by Jack Klugman, who was intense and passionate willing to go to any length to get the truth. People need such heroes to give spice to difficult economic and uncertain social times. I learned through an interview in "People" magazine that Mr. Klugman is much like the character he portrays. He is intensely dedicated to social justice, and is involved in numerous community and civic projects to which he devotes much time. We need men like the character "Quincy" in our midst; a man who has the courage of his convictions and is willing to battle the system for betterment and change. Such men are intensely involved with others, they care deeply, and get angry at injustice, and are passionate thinking individuals who do not let their thinking processes overrun their caring for others and their zest for life. They are more comfortable relating to people than machines and are able to experience their whole reality. His actions are positively personally and socially motivated.

Scientists who *feel* their theories and their social consequences, as well as constructing them rationally, will be of true benefit to the people whom they are intended to serve. Technology, produced with heartfelt purpose and service to humanity, is a technology worthy of true praise. Men who use their hearts as well as their minds will have the foresight to ensure their designs are beneficial to the consumer. Perhaps then the consumer will have reason to have faith in a machine-economy.

We have become a society too dependent on the thinking process as a means of defining our place in the world. We have sacrificed what Allan Watts called "instintual wisdom" in **The Wisdom of Insecurity.** He advised:

> "We have allowed brain thinking to develop and dominate our lives out of all proportion to 'instinctual wisdom,' which we are allowing to slump into atrophy. As a consequence, we are at war within ourselves — the brain desiring things which the body does not allow."

This conflict, experienced by so many of us, results in the head and rational process being the major controlling component of our functioning. This sets a rigid boundary between the head and body sense which is connected to the emotions. Eventually this split creates anxiety and insecurity. This in between place can be experienced as nothingness, which in effect, is our numbed passion for life. To be connected to our essential passion is to be joined mentally and emotionally so we can live our reality, our essence through our senses. Mind and feeling connected allows a more vital whole life experience.

When men learn to reclaim their instincts of knowing thought and feeling simultaneously, they will not experience such panic and confusion when bombarded with feelings. Men will not have to retreat to their familiar mental realms for security and control. They will begin to trust their bodily instincts and senses as well. Eventually, they will once again respond from their feelings and know the passion and intensity of their minds.

THE WHOLE BODY OF LIFE

When was the last time you noticed a spider web, a bird's song, squirrels gathering their winter stores; the beauty of nature? Probably not for a while, and for some not since childhood when nature was awe, excitement and wonder which sent our imaginations soaring.

We are too busy "being busy." I often hear businessmen complain of "never having enough time" in my workshops. When we discuss time management I explain that it is not that we haven't enough time rather that we are "out of timing." We have become so controlled within our lives, minds, bodies that we no longer know how to listen to our inner clocks. Our bodies are created to let us know when we have stretched beyond our natural limits. They tell us when to rest, to be active, etc. if we are willing to listen. We are accustomed to the external clock which regulates our daily activities. It would come as no surprise that some men regulate their love-making as they do the rest of their world. This can lead to premature ejaculation or impotence when they are out of sync with the body's natural rhythms. Most men either do not live in their bodies or they are so physically locked within them that they become a muscular prison. In the past, a potbelly was a symbol of affluence, not so today. Exercise is important and necessary but I believe that we go to extremes because we have lost the sense of our own rhythms. We are creatures of nature and as boys we were open to and in tune with natural living processes. As adults we have lost that sense and tend to push and stretch our bodies as we do our minds. We live mentally expecting our bodies to do the bidding of the mind. Working separately, our minds and bodies become fragmented. We often feel 'pulled apart' when under stress. The experienced tension winds us up like rubberbands ready to snap.

When working with men under a lot of stress in workshops, I ask them to check and see if they are breathing. They are often puzzled by such a mundane request but as they check they find their breathing is restricted. After taking a few deep breaths, they discover their tensions lessening and they take an objective view of what is really bothering them. This condition is a result of over controlling and not living within our bodies. Usually men carry their bodies as though they were nothing more than appendages to their heads.

Being out of sync with one's body often results in treating it as though it were a foreign object. Often this attitude will extend to other's bodies as well. Stanely Kelleman, a teacher in body psychology, states:

> "A person having contact with his own body is in contact with
> feelings, desires, sensations, and pleasures. And at the same time
> he feels related to the natural enviroment, of which he is a part."

A man with no respect for his body will abuse it. He will either be inactive allowing himself to become out of shape or he will over exercise and push himself beyond his body's natural balance. It is one thing to have a Charles Atlas build and quite another to appreciate the body for what it is.

This destructive external attitude causes some to negate their bodies regulating their lives through an external clock. They over-control and dominate their bodies and try the same thing in their interpersonal lives. The "bully" not only hates himself and is a coward inside but he hates his body. The "stud" prances around like a proud peacock obviously connected only to one part of his body. The rest of his body is numb and foreign to his experience. He lives in his image and forces his body to action as he would operate a piece of machinery. This might continue until the body in its own natural defence stops the machine altogether. Many men who have sexual function difficulties have tried to ride their bodies like a bucking bronco, making it a slave to their minds and societal image of what it is. The body's refusal to "get it up" is like the stallions determination not to be broken. The constant competition to conquer and control leaves many men with broken and unhealthy bodies as well as natural functions that are out of sync. We don't just have a body and we don't just have a mind. We are a body. A body of knowledge that is part of the organismic system of the universe. We are as much a part of the world of the insects, plants, birds and reptiles as they are of us. They cohabit with man everywhere and are in rhythm with nature's clock. When animals eat they stop when they're full. We often do just the opposite as many a ritual Christmas and Thanksgiving meal is evidence.

In both Eastern and Western religion our bodies are considered the temple of the living spirit. The way most of us treat our bodies would make it impossible for a "spirit" to live in our temples.

The authors Perls, Hefferline and Goodman, provide an illustration of man's inability to live in harmony with his body environment. They say: "... one fears contact with actuality - with flesh-and-blood people and with one's own sensations and feelings." What does happen when we fear contact with our bodies?

Bio-energetic analyst, Alexander Lowen believes: "the soul of a man is in his body." If so, and man is in constant search for salvation and freedom, the eternal happiness, why is it that he fails to see the marvel of creation in his own body? Why is it that he shapes his body into images and worships these at contests to see who has the "better" body? How can we have a contest to see who has the better body, negating the notion of the soul within that body?

Outside my cabin door, where I wrote this book, live a dozen tiny spiders on a rose bush. Each has a section of this rose bush where they have spun their webs. Each spider sits in wait for its prey to be entangled within its web handiwork. They don't compete they cooperate, for the rose bush is large enough for each of them to live and do their work. The rose bush itself seems to welcome these tiny creatures. Neither the rose bush nor the spiders have to be greedy in their need to be and exist. They co-exist, with each carrying on natural function season after season. The spiders function is just as important as that of the rose bush. It doesn't bother or interrupt the growth of the rose bush, it continues to be flushed with many roses in full blossom while other buds are just beginning their cycle. Years ago I would not have taken the time to even notice the spiders or the rose bush. If I had have, I probably would have grabbed a can of Raid to kill the spiders that were "disfiguring" the beauty of the rose bush — just as I would have had a mole removed from my body, or sprayed underarm deodorant in my armpits because these related to my natural attributes which were "unpleasant."

As men we have learned to view our bodies as images. We dress a certain way and expect it to fulfill our fantasies about the way it is supposed to be. If our chest doesn't measure to a certain size we pump iron to extend it, a symbol of what we believe to be true masculinity. Society dictates physical attributes such as hairy chests for men and large breasts for women as definitions of who we are. Some women resort to breast surgery to have to increase their sense of being "womanly." When I was twenty-one I bought a false moustache because I couldn't grow one yet, which is an example of being ashamed of my slow, but natural growth process.

Being out of tune with our bodies, creates imbalance with our minds, life and the environment. As long as we cannot accept the "parts" of us that are of the natural growth process we will be blind to this process and our function within it. We will miss the beauty that already "is" and will try to manufacture it out of some imagined concept. We will attempt to make our bodies over into some image that is dictated by society. We will be victims of these needs, fearing to move with our own rhythm lest we don't get approval. We will find ourselves measuring our images by some intangible yet powerful and controlling social yardstick and doing the same to others. Our lives will become regulated by the rhythm of this social yardstick as we strive to fit with the "sameness" mold. If we attempt to break out of the molding pattern it will arouse anxiety in others, for they have learned to find a false security in the "sameness" rhythm. If we dare to be different, we run the risk of being cast out as misfits. To break the tie with the societal life clock and tuning into the "body of life" clock is a risk. Without the risk, we continue to increasingly lose ourselves. It is our body that keeps us tuned into nature's pulse. When we are disconnected we become estranged. A re-connection with our body is like coming home. A busy executive who retreats to the mountains for a weekend knows that this is not enough time to feel part of nature's garden and will plan future visits. He needs more of this nuturing, getting in touch. When we are able to breathe fresh air, hear the birds, and the sound of natural silence, that "humming of activity," see the rows and rows of green, feel the warm rays of the sun, we sense once again the nurturing earth of which we human creatures, body and all, live as a part of nature's kingdom. The flesh is the spirit, the mind is the body, in union they are the environment.

MEN AND THE CREATIVE SPIRIT

When I was in elementary school I was a budding young artist. I loved to draw and was constantly sketching. School was exciting and I was thrilled to go there each day. Learning was a challenge and I always looked forward to what we were going to explore next.

By junior high I had begun to lose my interest and excitment for school and learning. It was becoming a chore to get up everyday and sit through the classes that I was beginning to dislike. I was restless and began to daydream a lot. I hated Math and found myself becoming increasingly frustrated. The 'D's' on my report card certainly didn't instill desire to overcome my disinterest for Math. I did like being around my friends and found this to be an education in itself. When I finished high school I had practically lost all desire to draw or be creative. My interests were being "cool", scoring with girls and fitting in to my peer group. My real interests and desires were camouflaged by the need to be somebody, though I didn't know who that was. While I was in college my concerns were with my fraternity. The supposed brotherhood stuff was actually an overated drinking club, R.O.T.C. and being B.M.O.C. — big man on campus! Most classes were boring and I seldom attended unless it was mandatory or the professor was semi-interesting.

This routine was common to most of my male friends and even some of the females. We are told that college is supposed to be such a big event in our lives and yet, when we get there we find out that it is often more of the same boring routine we had through twelve years of schooling only more sophisticated. My education became true learning for me when the student movement erupted in the 60's. Although I was a latecomer it was one of the most meaningful and creative events of my whole education process.

Finally, I was able to be part of something that had meaning, I could be involved in something that was affecting my life. The more I listened and communicated with others the more my curiousity and creative spirit were being born. I began attending classes again, and signed up for courses that through the grapevine I learned were taught by professors who cared and were willing to dialogue. Life was becoming interesting, I began to read and enjoy it. Learning was being born in me again and I could feel the effects of this new found creative pulse. This creative spark was turning me into myself; my mind, my passion, and the wonderous activity around me. At times I even found myself beginning to sketch again except something was missing, the "feeling" that I once had in elementary school. The contact with form had somehow left me. I was cautious, shy and unbelieving in this "feeling" that I once cherished. I even felt intimidated by the shapes and figures that were transposed on the sketch pad. Something was amiss. I was unable to connect with that artist part of myself that I had in the first grade.

As much as I tried, and frustratingly so, it was gone. Like an arm or leg amputated, I was handicapped. To this day I can only draw at about a third grade level, "stick people" is my standard expression.

It has been well documented that when children complete their schooling in the U.S. they have lost much of their innate capacities and talents to be creative, to be artistic. Creativity comes in many forms. It is a spirit of expression that is manifest in a variety of ways. It is more of a feeling, a human emotion that comes directly from the well-spring of life's continuous movement. It is an expression of the multitudes of one's beingness and and a kaleidoscope of what life process is. It has form and it has order — a natural structure that lacks rigidity, favoring balance and symmetry.

So, you might be asking yourself what creativity has to do with men and the theme of this book? As long as men are unable to re-tap the source of their creative passion, they will be destined to go through their lives half alive; hungry for this innate capability. They will become rigid, inflexible, eventually afraid of the creative desire within of them that periodically comes back to them in momentary "spurts" of excitement and playfulness. Sadly, they are often confined to their roles and images of how they are "supposed" to live their lives, and see these momentary "spurts" of imagination as mere intrusions. To focus and concentrate on this emerging life movement inside them leaves them frustrated and disappointed. Until, we are able to regain our creative spark our lives as men will be at best mediocre and conformed. Our vitality, once lived passion; that awe about everything that lives and exists, that pureness of imagination, will be missing from our lives.

Let us examine further how we lost this very vital part of our makeup as we begin to recreate the foundation, the process, to retrieve our creativity.

At one time, not long ago, it was joke to purchase anything with the label "made in Japan." It was considered shoddy and second best to the U.S. made materials.

Today people are buying cars, stereo's, cameras, and other goods imported from Japan. In twenty years Japan has risen as one of the world's industrial giants. Following World War II, their economy was next to nothing.

In many ways the U.S. has fallen behind the Japanese in quality production. It has become more concerned with quantity and profit and quality has taken a nose dive. Prior to this, the U.S. enjoyed a reputation for producing quality and products that bore the mark of craftmanship. Practically, every country in the world was buying our products. In recent years quality and craftmanship have disappeared. Prefab houses are falling down as fast as they're going up. Automobiles, are constantly having to be recalled due to faulty parts or workmanship. Law suits have been filed by many a consumer injured because of faulty equipment.

Recently, people plunged to their deaths, when a bridge collapsed in Connecticut. This is the second in two years. Another bridge in Florida sent others to their death when it crumbled. Reports have indicated that all of the fifty-one states also have bridges in need of repair and the future safety of these is questionable.

The Statue of Liberty has always symbolized a cry to the world to send us "your starving, your homeless." Today over a thousand of Cuba's "boat people," are labelled as criminals when some are only guilty of being opposed to the Casto regime. Some of these men are fated to spend two years in prison as "guests" of the "land of democracy." I believe that the government was shaken by what Castro did, and is still suffering from this shock. We send billions of dollars to other countries in foreign aide and still people in the U.S. starve. All this production, all this affluence and still people are being left out of the shuffle. And this is exactly what it is, a shuffle. The powers that be and big business are playing a card game and the people have become poker chips. It is obvious that those in power are more interested in destroying quality than in finding ways to bring it and creativity back to our nation and its people.

When the Russians sent up Sputnik in the late 50's, the U.S. became engaged in a technological race against them to not fall behind in conquering the frontier of space. Since this time the thrust of technology has influenced every aspect of our lives. From childrearing, education and economic development, our lives have felt the sting of the machine age. As the machines begin to dominate our lives, we have felt the deteriorating effect of the alienation of people. The creativity and the passion for living has gone from most of us. People hang on by their fingertips with only a glimmer of hope and optimism. Clark Moustakas gives a concrete example of this experience as he talks about the effects of alienation. "Alienation is a retreat away from self-awareness and toward self-anesthesia, where one's sense is denied as valid, and feelings are no longer felt and owned." I believe that alienation and apathy occur as a result of denied creativity. People need to express themselves. Life is expression in action and when this is taken away from us we become dull and numb. We lose our will to create, to imagine.

The education system fosters this decay and deterioration. Children go to school to broaden, to expand themselves and to find that they are limited by the system. The zest, the dynamism, the playfulness, the gushes of spontaneity suffer from immobilization. The education system does not exist for their benefit. Children are being prepared to keep the wheels of progress moving and the winning attitude toward the space race alive. They must learn the cognitive experience of the world. They must learn to use their minds for they are the technicians, the engineers and probably the future space travelers. It remains a male dominated world despite a few women who are joining the ranks of the machine-thinkers. Some of them are even sacrificing their natural creativeness to learn the game of the male world. I favor women developing their male side, but I hope that they won't get entangled and lost and trapped within it like so many men are.

As long as we continue as men to just go along with the robotized, calculated training for our manhood we are a part of the problem and offer nothing for a solution. When we march in rank through the assembly line process of education, we will for all intents and purposes do the same for the rest of our lives unless we experience an event that shakes us loose from the assembly line. We will pass non-creativity on to our sons in the attempt to ensure that they stay "in-line" just as we have. We will become the "storm troopers," aggressive, pushy, and arrogant believing that our mask-in-line is the way it should be through life. We will dismiss other aspects of creative expression, when they are seen as dissent, for we are unable to listen to anything that sparks of difference. This spark will be too much of a threat because we have settled for the humdrum of mediocrity. We will have become average, and will have lost our uniqueness. "Nature abhors same-ness," states Buscaglia. Sameness abhors difference and uniqueness. Those who conform to an image that they have come to believe in are a danger not only to themselves but to others who also desire to be unique.This rigid attitude tells them it is not necessary to look any farther.

To be born is a creative act, a magical dance that goes on between two rhythms of nature; the masculine and the feminine. The act of making love is creation in various degrees of motion. This motion creates tension that gives birth to the orgasm which in turn, if all is attune, is the beginning of another kind of birthing. Another creative act.

Life is creation. We are a living symbol of this action and it is our destiny to nurture this process. Creation is not a fixed, rigid or mundane process. Just look at the magic of what has been created. It is not mundane.

We are not mundane even though our lives dictate much of this. We start out free, moving, swimming into life and life still awaits us. Life is embedded in the hardened, blocked places of our emotions, our bodies, our minds and our interaction with the world. The primal ecstacy awaits those of us who are tired of pushing man's company clock, those of us who are tired of being put down for our expressed need to be more alive and creative. We are a gift to life through a creative act. By virtue of this we are a gift! To be a gift is to give ourselves back to that from which we came. This in itself is the highest of the creative acts.

HUMOR, SELF-ESTEEM AND HEALING

The energetic 80-year-old comedian George Burns once said about laughter: "You can't get an ulcer if your laughing." Norman Cousins, author of the bestseller **Anatomy of an Illness**, tells of how he cured himself from a terminal disease by watching Charlie Chaplin and Marx Brothers reruns.

Humor has been with us since the beginning of time. Court jesters were always present to soothe the tempers of a king, queen or emperor. If he wasn't funny, he often lost his head or tongue. I'm sure that cave men laughed when one of their followers was treed by a saber tooth tiger.

Laughter is a pleasant part of our life experience, reminding us that life is beautiful despite the prevailing conditions. Laughter, helps tame our seriousness and soothe our despair. It quells our loneliness and keeps us in touch with our vitality , the healing part of our self. Laughter acts as a cleanser as it clears away the nagging, punishing flavor of conflict. Laughter helps mend a broken bone, heal a broken heart and teach us the absurdity of certain unchangeable situations.

Yes, the gift of humor is a part of life that heals our troubled times.

But what about men and humor? I'm sure most of us have been the butt of some joke when everyone laughed like crazy while we just sat there stunned.

I'm all for having a good time, laughing and joking but I do draw the line. Humour is fine when it is not at the expense of others. In these situations what we think is humorous is actually destructive. Many a so-called prank has turned into mishap.

While in high school, a fellow in my biology class hid a bee in a girl's purse. When she opened the purse the bee flew out and stung her. She ended up in the hospital because she was allergic to bees and almost died. She even had to receive psychiatric help to deal with that traumatic event.

Several years ago in different parts of the country several young male students were injured and some died as a result of the traditional fraternity "hazing." Here, the initiate is put through an assortment of grueling tasks as the senior members of the fraternity proceed to humiliate the initiate as much as possible. This is the traditional masculine treatment for belonging to the so-called "brotherhood." On one occasion initiates were made to swallow pieces of sliced liver and were told they were live worms. One of the initiates choked on his piece of liver and was dead on arrival at the hospital. I was shocked to see this sort of treatment going on, and remembered when I was a pledge in a fraternity.

I know the scars that result from constant humiliation and teasing in the name of fun. My brother loved to tease me when I was growing up. Once, he put a pillow over my head when I was sleeping and when I woke up gasping for air, he laughed hysterically. Another time, I was awakened one morning by a continous stream of loud bangs. When I rubbed my eyes and brought my head over the covers, I had to duck quickly to keep from having a fire cracker go off in my face. My brother was throwing them on the bed while I was asleep. A dangerous joke.

I'm sure that my brother was really just showing me how fond of me he was; like the time that he and three of his buddies threw me into a patch of stinging nettles. I itched and burned for hours. This was all part of the ritual of being the ugly duckling, the one who didn't 'fit'. The aim is to drive him mad with fear and intimidation.

You can probably flashback to those times when you were the butt of a joke, or put someone else on the end of one. You can probably empathize with those who know the feeling of being bullied by someone who is releasing pent-up hostility through humor.

Men release their frustration through their anger, but I believe that they also release their hostility through their laughter. Most of the time when men make a humorous comment or tell jokes it is meant as a "putdown." Most jokes are forms of putdowns and overt signs of prejudice. I wonder if we realize how habitual our joke telling can be. "Did you hear the one about..." how often do we say this or listen to someone else say it. Women are often the brunt of the joke when men tell the "latest one." Men even say "fuck" in public as this goes along with the other acceptable means of release of their aggression and display of manliness. Swearing is a means of expression of the internal conflict that holds one in self-reprisal. For some men every second breath is "fuck this" or "fuck that."

Perhaps the meaning behind most joke telling is metaphoric. It's a story being told about the absurdities of life. Everybody tells jokes about the Pollocks even in front of the Polish. Some Polish people even tell these jokes but then they are about the Irish or the Italians or some other minority group. Someone, or some group has to be at the bottom of the heap. Nobody wants to be these people, even in a joke, because being unsuccessful in this country and not measuring up is a symbol of being a failure as a human being. This is especially true for men. Even a good joke teller is praised whereas a man who can't tell a good joke often becomes the brunt of it.

If we understand that underneath men's frustration and conflict is self-negation and self-denial, it is not too surprising that we discover jokes as a means of elevating our low self-esteem. Just for one moment, the laughter we experience from the humour soothes and heals us inside, even if it is at the expense of another.

Have you ever laughed so hard that tears came to your eyes? Or have you been so angry you began to cry? My guess is that laughter, anger and tears all come from the same place. Since we're not permitted other emotional expression but allowed our anger, we may use it to extreme. It is all that we have. Laughter, if coming from the same place as anger, comes rolling out mixed in with the frustration and lack of tears. I've noticed this in my own laughter sometimes. I can feel the rage from within my very being emerging from my throat. I specifically am aware of this when I'm feeling sarcastic. Each word is an attack on anyone who is my audience. The remnants of my displaced emotion is lodged in my jaw, welded in my teeth while my stomach is churning.

Humor can be used as an effective tool if used with perspective. It can be healing and can even save one's life as indicated by Norman Cousins. Joke telling can be a form of ventilation. I do not believe that the therapeutic potential of our humour will be fully realized unless it is used with aware-ness. If we stay hidden in the negative habits of our learnings we will be unable to benefit from the full use of our humor.

Bob Hope, Robin Williams, and Joan Rivers are artists in their use of humor. Like an artist they encounter and blend with the audience, touching them in the vulnerable and pained places that we all know. Those places include where we have been humiliated and been the butt of a joke. These artists of humor are able to move into our private rooms and like skilled surgeons cut through our defenses, turn our negative and hurt self-esteems, into positive and healed ones. They touch our humor button by touching our souls while they touch our minds, hearts and everyday events of our lives. They are artists because they talk to us from a loving place. Eddy Murphy, in an interview with Barbara Walters said that his goal in life was to make people laugh. Robin Williams, ad libs most of his lines. His gift of spontaneous wit makes him an artist bordering on genius. Again, he's full of love and concern and his humor is infectious.

Humour is a seed of our creativity. Comedians know how to nurture that seed in us because they are vitally aware of their own. When that humor seed sprouts our spontaniety grows and the natural artist who has always been part of us comes alive, nourishes and heals.

There are two kinds of humour and both can bring laughter. One is the hurtful, humiliating kind that comes from a repressed need to lash out from one's own hurts. The other is the spontaneous kind that comes from a loving place, that means to heal and build. The first kind comes from a sense of alienation, and being put down, while the other comes from a joyous feeling and wanting to share it. Both kinds live inside us. Unfortunately, the latter comes out most often with men. We might change our approach as we know the pain it brings. If we can learn to tap our hidden and denied creative spark, we will find the humor artist inside us. Our desire for humor will be in a different vein, rather than hurt we would rather heal, bring joy, share and enrich. As men begin to turn humor into something more than just a means of ventilation, the opportunity for release and the richness of pure humor will be ours.

The next time you are about to tell a joke pause for just a moment, look deep inside and ask your own humor artist how to tell it in the spirit of the creativity. You might be surprised or the joke might be on you.

COURAGE TO BE

As we are nearing the end of this chapter I have attempted to provide some maps and guidelines for un-becoming the "Supra-Man." We have journeyed into the minds of artists and thinkers of the past and today to build a foundation from which the new emerging male can spring. I have introduced the beginnings of a new kind of human male, calling him the, "Revolutionary Man." He is only the potential that has always been within our grasp beneath the hardened layers of masculinity training which is a part of our human consciousness. I have outlined the unique qualities that this evolving has. These traits exist within us already if we're willing to look, risk and have a sincere desire to change the limited and confining situation we find ourselves in. It is up to each of us individually, whether we want to budge from our pseudo positions as men and make the step that begins the journey back to our realness, our humaness. If we are willing to make the move, then this last part of this chapter will be the most important. It will take courage to begin the climb into our psyche, but it is this act of courage that will guide us back time and time again until we know the path backwards and forwards. It will not be a journey we fear and loath, but one to enjoy and anticipate taking again. If we have a desire to move towards that with conviction the courage, we will need will be the navigator of our process.

In **Tales of Power**, Castenada acquaints us once again with the special kind of character a man of courage must be. As Don Juan is talking to Carlos about learning to be a warrior spirit he replys:

> "I'm afraid that you are confusing issues, the self-confidence of the warrior is not the self-confidence of the average man. The average man seeks certainty in the eyes of the on-looker and calls that self-confidence. The warrior seeks impeccability in his own eyes and calls that humbleness.

"The difference between the two is remarkable. Self-confidence entails knowing something for sure; humbleness entails being impeccable in one's actions and feelings."

Pureness of spirit does exist within men and this has been proven to be true throughout history as men of greatness made worthy contributions towards humankind. Our founding fathers, as previously stated, being of the revolutionary spirit had those warrior qualities. Is it too much to ask that we begin the task of building a framework that we can align ourselves with that doesn't intimidate and make us feel uncomfortable and inferior? The old framework which tries to portray us as being superior is nothing more than falseness and unreality. The deep ache from that internal hollow place is a constant reminder this is so.

It is possible, if we desire it so, to begin turning the denial, self-abuse, and self-hate into respect, caring and eventually love. Yes, as we men express feminine attributes like caring for and loving ourselves we will feel better for it. I support what professor Buscaglia belief that, "Man loves himself when he sees himself with accuracy, genuinely appreciates what he sees, but is especially excited and challenged with the prospect of what he can become." This is the quality of the warrior spirit — an honest acceptance of who one is, and an honest movement forward to expand that possibility.

The man of courage draws from all of his resources, both known and those just coming to be known and experienced. A certain amount of faith in the process is necessary. This faith is a trusting in the creative transformation when the hardened parts of ourselves begin to dissolve into a more fluid flexibility. This fluidity becomes our opened awareness. We don't need to fear as much as we did before because we can see into our fears and realize that many of our fears are unfounded. As long as we hold onto fear, we lose our courage for we begin to trust the fear rather than the process of creativity that is part of the courage in motion. This doesn't mean we don't allow ourselves to fear, that would be another false perception, but if we can see fear with courage in our eyes, fear lessens its hold. Fear is strong when we believe it is strong.

When we move in the world with our eyes fully open, our hearts tuned to nature's, our feet on a firm foothold, a strong base, we are in a courage stance. We are ready to meet the world on mutual terms. We are able to be a creator and touch the world with our impact. Rollo May says: "Creativity, is the encounter of the intensively conscious human being with his or her world." With the openness and courage to meet the world with our wholeness, we generate vitality in the castaway parts, once dormant, now ready to emerge. By working with this desire to merge with our integrity, we bring into being more of our new self parts that are becoming our real structure for living. In a sense, we are creating a new form, a new order — one that allows us to breathe and enjoy the genuine quality of what we are becoming.

As we continue to embrace this living, changing process, we move closer to the artist who dwells inside. This artist is our "creator," our inner authority who has no recognized boss or hierarchy. It is a kind of authority to whom only we are answerable. It does not dominate or control but guides us through transformation and rebirth within a sense of order. This authority is more of a living experience of our creative power and this power feeds our courage.

Throughout this chapter the issue of creativity and its part in our development is highly significant. Creativity plugs us into our courage, love, our contact with ourselves and the world. When stripped of our creativity, people lose a part of their soul. They lose the rich contact with life, becoming blind to life's fullness. They live only portions of the whole experience. They become alienated from parts of themselves and begin to believe creativity no longer exists. A form of "schizoid" awareness takes over as a dominant way of seeing and expressing. People become limited and out of touch with the rest of their resources for living and growing. Piccaso, one of the world's most gifted artists, predicted this kind of deadening process in the 30's. Rollo May shares his experience when he viewed Piccaso works at a showing in a New York museum:

> "And here one was gripped in the exhibit with an ominous fore-boding — the prediction of the beginning of the time when people were to become impersonal, objectized, numbers. It was the ominous prediction of the beginning of 'man the robot.' "

I have already driven this point home intensely many times in this book. What is necessary now is to ask ourselves as men; are we going to sustain the status quo or move out of it? Ae we going to continue marching in line to the masculine machine or are we going to transform ourselves from being machines, breaking the mold of conformity and proclaim ourselves unique? Are we going to have the strength to say "no" to the oppressive force of our masculinity training and stand alone in our choice? We won't be alone for there are always other men waiting for someone else to make the first move.

Everyday we read or hear about another man who dies of a heart attack. In the past, the median age was in the fifties. Now men in their thirties are suffering from coronary ailments. When does it stop? When do we as men choose to get off the destructive treadmill and start plotting a new course?

I believe that men who touch base with their true courage will begin moving towards a refreshing new attitude for which they have searched for so long.

BE A CONSPIRATOR - A HUMAN REVOLUTIONARY

Marilyn Ferguson's **The Aquarian Conspriracy** was practically selling off the shelves before it came off the press. This book describes a movement that is developing worldwide. This movement is not a violent movement that seeks to overthrow government. And it is not just oriented to a special group. It involves people of all walks of life, all professions, all ages, all classes. This conspiracy as she calls it, is a consciousness shift from an old worn out human image form into a new one. She describes in **The Aquarian Conspiracy:**

> "The paradigm of the Aquarian Conspiracy sees human kind embedded in nature. It promotes the autonomous individual in a decentralized society. It sees us as stewards of all our resources, inner and outer. It says that we are not victims, not pawns, not limited by conditions or conditioning. Heirs to revolutionary riches, we are capable of imagination, invention and experiences we have only glimpsed."

The revolutionary man model that I have introduced is in alignment with the new conspirator. I believe that the only way we can survive these times as people is to unite in a common purpose and direction. If men are going to move out of their entrapment, they need to be part of an idea that has meaning, hope and options.

The possibilities are endless for what we can do if we set our minds to it. We have to move in another direction, to desire to transcend, make a shift and awaken from our deep sleep. Once we make this conscious effort and choice, people will begin to appear in our lives with similar ideas. It is like a synchronicity, a meeting at the right moment. It is ignited by our trust and courage to take a stand and tap our inner resources that open our outer doors as well.

Our choice to move and shift enables us to become a bridge to another man-brother who, if he is also moving forward, is another bridge. We are not alone when we decide to move. The community is alive with men like ourselves waiting to be found. If we reach out to them, our action creates the opening of another passageway towards another bridge to a man-brother. It takes the courage, the trust and the belief that something else beyond what we had is possible.

When we believe that other possibilities exist, then our thinking trans-forms, we feel the pulse, that passion deep in us, hearing the voices of our revolutionary fathers telling us to break free as they did two hundred years ago. It is up to us to hear their voices and re-write the "Declaration of Independence" calling it a "declaration of humanness," and be true human revolutionaries in spirit and actions.

CHAPTER V

Fear — Emptiness — Arrogance and Rigidity into Flexibility — Excitement — Aliveness and Richness

"None of us wants to be a fraud or to live a lie; none of us wants to be a sham, a phony, but the fears that we experience and the risks that honest self-communication would involve seem so intense to us that seeking refuge in our roles, masks, and games becomes an almost natural reflex action."

— J. Powell
Why Am I Afraid To Tell You Who I Am

"Mommy Mommy! Hurry home!" I yelled in panic, into the mouthpiece of the telephone. I was three years old and had just awakened terrified from a nightmare during my routine afternoon nap. I had reached for my mother and she was not there. I frantically roamed the house but she was not to be found. I ran to the phone, and when I picked up the receiver and put my little finger in the dial hole marked 'O' a woman's voice answered. It was a recording of an operator saying, "I'm sorry, all circuits are busy at this time, would you please try later." To a frightened little boy of three, the feminine voice was the closest thing to my mother's and in that moment of fear it made no difference who she was. I did not know how to use the telephone but had watched my mother do so. Perhaps the 'O' was an unconscious connection. I was able to retain one simple digit number but certainly not all the numbers of the next door neighbors' phone number. This was where my mother was having coffee and thinking I was sleeping peacefully. I was experiencing the panic of waking from a nightmare to discover my nurturing support person gone. This naturally magnified my fear.

My mother had left the house for fifteen minutes and to me it seemed like an eternity. I told her what happened and though she listened and tried to understand the depth of the trauma of the event, she could not. To her she was only gone a few minutes but, to me that fifteen minutes was an eternity. To a young frightened child, time in minutes or hours does not make any difference. Children live each moment fully, embracing time as though it has no limits. Adults often forget this and their moments of childhood fear which made them even more vulnerable. The nature of the fear is irrelevant. It is terrifying simply because it is unknown.

Men, once young, still carry with them the early fears experienced during their years of learning to be men. This chapter is an exploration of the world of rigidity; of being welded into a role and expectations which confine, strangle and lessen vitality. It can render one lifeless, without enthusiasm or zest.

We are going to view the origin of some of our fears and learn to distinguish between "our" fears and "their" fears, old fears and new fears as well as other aspects of fear. We will journey into the kingdom of fear which I refer to as "Feardom" because sometimes our fears are so intense they seem to originate from within the very "pits of hell." I want us to use our imaginations in a positive, healing manner and explore the real and unreal aspects of our fears.

Following this presentation of fear, I will look at fear's sidekicks — emptiness, arrogance and rigidity — and explore their relationship to fear.

Finally, we will look at some alternatives to our paralyzing fears and what we can do as men, to lessen their stifling effects. We will draw upon the resources which we are beginning to reveal in ourselves as we continue to look at our life's situations. Fear can cause anxiety and paralysis rendering us helpless or it can be our ally, a friend that prevents us from being subjected to danger. Fear is healthy to experience but it is unhealthy to live in fear when we are unaware of its origin or how to work through it and change its effects.

It is fear that prevents men from changing and it is knowing fear as a potential friend that will help us change.

JOURNEY INTO "FEARDOM"

If we could make a list of some of the common fears that men have, it would look something like this:

Fear of growing bald
Fear of not "getting it up"
Fear of failure/success
Fear of not being liked/understood/heard
Fear of loneliness
Fear of death
Fear of feelings
Fear of revealing to others our true selves.

The fears that men have about themselves and life could fill a book. Where do these fears originate? Is there a place inside us or outside that these fears we experience hang out and live? Let us imagine that there is such a place rather than have others tell us that it's only in our "minds" or we're over reacting. Let it be fact that a fear kingdom does exist, within it are many different kinds of fear. Big fears, little fears, powerful fears, phobias, etc. Let us assume that there is a hierarchy to this kingdom, i.e, "top-guy fear" and a "top gal fear" which are similar to a king/queen of fear or parents. Throughout this kingdom there are various subordinates or "lieutenants." The way this kingdom continues to exisit is find people to believe in its powers and that it has a collection of all the events in our lives that have made us afraid. This kingdom has a whole library of every fear we have experienced since we were born. During our more vulnerable and stressful times, the "lieutenants" enter the fear library, pull the most appropriate fear from our memory files, and by pushing a button on the main terminal of the fear control room of this fear library, they are able to have control and power over us. This is how the fear kingdom works.

The kingdom has existed for as long as man has and the operators living within know their work. They have had a lot of practice. They excel at convincing us that a little fear is larger than it appears by pushing our memory button that which reminds us of the original fear.

This fear kingdom is active at all times even when we are sleeping. If any of the operators of this kingdom sleep, they will disappear and then awaken and find themselves working for the courage kingdom which also lives within us but, obviously, has a totally opposite function.

So there it is, a fairy tale version of our world of fears and how it might possibly operate. If we were told in our earlier lives how to deal with fear in a healthy and respectful way, we might have an easier time today.

As I began to describe the kingdom of fear, it started to resemble what I had learned Hell to be as a young boy in church. As a youngster, my greatest fear was that I would end up there. Like so many other youngsters I was brainwashed with the reward/punishment ethic. If you're a good boy, you go to Heaven and if you are bad, you go to Hell. Descriptions of Hell from a well-intentioned Sunday school teacher frightened me. The thought of burning forever was terrifying! To a little boy who couldn't even tell time yet, forever was hard to contemplate. I just knew that it was a long time.

"Fear!" Where does it come from? Once I believed that man's greatest fear was death. Ernest Becker wrote a pulitzer prize winning treatise on this idea calling it **Denial of Death**, presenting a powerful argument suggesting that man's fear of Death, and his need to deny it, is the sole contributor to man's unhappiness. I must admit that he had a pretty strong case and his book launched a new frontier of man attempting to understand himself. A few years ago I began to think that man's greatest fear wasn't death, it was fear of being abandoned. This would fit into the existentialist idea and a combination of other beliefs and schools of thought, Eastern and Western. A long dissertation about this is not necessary because I no longer believe this fully either. In all the years that I have studied, experienced my own changes of thought and ideology, I have come to believe that man's greatest fear is not death, not abandonment, but "birth."

There are two kinds of birth so let me explain. Otto Rank, one of Freud's most promising pupils, believed that the worst trauma that we have is being born and the effects of this experience last throughout our lives and contribute to our deepest personal conflicts. So, the first kind of birth is our actual physical transformation from the womb to the glaring lights of the delivery room. The other kind of birth that I see as a contributing fear and especially for men is the "birth of change," the death of an image of who we are, the release of fantasy of who we thought we were. Some schools call this the spiritual death of the ego, and others today might suggest that it is transformation or transcendental change. I believe that it is simply change. We can delete the terms and labels of the various models flooding the spiritual marketplace. I do not believe that one has to sit crossed legged for hours or chant 'Om' or perform a number of other kinds of tasks in order to be re-born or to change.

There are basically three approaches that exist in our "change the person" marketplace — those that focus on the past such as primal therapy, psychoanalysis, T.A., etc.; those methods that relate to the here and now, including Gestalt and Zen, etc. and those that focus on the future such as behaviourism, rational, and emotive therapy. There are also those in the spiritual or transpersonal range who believe that the spiritual aspects of one's life need to change. There are many approaches. Some create their own, based on aspects from the others. I do not subscribe to any one model anymore, although I have a strong leaning towards Gestalt, Reichian therapy, T.A., Family therapy and "flying by the seat of my pants" therapy! I'm always open to something new and attempt to be as creative as possible. I believe that a person needs to find a way to change that fits his or her needs, personality and situation. I don't think any word by anyone is "written in stone". As for learning about changing and being 'born', we have to explore how we learned to understand change, the value we gained from it and the results when we did or did not. We also need to see the relationship between being born (change) and the fear connected to it.

Janov believes that fears occur when we are alone in bed at night, when the activities of the day are over and the house is still; when we can hear the sounds, such as water dripping, wind and thunder that can drive our imaginations wild. Janov discovered through primal therapy that people report memories of being in their beds or even cribs being terrified that Mommy or Daddy were not around. The strength of his therapeutic approach is that the fears we experience now were learned and experienced in earlier life:

> "In primal terms, a current, persistent, but seemingly irrational fear is generally a manifestation of an older and often deeper one."

Although I have never been in a primal therapy group, I have had breakthroughs in my own growth with other kinds of approaches that helped me to see my present fears as remnants from earlier ones. I have been through many Reichian therapy sessions, which is similar to primal therapy in that it helps a person release deep fear and experience memories of the events that caused it initially.

Harvey Jakins, founder and leader of the Re-evaluation Counselling Approach, works similarly. His belief is that we have stored pain in our bodies from past hurts and that our brain stores these memories. The process of "discharging," through a series of movements, gestures, yawning and talking moves us closer to freeing ourselves from the stored up past pain.

From my own personal experiences of growth and using these approaches in my work with others, I would definitely agree that we carry with us a great deal of stored pain since childhood. How we approach this in understanding men's learning about pain and how this relates to fear is another matter worthy of focus.

In 1969 I was in a very serious car accident which was nearly fatal. For years after, whenever I rode with another person who was tailgating another car, I would panic. I was a passenger in the accident. All I can remember before the impact of twisting metal which was the rear end of a car ahead of us, was that the driver of our car was following too close. As I write about this, my stomach quivers as I can recall the events of that morning over ten years ago. Since I have been working with myself, whenever I have the panic feeling while riding with another person, my memory floods with images of when I was in panic or some kind of fear. As I go deeper into the patterns of my life I begin to see streams of interconnected events that are related to pain, fear and panic. The more I see these events for what they were and can distinguish the fear and pain from "then" and "now," the more I am able to relax and let the panic subside.

One of my other fears is to show that I'm "needy." I have always been what is commonly called a loner. I learned at a very early age that if I wanted something done, then I had to do it myself. I still struggle with this. Only recently, have I been able to depend more on others. My dependency fear, especially regarding women is that they will become dependant upon me needing them and then I feel smothered and so I withdraw. I've reacted this way for years with women, and men as well. I'm afraid to become dependent on others for fear of losing myself and being trapped. A lot of men have this need to be free. Underneath this, I believe I have an idea of dependency but it's become distorted and foggy. Little by little I've been risking expressing my needs. Sometimes I get a positive response, other times I don't. Most of the time I do.

While writing the chapter, I felt some anguish and fear. As I wrote about childhood experiences so many of my own came back vividly. For two days after working on the chapter I was irritable and anxious. I was extremely restless and bitchy but since I was alone, I couldn't communicate my feelings. I progressively became lonely, from being alone but also from a prevading sense of isolation. I was feeling empty inside with a knowing "sense" right in the pit of my gut which felt like a deep hole that was getting larger daily. I was even getting scared that I might "freak out" or do something crazy. My mind was filled with memories of my learnings to be a man. The Death Script theme was weighing heavily with me.

One night a lady friend whom I had been dating for several months came over. Catherine and I planned to go to a movie. When she arrived, I was aware of my holding back quality. My shoulders were tense and my eyes looked away from or through her when I greeted her. We sat around briefly, had some wine, and discussed portions of my book and the movie schedule. We began to discuss our relationship and what it meant to us. We hadn't seen each other for over a month as I was out town conducting some training workshops. As we talked I became increasingly aware of that hole in the pit of my stomach. At times it felt like it was a lump in my throat and then, a heaviness in my eyes. We continued to talk and my voice began to get loud and demanding. I realized my anger wasn't directed towards her. The more I tried to explain, the larger the lump in my throat became; the hole in my stomach seemed deeper and my eyes ached. I was in pain and as much as I tried to tell her what I was experiencing I could not find the words. I felt "needy." I felt terrified. The facts I wanted to express were swimming in my mind, but they were stifled, I couldn't speak. I sat there motionless, stunned and I wanted to reach out to Catherine and just tell her to hold me. I was frightened; reliving past events and I needed contact, support and nuturing. While simulataneously needing to "keep it together" allowing this seeming crisis to work itself out. Additionally, I was aware of her reluctance and resistance to be part of my process. I experienced her distant, "cool" and detachment. This made me feel more anxious and as though I were being pulled apart. I was going through another re-experiencing of a deep need which I had kept hidden from my awareness. My lady friend was another catalyst for this. The more she kept responding to me in her "cool" detached tone, the more angry and withdrawn I became. Finally, it became too much for me to handle so I withdrew completely into myself as much as possible.

We later went to a movie. A week later we talked about the experience and were able to shed some light on it from both our perspectives.

Catherine was a catalyst for me, just like a therapist serves as a catalyst for a client. Sometimes a therapist becomes part of the client's past experience, normally called transference in therapy language. She was part of mine. She was my mother, my locked away feminine part of myself, as well as a friend. To her I was the "needy men" in her life, and she was trying to change her habit of mothering or rescuing them. Also, I was her male friend who usually didn't seem like he needed anything from her. For both of us, it was a journey into our fearful places. I was a reflection of events in her earlier years when she learned how to be a child-mother to men in her life. She was the cold, distant mother or father of my early life which marked the beginning of my years as a "loner." Each of us gained new insights into our lives as a result of that unusual dialogue.

I've talked to a few of my close male friends about this experience. They could emphathize with it. They found it hard to express their needs to their wives or girlfriends or even to admit that they existed. The few times that they did try to express themselves from a deeper place, they too found it difficult to find the words, and were often left frustrated, angry, feeling as if they were not being heard or understood by their female partner.

The number of men who could attest to this are many. Learning to express ourselves from a truly needing place was blocked early in our lives. The more that we denied those needs, the more they returned to us in moments of crisis or vulnerability.

We have learned to pretend that we are strong because this is "manly" and conforms with our societal script. It does not mean that our bodies and minds have not collected the many painful events we experienced in our beginnings. The stress accumulated within our physical bodies can send us to an early grave. Our minds, during our most vulnerable moments, punish us with an exaggerated picture of events, ourselves and our crisis situations making us feel even more miserable.

As long as we attempt to control, "keep the lid on," those memories of our early days mixed with pain and fear will come back to haunt us during our waking hours as well as during sleep. They may deprive us of sleep.

We learned early as "little men" to be strong and fearless. What did we do with those times in our masculine training when we were "scared to death"? The father who "throws" his son into deep water to teach him how to swim, is forcing a terrifying experience on his son that he could carry with him for the rest of his life. Each time I've talked to a man who learned to swim in this way, fear was embedded in his eyes.

Until society stops setting men up as strong, fearless, the warrior in battle while separating them from their need to express themselves deeply and with feeling as does a female, it will produce men who are fearful and restricted.

Those who are taught fear do indeed fear life itself. If a child is taught that "Hell is forever" and if we don't conform to what we should, we will go to Hell, then it is no surprise that a world of conformists arises, with no individuality, no uniqueness. They fear being disobedient and going to hell when they die, so they live each day, with the thought that hell or the kingdom of fear is always there to control and inslave them.

These fears that plague our lives are not imaginary, they stem from when we were young and vulnerable. We relive these, or experience another event that sets off a chain reaction which returns those events to us as if they happened yesterday. Unless we are free to accept our fears as real events, we will not be able to get at their source.

Beneath the fears are the real feelings that we have hidden from ourselves. Existing within those feelings are the needs that were never met. Our fear is that they still will be unfulfilled and it reminds us of the holes or wounds left from those times when we needed and no one was there.

Before we can be expected to change to a new attitude, a new prespective, we have to be free to see the true source of that fear. We have to stop believing that something is wrong with us and that we did not measure up.

When male children are raised in a less threatening, less fearful manner and are allowed to be whole persons, we will have a society of men with more courage, a sense of humility and vulnerability. They will learn to appreciate what they are and appreciate others as well. They will embrace change as a continuous "birth" of life's majestic action.

THE DEEP PIT OF EMPTINESS

"Loneliness is learning there's **"emptiness"** inside and not knowing how to fill it but fearing no one can."

Being alienated from one's own true self leaves us feeling empty and lonely . The more we settle for this existence the more we have fear when someone becomes too close to that place or we trigger something that opens that place to us. "The origins of alienation," says Moustakas, "are a lack of recognition and love in childhood; obedience to external "shoulds," rather than to the preferences of the inner self, the absence of growing identity that comes from self choice."

Most men who have grown up in the shadow of the masculine fraternity did not have the choice as to whether to move in the direction of their true self or to settle for what was being dealt out to them. Before they were old enough to know the difference, their life and role in it was determined. They took on this role willingly, even though a still, little voice inside them questioned what they were hearing. A male should not question what he is being directed to do, he just does it. If he does not act, he stands the chance of being denied, rejected and punished. If a young boy has to make a choice between trusting his own feeling or following the commands of the outside authority, he will usually conform and follow an adult's directive. He, as a child, does not know the ways of the world. If children persist in the non-conformist choice they run the risk of not getting the love, attention and recognition that they deserve and desire.

Men live life having gone through the process of deadening themselves to their feelings and desires for true choice and selfness. This is the traditional socialization ritual that they go through to be men. This process is so powerful that they are unaware of its impact. As a child they accept it because they are dependent on this teaching. As adolescents they rebel, often losing their battle because their social environment demands adjustment and conformity. If he cannot adapt there are places he can be sent for "rehabilitation." It is his duty as a man and citizen to fit the mold defined by society.

Often, during the quieter time periods, men feel a numbness within themselves. It feels like a gigantic, infinite pit. This is what they are facing when they try to "get to the bottom of it" with their logic and limited emotional exploration. it feels like something "ripping and gnawing," like something trying to escape from the pit of the stomach. This is most unpleasant and frightening. Men's customary reaction to deal with repressed desire, feeling or action is to keep it locked away. It is not fitting that he question the existence and nature of this "gnawing" and "ripping" sensation. He is living the way he "should," as vividly portrayed by Becker:

> "This is superb characterization of the "culturally normal" man, the one who dares not stand up for his own meanings because this means too much danger, too much exposure. Better not be oneself, better to live tucked into others, embedded in a safe homework of social and cultural obligations and duties."

This is the rule more often than not. I must be repressed for fear that it may topple the system and bring chaos into the established order. It's much safer when the masculine system does not have to view itself, it's empty theories and or it's policies. It is thought better to keep the prison doors closed than to give credit to the wisdom of the denied aspects of the self. The rule is "do not open the door" simply add to the garbage already held by those prisoners of difference.

This is how it is for most men who have grown up in our society. They lose their true selves to gain the world when young, and join the other lost souls who do not know or want to accept that they too are lost. They travel life's journey, occasionally hearing the rattlings of their chained "soul brother," and often panic, doing everything they can to muffle the sound. This sound is painful as it is a reminder that parts of their life spirit are lost and shackled, yet still alive in the dungeon within. The knowing sound only aggravates the emptiness they feel inside. It is the wound inflicted early in their lives, the wound of self-denial and self-death, a masochistic effect that leaves them half alive and living a life with partial meaning. Fromm put it like this:

> "The greatest tragedy in life is the fact that most human beings die before they are fully born."

ARROGANCE — THE PUFFED-UP BULLFROG

When a man is told that he is being arrogant by someone who sees this, his thoughts probably are: "How arrogant for someone to say that."

During the rise of the human potential movement, many of the "super stars" of this movement were allowed to make outlandish remarks about other people that threatened their beliefs or awareness, and this was accepted as being okay because they were the guru's, the top dogs. This was accepted even if their statements were hurtful and demeaning to others. They could not be reprimanded as they deserved respect in ways that a father demands respect from his obedient son. Their words were taken as gospel and to question them would be an insult to their brilliance. They could speak about people being vulnerable and risking spilling their guts, while they didn't have to move an inch from their pedestals if they did not choose to. Like some super human they could stand in front of their podiums, puffed up like bull frogs, espousing how people "should" lead a better life and not become entangled in the "shoulds" of a stifling society. In some cases, this meant that their ideas would be the new "shoulds" that we ought to incorporate into our lives. Through our naivety and learned obedience we went out and practiced their models, negative and positive. If they did something in a demonstration that was clever, but hurtful to others, we often would try their technique to see how it worked for us, even if we hurt someone too. In the beginning, I did the same and hurt others even when my intentions were good. The more we listen to our inner selves the less we will get caught up in the personal hangups of the teacher which we do not need to model.

People often, out of desperation, are willing to swallow what they are being told in the hope that new ways and answers will lead them out of their unhappy state of mind and affairs. Mentors and pontiffs become the new parents of the people-children who are seeking a better way to live and to know themselves.

There is much contradiction between the ways that we are told to be and the manner in which those who do the telling live their lives. It is often a repeat of the old patterns of authority and obedience but presented in a new way so as to hide the reality of how it is.

Whenever I read a new book or listen to a speaker on a new way of being a more effective human being I always look to see if they really believe in what they're saying or if it is just so many words, based on a new idea they have come up with. I ask myself if they live what they preach, or is this just another good idea that's supposed to work because they say it does. Do they live what they speak?

Many great men have made it possible for us to move forward in our pursuit for new knowledge and have created unique paths for us to follow. I believe that it is time that we begin using our own senses and feelings to meet what we are hearing and learning with a mutual discourse and evaluation. For, if all we do is imitate what we see without drawing on our own creative powers, we still remain the followers and not leaders or directors of our own lives.

In the last twenty years a preponderance of methods have been presented to the public in "cookbook" approaches to living. "Follow this recipe and your life will be full and meaningful, use step by step process for becoming more human." Human beings are not created in an instant. Babies are not purchased, like boxes of minute rice, placed in a saucepan and a few minutes later, presto! A new human being. Babies, go through a process that can only be described as a miracle. I realize that test tube babies are possible now for parents who cannot conceive. Does the future hold test tube babies as a possibility, marketed for any consumer who doesn't want to go through the pain of pregnancy, which may interrupt a busy schedule?

There has been much talk about how destructive humans are to one another and how child rearing is a task that should be taken away from undeserving adults. An idea being suggested is that children should be raised utilizing a strict scientific formula. By thinking in such a way are we adding to the problem, rather than drawing upon our humaness to generate solutions?

Though technology we have invented some incredible tools for enhancing peoples lives. Man has begun to believe he can tackle the "unthinkable." The concept of unlimited nuclear war derived by Kahn, mentioned earlier, is a ridiculous, bullish and arrogant example of the masculine immaturity that plagues men today. It is a small minded attempt, despite Kahn's better than average I.Q., to contact the universal mind which is not composed of only the rational. As Neuman and Berkowitz suggest:

> "Someone who thinks he can do anything he has a 'mind' to is not in contact with himself. It is an arrogant belief because it sets no limits. The struggles of our real selves are open-ended, but they are limited by our actual capabilities."

Men who grow up in society believing they can do anything, can reach any height and be a success by merely believing it possible and then going for it, are men who live in their dreams which exist only within their head, and they are sacrificing any contact with the rest of themselves. They probably are great achievers, able to make thousands of dollars and are the 'success apple' of everyone's eye. What are the costs?

Many millionaires die unhappy and lonely. One of the wealthiest and most influencial men in the world, Howard Hughes, in his last years lived the life of a broken down man. His wealth and power went to his head, and made him completely out of touch with his being.

I believe arrogance is a display of false knowledge. It is an inflated belief in the importance of oneself. However, a man who does live his beliefs in his own life is aware that anyone can teach him about himself and his ideas. He does not have to stand on a pedestal hiding himself from the true contact with his audience. He can touch and communicate, because he knows what he says is met on a common ground of mutuality and this heightens his beliefs in himself and in his visions.

RIGIDITY —
"I CAN'T LET GO" — "WHAT WILL I BE?"

The last rung on the ladder of fear is rigidity, which has its unsolid connection in holding onto the fragmented pieces of our false male self. Although it tends to be the strongest fear, it is the closest path of awareness to freedom and liberation. It is the last outdated male process image sitting at the edge of change and capable of being born more fully into a healthy human male. It is the pivotal point where the old image of self begins to blend with the new emerging self. This place is where memories, pain and experience of childhood and adolescence join.

Once, while I was preparing a stress seminar for some employees with a large Canadian oil company, I was writing ideas on the blackboard. I heard a voice in the back of the room shout "your lines are crooked." I turned to see an older company engineer staring at my handiwork. I commented back to him out of part surprise, and impish humor "I guess they'll have to put lines on the board next time when I write."

During the workshop I noticed him watching me out of the corner of my eye. Listening to a meditative kind of music, I asked the group of members to close their eyes in order to really feel the music and the effects of the relaxation. He was the only one in the group of thirty-five, who had his eyes open. He was having difficulty letting go. The others were allowing themselves the luxury of unwinding and many had the look of serenity on their faces. Our friend could not release his correct posture. He sat rigidly, firmly holding his body to the chair, unable to gain any value from the exercise. He left the room probably feeling the seminar was a waste of time. He probably went back to his office, to see if he could find some logical, mathematical formula that would help him to make sense of the effects of music in its application to relaxation. He held on so tightly to his conceptual view of life that he needed to put others in it as well. When I didn't fit his mold or what I was presenting did not correspond to his limited viewpoint, he was puzzled. At the same time he became threatened and afraid. He had what Van Dezisen sees as a limited awareness.

"We are locked up in such a mind castle, yet we have explored little. Many know little more than a sitting room in the east wing and assume this is the whole."

When I was making a presentation to the staff of a T.V. station in a small midwestern town, one of the executive managers kept hinting how I could better my presentation. The resistance in the group was so thick you could cut it with a knife, so I was open to his suggestions. However, he had an aura about him that he knew the score about stress, often sharing with the group how he dealt so successfully with stress. Two months later this self-appointed, thirty-nine year old authority on stress, died of a heart attack. Everyone was surprised because he was so young, active and the picture of health. Everyone felt he was "calm," "cool" and "collected," living a stress-free life. As Janov would say, "as long as he keeps himself in control and cooled, he won't have to be afraid anymore." This is the worst kind of self-deception because it cuts us off from listening to our inner healer.

Both men are caught in the "rigidity plateau" of self-deception, believing what they're holding on to on the surface is real and sufficient, and this gives them a self-confidence par excellence. What they're unaware of is that, part of their feeling of wellness that is real is the emergence of their new identity, but the other part, which is the old patterns still, lives in the realm of its "old self." This old self still controls the show behind the scenes and continues to practice its limited sense of wellness. A similar concept is a "wolf in sheep's clothing." It seems so real and honest and this intensifies the rigidity of holding on while underlying awareness is still chained to a very narrow perspective. Basically, it is living a lie projected as the truth.

Rigidity, can hold a man in its grasp forever. It gives enough of a reformed picture of well-being and being in charge, but not enough to ensure integration and transformation.

Through the legend of "The Holy Grail", Robert Johnson in his book on masculine psychology helps us to understand the depth of process men must experience to regain our full sense of self in becoming whole and integrated.

Briefly, the legend tells of a wound that is inflicted to the Fisher King. The Fisher King is a symbol of man touching his christ-self in adolescence, but discovering he has only had a glimpse of his integrated spirit, and is left with this wound deep inside. The legend describes a young boy who happens on a fresh salmon being cooked over a fire deep in the woods and since he's hungry from searching for food (his essence) grabs onto the fish, burning himself, hence the Fisher wound. Later in life when the boy grows up to be a King (adulthood) he begins eventually to feel weary and empty. He feels the wound inside of him and desires to heal the pain. It is such a painful wound causing great suffering, but he is incapable of dying because the wound does not heal even in death. In practical terms, the legend depicts the emptiness in men who have not been able to fully integrate themselves into wholeness. The legend is from the system of Jungian thought that suggests men experience an inner wholeness in early childhood and they must separate from this wholeness to move into a time in their adolescence to be born into another cycle of becoming whole. This is a time of pain and anxiety because of the separation experience. This is necessary for complete growth and emergence into the fullness of being a man in their middle years of their adulthood. This process, which Johnson describes, was developed by Carl Jung and is a vital aspect of man's healthy development. This process began in the male youth's childhood and it must be rekindled in order for a man to be born totally into himself. Johnson states:

"His ultimate healing comes only when he completed the process
he inadvertently started as a youth."

The tenets of this theory and legend hold that men's internal wound has healed by regaining the childhood portion of their lives that were unfulfilled and were unable to capture enough of in their adolescence. This period of "human metamorphisis" has carried into their adult male lives. When men can do this, they are on the road to their healing and rebirth.

Johnson adds:

"He must be humble enough to look to the young, innocent, adolescent, foolish parts of himself to find the beginning of the cure of the Fisher wound."

Rigidity is a hallmark for living for men in a society that holds adolescents as a "pain in the ass" for adults who are able to endure raising "those terrible teens." Yet it is the connection with this part of our developmental process that is vital to our birth as whole men and complete persons. Rigidity holds the child and adolescent part of ourselves intact and in control. We were slowly being coerced to do so when we were reminded of our childish, adolescent actions and being told to "grow up and act one's age". Then we are to arrive at some magical time when both those periods are supposed to be behind us and "acting our age" is not a suggestion but a command.

Those men who can weave throughout their natural periods of childhood and adolescence stand a far better chance of being happier, healthier and more awake to life. These men embrace life with an acceptance and curiosity that began in their childhood, was refined in their adolescence and savored in their adult years. These men have no need to hold onto rigidity, to their images and masks of who they are because they know that the best is yet to come and they welcome the future with open arms. They are not pulled into it "kicking and screaming," fearing that they are going to be dropped down some deep infinite abyss of the unknown.

"Loneliness is the best excuse for dying, but more the reason for Risking, for Reaching, for Growing for Becoming."

A psychologist, Dr. Mary Biaggis, University of Idaho, who has studied male and female anger, has found that women and men respond to anger in different ways. Women get angry when they're criticized, rejected, humiliated, embarrassed or disappointed. Men get angry most when annoyed by people they consider ignorant, careless or displaying socially inappropriate behaviour. Men, like women, do get angry when they're criticized, and so forth, but they react with a greater degree of hostility and hatred. This tells me that the "chained" effect of men's conditioning in our society forces men into a staying-in-line, conformist view point. When they see others not towing this line, they get upset. If they are going to play by the rules of the "dead men," then who can dare not play by these same rules? As long as everyone plays by the rules, the reality of our self-denial can be maintained. It also shows that women, being more in touch with their feelings, respond to a deeper part in themselves that is more real. Men get angry, then hostile, as the denied parts of themselves express their contempt for being imprisoned. This hostility is expressed through repressed resentment towards others in our life's beginnings; parents, teachers, other adults, etc. who made us "tow the line" and refused to acknowledge our being and uniqueness. Women have similar experiences but being allowed expression of their feelings provides easier and healthy access to those places where they live in denial. Women are able to go within their being and those denied areas, release and heal. Men stay on the outside looking away from this same place, for fear of being engulfed in this place of emptiness which is alive with exhausted parts of ourselves that are tired of not being expressed.

Another personal experience follows to illustrate the above point. It is one of the most painful times in my life as it recalls when I almost lost my life trying to get love and recognition and almost taking the life of my own brother.

I was born a junior — meaning I had my father's whole name. (I have changed my name recently.) To be named after your father as a young boy in our society was a special honor, "a chip off the old block." Being named after my father was more of a curse than a blessing. My brothers resented me for having this honor while the rest of the family saw me in the likeness of my father. My father, however, did not like the idea and many of his actions indicated this. I almost set the house on fire when I tried to start the morning fire in our wood burning stove for which I got a beating. This task was my older brother's, to awaken every morning before the rest of the family and start the fire. I resented him for this because he always got recognition from my Dad and the family. He was always working with Dad doing the plowing and running of the farm while I had to settle for feeding the chickens. This resentment was expressed when my father and brother were busy repairing some farm machinery. I was playing inside the old farm truck that had no engine pretending I was driving it. I was plotting a way to get my brother away from my dad so I could be with him. I began kicking the door, slowly at first, then more rapidly as my resentment grew more as I thought about my brother and my desire to get between him and my father. The door latch was broken so it made a loud and irritating squeak. This continued for some time, my resentment building, my plot becoming imaginable as I shoved on the door with my feet. Finally, my dad, irritated and annoyed by the commotion I was making, told my brother to come and settle me down. As he approached the door, I aimed and with one kick slammed the door into him catapulting him back onto the first object that broke his fall, which happened to be the blade of a disc-hoe, used to break up hard ground. My brother hit the blade of the machine with the side of his head, slashing a deep gash just next to his eye. By the time my dad got him to the hospital he had lost a great deal of blood and almost bled to death. As I describe this event, I only have a very vague picture in my mind. Much of this event was told to me by my mother and grandmother. My brother has seldom said a word about it but he still has the scar to this day. I'm aware of a painful nauseous feeling in my stomach as I tell the story. To know that I had almost killed my brother to have my father's recognition makes me sick to my stomach. This could be one of the reasons that my brother was always trying to burn me with firecrackers, throw me into the stinging nettles, and smother me with a pillow. Deep within he remembered the event and wanted revenge.

At three and four years old, I was a clumsy, dumb and a "pain in the ass" nuisance. This is what I began to believe and this was confirmed by my father and others. Each day, I tried to find some way to get close to my dad. After all I had his name and I was supposed to be special, right? Once when we went fishing, (the whole family clan, including uncles, aunts and cousins), I decided that I would catch more fish than anyone else and maybe this would get my dad's attention. Well I did catch more fish than anyone. "Thirteen prize trout," I said presenting my catch to my Dad and hoping for some show of praise. I was met with an, "Oh, hum..." instead as he continued his conversation. I felt hurt, crushed, but not defeated. I still was determined to get his attention.

One afternoon, my dad was sitting high atop the seat on the John Deere tractor guiding the manure spreader through the rows of beets that he was fertilizing. With bucket in hand, I was heading away from the chicken coop, completing the last of my rounds of live stock feeding, when I spotted him alone plowing. This was my chance. No one was around, not even my brother to take his attention. If I was going to get an opportunity to be a part of him, even for just a moment, this was it.

I slowly, cautiously moved towards the tractor and with determination in my heart and soul, lept upon the back of the tractor. My father was startled, and when he realized that I had interrupted his concentration he yelled for me to get down and stopped the tractor for me to step down. He started the tractor again, getting back into the rhythm of his manure spreading, thinking that I had moved away from the tractor. In one last attempt at pushing through my feelings of rejection, I lunged for the back of the tractor seat on which he was seated. I missed my mark and fell down under the large wheel of the John Deere and my father not knowing that I was even "underfoot," backed up over my head crushing it into the soft manure that he was spreading. I heard from others what happened after because I was knocked unconscious. I was told that my dad came running into the house, my limp body in his arms, and that he was white as a sheet, believing that I was dead. I do remember, however, regaining consciousness briefly and seeing my dad, mother and a room filled with relatives on their knees and standing above me in a room dimly lit with candles. This must have been my "last rites," because the room was silent and my parents were on their knees by my bed praying. The doctors told my parents that I was lucky to be alive. If it was not for the soft manure that my head was cradled in, which lessened the force of the wheels' impact on my head, my head would have been split wide open.

To tell this story brings tears to my eyes. I have had years to try to understand the meaning of that tragic time in my early life and piece together the reasons that so much violence was present in my life.

I realize that this story of my own childhood is not much different from other's stories told by various friends and clients. Several speak of unintentional violence they experienced in their early years as they tried to get respect, recognition and a feeling of connection with their fathers, only to be met with punishment, denial, control and domination. Few have been lucky enough to get what they needed.

I have no malice in my heart in speaking about this painful time and do not hold a grudge against my father. I realize he was doing the best he could with what he had. He had been denied so much of his vitality when he was growing up and had been taught to play by the rules. Like other fathers, he resented my determination and my will to go after what I wanted. He had settled for something less than what he wanted in being married so early in his life, and being strapped with the responsibility for raising a family when he was no more than a child himself.

This emptiness we experience in ourselves, is the manifestation of trampled dreams to become what we uniquely can become. We have learned to believe that it is our just reward but the wound stays and continues to hurt as we travel through life, occasionally feeling the "ache."

TURNING 'FEAR' INSIDE AND OUT INTO A RESOURCE

I stated at the onset of this chapter we would first look at the dimensions of fear along with its sidekicks - emptiness, arrogance and rigidity and how these affect our lives as growing functioning men. We will explore some alternatives that could be used in reversing the paralyzing effect of fear making these work for us rather than against us. I will present these alternatives and show how they can be applied in lessening the anxiety that fear brings into our lives.

Our major fears are things that occur within us. These are mirrored externally in our lives. By learning, or re-learning to turn these inside out, we are able to use them as resources, rather than letting them dissipate our energy.

I do not adhere to a cookbook approach in learning, but I feel that we can benefit from useful guidelines. These guidelines will get us started until we feel more comfortable taking charge ourselves. I encourage you to sift through my suggestions, allowing your own creative powers to emerge. Build your instincts and ideas as you go along and use my guidelines as a bridge to your own which await your contact and use.

GUIDELINES

1. **Befriend your fear** — Sometimes fear can be our greatest ally and friend. If we step into traffic unaware of a fast approaching car, fear sends a signal to us to look and be aware. It is like a sixth sense, alerting us to a dangerous situation. Fear and pain are cousins. Pain is a natural alert button that tells us to be attentive. It lets us know when there is a dysfunction in our bodies, in an interpersonal encounter or other areas of our lives. If we have not numbed our senses with drugs, alcohol, nicotine or denial, pain tells us to take notice. Fear often comes to us as a secondary response. If we have stopped listening to our inner self, fear becomes a more intense signal of disharmony. If we choose to see fear as our enemy, we remain unaware of its powerful role in helping us tune into our inner self. A man who experiences fear when he has a pain in his chest, perhaps imagining that he is having a heart attack, could just be receiving a deeper message that he's over working and requires rest. Fear connects us to other vital functional processes.

2. **Know your different kinds of fear** — Sit down and brainstorm a list of all the different kinds of fear you experience. Place them in columns of monsterous fears, reasonable fears, past fears - childhood, adolescence, future fears, present fears and ridiculous fears. Then make a separate column for your unknown fears. From these lists decide which fears, if you had to pick three, would you be willing to look at and know more about. I do this exercise in my stress workshops and people often realize that certain things they felt wary of were not to be feared. They had just never bothered to look and see if they were real.

3. **Know when you have courage** — After making a list of your various kinds of fears, make another list of the different traits and gifts you have which show your courage and self-confidence. When we do this we often discover skills and resources we take for granted or have denied ourselves because of judgments and negative use of fear.

4. **Situations we fear and situations in which we show courage** — When we lack the awareness of our various skills and resources, becoming locked in the grips of fear, we lose our ability to be aware when we experience these in our daily lives. Write out three or more situations in which we experience fear and three or more in which we experience courage in our daily routine. These can be situations with our boss, colleagues, secretary, women, friends, police, our children, etc. Out of these, which are monsterous, past, future, etc? How do we feel about ourselves in these situations? What happens to our self-worth. Begin to know when and how these relate to our daily experiences with others.

5. **When do we make others fear us** — As men are so often used to being aggressive, explosive with anger or quiet and withdrawn, we make others

around us feel uncomfortable. This can hurt us, magnify our fear and trigger memories of when others made us feel discounted or afraid. People can serve as catalysts that put us back into those times when we were afraid or were intimidating others. We all can share in this experience because we have been there. If we can begin turning "trigger situations" into positive learning events we can lessen some of the overwhelming emotions of the "repeat" situation. Sometimes we can get hooked by someone else's mood or 'bummer day' and become part of something that has nothing to do with us. Listen to your inner self. It will tell you what is going on. A dispassionate approach to the situation will only make it worse. Everyone needs a sounding board once in awhile and a caring heart.

6. **Be yourself and allow others to be themselves** — Everyone big or small, old or young, desires and needs to be their complete self. Living in a society that molds people to fit an image that is predictable and controllable makes it a struggle to be our full functioning selves. The more we can be ourselves the more we can allow others to be. We all are trying the best we can with what resources we have and we often collide with one another in the process. If we can be honest with ourselves, trust our intuition and feel a common bond with others, we have a framework for growing as individuals male with other males and women as well. We are all struggling to learn and grow. We move at different paces and have various methods of approach. Allow for similarities as a common thread and appreciate the differences that make us unique.

7. **Look beyond manipulation** — Manipulating to get our needs met has become second nature to us love-starved, child-adult men. We learned to control, compete, dominate and treat people as objects based within a society that sees people as products. People are not products and are not to be "folded, spindled or mutilated." They are flesh and blood creatures. If we continue to devour one another like hungry wolves eating sheep, it is we who will suffer from indigestion when no one trusts us. We are the losers not the winners.

8. **We are humans not machines** — So many men have learned to use the "slide rule" approach to life. They measure and calculate everyone and everything. Everything has to fit some prescribed formula. If it does not, they become anxious. For example, the engineer in the stress workshop who was confused when asked to relax and let go. For him this was an impossible task. It takes people and all aspects of life to fit a formula that is a creative process; forever changing. Leave the formulas to the laboratory experiments and machines, not people. We have to be sensitive, flexible, trusting and open to accept people as people. Most people are tired of fitting formulas and molds. Are you?

9. **Get back in touch with common-sense-itivity** — Although we are unique

as individuals we have common roots with our human neighbours. When we use, once again, our senses - hearing, seeing, smelling, touching - we discover a magical, alive world. The whole world becomes vital again, like when we were boys. The world becomes our teacher and we realize what we have been missing. We long for our contact with our natural place in our environment. When we do know this place again, we are surprised to meet other people in our lives who have the same longing. Being at home with nature is our common ground for contact with others, ourselves and our natural living domain.

10. **Be a body-mind** — Before reading any further stop for a moment, sit back, take a few breaths and as you do say to yourself "I am a body of life." Keep saying this quietly outloud and then to yourself. Now just let any thoughts, feelings, memories or images come into your awareness. Then close your eyes and do this again, continuing to allow anything that is happening to occur. Your thoughts, feelings, memories, breathing, movements, etc. Then imagine yourself in your daily situation, at work, at home, on the bus, subway, in the park, making love, as you repeat over again "I am a body of life." Be aware of any images or memories indicating when you were split between any aspect of yourself. Imagine when you were frantically working to meet a deadline and you felt hyper, and anxious and your body felt like a dead weight. Imagine yourself going into that memory and moving into your body. Be there as you experience your breathing and bodily sensations, thoughts and other processes that are occuring. What happens? We can change the image of our numbed bodies by focusing on that image-memory with our present awareness and resources. We can change our consciousness by being there totally and we can retrieve our energy into a "now" feeling bringing about relaxation and integration. When we take the time to focus with aliveness and awareness, all of our body life resources open up, responding to our need to heal.

11. **We are our feelings** — We do not just "have" feelings. Feelings are not a part of us that are attached in some way. "We are our feelings!" Most men already know how to get angry and anger is an emotion, a feeling. Let's go on a memory journey so we can explore the realm of our feelings. Go back in your memory a week or two and see if you can remember a situation when you became angry. Who were you with and what was happening? What was the reason for anger? Stay in that moment and see if you can go beyond the anger and see what other feelings you experienced at that time. Sadness? Fear? Confusion? Pain? etc. Can you find any joy or excitement mixed in with the other feelings? If not, what was the predominant emotion being experienced? If anger is the predominant emotion, what was the other person doing? What was your immediate need at the time? To be listened to, to be understood, in control? etc. Now go back further in your memory and repeat the exercise. Then go into your childhood and teenage years repeating the exercise again. In each cycle see if certain emotions begin to emerge,

as well as similar memories of other events. See how and when you started swallowing back your feelings, and how this made you feel about yourself, your needs and your emotions.

12. **You have needs and a right to them** — We become overly "needy" when we have been denying our needs or have been used to having all of our needs taken care of — mothering aspect. Either way we sacrifice those real needs of reaching out, growing and being self-supportive. From the denial place we become locked in and cannot reach out to others. If we have experienced the latter, we forfeit our own desire to be responsible and self-directed. We become dependent and demanding of others, especially women, to be our substitute mothers or sisters.

Both situations leave an infinite gap within us that cannot be filled by anyone. It takes practice to distinguish between our real needs as an adult and our needs as a child. We often find ourselves driving people away or testing them. Or we may draw people to us who will cater to our needs because initially it is their need also. Eventually, they tire of this. Recognize your small needs and see how you approach getting them met. Practice and experiment, trying different ways of using your abilities to have your needs fulfilled. The direct approach is not always the best. People can become overwhelmed due to their own unmet needs, and will often back off or become completely frustrated. Gradually work up to larger needs while practicing with the smaller ones. Also, practice responding to others needs by listening to them and to your own inner guide to help you assess a situation. By practicing knowing your needs and finding ways to meet them in adult, realistic ways you will be less needy and be able to discern between childish wants and adult-child needs. Not all of our needs can be satisfied, nor are they required to be. In time we can distinguish between important needs that we can respond to in our own self-caring ways and those we can receive from others through reaching out.

13. **Learn to be alone and enjoy it again** — As young boys we enjoyed our alone time. This was our private time and it was "our own." We used it to think, play, plan and find understanding of various events of our lives. As adults we have taken on our responsibilities as parents, husbands, employees, etc. We have very little time for ourselves. We spend time doing our countless activities and responsibilities. When we do find alone time, we're so used to having no spare time that we either are uncomfortable or we fill it with work or try to ignore it. We need to find the time to be in our private spaces again. It is crucial to our health and well-being.

Begin setting aside an hour a day or every other day just for yourself. Go to a movie, take a walk, go for a drive, see an art exhibit, but do it by yourself. After three weeks of this, allow more time to work on a hobby, read a book that you wanted to for sometime, sign up for a continuing education course in an interesting topic. The point is to learn how to entertain yourself again. You knew how to do this when you were a boy. Begin reclaiming that need, desire and ability. You may find yourself feeling less pressured and fatigued or yearning for that undefinable "something." You may find yourself enjoying your interactions with people more.

14. **If life is one big joke** - If you find yourself not taking anything seriously and can't put yourself into the responsibility of work or parenting, maybe it's time to look at growing up. This does not mean that you have to give up your playfulness, which is a gift that is not expressed often by men. A healthy, mature life is composed of some type of commitment to a stimulating interest or career. We need a balance in our lives or we become entangled. Initially, you have to desire to change your current pattern. Until this change occurs nothing can be done that has lasting value. Secondly, there is probably someone in your environment that makes it easy to stay in the little boy place. This person may want to keep you there because of his or her own need, or you may be tempted to remain there due to your own insecurity or fear. We are expected to be "grown up," but it is possible that someone may try to prevent that from occuring. You may be in a position of being "damned if you do," or "damned if you don't." Begin by seeing a counsellor, taking a course, talking with a trusted friend and/or your spouse or girlfriend and find some way to begin building bridges for change. Again, you sincerely have to want to begin the journey of change. You can start slowly but be committed. If nothing of these suit you; buy a pacifier, hire a nanny and then marry her.

15. **"Change" — find a way to grow and move that fits you** — Your community is probably full of continuing education courses, interest groups, action groups, and an array of different kinds of counsellors, healers and therapists from all kinds of schools of thought — body work, gestalt, T.A., family therapy, Rogerian, etc. Decide first what you want to work on, what your needs are, how much time you can set aside, etc. Then shop around and explore what your community has to offer. Begin talking with friends, male and female, who are sympathetic and support your desire to learn and grow. Find the situation that fits your needs and experience. If you choose a counsellor or therapist, make sure he or she is someone you feel comfortable with and supported by. We will feel comfortable with one therapist's approach and not another's. The best rule of thumb is to find one who is open, aware and to whom you can relate. The key in a healthy therapeutic relationship is to work with someone who encourages you to be aware of your own self-worth as well as having certainty in their own. Therapist's are human beings too. The better ones are those that can live what they practice. Choosing a way in which you want to grow helps you find a path that enriches your journey.

16. **Forgive others for hurting us** — When I work in private sessions and

after clients have gotten in touch with the people they have had resentments towards, I help them complete the process by encouraging forgiveness. Then I have them say "goodbye" to that person, close their eyes, pause for a moment, holding that feeling of loss inside. Then they open their eyes saying "hello" to that same person in a new way with a fresh, different insight. Sometimes individuals break down in tears, while other times they may feel elated. I encourage the emotional experience. I often have them write letters to express themselves. Of course, actual mailing is unnecessary. The idea is the essential expression of long-held emotions; a release. Other times I have them dialogue or role play with the person while trying a new perspective. If possible, I encourage the person to set up a face-to-face meeting with the person.

When we forgive others for pain or difficult experiences, regardless of whether they truly had anything to do with our experience or feeling then forgiveness starts the healing, the integration that allows us to close an old wound. In time it can become a new resource for our use in our lives. Until we can do this, our pain remains unhealed and the possibly for growth is limited.

17. **Sharing ourselves with others** — There is no greater delight than receiving ideas, resources and warmth and love from others. We are all teachers and learners of life and can reap the rewards of a mutual exchange of information, caring, skills and support. "People do need people" as the line in Barbara Streisand's song indicates. Despite the shams, unfairness and dilemmas of life, there are always people to know, share and grow with. When we share our gifts with others, they blossom as do we. "Looking out for number one" may gain you success but everyone needs people. If those at 'the top' feel otherwise, then many will suffer the consequences of their power hungry, dictatorship attitude. The more we share ourselves with others the more they will return it. We all know and believe this deep down inside even if it is hidden by fear and pain. We are all in this together.

18. **Become a child again** — This advice has been given in countless self-help books. There is truth in its message. When we are able to regain the simplicity; the awe of wonder, and the spontaneity or our childhood it transforms our lives. It lessens the drudgery of the day-to-day hassels and revitalizes us. It brings back our laughter, it enriches the laughter we have now. To be a child again opens the doors of our memories full of magic and surprise and this softens the rigidity of our lives. We recognize parts of ourselves once denied, and this eases the imposed adult role of being parent, husband, boyfriend, etc. It opens the world of children to us again that helps us understand the world of our own childhood. If we have lost it, we can get it back if we want it. Becoming a child again helps us see, feel, and touch the world and others with a sense of clarity and unity.

19. **Be humble, have integrity** — A man without integrity is like a lost sheep in the wilderness that will never find his way back to the flock. He cannot tell the difference between a wolf's open hungry mouth and another lost sheep like himself. He has lost his center of life and can be sold lead as gold because he can not tell the difference. He will sell his soul because he has put a price on it. He will sell to others his false soul, and for the right price will sell their souls too. A man who has no integrity does not know who he is or even what he is. A man without integrity has not been born yet and wanders through life trying to bargain for what he doesn't know he has lost. Need I say more? Dead men have no integrity!

20. **Live by what you are** — The only time we can start being ourselves is RIGHT NOW! Each of us as men, has lived through periods of our lives that contained pain, joy, fear, excitement, wonder and we have gained from it. We are not the same people we were five years ago, ten years ago, twenty or more years ago. We are not even the same as we were yesterday or five minutes ago. We are constantly moving and changing. This is how life is. Even when we're not moving and we feel we are "stuck in a rut" we are moving and changing. Nothing stands still, especially life. Change is the only constant there is.

Throughout this journey we have learned about our strengths and weaknesses, and things we never thought possible before. We have met people who have challenged us, hurt us, comforted us as well as those who became our mentors for life. We have engaged in adventures of daring and learned the pioneers' way. We have travelled to the stars in our minds and into the middle earth with our imaginations.

All this has brought us again and again to the inner place from which we embarked. Each time we leave this place and gain wisdom in our travels, we come back knowing this place more clearly. Each time we bear the fruits of these journeys to and from, we feel more enriched by our return and departure.

No matter how far we travel or how long we are gone, or how much we learn and come to know about this place, we always return. This place, our real home, is here, inside us. No matter where we go or what we do it is always with us. Living in our 'home' and caring for and providing its maintenance allows us to travel and return.

All and all, we are our home, here and now and in our journey as men or women, as humanity.

Take these guidelines and use them in ways that fit your personality, situation and lifestyle. Build on them and begin creating your own guidelines. You are ultimately in the driver's seat. Perhaps now, you can begin to release the chains of rigidity and move through 'feardom' with more courage. The empty place inside us is not empty, but rather, the gap created by unmet needs, or parts of ourselves we have denied. Bring more richeness and aliveness into your lives as men. The emptiness will begin to fill up with excitement for living and building a more humane world.

Learn to be a friend to fear and it will help guide you through the dark alleys of your being and teach you how to turn these alleys into gardens. Let go of your arrogant pride because it is a false representation of who you are!

Be humble, be happy and join with your brothers in a new way. This is our time as men to grow, reach out and touch the love inside of us, and in the world. Bridge the gap between the feeling and the rational; the mechanized mental plane of linear thinking and the body of life as a whole. Without this bridge, this balance, we will ultimately perish from this earth.

CHAPTER **VI**

Completion
Instead of Competition

"As we are to each other, so is God to us. If I separate myself from you by
believing that I have some special spiritual connection, I have, in my own
mind, **cut myself** off from what joins me to you and therefore to love itself. If
light allows us to see the spiritual, it must also provide the gentle recognition
of what encircles us both.

"It must shine on the road we walk and show us how blessed we are to travel
together."

There Is A Place Where You Are Not Alone

— Hugh Prather

Vince Lombardi, coach of the Greenbay Packers, took pride and was
famous for his remark, "Winning isn't everything, it's the only thing." Once,
during a volleyball championship play-off the commentators were discussing why one team was falling behind in points and one narrator calmly said,
"They just don't have the killer instinct." On another occasion I was reading
about a planning meeting in President Johnson's Whitehouse. He was
surrounded by his cabinet members and he was asking for their thoughts
on a decision to bomb North Vietnam and one cabinet member's remarks
indicated a softer strategy to be taken. Later as Johnson was talking in
private with one of his assistants, he spoke of this cabinet officer suggesting
he was weak and probably had to "squat to take a piss." And of course we are
aware of the lengths that Nixon would go to 'win', believing deeply in the
American competitive spirit. Competition has been the life blood of our
nation.

As American males we grew up with competition. Soon after birth our
veins began to flow with the "spirit of winning." Competition has become a
way of life. We were primed in school to compete for grades, awards on the
playing field, in the back seat, and in our own homes. Boys, who were our
friends, became our adversaries when it came time to win a contest. "May
the best man win," became our slogan and our relationships with one
another became secondary. Competition is as American as apple pie. This
way of life in western society has been a curse as well as a blessing. People
will do just about anything to win a contract, sell a product or sell themselves
often resorting to lying, stealing, cheating and sometimes even murder to be
on top. Competition has become a disease similar to cancer and other

terminal illnesses. Our way of life may indeed be killing us. Competition for some may result in a winning streak, but for others it is fatal.

COMPETITION — A DISEASE

The goal of competition is to win, the mainstay of competition is "to be somebody." This means you are a success. Book stores are full of techniques and methods on how to be a success with the gurus of the success empire laying out grand plans and strategies for making it to the top. They seduce the reader with promises of glamorous lifestyles, fancy homes, and all of the accoutrements that "success" offers.

Some of these pleasures also include fulfilment of special needs. The following is from a book by the "Master of Manipulation," Michael Korda. He is so called because of his clever wit in telling people how to succeed. In **Success,** he says:

> "Now the motion picture company is the heart of a growing conglomerate and Larry has not only 'turned it around,' but is clearly on his way up even further. A Lockheed Jetstar II waits for him when he needs to fly to the Coast, and a limousine is at his disposal twenty-four hours a day. Money is a meaningless concept, so much so that he never carries any, which is the ultimate mark of success. What could he buy, after all? His secretary places a pack of cigarettes on his desk every morning next to his coffee. The newspapers are ready in the back seat of the limousine that picks him up. After lunching in his private dining room, where a French chef prepares low calorie foods, he can exercise in his own squash court. Wherever he goes, the bill never appears: it is sent on to his office with the appropriate tip added — he doesn't even have to sign anymore, let alone pay."

Throughout the book he tells the stories of people who have "made it" with all the unique privileges and rewards they receive for being men at the top.

I pay particular attention to his definition of success as I believe it points out the qualities, needs, and desires that one requires to be a winner, at least in his terms. He writes:

> "How you become a success is, of course, your business. Morality has very little to do with success. I do not personally think it is necessary to be dishonest, brutal or unethical in order to succeed, but a great many dishonest, brutal and unethical people in fact do succeed."

At least he's one of the few successful gurus who is honest about what it takes to get to the top. Many people who have made it to the so-called top did so by stepping on the fingers of those who happened to get in the way during their process of succeeding. His book is probably a best seller because he tells it "like it is." Those who are on the success ladder like his approach as it caresses their egos. Interestingly enough, his honesty and "egomania" are what makes his book stand out above the others who talk of playing the "nice guy" in their strategies in "getting there." For the most part, the road of competition is usually brutal, painful and constantly keeps one on his toes. The best way to win in his success example is to "strike the first blow," don't let your opponent know what you're up to, always stay ahead of everyone else and when there's a crisis or someone fails —"go for the jugular." The code and ethics of manipulation are as follows: Hang in there, "never give up," play as though you are loyal and look out for number one.

It saddens me to see what the competitive gamesmanship does to people. It's like playing Russian roulette, with one of the bullets meant for you. It may take years or it might happen suddenly, but sooner or later the man at the top comes falling down. He does not have to fail financially. His failure can be in his health or the destruction of a close relationship with someone about whom he cares. The eventual emptiness he begins to feel inside, is expressed when he wakes one day to discover that he cannot trust or rely on anyone as it would show human weakness. Then he becomes the unfortunate "loser." There's no one there to care. Jimmy Durante was noted for saying, "Be good to the people on the way up, because you might meet them on the way down." Eventually even the guys at the top need someone to remind them they are still only human regardless of their expensive cars, their charge cards, or how lavish their homes are. The truth is, "You can't take it with you," as well as "it gets lonely at the top."

We idolize stars so much that they have to live private, isolated existences. Celebrities may live like kings on their million dollar estates, but have to spend thousands of dollars for sophisticated security systems to keep them safe within the palace. Elvis Presley, the "King of Rock and Roll," finally died lonely and out of touch with the world. We honor their success, but force them to imprison themselves away from contact with us. John Lennon, became the victim of his own success, when all he wanted was to "give peace a chance." Freddy Prinze, John Belushi, Marilyn Monroe, Jimmy Hendrix and others have paid with their lives for "making it." And as their fans, we drain their souls with our own secret hunger for stardom, wishing we had what it takes to make it to the "big time." We cling to their messages of love and human passion but don't really hear what they are saying. We have lost our own centers so we place these stars on center stage, worshipping them as the fulfilled forgotten shadow of ourselves.

Competition has blessed us with a thriving economy and an affluent lifestyle. We have things galore to satisfy our every "want" but they seldom touch our deeper needs. We have the most leisurely life-style in the world, but we are constantly restless for more material possessions believing that the more we accumulate the more secure we are. That emptiness exists inside and grows larger every day. Mother Teresa, the world renowned healer of the sick and poor of India, says that westerners are missing their soul's nourishment and are spiritually deprived. Competition has created a unique material world for us. But it has left us deprived, lonely and alienated.

When I was growing up, I wanted all the finer things in life even though we were poor. For a long time, I blamed my parents for divorcing, feeling if they had stayed together, we would have had a more comfortable life-style. I was ashamed of being poor and hated having my stepfather give me a haircut because we could not afford haircuts. I was embarrassed to go to school with a "pig shave." That was all my stepfather knew how to give. My male friends at school would always notice my newly shaved head and tease me. Their parents could afford a haircut! I always wanted more than the rest of my family. I didn't want to be poor and feel miserable and ashamed. I wanted the finer things in life, nice furniture, cars like my friends' parents had, and new clothes like the rest of the students instead of hand-me-downs. At the beginning of the school year I seldom had new clothes while the rest of the students were all decked out, showing off their fall back-to-school clothes. We just could not afford it. At Christmas time, my siblings and I received one present apiece and were grateful to get that. We would go to our relatives every Christmas as my cousins would show off their multitude of gifts. I was always disappointed I could not have more. Every Christmas until I was eleven, I asked for guns and holster outfits, but because I could not wear these to school I would go back after Christmas empty-handed while the rest of the kids were looking smart in their Christmas clothes.

When I was nine years old, I began sneaking into Salvation Army thrift shops and buying things that I could purchase cheaply. God forbid if one of my friends at school saw me, I would have been the laughing stock. I bought a pair of girls saddleshoes once for fifty cents and dyed them jet black. They looked like new shoes and my friends asked me if I had bought new shoes. Of course smiling with a self-assured look on my face, I told them these were indeed new shoes. One afternoon during recess, while I was playing fastball with my classmates, it began to rain. I didn't take notice of the rain as I was having too much fun. By the time we were ready to go back to class, one classmate asked what happened to my shoes. I looked down and saw that the rain had dissolved the black dye revealing that I had on girls shoes which had been dyed. The guys in the class started yelling, "Frankie has on girls shoes!" "Frankie has on girls shoes!" As much as the evidence was plain to see, I flatly denied it. I wanted to hide in a hole I was so humiliated walking back to class, my face red and flushed with tears of agony and a lump in my throat. I swore I would never be caught again wearing girl's shoes. When I got home I ripped them apart, and hid them in a neighbor's garden. The next day I wore my older brother's tennis shoes. They were two sizes too big but I stuffed old socks in the toe so they would fit. They looked terrible but at least they were boys shoes.

Later on, I learned to steal from clothing stores by putting new clothes underneath my own after selecting several garments of the same size. I got good at it and hid the new clothes in a concealed place in our attic. My mother sent my older brother and me to the department store to buy his winter coat and as the cashier wrapped up his coat, I took another off the rack and put it on and then remarked to her that we were buying my brother a coat just like mine. To this day, I do not know whether she believed me, was too busy with other customers to notice, or she just took pity on me, knowing that it was in the middle of winter and knew I needed a coat. When I started working I stopped stealing. I was lucky that I did not get caught. Like everyone else who had "things" I wanted them too. I was shaping my identity by comparing myself to kids who had material things and saw this as a means of defining my own personality. If I had nice clothes, toys, lived in a nice house and my parents drove a nice car this meant that I was "somebody." It does not take "clothes to make the man," although this was the value system I was creating for myself.

By the time I was out of high school, I had been paying for my schooling and the car I had bought with my father's help by working sixteen hours a day, seven days a week in our gas station, which we later took over. I also worked several different kinds of jobs. I had been going out with the daughter of a wealthy farmer and was planning to marry her. I had worked hard to climb up from poverty and was on the road to success, or so I thought.

I went on to college, paying my own way from summer jobs. Sometimes I worked two jobs, plus working in the dining hall washing pots and pans and scrubbing floors during spring break. I was willing to work hard and long to get what I wanted. What did I want? My goal was to be a lawyer or a business executive. I wanted money, status, power, prestige, and influence. I wanted all the things I never had while growing up. I was going to marry a girl who wanted the same things. It all sounded so promising. I was determined to succeed, because I believed that this is what life was all about. Once when searching for a part-time job after starting junior college, I knocked on twenty-six doors on both sides of a street. The twenty-sixth door was a car dealership and the manager was so impressed with my ambition that he hired me.

Another example of my determination to make it was when I worked as a campus cop. I would ticket illegally parked cars and find the owners in the student cafeteria. I knew most of the students by the cars they drove. Then

I'd make a deal with them, if they would buy me lunch I would tear up the ticket. I ate pretty well for two semesters. I was not only determined but I was clever as well. I had all the makings of a young, aspiring, corporate executive who surely would be a prime candidate for grooming for a company vice-president. I was willing to take advantage of others, manipulate if I had to, and be there at the right time ready to move in for the kill. People were objects of my quest and I would use them if I had to. I was aggressive, driving, intelligent, hardworking and "wanted" more out of life than what I had grown up with. I was an 'all-American' boy with all the qualities to make it in the fast lane of the corporate world.

I have pointed out here how my life script was similar to many of my male cohorts who grew up in the land of plenty and on the competitive edge. Like them, I had learned to value things over people and saw getting my needs met through acquiring material things. In order to have things I had to have money and to have money I had to find ways to make money. I needed to have all the necessary ingredients to earn an income in the winners way. I had to possess traits rendering me more capable, as well as cunning, so that I could play the game better than others, my opponents. If the goal I was seeking was really important to my quest then, I had to view my opponent as the enemy. They say in the business world, "all's fair in love and war." This was my motto for playing the game on the battlefield of life. To be a competent competitor, I had to refine my living skills so that I was equipped with a more effective, efficient arsenal than the next guy. To be a winner in the corporate world I had to be in charge, on top of it consistently, and view people as pawns for my next move. I had to be a champion among champions and to believe that I was the better champion. I had to look good and use all my resources of determination, hard work, communication, and drive to not only stay in the race, but to win it. If I was going to be a corporate game player I had to be more than just a man or a human being, I had to be a "man's man," a superior specimen.

My relationships with other male friends were concerned with qualities of "doing." We were always moving, always in the race. If we were not out drinking and talking about who we "laid" or who was a likely candidate, we were playing poker, pool or some kind of sport. We never had time to just "be" with one another or to appreciate one another in a respectful way. Even as friends, we kept a safe physical distance. We could pound each other on the shoulders until they were red, and sometimes had contests doing just that but as much as we deeply cared about one another we were never able to show it. Two guys hugging is not permitted. A strong handshake, a pat on the back, or even a kick in the ass was permissable. Beyond that, we did not get close in an intimate supportive way. Men do that with women, but they do not do that with men, not even their fathers or brothers.

Men have been taught to guard themselves in a competitive society, to not trust anyone, not even their men friends who are more special than they would likely admit. Do not touch, do not get too close because I might have to compete with you for a girlfriend or a job, is the unspoken warning.

Competition, like an incideous disease, affects everything that we do, it shapes our values as persons and affects the quality of our relationships. It feeds our "wants" and moves us, estranged, from our deeper needs as human beings. It feeds the brutal and greedy parts of our nature, leading us on an endless chase seeking something that is often elusive. We have been told that success is the top and failure is the bottom, but we were never told how to achieve an integrated middle; a place of balance and contact with a realness and richness. We are brainwashed into believing that status and power give us what we need. We find we have to hide ourselves from the world to keep from being bothered by those who are our "inferiors." We are taught that success is where it's at. We discover it is often a lonely alienating place unless we're with the success-elite, who do not really see us as persons anyway.

The competitive spirit, perhaps once was composed of fairness and sportsmanship. It has become tainted and decayed, souring our souls, turning us against our fellows and most of all ourselves. The competitive spirit has become a ghost that seeks to drive us into our own dungeons, haunting us throughout our lives. Competition is a disease that turns us into enemies to one another.

We see this epidemic rising in the corporate market place, on the grid iron, the media, world trade and even in the lives of our young. To keep up with the demands of their parent's need for their kids to be winners, some young people have resorted to taking pills to lose weight or participating in games despite injuries or imitating their pro stars by becoming addicted to drugs to keep up the stamina to win. Universities compete to get research grants and will bring in top names to guarantee project funding. Therapists compete for clients and are discouraged when not enough people are asking for help. The competitive spirit is everywhere and it is slowly and methodically turning people into ghosts, mere shadows of machines.

A MAN WITHOUT HIS CENTER

Those in the winner's circle are addicted to the belief that the remarks of success outweigh the failures. They proclaim that their needs are fulfilled, since they do not want for anything anymore.

Possibly, having people wait on you hand and foot, catering to your every whim must be the height of a healthy self-concept, as described in this situation:

> "You only have one life to live; you may as well live it as a success,"
> said my friend Laurence, looking out from the back seat of his
> chauffeur-driven silver grey, Cadillac limousine, complete with
> T.V., radiophone, at people huddled in the rain around bus
> stops."

Darwin said that the most fit should survive and rule, and "I'm the most
fit." I have the comfort of my limousine while you "freeze your asses off"
standing in the rain, waiting for an overcrowded bus. I should rule, and like
royalty, have all the comforts as well.

We have seen this situation in movies, on T.V., read it in books, or
experienced it when someone in a crowd, steps to the front of the line and
shouts, "Hey, don't you know who I am?", with an attitude of "step back you
inferiors of the species and let me through!" These may not be the exact
words expressed, I could be slightly exaggerating. These 'somebody's' do
demand special privileges. When one has power he can play out any fantasy
regardless of how others see it. Here we have a man who has fulfilled his
fondest dreams:

> "In the mean time Carlson motivates his senior executive by
> giving each of them a new Cadillac every year, all the cars the
> same colour (presumably to avoid jealousy or the complications
> of taste). In 1976 the Cadillacs were smoke gray."

> "One of the biggest prides I've got is my executive group driving
> Cadillacs and living in nice homes," he says, nicely combining
> motivation and leadership. One suspects, however, that Carl-
> son's real pride lies in having built up a monument so big that it
> answers, finally his own passionate need to succeed."

Mary Kay cosmetics founder has created a multi million dollar enterprise. She also gives her top sales people Cadillacs, they're pink not gray.
Playing "Big Daddy" and "Momma" is a privilege indulged in by the super
rich. Elvis Presley once called up a dealership in his home town of Memphis
and ordered motorcylces for all of his staff. It takes a special breed of person
to relish such indulgence, but this is what these elites of the corporate
market place can do and enjoy doing. Personally, I have my doubts. I see them
filling the gaps in themselves with gadgets and material wealth, in hopes of
buying love they never had.

I believe it creates the opposite of what the "status seekers" proclaim that
it does. I see the process of climbing to the top as regressive, rather than
progressive. As much as these climbers would like to feel that in Machiavel-
lian terms, that this brings them closer to "how it really is," it takes them
deeper into an unreal world of the "spoiled child" who finally gets his long

lost needs of his youth fulfilled, but in immature ways. To make slaves of people, rationalizing that all people have their price is nothing more than being caught in a similar state of the newborn child who is still unaware of the true pleasures of the natural life process. The author of **Competing**, Harvey Rubin M.D., points out that rather than fulfilling one's true and deeper human needs, it does the contrary. He states:

> "They may give a venue of self-confidence, but their use suggests that the person has lost sight of the real goals of competition and is beginning to compete for images rather than substance - because, in his highly refined world, that is all he perceives is left him."

Rubin describes a case study of a young man who grew up in a wealthy family, but was unable to get the recognition he needed and desired. He was never seen as being good enough or measuring up to the family name, and by the time he was in his twenties, his goals were to drive the "right" car, travel in the "right" circles, and belong to the "right" club. His whole life was governed by his deep need to gain needed recognition which caused him to forfeit his rightful place; his own center of himself. His life, his goals, his achievements and values were lodged inbetween his family's acceptance of him for what he was, and his own acceptance of himself. His life became externally motivated and his drive to be a success was a hidden need to be a success in the eyes of his family.

I have worked in therapy with several men in business whose goals were hidden, left over needs from their childhood. Even once they achieved success, they were unhappy. Something was missing inside. If they failed along the way, this was even more painful, leaving a deeper scar because on another level they had proven to their unresponsive parents that they weren't able to measure up. This is the kind of trauma that drives men to suicide. By taking their own lives, they show their parents that they were driven to suicide by having been placed in demanding, impossible situations. Also, the taking of one's life is liberation from the agony of never having felt fulfilled inside and believing no matter what was accomplished nothing would prove to parents that one was worthy of recognition and love.

Whether the goal of competition and power seeking is connected with left over needs, being blocked from one's own personal potential by parent's needs or a culture conditioning that pushes winning at us as soon as we can swing a bat or get a grade, the effects are eternal and contaminating. It destroys our soul, driving us like predatory animals in a quest for fulfillment. We believe it is our right to take what is ours, what we deserve and this is the game of survival. Another perspective on this condition is explained through what Herber Kohl calls "tension of perversity." He defines this particular kind of tension as this:

"A closed center strains to keep out threats, to maintain its preoccupations and ward off collapse."

In this light, the competitive person is hell bent on achieving the image that he carries within, which is mirrored in the outside world. Anyone who challenges this image of reality becomes a threat making him suspicious of anyone that threatens his reality image. The more their believed vision of reality is challenged, the more they pull their resources into themselves, to protect and guard their image of right. Anyone in the way is used as an object, a stepping stone to the realization of their fixed goal to fulfill their reality image. Any person who is a weak link in the ladder they are climbing whether it be in the corporate world, on stage, or in academia can be exploited in order to strengthen their hold, their drive which also streng-thens their image. A competitor in the race has to stay on top of it never giving up. If they do release themselves from the competition game, this is perceived as a weakness by his opponents, who wait like hungry vultures until their prey finally weakens, unable to stay in the race. The promotion game of business, military and just about every segment of western society has this flavor. Again, "may the best man win," the left over motto of our youth rings loud and clear. Once you slow down, or give an inch, your dead.

Is it natural to compete or do we learn it? Studies and theories suggest both. The way that competition is viewed and practiced in western society leads me to suspect that it is neither natural nor learned, rather it is a result of "over learning." Men justifying actions for getting their needs met, whether these needs be real or otherwise, will become primitive and brutal in this trek to the top of the ladder if necessary.

Those who "make it" assure themselves that this is just the way it is, that it "goes with the territory." "Survival of the fittest" becomes the game playing philosophy that justifies any action, no matter how damaging it is to another's physical or psychological well being, as well as to one's own.

The unfortunates of this drive for success are considered not fit enough which further feeds the prophets of success belief that it is true to human nature that the strong should reign, holding powerful positions and so have rightful domain over those who are excluded from the elite group.

I see these corporate climbers as floundering infants, pushing, driving and manipulating their way through the assortment of toys, trinkets and people, while their sense of true self is disconnected from them. They are forever trying to manipulate and control their playpen world of gadgets and attempting to manufacture ways to climb out and up out of their confining cribs.

The more they accumulate, the more power they possess and the more they regress. Eventually, they become frustrated by all the things and people they have to control and reorganize. Once they are finally free, at the top of the crib looking out over the rungs into a whole new world to see and organize, they demand recognition for being able to go through the whole ordeal. As infants they cry, demanding attention and nurturing. As executives they "shout" and belittle others to secure their power positions. The successes and failures of competing are analogous with the natural process of learning how to stand on one's own two feet. The next step is to crawl, then to walk, then to run, maybe even believing that one can fly someday.

The man who learns how to achieve this natural process of growing up, gaining support and love, will grow from the life center into his own center. The man who does not will take on the world shouting orders from behind his desk, stuck in his infantile crib, lost in the search for his own center by creating his reality externally, estranged from his true self. The mature male working from his center becomes involved with others as a way of expanding himself. The unaware male withdraws from people, mistrusting others and ignoring potential support. "Mommy, I'd rather do it myself!" he cries triumphantly standing on his own unassisted, clutching the rungs of his crib.

THE WOMAN AS PREDATOR IN THE MARKET PLACE

Since the advent of the women's liberation movement, increasing numbers of women have left kitchen and household duties to enter the work force which is still thought by many to be a "man's world." Women have returned to school completing bachelors, masters, law or doctorate degrees. Women are moving up from their once defined feminine roles as mothers, wives, secretaries and clerks and are pursuing the success rewards that men have enjoyed for years. They have set their sights on top positions and are even more determined to "make it" than some males. They are coming out of the starting gates not only ready to run the competitive race, but to win it. They are changing their feminine socialized traits of passivity to ardent and assertive qualities which make them equal among men. One such executive on her way up states:

> "I want it all — the Lear jets and the corporate headquarters with
> my own private elevator, and the limousine with two telephones.
> A lot of it may be silly and funny, but men have had it all these
> years and now its my time to enjoy it."

Like the predatory male in the competition game who is often the "ego hunter," many women are becoming the predatory female. They are out to conquer the male dominated world and to nourish their egos.

They are discovering that there is a price to pay for making it. Once it was more common for men to have heart attacks and other stress related illnesses. Now women are being stricken with similar problems, more frequently and at a younger age. The glamor that goes with the image takes its toll in reality.

I am not suggesting women should not have a piece of the pie and become part of our society in a more active way. I have supported this movement personally for a long time. However, I am concerned about the extremist way that some women are going about it. Like so many men, they are becoming trapped by the seduction of power, status and acquiring material "things" that they are losing sight of their original goals and are competing for competition's sake. Many men do not encourage women's striving and are continuing to throw chauvanistic slurs to discourage, confuse and sabotage. Many women have resorted to becoming hard and guarded to protect themselves from the dirty infighting which occurs in the drive to climb the status ladder.

While many men want to continue to think with that which they sit upon, women will not do the same. Women are more in touch with their feeling nature and do not have to ignore or shun this aspect as they become more attuned to the mental, assertive male sides of their natures.

As a male, I wish to thank women for taking a stand and making the first move towards a human liberation. I sincerely doubt that males would have done so. There is a chance that males will continue to fight it out globally seeing who can knock out whom from the race, the human race.

As men begin to move through their own transformation, women have to be mindful of their own evolvement. A lot of women still hate men and want revenge. This is just as immature as men who are still trying to "score" with as many women as possible.

Use your common sense, your human heart to guide your continued liberation. Thank God, one of us in the socialized "corral" is still guided by feelings and are not repressed by extreme overuse of the mind. When the two are unintegrated, a dangerous imbalance exists. If you are a feminist in ideology, be a human at heart.

In these times of economic and world strife, males and females alike are called upon to choose a better tomorrow. Together we must support one another's liberation as we move towards being healthier human beings and realizing a more humane society.

If you turn your back on the reality of corporate wastes, exploitation of people and the production of unnecessary, harmful goods to make a profit, then you are poisoning your fellow man's heart and mind. If you begin your quest for stardom and status unaware of such realities, then by the time you reach the top, it simply may not exist nor may anyone or anything else for that matter.

RUSSIANS INSIDE US

Ever since I was young I have heard how evil the Russians are; the true enemy of the free world whose main intent is to enslave us. Until college, when I became involved in the student movement of the '60's, I knew very little about Russians or about Communism. I had never met a Russian. I had met Communists and those who called themselves Communists, Socialists and more than my share of Capitalists.

I was taught that we are living in a democratic society governed by a democratic system. I agree that we have more personal freedoms than most countries and enjoy the highest standard of living of any free enterprise nation, but what was started when this country was born has moved a long way from democracy. What we live in is a "demagarchy"; an oligarchy ruled by a few and disquised as a democracy.

Gore Vidal has brought into view in his many writings, that our so-called two party system is really a one-party system flying two different flags.

We shuddered when Krushev said, "We will bury you." The resultant nationwide panic found us digging fallout shelters and practicing our civil defense drills.

Are we so different from the Russians? As the beginning of the Industrial Revolution, both Capitalist and Socialist countries seized Darwin's theory of evolution as a mandate to launch their industrial empires. Both used the "survival of the fittest" premise to conquer and dominate less technically advanced, weaker nations. Each believed that the industrial state was the highest order of societal evolution. Though Marx wrote it, Hegel, Engels and other philosophers on both sides of the ideological fence, believed and supported it.

Both capitalist and socialist utilized Newton's theory of a mechanical universe where in all its parts, including humans, allowed the machine universe to function, thus building some of the largest industrial systems in the world. People were working on assembly lines and products were mass produced for the world market. Both latched onto the progress principle first laid down by Darwin, which gave purpose and meaning to man's evolution of climbing the ladder to reach higher forms of being.

Whether capitalist or socialist, both set out to exploit nature to the hilt. Toffler states in his chapter on the meaning of the second wave, the Industrial Revolution:

"On both sides of the ideological divide, therefore, one found the same image of humanity standing in opposition to nature and dominating it. This image was a key component of indust-reality, the superideology from which Marxist and anti-Marxist alike drew their assumptions."

The Marxists were moving to the beat of their own drum and the collective enterprise system controlled by government and the anti-Marxists marched to the beat of their own drum with the individual's freedom at heart in the name of free enterprise which eventually became the enterprise of the privileged few. Both supported Darwin's theory that the fittest should have dominion.

Whether Capitalist of Socialist, Russian or American, at the core, we are not that different in our actions and attitudes. We both have goals to spread our way of life around the world exploiting others to do so. We both have visions for space travel and spend billions of dollars for this purpose. We both have emassed an arsenal of weapons that can destroy one another twenty times over, taking the rest of the world with it. We both have an elaborate intelligence network to spy on each other, our own people and others in the world. They call theirs the KGB, we call ours C.I.A. and F.B.I. Both of us will launch campaigns to oust other third world country governments and support those that will embrace our style of government. Both of us have corruption in the highest offices in the land, in the military and other levels of society. Both of us have men in high office who push their countries closer and closer to nuclear war. These predatory hawks on both sides believe that people are expendable in order to prove a theory or ideology. Both of us are ignorant about one another and rely on what we've been told by others or our governments. Finally, we are both highly competitive, aggressive but believe and practice it differently. How are we different? One way, is that the Russians lost 20 million people and fought a bitter winter war on its own soil. We have dropped two atomic bombs on Japan that completely destroyed two cities and hundreds of thousands of people. They have not.

Before we begin judging the Russians and listening to our own government's propaganda, it is time we looked in our own back yards. More essentially, it is time that we as human beings, begin to discover a way to coexist on this planet.

Two wise and compassionate human beings advocate: Norman Cousins, author of **Human Options:**

"The enemy is any man in government, high or low, who keeps waiting for a public mandate before he can develop big ideas of his own, but who does little or nothing to bring about such a mandate."

Sam Levison, author of **Everything but Money:**

"For the world in which you are going to live, tolerance will not be good enough. We are now in the 'live and help live' era of democracy. Like your immigrant grandparents who sent for those left behind, you will have to help others to cross over into freedom."

WE ARE EXPENDABLE

I sat back in the rocker, a cup of instant coffee in my right hand, and glanced out the window at the midnight moon, then I lit a cigarette and began to read a chapter from Toffler's **The Third Wave**, entitled: "The Corporate Identity Crisis."

As I took a long relaxing drag on my "special light," the nicotine began to swell up inside my lungs. I began to feel dizzy and nauseous, momentarily the room started spinning and I thought I was going to faint. I had not smoked in weeks and did so only rarely. Writing a book provided additional nervous energy which was expelled during the agonies of its creation. A cigarette helps to alleviate some of the stress — or so we are told.

Still half dizzy, I suddenly had a very profound realization. I was wanting to relax and had grabbed two of the most widely used drugs in society to give me a false sense of calm. Yet, I was doing it with such acceptance. With this, I realized how habitual and unconscious our learned self-induced poisoning can be. As long as we stay in a fog about our self-induced toxicity, we will continue to keep the wheels of free enterprise rolling. The "American way," billows from corporate smokestacks polluting our air as well as our minds. When we stop feeding their assembly lines and "bigger is better" and "faster brings more profit" attitude, we will move out of range of their destructive progress arrow and cease to be the target.

We are well conditioned to reach for something that is harmful to our health. We watch our parents and other adults as they model self-destructive behaviour. It is manly to smoke as so many of us learned in our puberty years. I know of no one who enjoyed the first taste of a cigarette. I remember being told by a twelve year old smoker, "you'll get used to it, everybody does." If I didn't like to smoke, I was considered a "sissy." Eventually I did get used to it like everybody else. Coffee was similar. I hated coffee initially. I used to fill a cup with loads of sugar and cream to mask the coffee taste. It is not the coffee or the cigarettes per se, it's what they do to us. These drugs help to numb us to the society's reality which lacks love, understanding, and sees us as expendable.

We become guinea pigs for nuclear blasts, being told that it is perfectly safe to watch an awesome mushroom cloud climbing to the heavens. Later we may die of cancer just like most people in the town who witnessed the blast. It's okay to send soldiers into the danger zone, to learn what effects the bomb blast has on troops and later, to expose others in Vietnam to the dangers of agent orange. Drugs are permitted on the market that have caused women to have deformed babies as a result. Deaths of several women to toxic shock syndrome, were due to some foreign chemical not tested thoroughly.

Everything is "okay" as long as corporations, governments, military and other political-economic groups can test their theories in the market place even though people are unaware of the potential dangers. To them, people are expendable — the marketplace is the laboratory and people are the rats to be experimented with.

Healthy people will not require artificial hearts and other organs when they are educated in the care of their own physical health. This is not a priority in the minds of the ego-starved technocrats who envision a mechanical world; a world of which Newton would be proud.

How can a society justify genetic engineering cloning and cybornetics, when it has failed in keeping its people healthy? Those elected for cloning would be the strongest, the most intelligent and those who would fit the grand plan for creating a master race of humans. Darwin's ghost is alive among us as selective breeding becomes a possible wave of the future.

The free enterprise system has high hopes for the space age industry. It is all mapped out as to how we can colonize in space and farm the oceans. The visions are into the dreams of the future, and these space age projects hold priority because the strong will of the "fittest." The strong shall reign, inheriting the earth.

Hitler is alive and well with us today as his dream of a master race is being explored. Those of "impure" blood not of the "right" stock, must be liquidated. Since the free world practice is to hide their atrocities under the guise of a justifiable purge to stop communism, we will see none of the overt displays of Dacha and Auchwitz; ovens, gas chambers, and mass graves. We, who are thought to be expendable, the everyday citizen, from every profession and even from the corporate and scientific community, will succumb gradually. We will be suffocated by the gaseous fog from the smoke stacks of the corporate giants, burning with half truths and deception, while deadening ourselves to the real truths. Our deaths will come slowly, agonizingly, as we choke on hollow promises and swallow self-induced poisons from our internal and external environments. Our healthy habits, our desires for images to replace our worn out misused spirit will not be realized, our human needs will remain untouched. These slow debilitating processes can invariably send us to our early graves, en masse. As in Auchwitz, we who are the expendable can strip nude, throwing personal possessions of identity into large piles, and march in line to the beat of a drum you cannot hear, into the crowded shower stall. We stand, waiting for the gaseous fog to come steaming out of the shower nozzle. There is no choice; "you are expendable."

MOVING TOWARDS COMPLETION

Crossing the bridge from a competitive outlook and practice to one that makes a man feel connected with life, rather than estranged from it, is difficult if one refuses to take action.

The 60's were a time of unity and embracing one another. The 70's was the decade of "me-ism" focusing on "doing your own thing." The 90's is yet another time to join together, but in a way that has never been experienced before on this planet.

Toffler speaks of a "new age of synthesis," whereby technology can help bring us together as a world community, a global family. Marilyn Ferguson defines this growing momentum toward global consciousness as a "conspiracy." Others have talked about a new step for humanity and see the 80's and 90's as a time of the cross over to an entirely different kind of world. Man's dreams can be manifested in a new world order that for once shares in harmony with nature.

Men and women share the responsibility of preparing ourselves, teaching ourselves and others to make this humanitarian leap to a new age. We have to learn alternatives and to think differently from any manner experienced in the past. It is necessary to probe our inner space and locate the necessary tools to carry on with this new age transition.

The challenge of this quest requires people who have reached a state of integration and harmony within and outside themselves. The super competitive, driving, bullying man, is beginning to be passe. He is aiding in his extinction by draining his psyche motors with the belief that he can go on indefinitely. This kind of man is a collection of fragments with no sense of direction or connection to an integral relationship.

The kind of man who is capable of transformation is the man who is fully aware of himself, and all of his functions on a physical, emotional, mental, social, and spiritual level. He will be able to draw resources from these areas individually and together as a unified whole. Each of the parts will work in support of the others and combined, they will provide multiple resources for the total function and action of the man. The catch phrase for this new emerging age will be; "The whole is greater than the sum of its parts"; rather than the premise that separate parts, in isolation, provide the best order and function.

The new kind of man will possess the qualities described of the "revolutionary" man. Briefly, he will be a man of synthesis, integrating both masculine and feminine parts of himself into a whole and healthy human being. This new male will also be able to operate on several levels of the conscious and unconscious. He will be able to be as alive in his adult ego state, as he is in his parent and child states. In fact, he will probably unlock a new state of awareness, not yet discovered.

Men today are struggling and beginning to feel the pains of transition as their function has become too limited. They no longer gain satisfaction from just living in a mental world and experience the blocked passages of their feeling-world. They are asking for more than images of people, feelings and themselves. They desire tangibility and substance. A fantasy world is just that, fantasy. A real world continues to be real, becoming more challenging the more we know about it.

The man who makes his journey will be a strong, compassionate man. He will be one who has travelled as much within himself as externally. He will have viewed the depths of his childhood, remembering with accuracy of how his life was. He will have gone back to his prime years of adolescence, reclaiming the essence of himself that he had forfeited by conforming to the measurements of society's yardstick. He will have re-journeyed through this wonderful vital time in a man's life, and rejected all the rules and regulations that restricted the expression of his own self-direction and self-healing.

He will have soothed his "Fisher wound" through befriending the child and adolescent parts of himself that have much to teach him about rebirth and being whole.

The man of the future can see the future in his visions, viewing the good of the past, and experiencing this in the ever present moment. The present can expand ten thousand years and turn back the clocks. The present is the peep hole through time and space in our eternal journey within the universe. The man of the future is not impatient with the movement of one time frame to another because he trusts the center of the universe which exists deep within his core. He has a faith and respect for the movement of life within and externally aware he is part of this rhythm, not separate from it.

This man has given up the endless war inside himself and is at peace with the world. He no longer has to compete with others as he no longer sees others as projected images of parts of himself with which he is at war. He accepts others for what they are, not expecting them to be what they are not, or cannot be. He appreciates the ability to truly touch, feel and experience people as real and lovable. He is able to give of himself not having to manipulate and destroy to get what he really needs from others. He knows the difference between his wants and his needs.

The man who crosses over remembers when he was at war with himself, and through others how he learned to be at war with his human neighbor. He remembers his pain and how he had kept it to himself and how that hurt him even more. He remembers when he carried the hurt in fear and guilt. He remembers seeing other men mirror his hurting style and deep inside, although he did not say it, that hurt him too. He remembers when he chose to give up the fight and let both sides rest, learning there was a third alternative to the constant battle, which was no battle at all. He learned to live in harmony with others and this brought harmony into his life.

Lastly, he is aware that the goal of completion is a never ending pursuit. Completion is something that is always in a state of becoming. The more we discover, the more there is to learn, and so on into infinity.

Completion as a way of life, can teach us as men to learn to trust our nature, instead of trying to control and harness it. It will give us more gifts than we could ever imagine. The bridge to completion begins with ourselves, and learning to integrate all our disparate parts into a unified whole — then we can begin functioning in harmony with others and viewing the world as a friend not our enemy.

MEN CAN BE A BRIDGE

When we love ourselves respect and believe in our true selves we are becoming our own best friend, a natural human bridge to ourselves, others and the world.

The lines in Helen Reddy's song illustrates this so well:

> "Would you take better care of yourself? Would you be kinder to yourself? Would you be more forgiving of your human imperfections? If you realized your best friend is yourself..."

The more we are able to dissolve our body image of "macho," the closer we are to freedom. If we can realize as men, that to be moving "into" ourselves and the world in a less driving, pushing manner then we are not giving anything up, but gaining a great deal.

We have been taught to fight against the negative side ourselves labeled as weakness. The more at war we are with ourselves, the less peace we will have. Our government officials talk of peace, when as men they are living a personal and tormenting existence. How can there be peace in the world when we are warring within ourselves?

We have been taught, not to love, or even like ourselves as men. We are unaware of the difference between our image and our real self, so why love something you know nothing about! It has been drilled into us that we are an image of manhood, an American male, that should be enough and we should be damn proud of it.

A few years ago the 'Duke' John Wayne finally died after a long fight with cancer. John Wayne, a legend in his own time, influenced the minds and attitudes of the American male young and old. He represented the male American hero, the silent, but aggressive spirit of manhood. His walk and movements were mechanical, his voice was harsh but soft, hiding an under-current of anger and violence that exploded when he was pushed. His movie roles symbolized the gentle protector giant, the ultimate in the good guy, marshall freedom fighter, preserving peace with the might of his big fist. He was a living symbol of the American way in the world needing to be protected from the bad outlaw of communism.

His impact resulted because he believed in his image. In real life he was similar to the characters he portrayed on film; he was a hard-driving, hard drinking man. He became his role, and his true identity as a man was hidden behind his chewing tabacco facade. He made the movie the **Green Berets** because he believed that the Vietnam war was necessary to keep the world free of communism. He even stated to the national press his support for the war in Vietnam.

I respect the man for his conviction, but he was so wrapped up in his "All-American" image of a man that he was blind to other human features that finally became the deadly cancer that took his life. He fought within himself against another side of his human nature and turned it into the enemy which finally ended his long enduring battle.

His death, marked the end of an era of the Teddy Roosevelt, Custer, Daniel Boone and Davey Crocket image. When he died a part of a national image, hard-driving American male died with him.

His death marked the beginning for a new kind of male image, one of androgyny. A man who could be tender, passionate and nurturing, while possessing dynamism and a zestful spirit. Males no longer had to be saddled with images that modeled "man against himself." Young males can grow allowing both sides of their natures to emerge. They could begin to draw on all the unique and multiple human talents and resources that live within them, without systematically shutting some of them down.

Men today can choose a softer, more flexible and integrated style without forfeiting their strength of maleness. They can lessen the taut and rigid posture, choosing to trust life's rhythmic streaming within and among others around them. They no longer have to fear the invasion of others and can embrace them in shared contact.

As men we can reach out to one another, supporting, caring and becoming the fathers we never had to ourselves as well as being the sons we were unable to love with wholeness and integration. We can communicate, listen, and be heard in ways that have before been foreign to us because we either feared that no one would understand or did not know how to act when someone did.

As models for future young males, we can teach them that it is not only okay to shed a tear when hurt, it is healthy. Our modelling can show them that size and muscle strength is not complete strength and that depth, awareness and compassion must be included. We can demonstrate a shared relationship with other males without making them our competitive enemy. We can model true sportsmanship by teaching them fair play and that the integrity of playing is much more important than winning.

The choice to be our whole male selves is following the path of the heart. A path that connects us to others, the environment, the world society and most importantly to ourselves in a loving way. Men who resurrect the love hidden behind the walls of deception, socialized through our well-meaning society fathers, will be guided by its force of healing and wisdom. This love will fill and light their empty dark places.

Everyone needs love. This is especially so for men. We have learned to settle for "objects" as love subsitutes or living out our needs through others, marching through relationships in an overtly aggressive fashion.

The time has come for us to bridge, to be living models of a new and healthy male. Allow the archetype hero portion of ourselves, the John Wayne image, to die. He and his kind are now part of history. They had their time, now let us begin to embrace ours. We have the option of becoming more complete males, stopping the war-like conflict against ourselves and unhealthy competition against our fellows. We must be aware of our strengths, our weaknesses, all the ingredients that make us men and most of all, human.

CHAPTER **VII**

'Brothers': Men Need Close Male Friends

"And let there be no purpose in friendship save the deepening of the spirit. For love that seeks aught but the disclosure of its own mystery is not love but a net cast forth: and only the unprofitable is caught.

"And let your best be for your friend. If he must know the ebb of your tide, let him know its flood also. For what is your friend that you should seek him with hours to kill?

"Seek him always with hours to live. For it is his to fill your need, but not your emptiness.

"And in the sweetness of friendship let there be laughter, and sharing of pleasures. For in the dew of little things the heart finds its morning and is refreshed."

— K. Gibran

Last Christmas, I found myself moping and being somewhat depressed. I was working on my book, and beginning to write the seventh chapter entitled "Brothers: Men Need Close Male Friends." I was having difficulty starting, and felt disoriented and out of touch with not only the book's process but my own everyday process. I thought that I was experiencing the routine "writer's block" which is customary in any writing process. But, this feeling was like a grieving, a loss. All I understood was there was a hole inside me that was sucking my energy and draining my enthusiasm for writing.

I spent an evening with a good friend who immediately sensed my sadness and weariness. She listened intently while I attempted to unravel my thoughts and buried feelings. I talked while she gave me impressions of what she heard me saying beyond my words. She confirmed that I was indeed experiencing grief having to do with a loss of someone or something. By the end of the evening, although several glasses of wine had numbed my pain and warmed my insides, I was realizing that I was sincerely missing my friend Rob who had moved to California only a few weeks before. Since I was out of town when he left we were unable to say goodbye. I missed our times together, sharing our thoughts, feelings and humor. When we were together

I felt good, excited, enriched and nurtured. Our relationship was a special kind of relationship, uncommon for most men. We could talk about anything, sitting for hours and philosophizing, we literally created beliefs and theories as we engaged in mental discourse. I loved his mind, his brightness and wit. At times, especially in the company of others, we had fun fusing our wit by throwing out lines that sometimes only made sense to us. We were actually quite humorous, and turned our friends into the audience, getting them going, too. To have a whole group of people on the same wave length of a fast roll of humorous dialect is great fun. Rob and I would do this often when we were together. He fed and nutured my soul as I did his. We had a special way of rolling off any sparks of the competitive which is so characteristic of men's relationships. We both were able to use these moments and turn them into opportunities to expand our boundaries. This became a challenge to find creative ways to use our limits and conditioning and roles to go beyond ourselves. We were able to touch and ignite the child part of ourselves and launch into hours of playfulness. When necessary, we would shift into a serious mood and respond with caring, attentiveness and resourcefulness. We were able to accept and respond to one another, not only as men, but as fellow human beings. I admired, respected and believed in him as he did me. We both cared about one another's separate lives. It was such a joy to embrace him whenever I saw him. It felt good to hug another man that I cared about and loved. We did not let social etiquette dictate to us, greeting each other with a hug in the office where we worked, on the street and in restaurants. We were not afraid to be different and challenge the entrapment of our socialized male roles, and strengthened each other in doing so. I admired his challenging, risking quality as it strengthened my own. We could be close as men, loving, caring, challenging, learning, and teaching with one another and we did not fit any sexual stereotype. Just because we were physical, feeling good with each other expressing human and loving embrace, we were not sexual in that sense, yet we were unafraid to feel the energy within us when our bodies touched during our embrace.

Rob and I were able to be the way that many women are able to be with one another. We could be close, loving, interested and supportive. We were able to be like brothers, as expanded as that word can be defined in human relationship terms. Our backgrounds were very different and so were some of our interests. He grew up in an upwardly mobile family, the son of a doctor whereas I came from a poor family. We were rich in spirit. Even though Rob and I came from opposite ends of the social spectrum, our friendship was somewhere in the middle; in a human place that stretched far beyond our social roots, and our upbringing. We met in the middle zone of human relationships; the place of acknowledgement of human worth and dignity. Our relationship has enlivened and touched me beyond my maleness. We have shared mentorship roles while being the active learners. Our relationship has been the spark of humanity that I believe exists in men, between men, and that lies hidden behind all the layers of misinformation and distortion.

It was painful to say goodbye to a dear friend who had brought much joy to my life even in such a short time. I felt the grief and was glad to know that it was possible to feel such depth for another man. The war contest is over-emphasized as a way to deal with human misunderstanding. I'm so glad that it is possible to share and know love between men and in our daily lives. It is one of life's special gifts. Rob is my brother and I ache inside with the knowledge of my loss.

Most men's relationships are externalized; defined by relationships in business, sports, hobbies and with the contact of male friendship inter-mingled within these. Beyond these regimented relationship styles most men have few, if any, close contacts with other men. To be open and trusting without some practical agenda usually does not exist. We have been so brainwashed that other men are our opponents in a competitive man's world on the sports field and in the market place. The cues exist for the right behavior we must practice in our dealings with other men. Everywhere the effect of this estrangement among men can be seen in the isolated, lonely lives of men who have become part of the slow death process of limited unhealthy contact. Men need the deeper contact with other men and to release homosexual fears. They need to re-learn or perhaps learn for the first time, how to freely and gently reach out and touch other men. To be able to reach out and be comfortably embraced by an accepting hand, touches that common brotherhood place in all of us.

This chapter provides some opportunities for men to explore and exam-ine their relationships with other men and to seek viable alternatives that move us towards healthy bridges between ourselves and other men. It is only when we look, listen, and dare to ask important questions that we are able to alter some of the self-destructive patterns we have learned from our fathers and their fathers before them. Once we get to the roots of the problem, we can hope to heal, starting a new kind of developmental and alternative pattern for living as a male.

Our choice is either to remain enslaved in our rigid styles of relating as men or to choose a new way of being with men. Perhaps by planting new roots and healing our wounds we can bring more choice into our lives and challenge the compartmentalization of the usual conformist male position of relating.

INTIMACY BETWEEN MEN

I once offered a men's workshop in Salem, Oregon that was to be held in a secluded setting between Salem and Portland. The setting would give participants an environment of support, safety and a chance to be free of the hassles of city living. Shortly before I was ready to leave, I was called by the workshop's organizers who told me that it would have to be cancelled due to lack of registrants. They shared some of the reasons that they felt the workshop did not materialize. There were well-presented brochures and newspaper advertisement support. Some of the men who orginally stated their interest in attending gave the following reasons for not registering; previous engagements, being out of town and lack of cash. The director of a counselling center and a friend and colleague of the organizers, stated the main reason for lack of registration was that men did not want to commit themselves, that is, they were wary of being intimate with a group of strange men in an isolated setting. He had attempted to organize a group of single fathers to help deal with the rising issues resulting from single parenting, but found these men unable to commit themselves to a group activity with other men, even though the purpose was healthy and meaningful.

After the conversation, I thought about the director's feedback. His comments matched the findings already presented regarding men's groups of any kind. Although a pocket of men have set up men's support groups across the country, many others have failed. In talking with some who had been part of a men's group, their experience was that they found it difficult to commit themselves to an ongoing group experience for more than a few sessions. They found it difficult to reveal themselves beyond the intellectual "verbal masturbation," and when they did allow themselves to be vulnerable, they either found it to be a very positive event or one that was terrifying. Those who were committed to finding alternative ways of living and releasing some of the rigid, unhealthy attitudes and masculine behaviors in their personal lives, seemed to gain the most benefit from the group's support and bonding. Those who were searching for answers but were unable to stretch themselves beyond the security of their male role image only had a small taste and retreated back into the partial comfort of their masculine positions.

Obviously, some of the these attitudes would explain the lack of enrollment in my weekend workshop. The issue which requires further exploration is that the real reason for men's lack of participation is that men are afraid to reveal their deeper selves and to share themselves intimately with other men. Behind the excuses and rationalizations lie the sources that invariably block and sabotage men's ability to be open to other men.

Men need and desire close contact with other men but have been convinced through their masculinity training that this contact does not serve the best interest of the individual male. The strong messages we have been given are very much alive in our day-to-day living process. These are not growth-producing but serve to keep us confined within our pits of inner fears. As we attempt to break free, we come face to face with the ghost messages or our past masculine training that seem so real and yet do little but hinder our present reality, confusing and contaminating our thinking, feeling and perceptions. What we often preceive as real is nothing but a portion of the present reality steeped within our past learnings. When we see how powerful and alive these processes are, we can change some of these habits which prevent us from blossoming beyond our socialized roles of being a man.

One of the area where men learn to become blocked is their intimacy surrounding their sexuality. It is extremely difficult for a man with overly feminine qualities such as a soft speaking voice, sensitivity and creativeness. Whether he is heterosexual or not, his life can be very difficult because he is different. When a man possesses such characteristics it does not mean that he is gay. Some gays are extremely masculine in their self-expression. Many of us have swallowed the taboo messages that state if you are too sensitive and express it, watch out! You may be suspect! In my years as a professional therapist I have learned that most men have a very distorted view of their sexual selves. We have equated the size of our penis and our performance with it as the basis of our sexuality. The media portrays men such as Humphrey Bogart, as the strong, silent type who does not need anyone for anything but when he does want a woman, it is for only one purpose. The socialized message is that intimacy is something that occurs during sex. Beyond this expression, to be fully open and vulnerable is not the way of the "normal" male.

I wish to share a personal experience that taught me a very important lesson. While living in Santa Monica, California, I was involved in a professional training program as part of my graduate studies. While there I befriended a fellow trainee. We enjoyed one another's company and were very comfortable with one another. Harry was gay and very active in the L.A. gay community. He had been married for twelve years and was now in a gay relationship.

One day, Harry invited me to his house for lunch. When I arrived Harry was on the phone so I kept myself occupied by reading some of the brochures that he had collected from various workshops and courses. I picked up a leaflet that was published by the gay community and began to read it. I soon began to feel very uncomfortable and felt like I wanted to leave. I began to imagine Harry propositioning me to have sex with him. I saw myself feeling awkward. I did not want to be involved with him sexually but still valued our friendship. In the past I had had some negative experiences with gay men who had propositioned me. I realize now that they struggled as much as I between feeling good with one another as special friends and experiencing confusion in sexual areas. Those painful memories were now bringing out anger and resentment, which I was now directing towards Harry. I was restless, feeling overwhelmed by these past events which were making me uncomfortable in Harry's prescence. Finally, before I was about to explode from the internal pressure, conflict and mental images, I stopped, took a breath and told Harry that I needed to get something straight between us. He listened as I poured out my fears and my painful past experience with a gay which ended our friendship. I felt much better once I told Harry how I was feeling. Harry said that he was glad that I had spoken with him because he was picking up on my discomfort and did not understand what was creating it. He told me he was not in the least interested in me sexually and he was committed to a long-term relationship. He felt, as I did, that he wanted to have our friendship grow. He was aware of my sexual perference and saw no reason why we could not enjoy our closeness as friends. He shared a painful experience that left him feeling distant from friends. He had had a negative experience with a friend when he was married and both of them became frightened when they started to feel more intimate in their times together. It was a difficult time for both and their friendship ended with missing information as to why they felt such a struggle in being with one another.

I was much relieved to hear Harry's story and to know that I was not the only male going through sexual conflict in regard to my feeling close to men. Harry helped me see that I was only focusing on half of the issue and was absorbed by my own memories. He also helped me see more clearly my own hangups about my self-image and how this had been distorted into fears of homosexuality. I began to realize that one of the greatest fears of heterosexual men was to be gay. We are held back from experiencing more of our gentle, sensitive qualities for fear of being labeled as feminine. To express our feminine aspects does not indicate that we are gay or even potentially gay. Our images of homosexualitiy and heterosexuality have been so distorted by masculine "shoulds" and "should nots" that we are unable to distinquish between our sexual impulses and our desires for loving and nurturing.

This distorted view of our sexual selves has influenced how we feel about ourselves not only as men, but as human beings. I believe that it is vital to our understanding as we seek to know ourselves in healthier ways, to clarify what sexuality fears are real and which are remnants of our masculinity training that turn our fears into sexual concerns.

A men's organization in Chicago called "Men Against Cool" has incorporated a very effective re-learning activity that helps men work through those areas of inhibition and fear. They bring in men from the gay community to share their feelings and knowledge regarding sexual issues between men. This has helped men untangle some of the distorted ideas and beliefs held since boyhood. They have learned that many of their fears of homosexuality are unfounded and are actually self-images that have been distorted and twisted often due to repressed feelings which create an overly active imagination in the the sexual areas. Being out of touch with our feelings has a detrimental effect on our being intimate with other men and ourselves.

To break down the walls of inhibition regarding intimacy with one another as creatures who need closeness and physical nurturing, we must un-learn some of the destructive relating patterns which serve to keep us at a "safe" distance. We need re-education with proper information which provides a balanced perspective. It is necessary to confront many of the hidden images and memories and remove the fear from these areas. These fears come from the same cesspool that any form of prejudice is born. Prejudice comes from a denial of parts of our humanity which is linked with self-hatred that becomes projected upon the external world. In this light, our distortions of our sexuality that block our potential for intimate contact becomes a prejudice against oneself. Until we reclaim our power of being more fully alive and dissolve many of our unfounded fears which stem from misinformation, our choices for intimacy will be limited and short lived.

By sharing with other men we can lessen the common fears we have about the new males we are becoming. We need to let go of our guards of protection and be aware that we are no longer enemies, if we ever were at all. We need to remember our special shared intimacies with a boyhood or other friend and know that these were real and worthy friendships. We know that we lost that special essence of contact when we began our climb in the man's world, incorporating the necessary learnings that made us successful competitors. Loss as a result of this socialization is common. We still secretly yearn for such special bonding with a male friend. Some of us who are fortunate have been able to retain a lasting close friendship with another man which has outlived the pressures of society that dictate what is "normal." These men have committed themselves in the truest sense of the word as brothers.

Those who can commit themselves to learning with other men, supporting them in difficult times and honoring their growth as human persons, will find a lessening of the pressures now felt with women who ask for deeper contact and intimacy. They will discover their relationships with women to be more rewarding and less strenuous. Relationships become more harmonious when partners are not responding to one another as dependent children. Men need contact with other women beyond the principal relationship as do women. Women can develop special bonding with each other which is supportive for transformation and for retaining self-confidence and self-esteem. Men can also bridge gaps between themselves and other males and free themselves to enjoy more positive relationships. When men have relationships based upon trust, respect and honor for one another, the potential for improving their human condition is greater. To change this world of chaos and confusion requires a relearning of the intimate contact we once had as boys; when the sky was fresh, animals were our friends and our comrades shared our dreams and our imaginations. To be fully alive is to breathe the deepest of life's intimate treasures. An openness to this unknown which is beyond what we have been trained to believe as men, will change our contact with the world and our brothers of various colored skins, language and culture. True intimacy is being open to the fullness and richness of life.

THREE SPECIAL MALE FRIENDSHIPS

Little is expressed regarding men's friendships beyond the basic movie or television scene where two men are engaged in working together through a major crisis situation. Men's friendships are, at best, depicted in the kind of team work comraderie expected in the corporate marketplace to "get the job done." The friendship is merely a token exchange to utilize the human resources required for completion of a task.

Though very little has been written about close male friendships, they clearly do exist. It is my purpose to reveal some examples of such friendships which offer viable, real life models of deep, intimate friendships within the boundary of the masculine norm.

A book entitled **The Best of Friends**, by David Michaels, provides a dramatic account of fourteen men who braved the perils of poverty, natural danger and other unique events. These men began their relationships as school chums and roomates in college and they are reconnected during their careers. They committed themselves to their enduring friendships as important parts of their lives. Their relationships stood the test of romantic involvements with women. Michaels states:

> "So it has turned out to be a book about another kind of romance. In these profiles you will find men whose friendships have been strong, enduring and intimate, yet not complicated by sexual love. These men who have illustrated, with their respective recollections, the issues, conflicts and pleasures of intensely close male friendships; men who have characterized, in the language of their particular friendship, the personal history they share and the strengths and weaknesses of personality upon which these friendships have grown."

Michaels illustrates the fullness of one another's lives that each pair of friends were able to share. These men had a deep connection to enhance the other's growth and development. They were also supportive during times of despair and downfall.

These men's relationships could be placed in the archives of rare partnerships or "soul ships" of human experience. Michaels further illustrates this bonding through the words of someone expressing his deep love for another man in the 15th Century:

"If you press me to say why I loved him, I can say no more than it was because he was he and I was I."

What these relationships have in common is trust, honesty, integrity and love which are essential to any worthwhile relationship. Men can learn in spite of their conditioned training, to have solid, warm and intimate relationships with other men.

I have chosen to mention three of the seven relationships. I believe these do exemplify characteristics common to all seven relationships. I will highlight each relationship's qualities and describe briefly some of their histories. I will then follow with a brief evaluation exemplifying how the qualities contained within the relationship do exist in all men's relationships behind the "learned opponent contest."

The three relationships that I will discuss are as follows: John F. Kennedy/K. LeMoyne Billings; Buckminster Fuller/Isamu Noguchi; John Belushi/Dan Aykroyd.

John F. Kennedy/K. LeMoyne Billings

John F. Kennedy and "Lem" Billings came together at one of the East's most prestigious prep schools where graduates are expected to continue to Harvard, Yale and other Ivy League institutions. They were roommates at Choate and managed to get into more than their share of trouble. If any rules could be made, these two found ways to break them. At one point they were expelled and later reinstated and put on probation. Although both were students in high standing, their conduct was not befitting to the pride of their families or the school. Both had older brothers who had been awarded special honors in scholastic and athletic areas. John's brother, Joseph junior, had been chosen as the Harvard football pick for scholastic achievement, a high honor for a prep student. Lem's brother, Tremaine, had been president of the class of '29, captain of the football team and had lettered in three other sports.

John and Lem, unlike their older brothers, were not model students. They were seen as rebels and trouble makers. The headmaster referred to them and their kind as "mukers." The authoritarian headmaster and staff prided themselves in keeping "mukers" in line. John and Lem started a "mukers" club in their class, which consisted of twelve of their closest friends. These club members were lovers of excitement, adventure and most of all, mischief.

They became such close friends that Lem enrolled for an extra year in prep school to be with John. Eventually, they both graduated and up until that time were constantly in each other's company. Lem became "one of the family." He was invited to the Kennedy's estate in Massachusettes as well as to their Palm Beach summer home. The Kennedys were very fond of Lem.

Following graduation, John went to Harvard and Lem to Princeton. They still made time to be with one another. John continued on to Law school and then became senator while Lem went into corporate business as a top executive.

When John ran for President, Lem was very active in his campaign. After John's Presidential election, Lem was a regular visitor to the White House. He had a private room set aside for his use during these visits. Lem attended as many social functions and engagements as the members of the cabinet. Once while on the Presidential yacht, Lem was introduced after a general on the Chief of Staff, as Lt. J.G. Billings, a rank remaining from his days spent in the naval reserve. This introduction was an example of the President's humor. When Alan Shepard came to the White House to receive the Distinguished Service Medal of honor for his historic space flight, the President introduced Lem, with a straight face, as "Congressman Billings." Lem often found himself in deep water as he was expected to pull off being a senator, congressman or military person. This charade was the humorous and challenging type of game that John enjoyed.

When President Kennedy was shot in Dallas, Lem huddled in the corner of his office and cried. His tears joined with thousands more worldwide after hearing the tragic news. Some say that Lem never recovered from his best friend's death and that the event hastened his own. Lem died of a heart attack one day before the anniversary of John's birthday. It might be possible that his heart attack symbolized a broken heart which never mended following the loss of his dearest friend. The minister who gave the eulogy celebrated Lem as a "prince of friendship." His coffin was lifted from the plot and carried high off the ground as a gesture of final honor. Later, bottles of champagne were cracked as a final toast to Lemoyne Billings. Eunice Kennedy Shriver stated in an interview with a Pittsburg newspaper, "Lem was President Kennedy's best friend, and it is my impression that the feeling was mutual."

COMMENTS

It is difficult to capture the true heart that existed in this relationship. Much of their caring was expressed through the playing out of their wits. John seemed to be the mastermind behind many a shenanigan. Not many of the American people had a chance to witness the wit and genius humor of President Kennedy. Lem was probably the one man outside of the family who knew John intimately.

Their mutual deep devotion to one another is what stands out in this relationship. Lem was one of the few people, aside from foreign dignitaries, who accompanied John in the presidential helicopter to Camp David. It would not be a surprise if Lem Billings had had in some manner, a hand in shaping some of the Kennedy admininstration's policies. Friendship seems to have a strong influence upon shaping one's thinking, beliefs and feelings about life. It stands to reason that political policy could also be influenced by this special relationship. Kennedy's love for Lem was shown repeatedly in his sharing of his political and family life with Lem. Their relationship brought a richer, fuller life to both of them.

Buckminster Fuller/Isamu Noguchi

"Both men stood five feet five inches tall; both were self-reliant, aloof and vigorous; both were readily adaptable to any environment or predicament. Together, they were like a pair of cats who always landed on their feet."

Fuller and Noguchi's friendship spanned fifty-two years. Following a meeting in a Greenich Village cafe bar, where Fuller often lectured about his space-age technology, Noguchi and Fuller became as close as their independent, free-spirit dispositions permitted. Fuller, initially, took on the father and/or mentor role. Noguchi was fascinated by Fuller's ideas of design and the universe. They would frequently engage in philosophical dialogue each coming from a strong-minded and fixed perspective. Simultaneously, they were open to each others ideas and added to those ideas with brotherly support and respect. Fiercely independent, neither wished to go beyond the vulnerable ground which separated them. They shared a rare kind of mutual interdependence.

They shared a special friendship at a distance for to get too close, beyond the passion of their intellectual embrace, would have left them open for a potential parting of ways. Each was aware of his strong differences and nourished the common element that made him greater in combination with the other.

Fuller's relating style was to be in constant intercourse with the cosmos whereas, Noguchi related to the material shapings of his art through sculpture. Noguchi would say of his friend:

"That's his way. So let him be. I don't try to interfere with him and he doesn't interfere with me."

Their relationship embodied the '60's sub-culture slogan "Do your own thing." Their mutual gifts of creativity and wisdom, which gave their works world acceptance, fused into a greater collective sense of strength. This compliment of each other's special gifts surpassed the adolescent need for separateness.

Fuller, a scientist and technologist, perceived the world in such a way that he was able to supply the words, the content of a particular idea. Noguchi was somewhat limited in this respect as he held loosely structured, impulsive perspectives. Both felt that schools were "ignorance factories." Despite Fuller's time at Harvard and Noguchi's pre-med year at Columbia, they felt formal schooling served no real purpose.

Their relationship was a perfect blend of left and right brain compliment. Noguchi was a right-brain functioning artist while Fuller was a blend of scientific logic balanced with a definitive amount of right-brain intuition. As they engaged in their discourses, each provided the balance which kept each both teacher and student. Each gave to the other that which expanded his assets assisting him to become more whole, more integrated intellectually. Noguchi's intense emotionality, which was expressed through his passionate impulsiveness shredded Fuller's tendency to be locked in his idea patterns of logic. Fuller's ability to bring fragments of an idea together, was a teaching example for Noguchi's artist process.

Within their lives, both have been recognized for their contributions to the world. Fuller's "geodesic dome" and Noguchi's "akari lamps" are acclaimed all over the globe. They enjoyed common friendships with public figures such as Indira Gandhi who held each of them dear to her heart.

Once while lecturing, Fuller saw his dear friend enter the room. He stopped the lecture, moved into the aisle and embraced his friend revealing the true admiration and connection that such a friendship of great depth and time brings to flourish.

The acceptance of their unique individualities threaded a special friendship bond between them. Fuller called their relationship "omni active" meaning it was the quality of contact that existed among humans on an universal level.

COMMENTS

Fuller and Noguchi's friendship sparked of the usual pattern of men's relationships between persons of strength. Their strength existed in their thriving desire to bring the world to the depths of their seeing. Both ahead of their time, they were equally connected to the stream of reality of which the world today is just beginning to be aware. They both could envision a world that consisted of a global and cooperative exchange with one another and the universe. Each offered his visions in somewhat different forms. Through their differences they provided one another with the edge that balanced, preventing the other from getting carried away on a tangent. In many respects they served as one another's anchors.

Their conversations at times moved into the realm of debate, and as in most men's relationships the competitive spirit was bound to create no-win situations. The importance of winning an argument or stating an idea was not the most exclusive priority, however. Each was able to see the "friction point" or ego boundaries of the other, and rather than trample on these sacred grounds, allowed the adversity element and friction to disperse. Their friendship was worth far more than one single idea or philosophical treatise. As stated by Fuller, regarding their discussions, "It was clear that he wanted to make a point, and then I'd let it go because I really value our friendship much more than whether or not he wins those points." This statement exemplifies the character of a true friendship between people. How many potential growing relationships fall by the wayside when one or the other competitors "needs" to win an argument unaware of the justice involved in conceding or compromise. How many male relationships are doomed from the start because of our programmed desired to win and be ahead of the next guy?

Dan Akroyd/John Belushi

Dan and John were as close to brothers as was possible. During an interview about his first meeting with John backstage after his performance in Toronto, Dan recalled. "It was kind of love at first sight. The friendship was almost instantaneous." They were like two souls searching all their lives for something to make their lives more complete and upon their initial meeting knew this other person was what they had been searching for.

Their relationship was a full friendship where every dimension was explored except, sexuality. They were business partners, artist-comedian colleagues, mutual emotional supports and both mentors and students to one another. They both acted as protectors, this was more Dan's role towards John. John was the wild and crazy one on stage and he liked to carry on this hard-driving, hard-drinking and consuming style in his daily life. Dan the more practical, did not engage in such indulgences, other unhealthy practices which are part of the lure of the entertainment world.

Belushi and Akroyd's talents, together created a very unique chemistry which is necessary in the world of comedy. Akroyd was the introverted, mellow nice guy while Belushi's wildman, daring streak manifested itself in his extroversion. John polished Dan's "rough edges," bringing more life to his deeper and hidden "wild" parts as Dan brought some calm and softness to John's hard and speedy side. They each provided a special kind of "spicy persona" that illuminated sides of themselves that needed a broader, deeper expression. More than a relationship, they had a co-operative exchange with each other which placed them on stage and in life as, co-creators.

John and Dan's relationship had a kind life preserving and growing impact. Dan was the kind of loyal friend that John needed and his devotion taught John the value of a true friendship.

Even though they were of the blue collar, working class spirit, considered "man's man," they had a deep excitment for one another. Dan said once:

> "I'm not a homo, and neither was John, but when I saw him come into a room, I got the jump you get when you see a beautiful girl. It was that kind of feeling. It was that adrenaline — that pit-of-the-stomach rush. He was always exciting to be around."

John possessed the nerve or fearlessness that often held Dan back in his practical stance. It was John's persuasion that brought Dan to the cast of "Saturday Night Live." Dan had been reluctant to take the plunge into live television performance. Dan admired John's ability to take risks, leaping beyond logical, security and practicality. Had it not been for John, Dan might not have been the success he was on "Saturday Night." John seemed to have that second sense, that atunement that told him when to jump.

At times their friendship showed much of the same character as that of Tom Sawyer and Huck Finn. They travelled together, and though they could afford first class airline flights, they once elected to deliver a second-hand, 88 Olds for a drive away from New York to L.A. They turned their office-apartment on the 17th floor of the Rockerfeller Plaza into a dwelling that became a tree-house sanctuary. They even had bunk beds built in the apartment. This hide-away became the escape from grueling schedules of Saturday Night. On many occasions, their apartment-treehouse became like a club house, with many of their friends from Saturday Night's cast and crew using it as a retreat. This sanctuary became the place where they worked together to create many of their TV sketches. Each made special contributions to the development of their creative materials. Dan was the meticulous writer-inventor and could spend hours at the typewriter while John was impatient, hated detail and lacked the attention span required for a full creative evolvement. John provided his spontaneous train of comedic genius, an inspiring flash of the moment while Dan could produce every tiny morsel as thoroughly as a craftsman of Swiss watches. Dan undertook the mechanics and John provided the spark, the infectious juice. Both created sketch pieces that brought out the consistent electric quality when these two connected their minds and hearts. Dan was the brains of the creative organism into which John continually breathed life. It was this special sharing, this blending of spirits that made them so popular and great friends.

There were times that like any friendship, the friendship was tested. Akroyd, being a champion of the written word, grew tired of John's laziness and mistrust of words. They argued and ended up feeling the hurt. This had been one time that each realized that their differences could come between their friendship. They had argued before, but this one served as a message to save their growing friendship. Later, Dan moved to another office-treehouse, and like before had bunkbeds built, so that John could also have a place to share in his "private space" where he spent so much of his time writing.

John's wife Judy was not excluded from their friendship. Judy became Dan's very close friend serving as a surrogate mother or a big sister. When Dan first came to New York to do "Saturday Night Live" he slept on a foam cushion at the foot of John and Judy's bed. John included his friend in all parts of his life. This special giving of his "all" was a paramount example of how much he admired and loved his friend. John was a hit with Dan's Canadian family. On his first meeting, after leaving the car, John, did a somersault and landed on his feet in front of Dan's parents as if to say, "I'm Dan's best friend and here I am." Dan was also close to John's younger brother Jim, who automatically shared a similar kinship. It seemed that those who knew them or were family, immediately felt the closeness between these two friends. This quality of contact seemed to suggest that the same resonance that was felt between John and Dan also existed in the special feelings they each shared with other friends as if sharing a unique quality of human contact existed in all their relationships.

The greatest display of comradeship took place following John's overdose of heroine and cocaine and it marked Dan's last gesture of love for his comic sidekick. At John's funeral in Martha's Vineyard, Dan dressed in blue jeans, motorcycle boots, a police jacket and wore a confederate flag as a scarf around his neck, to pay homage to John's rebel nature. With the "Blues mobile" serving as John's hearse and the family cars behind him, Dan led the entire funeral procession on his Harley motorcycle, gunning the engine loudly as if to arouse John from his deep and permanent sleep. Those "buddies" riding shotgun in the Blue's mobile at one point, jumped out and urinated on a pine tree, having been drinking during the entire ceremony.

The service, presided over by a priest from Borton's Holy Trinity Albanian Orthodox Church, was a good one that left many weeping, including Dan. John had always said he had wanted to have a Viking burial however, Dan didn't feel bad about not fulfilling his friend's last wish. His careful way, and strong protectiveness led him to a more subdued last rites for his friend. He worried about all the press boats taking pictures of the funeral pier, or that the fire would go out, or some other disturbance to interrupt John's farewell journey. Dan, ensured his friend was buried in the Vineyard where they had spent many good times together, a place where their friendship had been christened many times over, where they had a chance to be alone, free from the madness of their fame and public attention, a place that seemed to embody the divinity of their friendship. John Belushi and Dan Aykroyd possessed the prototype of friendship that personified that rare breed of male partnership that envelopes the mental, emotional and spiritual ingredients that truly complimented their common traits, styles and blended their souls' depth. They truly were in all senses of the word, Brothers.

COMMENTS

John Belushi and Dan Aykroyd's relationship possessed certain characteristics that could only be possible with the qualities that each possessed. Their love and respect for one another blocked any possibility for the usual and routine masculine distance and competitiveness to get in the way.

Like other examples sited, they had a high mutual regard and rather than attempt to win over one another in some kind of competitive race, they opened their hearts with one another. Like two musketeers, they practiced their brotherly love with one another and as a service to their fellows as was seen in their showmanship. Both, in their own special way, opened their souls to the public, their audience, just as they had done with one another. Each was the other's audience and greatest fan. It is sad that John's self-destructive attitude stopped him "dead" on his journey to becoming more than just a comic star, but a legend in his own time.

Dan's sharing of that journey was probably for both of their lives, the highlight and the most memorable of their separate and shared journey.

A FINAL NOTE

The media and literature in the field shows that most men's relationships with other men are filled with remarks of outdated, distorted patterns and habits of repression, competition and unhealthy contact.

These three friendships among the seven the author wrote of offer a description of some men's relationships that are possible, positive, nuturing and healthy. However, these relationships are unique and they provide the "best" of the possibilities for men's relationships. The qualitites and resources existing within these men independently and interdependently, contain the ingredients that savour the depths of humility; loving their friends and loving themselves.

These relationships augment the characteristics that I believe exist in all
people, man or woman, statesman or scientist, fisherman or baker. These
human character seeds are a part of humanity we have thus far failed to
explore and understand to its fullness and breadth. We have only touched
the tip of the iceberg. Now its time that we go deeper.

FATHERS AND SONS RE-UNITED WITHIN

Can you remember when your father told you he loved you? Can you
remember when you told him you loved him?

Like most men, I can't remember ever hearing my father say he loved me.
Perhaps he did when I was a boy but I have no memory of it. I told my father
just a year ago that I loved him, having not seen him in years. I was an
anti-war activist in the 60's while my father was a medal winner in the
pacific campaign against the Japanese. This caused us to see the involvement in Vietnam quite differently. As a result we did not speak for eight
years. I tried a few times to cross the barrier, but it didn't do any good.

One of men's greatest areas of relationship difficulty is with their fathers
and most of us still carry the deep scars from the pain of distance and
alienation experienced in this primary relationship. I also share in this
burden. This vacuum that separates fathers and sons has escalated in the
last century taking its toll upon the healthy development of the young male.

As one man put it, "I think a relationship between a father and son is one
of the most, if not the most important in society today, yet it is probably the
most troubled."

Shere Hite, the bestselling author-researcher of female sexuality, has
completed another report on male sexuality. She has compiled one of the
most extensive nationwide commentary's from men regarding their ideas
and feelings about sexuality, relationships and love. From her report, I would
like to present several of the comments men have shared about their father
relationships which I feel will help other men reflect upon their own.

"He never shows weakness or strong emotion. I know he loves me
but I want a more explicit statement of that. We did not have a
physically close relationship. No hugging, kissing etc."

"I don't consider that I was a close to my father. All that I can
remember about my father was that he was always drunk or
beating me for something that I didn't do."

"My father is a dominant, controlling man. He accepts responsibility well, but is inept in interpersonal relationships, except on a very casual basis. I now have a comfortable relationship with him, but very superficial."

"We are not close. He is very quiet - distant. I respect his dedication to the family but I never talk to him about important things."

"I'm not really close to my father. I respect him more than he knows, and I know that he cares about me. But we did very little together. He is strict, and used to have an explosive temper, which has mellowed considerably in the last few years. He grew up in the depression, and refuses to throw anything away because he 'might need it some day'. I love my father, but I can't talk to him about anything but practical and mechanical matters."

"There were times of closeness with my father. The occasions of togetherness were generally working experiences. That's where I'd find him. The times of talking in more than just perfunctory ways were rare. I would not say we were especially affectionate. I sensed at times that I was his favorite, but my respect for him bordered on fear. He was a person not easy to know."

"My father and I rarely spoke about anything. It was basically a yes and no relationship, with 'sir' following each reply."

"I don't remember us having much of a relationship when I was a child. It seemed to me that the only time he would talk to me was when he yelled at me for something."

"I can remember being punished and corrected with a spanking but I don't recall being held or cuddled. There was always the younger brother or sister so things were pretty hectic."

"No memories in this area, except punishment and spanking, which I dreaded, probably from fear."

"Most memories involve punishment by my father. Humiliation was his forte. His classic was when I wet my pants slightly when we were visiting relatives and he told me to tell everyone present I had wet my pants and to show them the spot of urine near my fly."

"I remember being held very often as a youngster, but as I reached age five or six, it was expected that I played 'boy' games and would not be cuddled nearly as often. I definitely remember being spanked."

"My Dad was not physically affectionate, though my Mom was. Dad was very severe concerning discipline. The black belt loomed in our minds like the rack in the Inquisition. And he applied psychology that he learned in the military. He would draw back for the first lick, then not deliver. He would repeat that until we were almost relieved to get hit. I don't bear him any ill will over it (I usually had the spanking coming) but **I AM UNABLE TO TELL HIM I LOVE HIM.** I do him favors and give him stuff, but I'll never be able to say the words."

The picture painted here from the dozen comments displays relationships where the father is a disciplinarian, punisher, provider, and is silent and has difficulty in expressing deep feelings or talking about important matters with his son, rendering the relationship mundane and superficial. Many stated that they actually feared their fathers, never knowing when their fathers would explode with unexpected anger and/or rage. Most of the comments shared the common theme of a gap between their fathers and themselves and an inability to close this gap. Characteristic of these men's comments is the painful, deep longing, desiring of another kind of relationship with their fathers. This distance factor is also important as alienation, physically, emotionally, intellectually and spiritually covers such a ground of human experience, that a father and son standing next to one another in the same room, are actually extremely isolated.

I identify strongly with these comments. Similarly, I was unable to talk to my father about anything other than sports, working or other everyday routine matters. I feared my father and remembered the sting of his belt when I was being disciplined and punished. Once I actually had to lie, saying I had committed the theft of a neighbor's pop bottles when she had really given them to me. He was convinced of my guilt and was going to beat the confession out of me. I had friends who had their father's beat them until they were black and blue. Spankings were a part of many of our lessons in becoming men. Our fathers were the ones who dealt out our education in conforming to the rules of manhood.

For many men, we have a place inside of us that lies half-dead and numb. It is empty, yet consists of deep, pent-up and bruised emotions that are due to the hidden societal expectations. These emotions are also composed of longing for the loving close contact we desired from our fathers. We learned that being close to our fathers wasn't supposed to be part of growing into a man. We were taught to mimic our fathers. They taught us the best they knew how, modelling men we were to become. The ache we once felt, that urge to embrace our fathers, diminished in time because eventually we accepted that "that's the way it is." Fathers and sons were taught not to be close, at least in the physical sense, and eventually, in every way. By cutting off one piece of human contact, we eventually cut off the rest. For most of us men, this learned pattern of becoming a man was more of a rule than not. It was the acceptable norm and most father and son relationships modelled this kind of non-intimacy. The sons carry this kind of relationship into their adult and family lives and continue it with their own sons. It is no wonder that men are scared to death of close, intimate contact with other men. From the beginning we are taught that men do not become intimate with one another. Our fathers, brothers, playmates and the whole community continually remind us of this script. We learn that if the majority conforms to this conduct and practice, it must be right. To have differing feelings is a mistake and wrong. So, our nation has produced men who are practicing the "right way" of interacting with other men and this has made, and continues to make them miserable. When men reflect on the teachers of this "right" manly behaviour they know this teacher to be their fathers who were modelling what they believed was right. This was not only unhealthy for them but for us as well.

Freud and others, in their theories about father/son relationships, have created some problems regarding understanding and discovering alternative ways for sons and fathers to relate. If we believe and practice that fathers and sons are natural competitors for the mothers love, of course a son's behavior following such a script is going to reflect this attitude. A father who believes that his son is a threat to his domain, is going to use power tactics to keep his son away from his territory. The relationship evolved from such a belief system is full of deception, games, and intimidation. Freud theorized that, as long as a man's father was living, he was not a truly free man.

When we stop practicing and living outdated beliefs, and seek new and healthier alternatives we will not be doomed to the kinds of father-son relationships that cause us always to be at war with one another. Some men are trying out new alternatives of being fathers. Some are present at their son's birth and respond to him from a proud, loving and respectful place. Men will begin changing centuries of practice that create such a deep emotional and psychological distance between fathers and their sons by challenging their learned patterns. We who dare to open doors to within which contain the half-alive emotions toward our fathers, and pour some life, some new understanding into the past, will be the men who will start the chain reactions that will affect the whole domain of father-son relationships. Whether we are aware of it or not these relationships we had, and have now, still live within us.

When we meet a new man, we are reminded of the feeling of alienation and distance between us and our fathers which warns us to keep a safe distance. When a man, out of friendliness and love, reaches out to us, it recalls the many attempts we made in our lives to connect on an intimate level with our fathers. His gesture is a painful reminder of having been rejected and makes us guarded.

If we are lucky, we had a more positive and loving relationship with our father. In turn, this can be passed on to our sons and modelled with other men who accept male closeness. Some of us have been fortunate in having father substitutes and bosses, teachers, uncles, grandfathers and others became our mentors for a better and healthier way to be men. Many of them failed to establish this with their own fathers and perhaps their own sons, and desired a second chance at establishing closer, more vital relationships with men.

The more energy, love and understanding that goes into lessening the distance between the memory images of our father relationship that exists inside us, the more we are able to dissolve the unhealthy pattern that has hardened us in our man-to-man relationships. The inner images become the outer reflection of who we are in our relationships with other men. If inner images are father and son in battle, then other men will be opponents and warriors to one another. If the images are full of mistrust and lack of respect, the outer reflection will consist of caution and manipulation. If the images are positive, loving and respectful, the expressed behavior towards men will be of gentleness, respect and sharing. When we change the inner pictures of our past experiences, our outer experiences then have greater potential.

Many men are still blocked and confused regarding their relationships with their fathers. Some have attempted to close this gap with some success. Others have not been successful and many, both fathers and sons, take their unfinished business to their graves. Many men experience emptiness and suffering, and only another man who truly understands can help them heal this wound. Of course, many do not reach out, nor do those men who do understand come forward. This is another manifestation of the earlier alienation and distance experienced with their fathers.

Someday men will be able to provide the loving support to one another that we need. It requires much work, change and commitment to move towards better men-to-men relationships. It requires a re-examination of our most important relationship with our fathers. Honest appraisal of that relationship and a desire to release negative pictures of events we carry into memories is necessary. A deep understanding of our own father part of ourselves can be given to the rejected, angry, hurt and lost little boy within. Yes, we have been wounded but over time we will be better men as a result. We have learned what kind of relationship we don't want to have with our sons and men-brothers. It will take a commitment on our part to re-discover the nurturing, female part of our father part and to begin building the bridge to the child-son part of ourselves; a filling in of the gap that has kept us locked into positions of polar opposites. When we can be a proud father of the son inside of us, just as we would be of a son from a physical birth, we will be the nurturing and loving parent that our "son" needs. By healing our inside relationship, we do not repeat the old patterned, negative relationship. By changing with a deeper understanding of our father-son situation we can begin to see our fathers were like us, sons who once attempted to know their fathers, and the cycle continues back for generations.

We are products of generations of learning and have acquired numerous value and belief systems that were passed down. Now, our responsibility as men is to be the vanguards of a less rigid, closed system of men's relationships. We can heal ourselves, our relationships with our fathers and have an understanding. We can develop rich, vital and life-enhancing relationships among men. We can respond to other men as brothers, composed of the seeds of father, grandfather, son plus the nuturing and loving female parts of ourselves. We can become better parents to ourselves, learn to care for ourselves and can learn better communication. Someday, hopefully, we can forgive our fathers for the pain we experienced thus, ending the "oedipal curse." Its time to heal the wounds, close the gap, and resurrect a new way of developing relationships between fathers and sons. Our sons and their sons will reap the benefits from our actions now. Then what this man believes could be possible:

> "If only I had a warm, loving, physically affectionate man for a father. A father-son relationship must not be fraught with hatred and a tense tyrant-subject relationship — it cannot work that way. It will ultimately destroy one or the other or both.

> "It must be A WIDE OPEN RELATIONSHIP IN WHICH A MAN WILL GIVE OF HIMSELF AND OF ALL HIS LOVE SO THAT HIS SON WILL BECOME THE MAN HE WANTS TO BECOME.

> "The father should **not be afraid to touch and cuddle his son.** His son needs it. Also a father and a son should be able to express anger to one another freely as well as love, AND EITHER SHOULD BE ABLE TO SAY ANYTHING FREELY."

MY BROTHER MYSELF —
UNLEARNING PREJUDICE TOWARDS SELF AND OTHER MEN

> "There are no "mere" men — moral splendor comes with the gift of life each person has within him a vast potentiality for identification, dedication, sacrifice, and mutuality. Each person has unlimited strength to feel human oneness and act upon it.

"The tragedy of life is not in the fact of death but in what dies inside us while we live."

— Norman Cousins

Each time we turn another man into an opponent, we move closer to being his enemy. Each time we use another man as an object, a pawn in our mechanical games of climbing the success ladder, we lessen our ability to respond to life with our hearts. Each time we commit an act against others in the manner of policy or profit, we shrink some of our own potentials for being human and fully alive.

When we step on another man's idea, dream or feeling, we are also stepping on a reflection of our own chances for living. The more we dehumanize another man through our thoughtlessness and heartlessness, the more we move towards being less human and less a man. "Macho" is a shadow of the image of the decayed, unexpressed hidden and hardened facade turned inside out. It is not the healthy, human expression we are seeking through exhibition of bulging muscles and hairy chests.

Prejudice is a terrible thing. Prejudice or learned hate, as I refer to it, exists among men in Eastern and Western cultures, Latin American countries and those of the African and Middle East regions.

Various ethnic groups war against one another carrying on a learned pattern of hatred that has been passed on for eons. The young learn that those of a different group, tribe or culture are lesser persons. In North America the blacks, Mexican Americans and Indians are considered to be minorities. They survive in a society in which others wish they were non-existant. Although the white man's religion teaches equality among all races, proclaiming all to be God's children, some develop the idea that they're better than the others.

When I was fourteen I had my first lesson in prejudice. I was attending junior high school at the time and one of my best friends, Eddy, was a Mexican American. We had grown up together playing baseball on the same teams. One night I invited Eddy and his two brothers over to my home and introduced them to my stepfather and family. After seeing them home, my stepfather took me aside and began interrogating me about my friends and associating with Mexicans. Finally, he strongly suggested that I stay away from Eddy and 'his kind'. I was shocked, hurt but mostly angry. Eddy was my friend and I thought a lot of him. His being Mexican just made it more interesting. His family had different customs and I was keen to learn about them. From that time on, I found myself becoming judgmental of Eddy's behavior and finally I could not stand to be around him and stopped seeing him. My father's words had done their damage. I was beginning to see Eddy as a "Mexicano," whereas before I saw him as my friend. The seeds of prejudice had been planted and began to grow inside of me. Although Eddy and I spent other times together later on, our friendship was never the same. We moved from the close bond of friendship to the rigidity, and closed mindedness of prejudice, losing the human non-judgmental acceptance that goes beyond skin color and culture.

Use your imaginations for a moment and imagine race reversal. If you are white, think for a moment that you were born to another race. If you grew up where alot of blacks or Mexican Americans lived, then see yourself as either. Imagine being brought up in such a home and attending school as a minority person. How would it feel to be judged because of the color of your skin? How does it feel to be made fun of and called "nigger" and "chili picker?" One author who dyed his skin black, actually discovered the harsh reality of being a minority black in a southern white community. He had an entirely different perspective living in the skin of a black man. However incredulous, his story was true and he feared for his life in the community of whites.

Often we find ourselves as majority whites, even being judgmental and prejudice to our own kind. Sometimes we treat one another as "niggers". We exploit one another in industry, and in every other area of society. It surprises me that white skinned people will spend many summer hours baking their skins to the perfect golden tan to become darker skinned persons. Often they remain fixed in their learned, prejudice attitudes and practices, no matter how subtle.

Looking closer, even the developing men's awareness movement is composed mainly of middle class whites. Where are our brothers of black and brown, yellow and red skin? The human potential movement composed of mainly middle class whites and most other groups are white dominated except for maybe civil rights groups and NCCAP.

When we rid this planet of its many social diseases a priority should be to dissolve prejudice. Prejudice spreads its hatred and evil amongst us all. All races have a heart that beats and that has a passion for life, it is our minds that have been twisted and soured. Children are unaware of this decay and hatred until we teach them the scripts.

Upon embarking on a new path for men, let us not forget the true essence of what makes up brotherhood. It takes the touching of our souls, beyond our skin colors and belief systems to remind us we all came into this world free and innocent of the lust for hatred, and disgust for our fellow man.

We will leave this world the same way we came into it. Hopefully, we can walk side by side, with our fellow men who of any race knowing that true soul, spiritually, is all colors and races.

VIII

The Everyday Workshop

**PART I: PROCESS: Getting a Grip on Transition
Bridging Our Inner and Outer Experience**

**PART II: PRACTICUM: Strategies for Transition:
Coping with "Endings," and "Inbetweens," and "New Beginnings"**

The word transition is derived from the latin word meaning "to go across." It is often referred to as a kind of bridging process.

The theme of this book is male bridge building with each chapter continuing to bridge and shape the structural context of the male journey, moving from the archaic to the new. This chapter has even a more explicit focus on this theme. It deals with the "mechanics" of bridge building. Within this context it is the life process called "transition."

Today books, movies and studies attempt to explain the meaning of life's transitions. Various theorists such as Levenson, Vaillant, Lowenthal and others have expanded upon the earlier works of Erik Erikson, one of the first developmentalists to outline some of the steps of the human life cycle. Carl Jung, pioneer of the human psyche, can also be credited with contributions to the "individuation" of one's growth towards wholeness. With all such information, it is still painfully obvious how inept modern people are in fully understanding the significance of life stages and the changes that accompany them. While women are doing their best to outline, pinpoint and match their know-how with cycles of life changes, they have only touched the tip of the iceberg. Men are more in the dark still even though we have chalked up many hours of research on adult development stages and made our scholarly contributions. This we have done. What we are having the most difficulty with is the actual experiencing of episodes of transition. Our difficulty lies in the living through the turbulance of the process, even though we haven't much choice in the matter. The rate of change in roles, responsibilities and shifts in relationship styles such as single parenting, pushes us into it. Whether we are aware or not, when it becomes our turn to go a few rounds with nature's mentor of the life cycle, we must deal with it. Why?

Firstly, we have been trained, as men, to live in the world of the external. The domain of transition is internal so women are better prepared and more able to call upon the strength, wisdom and healing of the inner world. They know intrinsically and trust the inner rhythms of the self. Men have learned to conquer and control the urges and functions of these deep, inner places. Men have come to mistrust these feeling places and substitute the "rational" aspect, believing it to be superior. As a result, we have created a continuous masculine/feminine dichotomy that governs both the inner and outer realms of life's experience. Therefore, when we feel changes, these inner stirrings, we become confused, numb and have the urge to control for fear of what these feelings may release.

Secondly, we are not prepared to handle these periodic episodes of life change. Our ancestors designed elaborate rituals which were honored as rites of passage, for the male's life journey. Today, we have no such sacred ritual beyond getting drunk or having our first sexual experience. These offer no attunement to the deeper spirit of our maleness and speak only of immaturity and lack of respect for oneself and for life. We are without viable role models, tools or appreciation or spiritual sense of the meaning of being a true human male. If we look to our fathers, grandfathers or other men in our lives to give us balance and direction regarding our life cycle, they are often too lost or fearful to fill our need. They too, have been stripped of the meaning of the male bond and the wisdom of the inner meaning of the psyche. We are left on our own to discover the means to understand our transitions. "Flying by the seat of our pants" can bring with it its share of adventurous learning, but our core needs never get addressed.

Thirdly, we have been locked into our roles of what a man is supposed to do and be. It is frightening to surrender this script; the tendency is to hold on to these cemented images. We fear that in release of such, we will die or worse, become helpless, unintelligent and out of control. The "image" has given security and purpose in life regardless of what life has presented to us. It has become a means to our end. This is insufficient. It is a shock to look beyond these roles and external image trappings and see the pit of emptiness within. We seem to be able to take a loss, but have difficulty in acknowledging the emptiness which is too close to the truth we have learned to conceal, especially from ourselves.

Finally, we have too much investment and training in having women take care of us. Our mothers nurtured or smothered us sometimes leaving us needing genuine affection but resisting it for fear of being swallowed by the ghosts of our mothers or other female energy. We are basically novices when it comes to self-care particularly regarding inner wounds and past events that return to haunt and teach us. The reasons are numerous and are discussed in other chapters.

As men, we are searching for some very important skills and capacities which can aid us in our transcendence or major life challenges.

This chapter could be called the "tool box" of the book. It contains some strategies for living and working with transition. Without a doubt, we need tools to aid us in these times of transition whether these occur in relationships, careers, life styles or within ourselves. I see this need growing daily as I interact with men in my practice, workshops and in social situations. They are experiencing great difficulty in understanding the inner shifting of a transition period. I remember my own transition and wish I had some of these guidelines to help me. Please remember these strategies in no way substitute for deeper exploration which comes from therapy or some other discipline that brings clarity and development. They serve as maps or planks of a bridge that can help connect memories, feelings and insights that emerge during the transition process. These must be tailored to our needs, situations and style of learning and growing. I provide the skeleton and the indvidual has to build the frame.

This chapter is called the "Everyday Workshop" which is divided into two parts. The first section is called "Process" and outlines a brief description of the transition process and some strategies and processes for working with and identifying certain stages or phases. I also incorporate a model that I use in my personal life and work which has been born out of my own transition journey. I call this "The Wheel of Transition" which is used to identify eight separate, integral processes that occur within the overall transition process.

The second section is called the "Practicum: Strategies for Going Through Transition." Here, I provide some activities, exercises in the form of inventories, sentence completions, etc., which can be used in our daily routines as we deal with our transitional experience.

Transition, whether we understand it or not, is here to stay. The better equipped we are to handle it and work with it, the more positive will be the outcome, increasing our sense of life and our part within it.

"There are ways of facilitating transitions and they begin with recognizing that letting go is at best an ambiguous experience. **They involve seeing transition itself in a new light** and understanding the various phases of the transition experience. They involve developing new skills for negotiating the perilous passage across from the 'nowhere' that separates the old life situation from the new."

— **Transitions,** William Bridges

PART 1

PROCESS: GETTING A GRIP ON TRANSITION:
Bridging our Inner and Outer Experiences.

Within the following, I provide a description of the stages or phases characteristic of the transition journey. I have simplified this for easy comprehension. I prefer to work with a few in an effective, long lasting manner than deal with superficial, vague knowledge. I encourage fellow-journeymen to go beyond what I present and use these as a springboard for further focus and development.

TRANSITION: HOW TO RECOGNIZE IT

William Bridges has written one of the best books on the market regarding the transition process. It is easy to read and understand and I recommend it to anyone who desires further study in this area. In, **Transitions,** he identifies three main phases of this process: 1. Endings, 2. A period of confusion and distress, 3. New beginnings. Other authors suggest different aspects of pertaining to these primary phases, but I see Bridges as outlining these most specifically for this chapter's intent. We will focus upon these three phases in our investigation. I have used these in my workshops and find them to be invaluable guideposts for identifying the episodes of the transition process.

The first phase "Endings" is exemplified in the phrase, "Letting go is hard to do." It usually takes the longest to complete. It also is the most difficult and most painful to experience of the three so, it is often delayed or denied. As a man related to me while struggling through his divorce, "I know I have to let go, but I don't know how." To end a relationship that one has invested much of oneself in, does not magically happen overnight. The completion process has within it, a deep sense of longing coupled with resentment. Often we carry the residues of past endings with us into our beginnings. If we are unable to distinguish between the old stuff and our new merging desires and needs, we prolong our healing and integration of the process, even more so. These can continue to influence our choices for alternatives in habits, beliefs and feelings. They can take control, dominating and curtailing the potential development for vitality and flexibility. Many men experience "endings" as finality which causes us to hold on even tighter to the past. Our adjustments are often difficult experiences due to this resistance. Rather than accepting this phase as a necessary death of an old life pattern, needs and experience, we tend to respond with more rigidity and control of our processes and those of others. This can make a changing process almost impossible, even volatile or potentially dangerous. Men's violent expressions towards themselves and others are examples of men acting out this fear of letting go, and living through the death aspect of transition.

Statistics indicate that men remarry sooner after divorce than women. Often they do so within months of a break-up. This is now changing but does remain a solution for those who have trouble dealing with "endings." Theorists indicate that how we learned to handle endings in our childhood has a great deal of influence upon us as adults. Endings bring pain, and sorrow as well as assorted extracts of past experiences to the fore. If we are able to live through this passage with fullness, we will benefit in the end.

"I don't know whether I am coming or going," could be an apt description of confusion as one goes through the second transition phase. We may feel confused, disconnected from others, ourselves and life. We experience isolation like we have never known before. Feelings of abandonment are common. During one of my episodes, I constantly asked myself, "Who am I? What are my needs? What is my purpose in life?" When in the company of others, I was convinced I was transparent, that they could see right through me. I felt helpless to do anything about it. I had images of being in a crib, of wearing diapers and being as helpless as an infant. In moments of strength, I was able to gain perspective and learn. I chuckled to myself at the image of me wearing diapers beneath my three-piece suit. Another valuable picture of this "inbetween" stage was given by one of my workshop participants. He said,

> "I feel like two giant hands have come out of nowhere. One has me by the balls and the other has slapped me across the face and my head is still spinning."

This is a graphic description with which many can empathize. During this inbetween phase, we are like lost souls; our outer world does not make sense any longer and our insides are a churning swirl of past events and experiences. We do not know who we are because what we thought we were and believed ourselves to be, is dissolving gradually. Our mind plays tricks on us and we are unable to distinguish thoughts from feelings, memories from dreams or physical sensations from signals that we are coming apart. We ask, "What's it all about, Alfie?" and "Alfie" doesn't know either!

The second phase of transition is a time to reconstruct our psyche, change our perceptions, attitudes, beliefs and habits in our lives and how we view the world. We have no control during this time except for our daily routines at work and at home. This second phase prepares us for our resurrection. It is a time to roll away the stone which hides our fears and holding patterns, as we stand on wobbling legs reaching an awakening of our life's purpose and beginning the building of our bridges. We will eventually cross these bridges with renewed spirit and vitality.

The third and final stage according to Bridges, occurs when we have completed the first, ending phase. We may be experiencing new relationships, work or living situations, but it is only when our inner voice points "our way" that we are actually on the path to "new beginnings." This requires time and a straightening up of our lives, a taking care of unfinished issues. If these are still obstructing our path, we cannot hear our inner signals. It is essential during this period to distinguish between our wants and our needs. It is easy to become swept away by our past, immature aspects of ourselves. It is a time of re-alignment and giving a natural order to our psyche; a time to match our inner and outer processes and learn to center ourselves. During this phase, we can become highly creative, the sowers of new seeds. We finally can understand the meaning behind becoming self-nurturers. Our thinking begins to integrate with our feelings. Primarily, our illusions about the external world are revealed. We realize our own ability to set necessary limits; we become more accepting and see ourselves as having much to learn. We begin to feel an excitement, a zest for life, similar to what we experienced as young boys. New beginnings are highlighted by a zest for living, our energy says, "Go for it!"

The three phases are blueprints to be used for pinpointing where we might be at this time in our journey. They can also clarify and piece together what we experience during other transition periods. Whether we are dealing with an "ending" or swimming in the chaos of the "inbetween" or ready to begin the "cross over" to new direction, these are tools for use regardless of what phase you are in now.

THE WHEEL OF TRANSITION

As earlier stated, this model has evolved from my own transitional experience. I begin with a brief description of these eight processes, followed by a more in-depth presentation of their function including examples of how they relate to understanding one's own inner and outer shifting.

What it is and how can it be used?

The wheel serves as an inward and outward reality tester. It is comprised of the following eight processes:

1. Re-Discovering
2. Re-Evaluating
3. Re-Awakening
4. Re-Learning
5. Re-Organizing
6. Re-Affirming

7. Re-Cycling
8. Re-Applying

These are natural processes that we use to some degree in our lives already. Each process is governed by and connected to the mental, emotional, physical and spiritual systems of life and change. At times, we might move through these more rapidly than others and can move through several processes simultaneously. To understand these processes and their function, it is best to utilize our intuition. If we try to to find the scientific, rational base for what is happening, we become too analytical and can lose our depth and connectedness to the process. When we are able to be guided by our intuition these processes become more illuminated within us. We are able to "know" the workings of these cyclical processes by moving, shifting and re-organizing our inner selves. They are part of the re-alignment process which occurs during great change in our lives. They serve to match our inner experiences with our outer actions.

The characteristics and governing activities as they relate to the eight processes are as follows:

1. Re-Discovering - strengths, skills, knowledge
2. Re-Evaluating - actions, patterns, habits
3. Re-Awakening - physical, mental, emotional, and spiritual wisdom
4. Re-Learning - better use of skills, learnings of origins
5. Re-Organizing - time, life events, and use of energy
6. Re-Affirming - belief in self, others and life
7. Re-Cycling - already acquired skills and resources
8. Re-Applying - new learnings and skills in daily living.

THE WHEEL OF TRANSITION

These processes are the most recognizable following completion of the first phase of transition, "endings." These eight processes then become like a crew of re-construction workers whose sole task is to begin the renewal process and adapt to a new situation. Each process has its own function yet works in co-operation with the others. Each is a vehicle for facilitating strength, awareness and reclaiming one's power.

The following is a more in-depth description of the eight processes exemplified by vinettes and related events.

RE-DISCOVERING

To find new ways of living we must become seekers and challenge many of the beliefs and ideas that we learned and used as building blocks to construct our lives as men. Through this questioning, seeking process we challenge ourselves to look beyond what we have taken for granted as the truth or reality. This journey takes us into new territories which initially seem alien to what we have accepted as "right." This journey gives us a fresh perspective on beliefs and attitudes. We begin to understand ourselves and our relationships with others in new and refreshing ways. Those who have experienced a loss or deep, significant change know this to be true. It is through this process we find deeper meaning in our existence, strength and resources we did not know or believe that we had. We can now react to situations with certainty and calm that before left us anxious and afraid. We begin to see our vulnerability as the budding place of our strength and source for vital living. Here we must be honest with ourselves, and know our true strengths, gifts and limitations.

This phase or re-discovery guides us to our authenticity and the wisdom of our inner teacher-healer selves. As we re-discover, we also re-claim missing parts of ourselves, those we thought were no longer and were denied.

Re-discovery can be a time for celebration. I had been teaching a "Brothers" workshop in Northern Alberta in which Robert, a physician, was a participant. I was impressed by his gutsy ability to probe and take risks to discover that which was beyond his role as a man and a doctor. It was obvious that he was in the workshop to gain something and he wasn't wasting his time or energy in the process. He had set a goal for himself yet, I doubt if he was conscious of this.

He stepped forward at one point to work on an issue with his mother. I sensed his aprehension in expressing his feelings in this area. I asked him to choose two men from the group; one to play his past and one to play his future. He had one man sit in front of him and one sit behind him. Before I could even begin to work on the issue with his mother, he began to hyperventilate. I had him take long, deep breaths and finally he stopped hyperventilating. I asked him to express his feelings at that moment, and he shouted, " Mom! Let me go!" He repeated this again and I asked him to do so a third time. We stayed with this part of his process a while longer, but did not seem to be making any headway. Frustrated, I decided to alter the situation by switching the placement of the two men who represented his past and future. I told him to hold tightly to his "past" and yet try to escape while shouting, "Mom! Let me go!" Very shortly, his anger came out and he shouted, "You fucking bitch, I had to do it your way or you'd reject me! You fucking bitch!" Tears of release came; he sobbed loudly, his body twitched. I took him in my arms and held him as his father never had. His tears lessened and he began to express a series of insightful statements of which he had been previously unaware; "She took my balls and she took my old man's too! We were both trapped!" We worked a bit more in this area so he felt completed with what he was able to deal with at that time. His eyes were sparkling, his face was flushed with color whereas before his face looked as though it was part of a mask which he hid behind. He looked alive now and very much in the present. His discovery released the block that had prevented him from seeing clearly for a long time. That day, he re-claimed his male soul.

This dramatic account of one man's journey through the re-discovery process speaks for itself. It is an example of the numerous releases that can occur in this phase.

Bill, personnel manager for a large oil company, husband and father of three children, made a discovery in the relationship area. He was surprised when his wife requested a divorce, but did not object. Three years before her request, she had gone back to school where she met a man and had had an affair. This led to other affairs which Bill later discovered. They had a very traditional marriage and shortly after her divorce request, they sat down together and calmy divided up their material possessions. The divorce was uncomplicated, clean and smooth.

Bill, showing no signs of remorse, threw himself into his work. About six months after she left, he began to have nightmares in which she appeared as a witch-like entity. He would awaken from these dreams in a cold sweat. These nightmares became daymares shortly after. He resigned from his position after being told to seek help or take a leave of absence until he got himself together. Bill finally went for treatment and through group therapy learned he had never resolved his feelings towards his wife's leaving and having affairs. He learned from family patterns of being the eldest of five children, that he always put others' needs before his own. When his wife expressed her needs through her actions, he was at a loss as to what to do. Finally when he touched his stored anger towards her, his parents and others who had taken advantage of his good nature, his eyes really opened. Today, Bill has re-married to a wonderful woman whom he loves and the feeling is mutual. He has experienced Body Therapy and has learned to express his needs and feelings and he likes doing so.

RE-EVALUATING

During the internal process of Re-Discovery, as we seek and question, we are confronted with the values we have built our lives upon. These values are the anchors of our beliefs which manifest through our attitudes and behavior towards ourselves, others and nature. It often takes a crisis or loss of something or someone dear in our lives to bring us to a point of examination of the values which guide our lives.

For example: we have learned that keeping the edge on competition was the most effective way to get ahead in business or academia and suddenly, through no fault or our own, a recession makes it impossible to succeed in this manner. We become failures by our own standards. This failure makes us re-examine what went wrong both subjectively and objectively as well as what it means to be a failure. We begin to look at ourselves from a deeper perspective. We question our original scripts about winning and begin to question whether this is really worth the consuming time and energy required. Now, we begin to filter out some of these arrogant, inflexible messages, seeking new, healthier ways of being a winner in life. This process aids in the discovery of new choices which we do not have under extreme circumstances.

Anwar Sadat was forced to re-examine his role as Egypt's leader and the conflict with Israel, upon the death of his brother. He realized he had to find the courage to stand up against hatred and opposition in order to negotiate peace between the two nations, even if this meant his own death. President Carter and Menacum Begin also had to shift from some of their deeply ingrained beliefs to bring about the Camp David peace treaty. It was necessary for these great men to open their hearts and minds to new possibilities and proceed with the actions to break centuries' old patterns. Deep evaluation of past values and behaviors can change one's direction, lending new perspectives for thought.

RE-AWAKENING

It is common knowledge that man uses only a small portion of his potential. During times of profound, deep change, we expand the boundaries of our minds, emotions, spirit, memory and awareness of our body's energy. We begin to see **more** of what we possess on all levels and our greater capacities and talents. Disabled people are aware of this transformation when they are challenged to make use of other capacities in order to compensate for their loss. During a major change crisis, we discover some of our own disabilities that limit us comparably to a disabled person. We see that many of our human capacities are asleep and hidden within us and we have been living in a semi-comatose state for much of our lives. This awakening process illuminates our thinking, emotions, creativity and the meaning of life itself. That which was asleep and dormant now becomes fully, intensely alive.

Laughter was the ingredient that best-selling author Norman Cousins, in **Anatomy of An Illness**, found as a cure of his terminal illness. After being diagnosed by several doctors as terminal, Norman embarked upon a search which ended in triumph. He collected several Marx Brothers and Chaplan films, secluded himself in his private hospital room and proceeded to nurse himself back to health. Comedy was the exilir for his ailing soul. How did

Cousins know that laughter would heal him? He did not. When people are told they are dying, they can react in two ways. One is to passively accept the diagnosis and prepare oneself for the final hour and the second is to strengthen one's will to live. How often does one's life hang on the edge of the strength of the will? There are countless accounts of those who were close to death or were told that they would never walk again but miraculously they bounce back, renewed. Being on the edge of death can re-awaken a deeper appreciation and will to live. One is confronted with, "To be or not to be."

Not all end in triumph. I recall a patient in my group when I worked in a psychiatric hospital, my first job. He reversed the re-awakening process. Mack had attempted suicide three times, he was the model of a broken man. He had failed at three marriages, his career as a newspaper reporter and had drinking problems. One day he decided to kill himself by jumping in front of a subway. To his surprise, the driver saw him in time and applied the brakes. Mack ended up in the hospital with a broken arm, leg, a fractured pelvis and numerous cuts and bruises. I do not know what became of him. Perhaps, being immobile for months in traction gave him the direction to give life another chance. Often we do not get another chance or we miss the signal indicating that our options are open.

RE-LEARNING

Mark Twain taught us long ago, "to never let school separate us from education." In our modern world we have depended upon what we were taught in classrooms to prepare us for reality. It is painfully evident that this learning is insufficient and has even aided in limiting the growth and expansion of human knowledge skills for life. The powerful transitional shifting is required to shake us into the realization of this limitation of our learning experience. This process puts us back into the "kindergarden" of life, reminding us of this limitation. Transition re-aquaints us with the blocks in our learning and the disconnection from true learning. It is a renaissance process which gives us a second chance to start again, using choices more wisely while we experience the rebuilding of our beliefs, habits and potential possibilities. It is a chance to "learn how to learn" again and to appreciate life as a teacher and to respect its powerful guidance and lessons.

How many Ph.D. dishwashers do you know? Though the answer is probably few, these few most likely wash dishes out of choice not necessity. I am one of those over-educated pot-scrubbers. I had completed my Ph.D. in 1981 and had re-located to Marin County in Northern California, across the Golden Gate from San Francisco. I was broke and driving my 1971 Pinto with 95,000 miles on the odometer. The recession had hit California and it is said that when it strikes California, the whole country must also be in recession. I had been staying with a friend, later I moved to a cheaper place. I tried private practice and nearly starved. I took odd jobs and was working for minimum wage. I was used to being paid fifty dollars per hour. My car began to smoke and the highway patrol said, "Fix it or park it." I had fifteen days to do so. I found a dishwashing job in a nearby French restaraunt. When I told the owner, a Mexican-American, Jehovah Witness, that I had a Ph.D., he laughed. Initially, I was embarassed and my ego suffered for the first couple of weeks. I almost quit. Then, I began to relax into my job and proceeded to master the art of dishwashing. I became the best, most efficient dishwasher anyone had ever seen; I had it down to a fine art. After a month, I found another dishwashing job on my off hours. I was able to save most of what I made because I didn't have time to spend any money.

I learned a great deal during those months of having my hands submerged in dirty water. I quickly became very humble, realizing I was a survivor and could do anything I had to, to make it. I had sworn, years earlier, that I would never be a dishwasher again. I had done dishes in the unversity dining hall in exchange for meals. I learned that "never" was a useless word. Washing dishes re-introduced me to my survival instincts. I know now that if my career ever took a turn for the worse, I would be able to live. We never know when life will throw us a curve that challenges us to learn, once again, or to retrieve once learned, often menial skills. Someday, I might have to walk the streets until I find a restaurant sign which says, "Master Dishwasher Required: Only Ph.D.s Need Apply."

RE-ORGANIZING

All life sustains some kind of order to function. Human beings respond to a higher order of organization to adapt to living conditions and situations. Change necessitates adopting different beliefs, methods, structures, choices and a new, flexible order. This is particularly true when old forms are unhealthy, outdated, no longer serving one's needs or situation. Setting fresh priorities becomes a must. Men who are adapting to new roles and needs are forced to modify past routines, goals and actions. Their new choices must be less rigid. One alternative is learning to be less competitive and fearful. The re-organization process begins during the onset of the preceding processes. As these grow and mature, they shape the organization and facilitate the birthing of a new, less rigid, healthier system.

What quality of vision or faith is necessary for one to hit the bottom and then climb all the way to the top. Certainty and strength, which many are afraid to express, are necessary to pass the test.

Kenny Rogers, years ago, hit a slump in his musical career. His records were not selling and he was millions of dollars in debt. He borrowed more money, and determined to turn his career around. He once stated in an interview that he was prepared to lose everything and could live with such a consequence. His ability to take a risk paid off for him. Taking risks and a willingness to begin again does not have to be limited to monetary ventures. In Eastern systems, it is believed that change is the only constant in our lives. The more we can adapt to change and allow old forms to die and begin again, the easier life will be for us. Learning how to surrender to a new, evolving process is the mark of a wise, creative mind. Striking a balance between "doing and being" is a sign of a higher order of organization of our life experiences.

Those who are unable to adapt to change, often pay a very high price. John Deloren exemplifies someone who had to learn a hard lesson. His life modeled the "succcessful man." He was wealthy , rubbed elbows with the elite of society and was viewed as an innovator in the business world. When his company was near bankruptcy, he found himself caught in a F.B.I. scam that cost him his company, his marriage and his reputation. When he was confronted with signals to alter his course of action, he was unable to hear the message nor did he want to. His taste for his accustomed good life was strong. He did not want to let go and be seen as a failure. He had organized his life in such a manner that it allowed no mistakes. He had mastered the ways of the external world and had alienated himself from his internal self. He could not let go of what he had learned to possess.

Transition is a process that disintegrates "what has been." It is a re-ordering, a replacing of obsolete structures which must dissolve for the new to emerge. It is our choice to invest our energy into clearing the path for this emergence or to resist and hold on. Holding on, at best, only delays and inhibits the process which intensifies our fear and vulnerability. If the foundation that we have built for our lives is false, the transition will become a giant reflector of this pretense.

RE-AFFIRMING

During transition our attention is focused inward and by the time we look outwards again, we have undergone a deep, penetrating search from which we learn to distinguish more important priorities from less important. We become more selective in choices regarding our use of energy and how we invest in interpersonal, career and social areas. Our commitments to the important areas of our life become stronger. Our decisions are well thought out. Time and individual moments are preserved. Our place within the grand design of life begins to have more meaning.

One of the exercises I give participants in my stress workshops is as follows. First, I write this question on a chart: "What would you do if you found you were going to die tomorrow at noon?" I have people, individually, share their responses with the group. Initially, some do not take this exercise seriously and try to joke about it. Those who put more into the exercise obviously gain more from it. Some wish to be with friends and loved ones while others choose solitude. One person said he would go home and kill himself. This exercise helps to focus on the present and forget about the future. Future concerns often cause people a great deal of stress. People often feel they have so many things they "have or should" do, and expend energy worrying whether they will accomplish everything. This pace of modern society clutters our lives with excess activity. We become "space fillers" and then complain we do not have enough time. When faced with our deaths, our impermanence, we begin to appreciate those simple things in life that are valuable to us. Once we accept death as an integral part of life, we can gain more from living. Life takes on an intensity that lends us more vitality. Things and people which we took for granted become important. We see life as a gift for which we are grateful.

Rather than accept the gradual, cancerous deterioration of his life, Terry Fox, exemplified the courage of acceptance of his final days by becoming a hero in the face of the inevitable. With an artifical leg, he ran the equivalent of a marathon everyday with the goal to reach the other coast of Canada. He died before he could reach his goal. Today, each year Canadians take part in the festive Terry Fox Run to raise money for cancer research. So close to death, life was re-affirmed for Terry Fox.

An Eastern Canadian priest was ordained a few years after being in a serious accident that should have been fatal. Just before the car hit in a head-on, he prayed. In his prayer he vowed that if his life was spared, he would devote himself to his fellow man and become a priest. The doctors said it was a miracle that he survived. In a moment's flash he chose service to others over himself. When faced with death, he chose a new path for living.

RE-CYCLING

How often do we say, "I'll never do that again," only to repeat sometime in the future, "Oh no, that again! Why?"

North America is a fad-oriented society. We are always discovering new techniques, style of dress, art, etc. Of course, everyone has to indulge in these new trends. There is nothing wrong with this, but it becomes such a habit that we are not satisfied with what we have, always having to replace it with some new thing, of which we will tire eventually. We have done this with our elders, cutting off an entire inter-generational link to our past, blocking our young people from seeing the wealth of experience of our interpersonal history. If some ideas, behaviors and beliefs do not fit the fad consciousness of today, it does not mean we should let all of the past go. There are basic virtues that act as guiding principles for life. These are basic to our humanness and do not change. These basic principles have even more validity in times of stress and upheaval.

Hugh Prather's book, **Notes on Love and Courage,** tells of the richness of basic values. In the introduction, he speaks of the theme of the book:

> "I found I had been in a process of re-claiming much of what I had discarded when I was younger."

He talks, also, about the birth of his new book, **Dreams Left Burning.** He adds:

> "This was surprising because the novel was, among other things, an expression of deeply felt cynicism. At the same time as I had, with great pleasure, been turning things upside down, another part of my mind had been putting them right side up."

The way Western society deals with transition is often paradoxical. While our "New Age" thinkers and healers teach us to let go, seeing this as a remedy for unecessary suffering, we still have internalized the teachings of security and permanence. These two opposed teachings confuse us. Which do we follow? Do we give in to the "New Age" perspective or hold on tightly to that which we have always known and used? This is demonstrated in the following account.

Andy was once a highly successful finance manager in the automobile sales industry. His friends nicknamed him "The Wheeler-Dealer." He was good at his work, enjoying the benefits that come with being succesful; a beautiful home, a beautiful wife and son, two beautiful cars, etc. His life was surrounded by "beauty" he often said. With only his signature, he told me, he could borrow thousands of dollars. His favorite past time was playing the stockmarket which he was also good at. His "beautiful" life turned ugly following some large investments that bottomed out when he had been convinced they were "sure things." He lost everything. First to go were the cars, then the house and finally, his wife who asked for a divorce. The collectors were at his door, calling his office and he was being driven insane. Once he could enter a bank and sign his name for thousands of dollars and now, his name was not worth the cost of the lead in his pencil. Before he had lived like royalty and now he did not have bus fare. With no further options, he finally declared bankruptcy.

A friend suggested that Andy seek professional help and in time, he was able to pull the pieces of his life together. He went back into the industry, starting out as a salesman. Before he was training salesman in financing car deals and this time, he was on the front lines himself. He did this for some time but was having difficulty being aggressive in selling cars. He said he had lost his "killer instinct." Before people were just customers and now he viewed them as people just like himself. His values and his needs had changed, his heart was just not in it. He found himself being totally honest with his customers regarding the condition of the cars in which they were interested. His customers praised his integrity, but his boss did not. That which had once made him tops in sales, was gone.

Andy's story offers an example of a man who bought the societal message of how a man was a success. He had become greedy, selfish, mechanical, limited and driven as a result. As a youngster he was a "good boy," who was honest, enjoyed people and was friendly. As his business talents blossomed, these other qualities faded which were necessary for him to be a success in his field. Following his personal losses, these other qualities shifted back into his life once more. During his healing time, he had a chance to look at his life from the inside out. As his healing progressed, he became stronger and more human. These other qualities had not died, but only needed an opportunity to be recycled. These had been hidden beneath his success image.

Andy, to date, has not re-married and is not in a rush to do so. He now is driving sixteen wheelers which keeps him on the road most of the time. He quite enjoys this. He is not required to sell anything, not even himself. He can just be himself, "take it or leave it."

RE-APPLYING

The tail end of the transition process is the application phase. In this phase, we begin to "practice" new ideas, beliefs, attitudes and methods discovered throughout the complete transition process. We experiment with new learnings and seek the best way to incorporate them into our lives. In attempting a new lifestyle, business practice, relationships with men and women, the more we practice, the more valuable will be their use in our lives. We come to know, to understand that our lives are full of transitions which do not end. Accepting this basic life truth, we are better equipped and prepared to survive these life cycles that will repeat themselves in other times and in other ways.

The following are a few stories of what occurs in men's lives following a crisis or major shift in their lives.

Larry was in the process of getting his Ph.D. in speech rehabilitation. Following a trip abroad to "find out what he wanted," he returned and dropped out of the program. He decided to pursue his life-long hobby of pottery. Today he works as a special education teacher to finance his pottery business which has become extremely popular in Redlands, California.

Ned had been a police officer for six years in a small Ohio city where he was almost killed in a shootout. This shook him as it had been the only time he had used his gun in six years. He believed there were better ways of dealing with people. He later attended some encounter groups sponsored by the department. There he discovered some things about himself which he had not before acknowledged. He eventually became a sergeant and an instructor at the police academy where he taught "Human Relations in Police Work," a course he designed himself. It was a successful course and here he was able to pass on his belief in alternatives to force in police work.

Vick had been a land developer in New Mexico and had made a great deal of money in this business. After the death of his son resulting from a hunting incident, Vick went into a deep depression for five months. With the support of his wife and two other children, he came out of it. During this time he placed his land development business in the hands of his partner. After his bout with depression, he sold his share of the company and bought a nursery. Before it was second nature for him to bulldoze trees and destroy natural environments for his numerous commerical projects. As the owner of the nursery, he had to "baby sit" all varieties of trees, shrubs and flowering plants. He spends hours caring for his plants.

All of these men have a common story. Following a major life change their personal and/or career paths took different directions. Each went through the various phases of transition characteristic of those discussed in this chapter.

Presented here is a description of the multi-phase process which I have discovered in my own journey through transition. These can be used as a model-tool to assist **we** men in pinpointing and identifying what occurs during these phases that disrupt our lives, stir our thoughts and feelings and prepare us for a deeper experience of our self and our life.

PART II

PRACTICUM: Strategies for going through Transition:

Coping with "Endings." the "Inbetweens," and "New Beginnings."

> *"Experience is not what happens to a person. Experience is what a person 'does' with what happens to him."*

> **— Aldous Huxley**

Transitions are epic events in our lives. We, as men, are just beginning to explore just how important they are as more of us are becoming "initiates" of these cyclic life passages. To acknowledge and live through these passages brings both potentially healthy choices as well as limitations as we adapt.

We are still limited by archaic choices of self care, lack of preparation and skills for coping with the transition process. We are limited in our understanding of the workings, function and wisdom of the "inner" psyche. Our ingrained, scripted messages regarding our maleness still influence and limit our choices and actions. For many, these still control and entrap us, becoming blocks to further growth and change. However, even with these limitations, we do have some alternatives from which to draw. I believe it is time to make the decision to make "new choices" which bring healthy responses to change the readiness to partake and the acceptance of the transition experience. It is time to be a leader towards positive directions rather than a follower of outdated, stifling patterns of male conformity. To choose these new alternatives could be one of the most important moves we will ever make for ourselves and those we love.

The strategies (suggestions) that I offer here are to assist **us** through the "Endings," the "Inbetweens" and the "New Beginnings" of transition. These are not magical solutions or cure-alls; they do not halt or make the chaos of transition disappear. However, they do help to "bridge" our everyday experiences with the inner shifting of transition. They assist us in organizing situations; they connect us with our past and our present. They **do help** to lessen some of the overwhelming feelings of helplessness and insecurity experienced during periods of intense change. They can also open doors to dormant capacities and strengths and turn obstacles into positive supports.

I begin by introducing what I call a men's "LIFE INVENTORY" checklist.

This tool helps readers approach everyday aspects of their lives within a more total picture. It provides an overview which encourages identifying areas in our lives that need attention and putting these in priority, whether these be in the "Endings," "Inbetween," or "New Beginnings" phase. After completion of the checklist, I would encourage your choosing at least three areas to work on at a time. Perhaps these areas match what one is already doing. If so, good. If not, choosing at least three narrows our attention so we are not working on too much simultaneously. Then, proceed to the three sections and complete some of the activities/strategies selected and designed for the practicum purpose. It is not necessary to follow these in sequence. Try to match the activity with a need you may have for sorting out or working through a particular relationship, career or health area. I provide an assortment of activities some of which will be relevant. Choose those that fit and even try some that do not necessarily appeal to you. Use them to build upon your own skills and knowledge for dealing with change or crisis. Be inventive and create your own. All it takes is imagination, commitment, desire to change a circumstance, pattern or process.

MEN'S 'LIFE INVENTORY' CHECK LIST

Directions: Look over the various life areas in the left-hand column, put a check mark in **one** of the four corresponding columns on the right. (Choose ONLY ONE per area.)

	Change Not Needed "OK"	Needs Overall: Counselling, Therapy, etc.	Needs Information & Re-education	Needs Some Work
Self care nurturing & healing oneself				
Self Image positive & realistic				
Emotions healthy awareness & functional				
Relationships past & present				
friends, spouse,				

family, colleagues,
etc.

Life Stress
change, loss, pressure

Health
physical, mental,
well-being

Nutrition
eating habits,
diet, etc.

Spiritual
The purpose
harmony, in tune with
life, inner guidance

Note: Now Circle **three** areas that you need to work on to aid you through any stage of transition. Be as honest and specific as you can. We will return to this area at the end of this chapter.

The purpose of circling these three areas is to design our own self-contracts at the end of this chapter. Now I will begin the introduction of the three-part section of strategies for transition.

STRATEGIES FOR COMPLETING "ENDINGS"

Learning to say "goodbye" to past, worn-out thoughts, feelings and memories of ourselves, others and aspects of living involves creative thought, honesty and a willingness to look further within ourselves. Before we can begin anew, it is necessary to take care of unfinished issues. While it may not be possible to resolve all such issues, it is possible to finish some. How well we handle our endings does determine our abilities for inviting new beginnings.

STRATEGIES: **FREEING OURSELVES FROM EARLIER MESSAGES**

INTENT: As boys we were given certain "messages" by our world as to how we were supposed to be. These were subtle or direct "do's and don't's" of becoming a man. They came from our parents, relatives, teachers, people in the community and the media. I have designed an exercise that I use in my "Brothers Workshop" that is very effective in pinpointing certain message patterns that have become ingrained since our earlier days. During times of intense change, these become apparent as they come from their hiding places deep within us. Most men have found this exercise helpful for putting pieces of their lives into perspective.

What to do: Take a large, blank piece of paper and draw a small circle in the middle of the page; placing the letter "I" in the center. This figure represents you. Then, draw five other **very large** circles around the smaller, centered one. In each circle, write one of these words: Family, School, Church, Community, and World (media, ie: t.v., movies, newspapers, radio, etc.) Take a few moments to return to your earlier memories and begin to see the events, people and situations present as you grew up. Then, complete the following tasks:

1. Write **what** messages you received about **being male** from each of the five circled areas, placing these next to the corresponding circles. Write these in short form to give yourself some space. List as many as you can think of. Don't be concerned about duplication; we often receive similar messages from several different sources.

2. Indicate messages you received from men next to each of the five circles.

3. Messages you received from women.

4. Messages you received from males about women.

5. Messages you received from women about men.

6. **Who** gave these messages to you? (father, mother, teachers, boss, media, etc.)

7. **How** did you respond to these messages and **What** did you do? ie: accept them, reject them, rebel, question, become afraid or confused?

8. **Which** messages did you like? Dislike? Circle those you like and place an 'x' through those you did not.

9. Using + (positive) and — (negative) signs designate the ones that influenced your life either way.

10. Circle the messages and/or who gave them to you **three times** to show which ones still influence and shape your thinking, actions and feelings today. These can be both positive and negative influences.

This exercise is best done in a group setting as it evokes much dialogue. If this is not possible, talking to a friend, male or female, enhances the value of what discoveries are made about our earlier learnings. This exercise can be done numerous times as new information emerges each time.

STRATEGY: **RE-EXPLORING OUR NEEDS**

INTENT: Everyone, young and old, has needs and the desire to have them met. The ways we endeavor to have our male needs met is often dependant upon how we got them met or attempted to have them met in our earlier years. We may simply ask that they be met or we may resort to manipulation. If this doesn't work, we may give up trying to have our needs fulfilled. These tactics for need gratification are not new; they have been used and re-used at different stages of our life journey. We all have needs and the effectiveness with which we have these fulfilled determines our life's enhancements and disappointments. This exercise familiarizes us with many dimensions of our needs as men and how we may or may not be fulfilling the essential needs in our life.

What to do: Make three separate lists; one that contains **childhood needs,** the second is **adolescent needs** and the third represents those needs we have which are **adult needs.** Brainstorm, at least, ten needs for each list. Then, do the following sentence completion:

The way I got my needs met as a child was:

The way I got my needs met as an adolescent was:

The way I got my needs met as an adult was:

The ways I communicated my needs as a child were:

The ways I communicated my needs as an adolescent were:

The ways I communicated my needs as an adult were:

When I had my needs met as a child, I felt:

When I had my needs met as an adolescent, I felt:

When I had my needs met as an adult, I felt:

What I did when I got my needs met as a child was:

What I did when I got my needs met as an adolescent was:

What I did when I got my needs met as an adult was:

When I did NOT get my needs met, as a child I felt:

When I did NOT get my needs met, as an adolescent I felt:

When I did NOT get my needs met, as an adult I felt:

What I did when I did NOT get my needs met, as a child was:

What I did when I did NOT get my needs met, as an adolescent was:

What I did when I did NOT get my needs met, as an adult was:

Today, I get my needs met by:

Today, I communicate my needs by:

Today, what I do when I get my needs met is:

What I need to learn more about getting my needs met, today, is:

After completing this exercise, see if a relationship exists between past and present styles of need fulfillment. Are you still trapped in old patterns? Is it possible to change some of these?

Needs, are basic to our health, growth and humanity. The more skilled we become in having them met, the better off we will be.

STRATEGY: **ASKING OTHERS FOR HELP**

INTENT: In times of crisis or when we're hurting, we men often find it difficult to reach out and ask others for help. We have been taught to be strong and keep our feelings inside, unexpressed. This can be detrimental in our interactions with others and can prevent us from releasing past, ineffective behavior patterns. This exercise re-aquaints us with those whom we first reached out to for help and how they had a lasting influence upon us.

What to do: After reading the following sentences, select one of the three choices in the columns at the right. Then, fill in the sentence completion after each question.

(SELECT ONE ONLY)

	Often	Sometimes	Never

In times of crisis, I could depend upon father:

My most painful memory of my father was:

My most joyful memory of my father was:

In times of crisis, I could depend upon mother:

My most painful memory of mother was:

My most joyful memory of mother was:

In times of crisis, I could depend upon brother(s):

My most painful memory of my brother(s) was:

My most joyful memory of my brother(s) was:

In times of crisis, I could depend upon sister(s):

My most painful memory of my sisters was:

My most joyful memory of my sisters was:

In times of crisis, I could depend upon grandfather:

My most painful memory of my grandfather was:

My most joyful memory of my grandfather was:

In times of crisis, I could depend upon grandmother:

My most painful memory of my grandmother was:

My most joyful memory of my grandmother was:

Of all my family members, the one I could depend on the **most** was:

Of all my family members, the one I could depend on the **least** was:

Those of us who can, will turn to others when we need help. Some will choose female companions while others will choose male. This can indicate some hidden reason why we may choose certain people when we are in need of help, perhaps they remind us of a type of communication that we desired but did not have with our parents or siblings. We learn soon in our life the type of person to whom we can turn for help and subconsciously, we seek these people in others.

STRATEGY: **DEALING WITH ENDINGS**

INTENT: The difficulty and pain we experience in endings is often from earlier exposure to endings. What happens after we have ended a relationship, career or experienced a deep loss or failure? Do we enter a new situation immediately or take time out for evaluation, or do we withdraw for a period of time? This exercise will help us recognize certain patterns which we have for handling endings and will allow us to complete these past endings.

What to do: Select three of the **most** painful, difficult situations in your life that involved some type of ending, ie: divorce, death or failure or set-back in career. These can be chosen from childhood or adulthood. After your selection, see who comes to mind and note the feelings you experience when you remember them once again. ie: anger, fear, joy, calm, etc. Match each person to a feeling or emotion. As you do this do not be surprised to find you are talking to yourself, this is completely natural, occuring when we re-connect with part of our stored away life experience. Write down these people's names and the situations of which they were a part on a separate piece of paper, including the feelings that match that person or situation. Put this paper in a place at home or work where you can notice it, leave it there for a minium of three days and a maxium of six days. The purpose of this, is to give you some time to process what you have discovered during the exercise and to build your attention and focus upon the situations. During this time, it is good to jot down insights of these situations and to look for patterns in how you handled endings in your life. Within a few days, you can pinpoint and distinguish with whom you have unfinished issues. I use several methods to help people with completion. These are a few that aid the process:

1. **A goodbye letter:** Write a letter to each of the three people as though you were still in contact with them. Talk about the situation before and your feelings towards them and the situation. DO NOT HOLD ANYTHING BACK. Write as many pages as it takes. Be dramatic, sarcastic; whatever you have to be to release all of your feelings. Then, end the letter by thanking them for being a part of your life and wish them a good life. Follow this with a goodbye of your own style and end the letter. Then, mail the letter to yourself and once you receive it, re-read it once more and then burn it. The burning of the letter is a powerful symbol of release. Add further rituals to this process if you desire.

2. **Externalizing what is inside:** Place a pillow, empty chair or some other symbol to represent these three people as sitting in front of you. Take a few deep breaths to center and relax yourself and give yourself time to imagine those people are present in front of you. Begin with the following statement or one appropriate to you, "What I need to say to you is. . ."

From this point allow yourself to say whatever you need to, to each of the three people. You can even change places with them, imagining and giving back their replies. This technique can be modified to accommodate various styles of learning. Some people do not like talking to "empty spaces." If this is the case, ask a good friend to be with you and act as a sounding board, role playing the actual other people.

STRATEGY: **GETTING READY TO CROSS OVER**

INTENT: In Alcoholics Anonymous, one of the advanced steps of the program's twelve steps pertains to "unfinished business." During this step, the member must go back and make peace with a person whom he or she has hurt during the time of his or her drinking. This is a difficult step for many and often it takes years before a person is ready to attempt this step. Returning and facing those who have suffered because of your personal insensitivity or brutality takes courage. This completion is necessary before the person who has been a problem drinker can move on to more advanced steps. This is also true for we men who are getting ready to begin afresh, another phase of our lives. Here are some guidelines to follow to help tie up those loose ends.

What to do: Make a list of all the people in your life with whom you have unfinished business. Divide it into the most and the least important. Then, devise a means of contacting those who are under the "most important" heading, ie: telephone, letters, or personal meeting. Take time to thoroughly explore your personally held resentments and fears of those persons. Ask yourself which of these feelings are real and honest and which are exaggerations. Be honest with those people and listen to what they have to say. If they are unprepared to listen to you and choose to hold on to their own negative feelings, give them your regrets and if they are resistant to future communication with you, release them, let them go. Put your energy into people and situations that will strengthen you and your move to a more positive reality. Take an inventory of all our available resources for moving into a "Beginnings" phase. Are we emotionally ready to make the shift? If we are meeting new people, are our contacts honest and comfortable? Are we choosing people to be with that enhance our growth, rather then draw upon our energy? What about our needs, are the important ones being fulfilled? Most of all, we need to take stock of what we are leaving behind and what we are still carrying with us? What is beneficial? detrimental? Until we are stronger, and can be more discriminating, the ending process is composed of left over "bits and pieces" of thoughts, feelings and memories. The more energy we invest and commit to these "cross over" phases and finishing of "old business," the greater will be our reward and accomplishment.

STRATEGIES FOR THE INBETWEENS

The "inbetween" phase is a time of our greatest vulnerability. It is a time to re-discover the past and imagine the future — a time to open and heal past wounds; to re-organize our psyche and to prepare ourselves for new beginnings. This time needs to be approached with foresight, hindsight and above all, "inner sight" and an awareness of our present center. It is a time for commitment to one's self-care, re-education and healing. The following strategies have been carefully designed to facilitate this process. (Choose one that fits your situation.)

STRATEGY: **TAKING TIME OUT**

INTENT: We all need to break away from the hum-drum routine of work and everyday activity. This re-charges and re-vitalizes us. During this time, we take "stock" and prioritize the events and situations of our lives. During transition, this "time out" is even more essential. This is a time of **solitude** and reflection upon our communication with the past phases of our lives.

What to do: When did you last do something just for yourself? What enjoyable activity did you once do but now make excuses to yourself for no longer having it in your life? Perhaps you enjoyed a certain activity as a teenager but have now given it up because you are a "respectable" adult. It could be anything from going fishing to visiting art galleries. Maybe there is an activity you would like to try but are reluctant due to past and future expectations of success or failure in that area. Discover activities in which you would like to be involved and make a personal commitment to re-activate these experiences. Make a list of that which you would "like to do" and "used to do." Select at least **three** from the list and plan to do **at least one** within the next week. If you only have fifteen minutes of time, use it to get started. If necessary, use some of your lunch hour to begin. The essential thing is to get started with **one** thing. Pick a date in the following week's calendar and write it plus the newly selected activity down on paper, and then put this paper in a visible place. After comfortably fitting one activity into your schedule, use this same process to add the second and then the third activity to your life. Some people will be able to handle only one new activity at a time. What is important is to begin to develop a pattern that can be strengthened over time. **Do whatever is necessary** to evolve this process for "time outs."

STRATEGY: **SETTING PRIORITIES**

INTENT: The "in-between" phase is not a time to begin major new projects. It is not a time to take on extra work or activities, rather it is a time to lessen the demands upon our time and energy. We must re-organize our personal and professional lives to give us the space to read, write, meditate or walk in the woods. This time to reflect should be a priority. The following are some aids in setting priorities.

What to do: Draw two schedules of activities/tasks for a one month period, marking one as "personal" and the other as "professional." Within each category, make two columns marking them as that which "must be done" and that which "can be done." An example of this format is:

ONE MONTH SCHEDULE OF ACTIVITIES/TASKS

PERSONAL: PROFESSIONAL:

"must be done" "can be done"   "must be done" "can be done"

After placing a month of activities in the appropriate schedules, circle those which you enjoy, are interested in or have invested in regardless of whether they fall under the "must be done" or the "can be done" column. Now indicate which have to be completed within a certain time period or have been scheduled within a time frame such as appointments, etc. Those which **do not** have to meet a deadline, prioritize according to your interest and energy levels. If possible, rearrange these, beginning with those activities which excite and challenge you. Be certain you have "free time" for yourself in both the personal and professional schedules. It also helps to arrange a complete day of activities, hour by hour, to become accustomed to a timeline. Then extend this timeline to a week, and finally to a month.

STRATEGY: **THE ENERGY WHEEL**

INTENT: Sometimes when we have invested time and energy into a project or relationship, we feel drained as a result. Often, the more we attempt to change this feeling, the more futile it becomes. In time, the whole of our lives becomes clouded with this perspective, becoming chaotic and losing a sense of balance. This is magnified during times of transition.

To modify this effect, it is necessary to begin to take "inventory" of our energy distribution. We have to see where it is going, to whom, in what proportion, and what is coming back to us.

A tool I have used in my workshops is simply called, "The Energy Wheel." It pinpoints where our energy is going while providing options for reorganizing time, events, etc., to enable us to balance our input and output.

What to do: Draw a small circle with lines extending out from it in all directions. At the end of these lines draw small circles, writing within them, the various areas which you give your energy to in your life.

Choose from areas such as family, friends, work, community, etc. and write personally applicable ones in the smaller outside circles. Now, say you have 100% of energy to give in these various areas. Break down the areas as follows, ie) 10% community, 20% social, 30% family, etc. in percentages that apply to you. Then, indicate by percentages how much you receive back from these same areas. These arbitrary percentages help to pinpoint the energy you give with what you receive. Upon completion of this exercise, see which areas require modification. This exercise can be repeated and you will find that the percentages change.

STRATEGY: **WHAT CONFUSES ME ABOUT MY ROLE**

INTENT: Regarding the changing shifts in sex roles today, it has been said that women are overly certain of their new roles while men are merely confused about both. Transition magnifies this confusion of our male identities and our relationships with other males and with women.

I have designed a simple method of probing confusion and while it certainly does not remove confusion, it does clarify some of its facets.

What to do: First, brainstorm a list of issues or events regarding male/male and male/female relationships which confuse you. Then create some sentences which connect these areas. You can draw some examples from the following:

What confuses me the most about men's changing roles is:

What confuses me the most about women's changing roles is:

What confuses me the most about men's relationships to one another is:

What confuses me the most about male/female relationships today is:

After you have completed your sentences, circle those that seem to stand out. Of these, which relate to or add to the theme of confusion? Look for patterns. People will experience confusion in various areas. This exercise can be repeated many times. Other issues such as fears, needs, dislikes, etc. can be addressed in a similar fashion as was confusion.

STRATEGY: **VISITING THE 'SCROOGE' WITHIN US**

INTENT: Each Christmas season, Dickens' classic tale of "Tiny Tim" is aired on television. We watch as the ghosts of Christmas "past", "present" and "future" haunt the stingy Scrooge, taking him on journeys which show him the misdeeds and corruption of his life.

I believe the tale is a metaphor for the "inbetween" phase of transition. Like Scrooge, the ghosts of our life passages come to aid us in re-balancing our lives, deepening our attunement and strengthening our connection with life.

Two Christmases ago, while working with a male client, I followed an image I had about how best to help him. As a result of this image, I created a method of working with transition which I call, 'The Scrooge Process'. It was so named because of some of its content-structure and because it came to me during the holiday season. It is very effective in helping people sort through and bring some positive order to their lives. Anyone can do it. The best results occur when two people take turns doing it to each other or in a group situation.

What to do: Write on three separate pieces of paper, three events from the past (positive or negative), three goals you have for the future and three situations which you are presently involved in. Select three chairs or pillows to represent the "past", "present" and "future" and place them side by side with the chair representing the "present" in the middle. Place the corresponding pieces of paper in each chair. Pause, closing your eyes and focus upon your breathing for two to three minutes, allowing your mind and body to relax. Soothing music can be used here to aid this part of the exercise. Upon opening your eyes, ask yourself, "Which chair am I drawn to?" Take the time to discover which chair really does draw your attention. Once you know, sit in the chair and again close your eyes and focus upon your breathing. Allow any thoughts, feelings or memories to emerge. These can be both positive and negative. As the process continues and you recognize people's faces, ask yourself, "Do I have anything to say to anyone?" Again, take your time and see if words come to you. If they do, imagine that the specific person to whom they should be directed is sitting in front of you. This is an opportunity to resolve past conflicts, affirm a feeling towards someone or to get an issue straight with yourself. Continue with this dialogue until you have a sense of completion and release. Move on to another chair, when ready, and repeat the process. If you feel confused, return to the "present" chair and settle yourself by focusing upon your breathing. This exercise will work if you are willing to use your imagination and follow your intuition.

Note: This exercise may bring memories of sadness or anger. You are free to stop at any time. Remember: **You are in control, you are in charge.** This is an exercise, not a therapy. **You are your own judge.**

STRATEGY: **PEOPLE I MIRROR**

INTENT: When others comment that we are a "chip off the old block" or that our behavior is similar to someone else's, they are often not far from the truth. Though we may try to be a unique, separate individual, we do absorb certain traits from others as part of our socialization process whether we are conscious of this or not. This is even more apparent during a period of transition. Often a behavior or image that we once took for granted, now stands out "like a sore thumb." We become aware that we have incorporated someone else's trait often without being conscious of it. This can be perplexing as we ask ourselves, "Which behavior is part of the 'real' me?"

I have designed some sentence completions which I often get participants in my workshops to fill out at the beginning of the session. The positive feedback towards this exercise that I have had is an affirmation for me. I have done these same completions myself and have found them to be worthwhile in discovering how we learn to "mirror" another person.

What to do: Complete the following sentences and add those that fit your situation specifically.

I am most like my father when I:

I am most like my mother when I:

I am most like my brother(s) when I:

I am most like my sister(s) when I:

I am most like my grandfather when I:

I am most like my grandmother when I:

I am most like my son(s) when I:

I am most like my daughter(s) when I:

I am most like my teacher when I:

The person/persons to whom I am most similar is/are:

The person/persons from whom I am most different is/are:

When I act like other people, I feel:

STRATEGY: **WHAT I FEEL REGARDING THINGS IN LIFE**

INTENT: I would like to complete this part of the chapter with open-ended sentence completions which provide a broad perspective for our understanding of our journey as men today.

What to do: Fill in the following sentences:

As a man, I am:

As a man, I think:

As a man, I feel:

As a man, I assume:

As a man, I would like to be:

As a man, I love:

As a man, I hate:

To me, men are:

To men, women are:

To me, children are:

What I like the most about being me is:

What I like the most about being a man is:

What I like the least about being me is:

What I like the least about being a man is:

What I like the most about women is:

What I like the least about women is:

What I miss in my relationships with men is:

What I do not miss is:

What I miss in my relationships with women is:

What I do not miss is:

What men need to change in their relationships with other men is:

What men need to change in their relationships with women is:

What I need to change about my self to be more alive today and in the future is:

As this chapter comes to a close, our journey through transition is nearly complete. We have explored the dimensions of the first and second phases of the journey, gaining new perspectives on our changing roles as men. I hope it has also renewed our commitments to learn the necessary skills to become healthier travellers. The transition phase is temporary yet, it is an opportunity to learn, heal and grow.

The strategies just outlined have a three-fold purpose. Firstly, they provide methods and processes that activate our capacities for approaching and enhancing new beginnings, whether these be in areas of interpersonal relationships, career aspirations or facillitating a renewal or self-expression and creativity. Secondly, these provide a context for playing out some of the ideas generated thus far in the reading of this book and in the completion of the exercises in this chapter. Finally, they connect aspects of the chapter to the design of the "Life Plan" which is introduced at the end of this chapter. The "Life Plan" serves as a beginning blueprint to be used as a tool for growth in our daily, personal and professional lives.

This is a guidebook for renewal of a healthier life journey for men wih the activities of this chapter being the tools to aid this same journey. In combination they represent new perspectives and richer potential for positive growth. Hence, they are a symbol of men's "new beginnings".

STRATEGIES: **NEW BEGINNINGS**

In the fall of 1985, after completing a "Brothers" workshop in Edmonton, Alberta, I received a parcel in the mail which contained a cassette of songs and poetry for and by men. Two participants, Chris Bullock and Ken Dickson, stated in the accompanying note that they had been created in appreciation of the weekend workshop. Included, as well, was a poem written by Chris, the theme of which had come from the exercise conducted at the end of the workshop wherein everyone planted a sunflower seed which I had given them. This was a ritual for new beginnings. After rereading Chris's poem, I realized it had a potent message for men who struggle with the cycles of transition, particularly as to where to begin once more. The poem speaks of the "crying child" within us who does not know how and worse, is afraid of coming out of the dark. I thank Chris for his contribution and in appreciation I use his poem as a beacon of light to guide us through this chapter and as a shared message to his fellows.

Passing on the Seed

How to speak to the child inside that cries in the dark of an empty room?
The child's body grows. The child moves into other rooms.
Rooms full of people; his head is full of people.
He learns to smile, to read well, to sparkle in conversation, to help after dinner, to be the perfect guest, masquerading as the host.
The host, who, now and then, walks with a limp, or a strange pain around his heart, as he walks away from the crying child in the dark room.

The host serves dinner, his wife is in the kitchen.
The talk is of terrorism, senseless death in Lebanon, the collapse of small banks, pornographic movies, the spread of AIDS, the new cults springing up daily.
The host eats up the talk; it is his invisible dinner.
The host breathes in the talk; he is getting his second wind.
Tomorrow he will climb the steps up to his office and for a moment see only the darkness at the head of the stairs.

The men at the workshop sit in a circle, embarassed.
Hearing the voices of the dinner guests in their heads.
The workshop begins; around the circle voices begin to speak:
of distance from fathers, fear of imposture, late night panics, the lump in the throat, the pain around the heart, the crying child.
The mid-day sun slants through the window, the voices of the dinner guests begin to fade.

The circle becomes a medicine wheel: a wheel of healing
The wheel turns through evening, night, morning.
The men leave; each carries a seed.

Now the men are back in rooms full of people.
Now the voices begin again in their heads; the voices of the dinner
guests, and a new voice, asking:
"Where is there a space to plant this seed? Where is there a space
where the crying child can move into the light?"
The men move through the rooms of the present, carrying a seed,
looking for a planting ground.

Chris Bullock

To become better seed planters, "seekers of ground," — to plant our
beginnings, ideas, feelings, needs and dreams within, we must make a pact
with ourselves. This pact is a type of marriage contract with the self — a life
long commitment from this time onward to re-educate and do what is
necessary to heal ourselves. Anything short of this "contract" is a meager
attempt at changing our course and finding a "space where the crying child
(son) can move into the light." This starts with a deep, personal talk with
ourselves, call it soul searching if you like and the collection of all resources
we can tap both inside and outside of ourselves which can be used in our
re-newal journey. The strategies within are only as effective as we personally
make them. One exercise that I often use and present in my workshops is the
"Self Interview." It is a form of inner dialogue which helps to clarify and
sharpen our perspective. I will demonstrate this exercise by completing the
interview myself to give you an idea of how it works. Then, I will present the
rest of the strategies for "new beginnings," the "Life Plan," and the closing.
The "Self Interview" is as follows. Please try it for yourself.

Interviewer: Well, Frank, what does all this stuff about beginnings
mean? We are always dealing with beginnings, what is so special about your
message?

Frank: Firstly I agree that we are always dealing with beginnings in our
lives, but I do not believe that we handle them very well. As I wrote in the first
part of this chapter, men do not know how to handle "endings" any better
than "beginnings." It may seem that they do, but the evidence is to the
contrary. We lack the basic, instinctual wisdom to heal ourselves. We often
leap into situations before we are prepared. We lack structure and a sense of
timing. Many of us lack the ability to complete experiences and to give our
"all" to any aspect of life, except possibly to our careers. Women state that
men do not know how to give their all and we should acknowledge this so we
can begin to change it rather than continuing to pretend there is not a
problem. Though we are capable of changing jobs, relationships, thoughts

and feelings, major life shifts can "throw us for a loop."

Interviewer: Are you saying that we men can easily con ourselves into believing that we are more competent in such matters than we really are?

Frank: Yes, this has been part of the way we have been taught to believe and see ourselves. It is an image that gives us a false sense of confidence and security. When we are faced with major changes and/or loss in our lives, we are usually lost, confused or devastated.

Interviewer: If this is the case, what suggestions do you have?

Frank: We have to make growth and change a priority in our lives. We have to acknowledge that we have much to learn about ourselves and this knowledge lies beneath the limiting, scripted image we have of ourselves. We have wounds to heal, gaps to fill and myths to dissolve. We need to develop a more realistic picture of ourselves and the world.

This priority is a major step which is only the beginning. We have to start somewhere and there is no going back.

Interviewer: Thank you, Frank. You have helped me consider areas of my life which I have not given attention to before. At least, you have shown me how to "interview" myself.

STRATEGY: **DAILY NEEDS MAP**

INTENT: Men have been taught to feign their internal needs for the external attainment of power, money and prestige. This externalizing search for gratification can leave us shallow, superficial regardless of the image we are trying to project. It is time to shift to an "internal" focus and to learn how to bring our needs into focus. This exercise can get us started.

What to do: On a large piece of paper, using a felt pen, draw two large circles and write "needs I have" and "what I have to do" above each of the circles. In the "needs I have" circle, fill in as many needs as you can think of. For each need, write the necessary action to be taken in the "what I have to do" circle. Remember that though there is no limit for needs, each must be matched with an action. Upon completion, place this "needs map" in a visible location and each day, for one week, circle one need that you would like to work on that day. Also, circle the matching action. After one week, evaluate your situation; what did you learn about your needs? How do you communicate them? **What did you do to meet them?** Repeat this strategy for several weeks until you are ready to handle two needs per day. Be realistic and have fun.

STRATEGY: **SHOULDS, CANS AND WILLS**

INTENT: The following sentence completion helps to distinguish between society's and other's expectations so we can focus upon our real abilities and resources in our relationships and have a realistic perspective of ourselves.

What to do: Complete the following,

I SHOULD:

As a father, I should:

As a professional, I should:

As a husband/partner, I should:

As a friend to a man, I should:

As a friend to a woman, I should:

As a son, I should:

As a man, I should:

I CAN:

As a father, I can:

As a professional, I can:

As a husband/partner, I can:

As a friend of a man, I can:

As a friend of a woman, I can:

As a son, I can:

As a man, I can:

I WILL:

As a father, I will:

As a professional, I will:

As a husband/partner, I will:

As a friend of a man, I will:

As a friend of a woman, I will:

As a son, I will:

As a man, I will:

I AM:

As a father, I am:

As a professional, I am:

As a husband/partner, I am:

As a friend of a man, I am:

As a friend of a woman, I am:

As a son, I am:

As a man, I am:

STRATEGY: **AUTOBIOGRAPHY: A "WHOLE" DIFFERENT VERSION**

INTENT: We all have our stories, our versions of what our lives were like growing up male. We also have the memories, joys and past wounds that match those stories. Have we considered what those stories would sound like being told by those who shared those moments with us? What would be their versions? Would they sound the same as ours?

What to do: First, write your own autobiography and give it a title that fits your life's journey. Include events, both positive and negative, of your childhood, home, school, adolescence and adulthood to the present. Be as specific and thorough as possible. Take your time and make the experience worthwhile. Upon completion of your story, re-read it to ensure that you have absorbed its contents and then, put it away for at least two days. Think about what you have written. After two days, write the story from someone else's perspective. This could be your mother, father, teacher, brother or sister or anyone you choose. Then, compare the two versions. Does someone else's version change your own? Are you now aware of a perspective on the event that you had not considered before? After your comparison, re-write your own and discover what has changed.

STRATEGY: **CELEBRATE BEGINNINGS**

INTENT: Rituals have always been a part of our lives from birthday parties, graduations and marriage to placing a newly lost tooth under our pillows. Rituals are a means by which we tap into and sanctify special moments in our lives through lending depth and significant meaning to them. Rituals are necessary today as men experience life's changes. They need to be seen as times to celebrate our changes and accomplishments. Here are a few suggestions you can use. Create your own as well.

What to do: Pick a recent occasion which signified a new beginning. It could be a new job, home, relationship, discovery or a special personal or professional accomplishment. Select an appropriate reward to match the occasion such as a movie, treating yourself and someone else to dinner complete with cake and candles, or making up a "reward" certificate or mailing a letter of congratulations to yourself. You could have a seed-planting party, buy yourself a trinket or call in "well" at work. Be creative and allow the child within you to be expressed, if only for a day or an evening.

STRATEGY: **LIVING OUR DYING**

INTENT: Saul Alinsky, the 1960's radical movement organizer and mentor to Ceasar Chavez, stated to a group of three hundred clergymen that it is time to be concerned about "what happens after birth" rather than be obsessed with what occurs after death. His statement has validity twenty years later regarding living with death. Our attitudes towards death in general and our own in particular, can reveal some of the ways which we hold ourselves back from life and inhibit our chances for growth and change. This exercise will invoke your thoughts and feelings in this regard.

What to do: Answer the following and give yourself time to consider your responses.

1. If I knew I was dying tomorrow at noon, what would I feel?

   What would I do?

2. If I had six months to live and could do anything I wanted, I would:

3. You have been asked to address the United Nations after learning that you have a terminal disease. What would be your message to the world?

4. The way I expect to die is?

5. A belief that I would be willing to die for is?

6. I expect to die at age?

My Funeral:

The people whom I would want at my funeral would be:

The songs that I would want sung are:

A special ritual that I would want performed would be:

The way I wish to be remembered is:

Death to me is:

My death is:

A CONCLUDING MESSAGE

Many hours have gone into the designing, choosing and creating of the strategies and exercises that I have presented in this "practicum" section. The exercises have been "hands-on" activities as I feel that men need some new tools, processes and means to understand the changes that occur in our lives today. This chapter has provided, perhaps in a humble way, the opportunity for this to happen.

The "Men's Life Plan" is on the following page to lend some sound meaning to the "practicum." The plan is only a simple instrument that provides a context for viewing our lives from various vantage points and in a more wholistic manner.

I believe this is the only viable type of blueprint for us to use. We have been far too restricted and limited and our self-perceptions are colored by vague, mechanistic scripted images.

I leave you with the words of a great journeyman to help you in your travels:

> "We shall never cease from exploration and the end of our exploring will be to arrive where we started and know the place for the first time."

— T.S. Eliot

MEN'S LIFE PLAN

Note: This is only a design, create the a plan that fits your life.

SELF:

List three of your greatest personal strengths:

List three of your greatest professional strengths:

List three areas in your personal life that need growth and change:

List three areas in your professional life that need growth and change:

OTHERS:

Name three people in your personal life who support and validate you:

Name three people in your professional life who support and validate you:

NEEDS:

List three needs you have to make your personal life more rewarding:

List three needs you have to make your professional life more rewarding:

Name three actions you are taking to have these needs met:

TRANSITION:

ENDINGS: Name one unfinished situation that needs completion:

What am I doing to bring this about?

INBETWEENS: What am I doing to tap my inner strength and resources?

BEGINNINGS: A positive, realistic and flexible goal I have for myself is —

TAKING ACTION: CHANGES NEEDED

Three specific areas I plan to work with from now on are:

(Choose from the "Men's Inventory Checklist")

What I am doing to make this happen is:

(actions for each area)

TIME FRAME:

In one week, I will:

In one month, I will:

In three months, I will:

In six months, I will:

In one year, I will:

In three years, I will:

I, _____, in signing this, plan to commit my time, energy and intelligence to improve areas of my life.

Signed:

Dated:

** Revise in three weeks.

CHAPTER IX

Towards Being
More Whole and Real

'Daily Living as a Healthy Growing Male'

"On the other hand a characteristic of childhood is that, thanks to its naivete and unconsciousness it sketches a more complete picture of the self, of the whole man in his pure individuality, than adulthood.

"Consequently, the sight of a child or a primitive will arouse certain longings in an adult, civilized person — longings which relate to the unfulfilled desires and needs of those parts of the personality which have been blotted out of the total picture in favor of the adapted persona."

— C. Jung

Becoming a more real and healthy male is a journey towards wholeness. It is an opportunity to re-discover the human seeds and resources that we had at birth and misplaced along the way to adulthood. There are obstacles along the way which will set us back and derail us at times. Once the decision is made to undertake such a journey, any obstacle will merely be a hurdle that we can face as simply another challenge in living and growing as a human being.

As we explore our positive and negative memories of past experiences, how we deal with what we find is important. Some information is hidden beneath tons of social and self-imposed denial patterns. We must have a desire to change these unhealthy patterns and be willing to take new steps to penetrate habitual fears and beliefs about ourselves and the world. This will involve struggle but it is a struggle with a difference which involves breaking free of the rigid demands that suffocate us. We already know how to strive, how to fight and how to keep our feelings in check. We must now release ourselves from the weight of our male scripts which restrict our images as males and as people. Each day will bring fresh insights that can help dissolve the binding of our conditioning.

Whether we are just beginning or have been on the quest for some time, it is important that we stay alert to not only the effects that our changes are having on us, but on others as well. As we discover aspects of ourselves once dormant, other people will either adapt to our emergence, or refuse or have difficulty in responding to us in a different way. For others to view us alternatively they must also move through a shifting of fixed patterns of how they once experienced us. If they are willing to change with us in a positive manner, then our growth will be further enriched. If we meet with resistance, we need to know how to work with it. When "this is the way things are done" is challenged, whether it is for the good or not, others may respond with their own readiness to accept change or to keep us locked within old performance standards. Often this resistance to change is an attempt to remain secure as change often brings with it fear of the unknown and uncertainty. Without change there is no growth.

We must learn to protect ourselves to ensure that our growth is healing and educational for ourselves and for others. Before one can be comfortable with new ways of doing things, there must be a foundation of trust and understanding. Clear communication is the healthiest and most effective way of doing this. Sincerity and integrity are other human tools that make people be aware and listen. Until our journey is more regulated we must balance our desires and actions with common sense and realism. Our liberation will free some people and will threaten others. We will gain support from some and resistance, manipulation and sabotage from others. Maturity and love are necessary ingredients to want the best for another person and we must use these two qualities to help those who are frightened by our change so they can learn to trust and respect our new attitudes.

When moving in new directions, it is best to have a healthy sense of caution. This caution will make us aware as to the appropriate time to be more open and vulnerable. There are people in the world who are wounded and may desire revenge because of the experience they have had with male behavior. It takes time, forgiveness and understanding to heal such wounds but their venom must be dealt with or it can become toxic and infiltrate our personal and social relationships. Our desire for growth will naturally move us in directions where we can find antidotes to heal these wounds.

Be aware that the effects of male conditioning have caused problems for men and women, families, and other social and business contacts. The growing male knows that he is responsible for actions and deeds but not for the misdeeds of all males in society. It is unecessary to shoulder such responsibility and such action will deplete the energy needed to be a more creative, resourceful human being.

Men have begun revealing their needs and have been met with rejection, lack of support and understanding from their mates, lovers, friends and associates. One must change what he is able to change. To demand more is unrealistic and can create a heightened vulnerability which may erupt into violence or clamming up. The result could be an unwillingness to risk being vulnerable again.

I have heard men speak of the demands they feel from women. They should be more sensitive, but also strong and aggressive in a more positive manner. It is enough to attempt to swim these new uncharted waters without feeling one has to live up to the demands of some women as well. Stacy Keach, well-known TV and film actor, states that men need to "get tough again." He feels that women want men to be strong as this has always been the case. He believes that now is not the time to be vulnerable.

This is becoming more common as men discover that their vulnerability is not being met with encouragement from some others. Being unable to turn to other men for support or to women for acceptance, some men close the doors to their inner worlds as quickly as they open them. It is not easy to walk into a situation with one's guard down and reverse the usual way of interacting.

Three male therapists, from a clinic in Berkley, California that specifically serves men's needs appeared on the Donahue Show. These therapists represented a new way of dealing with men's ordeals. They had difficulty in speaking with the audience. Though they attempted to be authentic and develop a rapport with the almost all female audience, there was a definite atmosphere of hostility and tension. The comments of two professional women remain in my mind. One of them, an executive with a large corporation, said she felt it was good for men to go through the pain of changes. She recalls the rejection she experienced upon entering a male dominated industry. "Let them squirm," she said, "Its good for them." The other woman, a lawyer, spoke about her negative experiences of going to a male dominated law school. She was still bitter about her treatment by male students and professors. As I watched, I could see the anger lines etched in these women's faces which told of being hurt, invalidated and having to struggle to survive. These lines painted pictures of more than just professional struggles. In my mind I could see how these women had been hurt by other males, friends and lovers; plus the remaining disappointments of their father's lack of appreciation for their aspirations for careers instead of traditional female roles. These memories created pain and discomfort which these women were still experiencing. The three guest therapists and the perspectives that they were trying to present served as catalysts, reminders of the pain once received from other males. These women thought they wanted all males to "squirm" when really, they wished for revenge towards specific males for their discomfort.

Time will allow women's wounds and anger to be healed and foster a positive perspective towards comprehension and reality. Men can help in this healing by supporting women's transformation and growth. Relationships between men and women have to move closer to a basis of mutuality. "It takes two to tango" and it also "takes two to tangle." One's sex can no longer be blamed for everything and neither males nor females can "carry" the other. We can learn more about caring through a nurturing attitude and practice, permitting both to be nurturers. We have to practice more self-caring attitudes and learn to receive from one another. I believe that in these times, men need support, connection and sharing with both men and women. This is also true for women. These times necessitate becoming allies with one another and to see each other as whole, capable and loving human beings which give encouragement and support. Anger and blame patterns must be altered and dissolved. We cannot have total awareness if we only see a part of an issue because we will miss opportunities for connections that encourage us to learn, give and grow. Releasing blame and generalization lessens the gaps between the sexes and increases communication and understanding. Without this give and take and less defensive stance, the gaps become stronger and wider. Once we join forces we are both guaranteed more possibilities for leading richer, fuller lives.

Part of my work is aimed at finding ways to bridge the gaps with women and dissolve the "enemy shadow" that inhibits and distorts male/female relationships. Being unable to relate to the opposite sex in a positive way damages our own possibilities for growth and wholeness.

These past few years of my own transformation have put me in touch with more of the deeper wounds and scars of my childhood conditioning. It has revealed those caverns of deprivation containing the memories of when I felt I was not good enough, or did not have the right stuff to gain acknowl-edgement not only from my father, but from other family members. Those memories tell me that I did not receive sufficient strength to understand my pain, confusion and feelings of unworthiness. Everyday, I feel less like a "lost child in the woods" as I re-discover parts of my personal history of which I was unaware, or events I thought had happened certain ways and for other reasons. I am now learning to know the difference. I realize that everyone; my father, mother, brothers, cousins and playmates, were doing the best they could. I can now accept and forgive them. Those memories do not hurt any less, however, awareness and understanding removes some of the sting. I know that I can make life different for myself and do not have to repeat the cycles of those times.

I see more "light at the end of the tunnel" yet I still get caught within the darkness of my learned and inherited self-denial patterns. Today, at thirty eight, I am finding myself re-experiencing being afraid of the dark, just as I did when I was young. This and other fears return, teaching me to face them in more resourceful ways, in ways that I could not when I was young and inexperienced in the matters of the world. These fears are locked within my "image" of being strong and macho. I can now see alternative ways of responding to these fears. I am no longer a little boy unfamiliar with the unknown elements of the adult world.

Recently, I have tasted the sourness of desperation, the fear of being abandoned. In front of me stood a lover and friend who was leaving our relationship. What I felt was the past rejection experienced from father, mother, brother and school mates. This experience reminds me of the loneliness and anguish once felt long ago.

I feel so vulnerable at times, it is as if the whole world is conspiring against me. What is really happening is my deep fear of feeling unloved. I was not receiving the nourishment necessary to grow and develop healthily. I was not receiving the acceptance and bonding from my kin, my human support system. I continue to struggle and know that in time, the pieces of the puzzle will reveal themselves to me enabling me to reclaim lost parts of my journey in life.

Robert Bly, poet and storyteller and a popular spokesman on male issues, states that men today are struggling to get in touch with the "wildman" parts of ourselves. He also refers to this as the "animal twin" and that women have this part in their personalities as well. It is basic to both our natures but manifests differently through our psyches. The wildman serves as the deep, unconscious part of our psyche which re-connects us to our instincts, our creatureness. That kinship with all living things which Indians and other "primitive" cultures understand so well, knowing how to respect and live in harmony with nature.

Bly's wildman is not to be confused with the animalism of the abusive, out of control man who ends up hurting himself and/or others in his machismo displays.

The wildman concept refers to that deeper part of our humanity that brings wholeness, a sense of self and spiritual depth back into our lives. The lack of recognition of our wildman has actually created the abusive male mentality. Freud teaches us that we have paid a price in being "civilized" and cutting off contact with the animal part of our nature and that this has created psychic imbalance. Without this connection plus swallowing society's rules of conduct, we end up losing our respect for nature and our ability to resonate harmony with nature. Without our connection to our creatureness, we mindlessly slaughter animals, just as we continue to destroy the beast part of ourselves and keep it hidden within the shadows of our psyche.

The wildman is part of our souls. It is the center piece of our intrapsychic system that keeps us moving on track towards our individuation. To become completely awake, respectful and in harmony with life, it maintains the bridge between our passions and our intellectual selves. It is our grounding center, the gravity of our existence. Without it we are less human and less real.

Bly suggests that modern society men are unhappy and less masculine in the true sense because they have been isolated from the wisdom and strength of their animal selves. Men have been too closely bonded with their mothers, the feminine aspect and though this is important for their inner human development, they also need a stronger connection with their fathers and other males in their lives. Additionally, young boys need to experience important initiation rites which must have a base in the specialized rituals that were once a part of the male growth process and now only exist in some ethnic groups and "primitive" cultures. Bly states that young men need the experience, also of the nurturing aspect of their own maleness plus that of other men. Deep beneath our images, beliefs, fears, the "wildman" awaits our return.

I support Bly's findings and see his contribution as enhancing the growth and change of both males and females. I believe also, that the wildman concept is merely a symbolic image which has many faces and words to describe it. It is as old as humankind, itself.

I believe that it we are to understand Bly's concept of wildman, we must have several different descriptions relating to it. We need a multifaceted description to discover ways to integrate the wildman concept with other things we know and understand and with that which is still hidden from view.

The word that fits, which reflects my own style of relating, is "vitality." I see vitality as the source of energy that flows through all living things. It stems from the deep stream within that often overflows with joy, excitement and a zest for life. It is a passion for existence, kinship and being grateful for life. Most of all, it is a feeling of deep respect and love for the self and for others, the environment and all kingdoms of creatures. To be "vital" is to be a "blood brother" with all creatures of life; human, animal, plant, etc. It means possessing a spirit to challenge those who would threaten this life system. Vitality, that deep inner awareness and creative functioning, is to be balanced with outward expression. Great men like Picasso, Shakesphere, Blake, as well as women like Joan of Arc, Susan B. Anthony and others possessed a vitality which they expressed as part of their contribution to humanity. Vitality is synonomous with Bly's "wildman." Both are life-giving and seek to transform and free the "id" locked within the social armor and patterning as described by Freud. In fact, the imprisonment of our primitive, our creatureness, has caused us to abandon a vital part of our being which created the imbalance and the subsequent destruction against ourselves and nature. Regaining deeper relationships with our wildness increases the options we have for being whole, humane and deeply connected with life.

We are on the edge of our transformation journey. We must leave behind the old, and embrace, explore and discover how to touch the heart of our human destiny.

Whether we join forces with this sweeping, moving river of human evolution or not; whether we resist or invite it; whether we ignore the powers of this shifting change or accept them is no longer an individual choice. This change takes us towards a new understanding of ourselves as men. We can learn to meet women on a healthy, allied level of co-existence. We are being forced to look at our present course of destruction and to change our way of thinking and searching for solutions. We are having to look at our incredible disharmony with nature, ourselves and other people. We are being pushed to experience the possibility of even greater fears of abandonment and separation. We have to release, to let go of our false egos. We are being challenged to go deeper within our minds and bodies, penetrating through the armor shields of logic and rationality. We must probe into the "heart" of our minds and reach out to the feminine, the mother earth part of us which has always been there.

We are being asked to challenge the habitual patterns of thinking to discover the feelings within our rational process and to bridge the gap between mind, body and spirit. By challenging the old modes of structuring reality we are penetrating the outer worlds of macho conditioning and competition and those masculine edicts of male identity which are reinforced by the media, industry and the political system.

To become vital and richer in our lives, we are going to have to say "Yes" to life. We must make a commitment that puts us back into our own rhythm, emotions and facillitates our comraderie not only with men, but with women.

Finally, we must trust and listen to that still inner voice that sees the journey more clearly than we do. External answers will not provide direction to carry us along this new road that we are travelling. Simultaneously, the 'road' is only a reflection of what we abandoned long time ago. The journey to freedom will demand skill, faith and the surrender of the old guideposts of masculine security. Above all, it will demand that we become humble and begin to see how we are a vital part of this creation.

Our connection, our true birthright and finally our wholeness can be realized by acknowledging we are gifts of creation and have no dominion over it. This realization is the beginning of learning how to live in harmony.

NEW AND HEALTHY MALE

"Creativity"

The man who follows the crowd, will usually get no further than the crowd.

The man who walks alone is likely to find himself in places no one has ever been before.

Creativity is living not without its attendant difficulties, for peculiarity breeds contempt.

And the fortunate thing about being ahead of your time is that when people finally realize you were right, they'll say it was obvious all along.

You have two choices in life: you can dissolve into the mainstream, or you can be distinct. To be distinct, you must strive to be what no one else but you can be. . .

Author Unknown

CHAPTER

Mens' Transformation:
Workshops/Support Groups/Networks

"Men Supporting Men's Growth and Emergence"

"I can help you to accept and open yourself mostly by accepting and revealing myself to you."

J. Powell

Art thou lonely, O my brother?
Share thy little with another!
Stretch a hand to one unfriended, And thy loneliness is ended.

John Oxenham

"It is this that we all share — the emergence of a common destiny and the beginning of a perception, however misty, that something beyond the nation will have to be brought into being if the human race is to have any meaning."

Norman Cousins

It is seldom that men can converge with one another, sharing some of their darker secrets, needs and concerns. Often, we simply chat, or get into intellectual exchanges which can be trite and irrational. We stand on the competitive edge, pushing for domination and one-up-manship.

It would be a change to just be ourselves with other men and feel trusted and supported by each other. Such feelings nurture us with warmth, confidence and heighten our self-esteem. Can we let down our guards revealing more of ourselves without fearing being judged or manipulated by another man's need for power and control? Our learned behavior for control and power, when threatened, kicks in automatically. The chance for men to be open and real with one another rarely occurs or simply does not exist.

It is believed by many women and some men, that men already have natural bondng relationships. However, the evidence shows the contrary. Men's relationships are usually superficial, shallow and immature. The customary joke-telling or demoralizing of women, reminiscent of adolescence, is often the focus of men's conversation. During business hours, conversation is usually geared towards shop talk, politics or sports. When an attractive female secretary happens to cross their view, it is almost guaranteed that some glib or degrading remark will be made. It is this routine, habitualized attitude which is the result of centuries of male socialization.

Men's encounters with one another do not have to remain superficial. It is possible for men to join together and share with each other the opportunities for growth. We must dispel the myths that keep us isolated within and confined to our habitual patterns. The superficial, inharmonious relationships that we had with our fathers and other males do not have to be continued. We can free ourselves by changing our attitudes and beliefs about relationships and discovering new ways to connect with other men. We cannot do it alone. We need the support and kinship of other men as we shed the destructive scripts of our masculine conditioning.

In the '60's and '70's women banned together in consciousness-raising groups to help themselves deal with the inequalities they experienced in a male dominated world. For many, these groups provided a base of support, trust and nurturing which helped them to grow and become healthier human beings. These groups have evolved into other kinds of vehicles for political, environmental, social and personal education not only for women, but for others as well. Women have gained strength, power and growth through their close connection with one another. The consciousness-raising groups served as a viable support system that enhanced this growth. Today, it is common to see several women socializing together and this also serves as an important recreational connection for them. This is a special type of bonding of commonality and shared experience. Men can learn from the experiences that women have gained in their group connections.

In the last several years industry and other institutions have implemented the group process into their staff and employee relations. The die-hard hierarchial system is beginning to fade as the top chiefs who once held all the power and made all the decisions are becoming obsolete. A more humane and cooperative method is more effective as working together towards a common objective enhances production and builds self-esteem and confidence. Team management is one alternative means of organizational functioning. Increasingly, group power is viewed as a more viable and effective tool for not only the work place, but to provide need gratification for all kinds of people. Groups bring people together rather than isolating them. The energy created when people work together cooperatively with trust and respect, brings a sense of well being in all participants. As the adage goes, "Two heads are better than one;" from a group perspective, "Six or more heads are even better."

Men are so used to standing in isolation and being limited in their dealings, that they feel this is what life is all about. When they need help or support they are conditioned not to ask for it. So, they do not ask or if they do it is often after it is too late. Thinking of connection rather than isolation will enable us to share our needs, receive ideas from others which will enhance others as well as ourselves. Despite our learned competitive scripts, we do secretly desire connection with others. It is part of our natures as human beings to be social and connected.

In the last few years the needs of men and their changing roles and identities have come into the spotlight. Slowly, the nation is becoming aware that behind the external images of power and domination, men are trapped in socialized, rigid scripts. Women have helped bring this into the light by challenging the masculine values and attitudes that affect their growth as whole persons. As women become stronger and independent, men will be able to become more sensitive and intuitive. Everyone's strength is enhanced through group bonding and networking connections which empowers others by building self-esteem and personal well being.

Men can learn from womens' experiences that serve as models to aid in our development and growth as male human beings. It takes some unique tools to broaden and strengthen men's transcendence from the obsolete past habits and patterns. Without the strength of education and support, growth and change are virtually impossible. Most men find it easy to run when the anxiety of being alone hits them.

Three tools that serve as guideposts for men's transformation and offer a sound basis for developing a foundation for their change are workshops, support groups and networks. Each provides an opportunity for men to gain needed information, have access to information and resources and achieve stronger, healthier male bonding.

Workshops — Information and content for men's growth and awareness.

In the fall of 1980, I attended a professional conference in France where several hundred therapists and other professionals from all over the world came together to share their skills and resources. The schedule was filled with numerous workshops in family therapy, couples enrichment, personal growth and women's issues. Despite the fact that over half of the participants were men, there was not one workshop offered specifically for men. I decided to offer the first international men's workshop. This decision marked the beginning of my work and the writing of this book.

I have travelled across the U.S. and Canada and have discovered a lack of courses and workshops for men. Almost every major center and smaller city has courses for women in career development, single parenting and other areas pertaining to women's growth, information and education. Many universities have information facilities concerned with women's isssues. There are a few men's programs, but these are insufficient to ensure that enough is being done for men's positive growth and education.

To re-program many of our unhealthy attitudes, habits and behaviors, we need a full scale education program. Courses and workshops in the following areas need to be offered: fathering, single parenting, men's conditioning, war, incest, sex roles, mid-life crisis, divorce, stress, wholistic health, relationships and other relevant areas to men's needs. Men need new information to assist them in their transformation to a new, healthy human authenticity. Communities, agencies and especially universities and colleges through continuing education programs, should be concentrating on the developing of courses and workshops that enhance men's awareness, growth and changes. In areas where this is occuring, I commend those who are alert and aware of the needs for these times. For those who have not as of yet made steps, I encourage you to begin. Men's issues and changing sex role responsibilities are an area which require attention.

If you, the reader, are unable to find the courses, etc. in your community that will answer some of your needs, then find a way to get them started. It takes only one person and that person sharing an idea with another and that person passing the idea along to get something started. The desire for this must become a major priority in our lives. Men who are breaking free from their false imagery patterns need guidelines to help them on their journey.

Support Groups — A vehicle for ongoing education and growth.

Warren Farrell, in his new book **Why Men are the Way They Are,** shares a story of a forty year old attorney and senior partner of a law firm who became a member of a men's support group. The attorney, after 2 months of attendance and no communication, decided to share his reason for being there. It was the result of his wife joining a women's group and threatening that she would leave him if he did not make some changes in his life. He initially thought that the group consisted of a bunch of "fags" until he listened to other's stories and discovered he was not that different from them. After expressing similar needs concerns for some time to the group, he admitted: " I guess maybe I am holding something back. I feel like I spent forty years of

my life working as hard as I could to become somebody I don't even like."
Many in the group could empathize with him as they too had learned to
commit their lives to playing out a societal male script resulting in a loss of
much of their genuineness and gentleness. He spoke of his attempt to voice
his concerns with his law partners and found they were uninterested. He
relates:

> "I was mentioning some of my doubts to a few of my buddies at
> work. They listened attentively for a couple of minutes, then one
> made a joke, and the other excused himself. Finally, I mentioned
> this men's group - which I never should have done - and they just
> laughed me out of the office. I've been the butt of jokes ever since:
> 'How are the U.S. Naval Gazers doing Ralph-boy?'

> "Suddenly, I realized — Ginny has a whole network of friends she
> can talk with about all this. And me, the men I've worked with for
> seventeen years, sixty hours a week — they hardly know me. Nor
> do they want to."

Farrels account is of a man who discovers that much of what he had
worked for to be recognized as a successful male was false and empty. This
plight is characteristic of so many males in our society who are now awakening from their numbing coma and discovering they were sleeping as their
lives passed them by. The negative response he received from his associates
is another sad story of the lack of support and understanding that men have
for one another. However, this does not have to be the reality. Men can gain
support, trust and sharing from men's support groups.

There are many kinds of support groups which have been adopted in
fields of business, education and social services. Support groups help alleviate stress and facilitate the development of ideas and projects to enhance
people's personal and working lives.

Support groups are not a new entity. People have always found a way to
connect for personal and professional support. In times of crisis and need
for social change, the gain of the everyday citizen is often enhanced through
groups which provide support for common objectives. The family has always
been the strongest support group, however, in modern society when families
spend little time with each other, its usefulness in this regard is lessening.
These groups do provide an opportunity for those involved to bond with one
another with a special kind of loyalty. This generates trust, communication
and positive education from which all benefit.

We are living in a time when collective energy and team effort are the only
sound ways to deal with the stresses of this modern era. We cannot stand
alone. We must join forces and strengthen our resources by providing a

variety of information sources, skills, experiences, and so forth that many can share and benefit from.

The support group offers men the opportunity to continue with the development of a growing awareness of themselves and their dilemmas as well as a means to pool resources to educate, heal and expand their growth.

Networking — A link to resources and empowerment

For centuries society was organized and managed by the pyramid system. This system consisted of power distribution levels whereby those in the top positions hold the most power. They were in control of functions and decision making, and those beneath the powerful few were the subordinates, having slightly more power than those underneath them.

The pyramid system reigned over industrialized societies as it evolved massive bureaucracies. Now computer systems and technological advancement encourage new ways of running organizations and other institutions. A system or model had to be found to fit the needs of a growing high-tech society. The old systems were inefficient and the information flow and product process was too slow.

The system was selected as the most effective for organizational growth and replaces the hierarchial pyramid system. This model serves as a "kinship" system drawing people together with each participant making a vital contribution for the development of all. This kinship system is as old as humankind itself and is still practiced by many "primitive" tribes and ethnic groups.

The network model is based upon cooperation, self-generization and realization and bridging with others through sharing of resource information. The network is an "antedote to alienation" states Marylin Ferguson author of **The Aquarian Conspiracy.**

It broadens the scope of individual's effectiveness and resourcefulness in the community by connecting with others who have similar needs, concerns, goals and information. This interaction creates an incredible package that is more complete than if a person stayed isolated. Networks stretch beyond to include communities and members of other similar groups. It can go beyond geographical boundaries to connect communities and groups throughout the world. Others have information, skills and resources from which we can learn, as they can learn from us. The network system creates the way for like-minded people to share the benefits and wealth of their knowledge. It is greater than the whole which links the integral parts, each offering a special gift that offers the whole its greatness.

Gandhi used a form of networking called "grouping unities" which eventually led to the people of India achieving their independence. Without the sophistication of technology, the millions of people of India joined together each in their own way to do what they could. Villages were connected by running messengers who moved from place to place passing on information, letting people know when to march and when to wait. Essentially, they worked together, keeping their communications channels open.

Social action groups, have and are using networks to carry on their causes. Networks are serving as a means for citizens to increase their strength and purpose. The individual's needs are not only being dealt with, they are joined with others who have similar concerns.

Two organizations have been started to help males — each calls itself The National Organization of Men. Although their focuses differ somewhat, one is quite political while the other has a broader perspective, each has something to offer the other. The combination of the two could reach men both nationally and globally.

Many cities are establishing centers which deal primarily with men's issues. Other agencies are offering courses or providing resources and facilities to begin courses and workshops for men and others needing information and exposure to men's areas.

Networking is the model for these times in creating processes not only for men, but for all people who are humane, just, effective and resourceful. It draws people together and empowers everyone and this increases the strength of the power of the process itself. Networking is like a giant support group in action. *

The three vehicles of workshops, support groups and networks offer men the chance for an extra push required to take the journey towards being a healthier human beings. It is unnecessary to become a member of the male liberation movement or to join either party of The National Organization of Men, to become active in your liberation. It is not necessary to attend workshops, etc., which address these issues, however, these do offer opportunity and information and perhaps a place to get started.

To aim at attainment of our own liberation, is to work towards the liberation of others. New ways of responding to people in our daily lives can affect small, but essential changes in our selves and in our relationships with others. A simple smile to a stranger, a kind word on the telephone or to a store clerk are small, effective places to begin.

* See resource section at the end of this book for further information.

Perhaps a Sunday brunch with a few close male friends, playing basket-ball or taking a walk is the beginning of a men's support group. An evening with a couple of divorced friends talking about single parenting is a quality way to spend some time. Writing a letter to a member of another men's group or a social action group which focuses on men's needs is a communication link and the beginning of a network system.

It is easy for men to remain distant from any attempts at mutual sharing about that which is really important. Do not wait until a crisis is the signal to get you started. We can begin now in thinking of ways of prevention through education and action.

We have choices. It does no good to sit and watch and wait for others to make the first move. We have to make that first important step. It will open a whole new world of possibilities.

Maybe **you** will be the one to get a course going, create a project or start a group. Maybe **you** will be the one to take a risk, to be seen and heard. To take such action will symbolize the love you have for yourself and for our human family and the survival of the race.

CHAPTER XI

Androgyny and Beyond:

Healing the split and re-discovery of
the masculine/feminine compliment in us all.

"A new consciousness is rising out of the morass of a declining society that has bent too far towards rationalism, towards technology and towards the aquisition of power through unbridled competition — or whatever other means have been considered necessary by those in charge to achieve dominance and control over less-sophisticated people.

"The new consciousness takes note that our society has become over-balanced in favor of the so-called 'masculine' qualities of character."

June Singer, **Androgyny**

"Go to your bosom; knock there, and ask your heart what it doth know."

— Shakespeare

In western Canada, in the fall of 1983, I attended the preview of the "Dinner Party," by artist Judy Chicago, sculptor/artist and feminist. I viewed the triangular table with thirty nine unique plates and place settings representing women throughout history such as: Theodora, who co-ruled with her husband during the Byzantine empire; Molly Pitcher, heroine of the revolutionary war; and celebrated author Virginia Woolf. Each piece represented the contributions of women throughout history to the growth and knowledge of humankind. Additionally, covering the floor were the names of 999 other women contributors.

I felt that I was seeing a side of history that had always been foreign, now unfold before me. The "Dinner Party" was far more than an artistic display. It

243

was symbolic of the shadow of human history, once denied, now coming to light. It acted as a vehicle bringing to light the feminine half of humanity, revealing the essential human spirit which was covered beneath the rigid structure of an overly-masculinized world consciousness. It was far more than "female genitals on plates" which was one fellow's comment that I overheard. Through the power of metaphor and artistic genius, it provided a picture of life that went beyond the physical. It is a masterpiece of historical evolution symbolizing the messenger from the unconscious which previously has been denied expression.

The "Dinner Party" was an event that challenged all who viewed it to witness a reflection of the human consciousness which has been smothered under tons of falsehood and distortion throughout human history. It serves as an epic reminder of how we have continued throughout history to disconnect ourselves from the whole of our consciousness.

It is time for men and women to move towards a complimentary existence and move beyond the battlefields of the sexual revolution. New relationships between the sexes must come into being. We must declare an armistice. Our differences need not fragment and separate us. The challenge is to share tasks, learn from one another, to participate in healing the wounds and splits of centuries of habitual psychological imbalance.

I alone, do not have the answers. I would like to attempt in this chapter to broaden the aspects of male/female relationships in the hope that what I share here will whet the appetite of the reader and provoke some thinking. Like you, I am searching through the remnants of past ideas and practice hoping to find pieces of the puzzle that fit together. It is premature to claim that we have found the answers when we are still asking the questions. Through discussion and dialogue we can create the context which involves both male and female energies, plus intelligience and wisdom. We need the balance of these complimentary qualities to gain a wholistic viewpoint and system necessary for healthy and realistic male/female relationships.

I will begin this discussion with these goals in mind. The first is the review the concept of androgyny and its implication in comprehending male/female relationships. The second goal is to expand this concept by borrowing ideas from the Jungian system as this relates to male/female relationships. The third, and final goal is to discuss the application of these concepts in everyday life and to offer a blueprint that can be utilized in helping men and women construct the ways and means necessary to develop healthier interactions.

In these chaotic times, we have to be both "seekers" and "finders" as we build honest, complimentary and   healthy relationships. The journey is uncertain and fearful at times, but I believe eventually, well worth the effort.

ANDROGYNY — A STEP TOWARDS WHOLENESS

If we were able to travel back in time through the use of a time machine as imagined by novelist, H.G. Wells, we would discover a world less fragmented than the one we know today. Today, men and women are separated by gender; sex is isolated from love; death from life; material from spirit; body from mind; and the multitude of races are separated by color, language and culture. Political parties are divided, each representing a differing ideology, though, at times, it is difficult to tell one from the other. Everywhere the elements that qualify "difference" reign as a great social and moral web which blocks the possibilities for the recognition of similarities. There is no suggestion here for universal similarity.

This obsession with separation and difference has removed us farther from our natural roots. Within our "differences" lie the seeds of commonness which exist beyond this world's similarity. Within the polarity threads of unity and relationship do exist. To discover such we need to transcend duality - the "dialectic," and find the symbol of unity in the "trialectic." Within such spheres of reality, differences no longer make sense and the uniqueness is seen as a compliment to an integral part of the whole.

History explains that prior to the thirteenth century a more visible balance existed as tribes and/or communities functioned within the laws of nature. Women were accepted and respected as were men for their contribution to their tribe. Often those with special talents and skills, such as healing or mediators etc., carried out these functions. The tribe or community was seen as a social collective with all participating and contributing their skills. Men and women were not seen as separate entities but as contributors in the growth, education and survival of the community network. These social groups were regulated by a patriarchical or a matriarchical system. Each member was viewed as a very important link in the greater whole and survival of the community. The feminine and masculine principles provided the balance. Neither was seen as being superior, each functioned within natural rhythm with the other as the roles enacted by men and women were determined by the needs of the tribe and the evolution of the species.

In a sense, earlier people were androgynous in their perspective meaning that both men and women carried the opposite traits and characteristics of the other. They were neither male nor female, as we have come to understand today. Sex did not dictate duties. Identity was not carved out of some socialized blueprint. Men and women were aware of the spirit of the land and all aspects of the natural system. They understood the environmental relationships between themselves and nature and how both male and female principles are evident in nature. All life kingdoms possess androgynous relationships. Androgyny is a natural blueprint which provides order. Nature in its abundance is sexual, vital and full of creative purpose. Humans are sexual, creative, just as are the trees, birds, insects, fishes, etc. Life streaming through all nature's kingdoms is androgynous.

Now let us hover our time machine over a climactic period in our history. Here we find the beginnings of the rigid patterns that have continued their influence to the present and these core principles became magnified. The church was becoming more powerful and the merging of church and state was becoming inevitable. Politics and decision making became sanctioned by the church. Through chaos, fear and greed the balance of masculine/feminine principles began to disintegrate and the institutions of "rational thinking," the church and the state became second to none. Through force and coersion, the masculine principle became the dominant power resulting in the feminine being the underdog. Changes proclaimed as political acts were referred to as spiritual necessities; the feminine was pushed into the shadows of nature.

The understanding of the essential need for both principles of masculine/feminine to provide order and balance was lost and rationalized away. From this point on the church/state went beserk. During a four century period men and women who lived and practiced the natural laws, these being priests, priestesses, healers, etc. were tortured and put to death. Many women who once were honored for their healing abilitites were accused of witchcraft and consorting with the devil. People had become afraid, estranged and blinded from their kinship with nature. That which was once natural now was part of the dark kingdom. For four centuries, the reign of terror and interrogation spread across Europe and eventually America. Out of the thousands who were brutally tortured, hanged or burned at the stake, the proportion of women and men was 5 to 1. For the power structure of masculine order, the death and destruction of the feminine aspect, unconsciously became a campaign as vehement as earlier crusades to the holy land. Through fear, suppression and violence, the imbalanced masculine element succeeded in "raping" itself and turning that which was once a partner into the dark enemy.

My intention is not to give a history lesson, as I'm not a historian, nor do I blame the males of history for upsetting the masculine/feminine balance. It takes a few power hungry, insecure and fearful human beings of either sex, to start a movement which eventually affects everyone, injecting their poison into the bloodstream of humanity thus creating a cesspool of disease and further stagnation throughout human and social development. It is the power of the vacuum created through imbalance that continues the destructive effect felt for generations to come. What is important here is that before this upheavel, the feminine principle and the masculine principle were accepted as part of the natural fabric of which communities and other social groups were constructed. These principles, alive within the hearts and minds of males and females, were natural contributors to social evolution and the co-existence of partners in androgyny.

Virginia Woolf was one of the first women in the 19th century to recognize and write about the lasting effect of earlier times. She remarked:

> "...everything was covered up or disguised, except the sexes, which became more divided than they had ever been, more distinguishable."

It was those patterns of centuries of suppression of the human feminine spirit that Woolf was able to see. She became one of the outspoken forerunners of the women's movement.

The women's movement was the first collective of driving feminine force that penetrated centuries of masculine domination. It provided a channel which opened the prison doors so that the hidden femininity could be reborn into the world again. This re-emergence touched a missing part of the wholeness of humanity. This marked the beginning of men feeling the stirrings of the deeper feminine pulse in themselves, while women now were able to experience their maleness. Creativity was again being reborn while the fixedness of logic was starting to melt, revealing the whole, wherein male/female were once integrated with life's creative movement, balance and co-existence. It severed past centuries' fixed, distorted image of humanity's wholeness, and the functioning imbalance of gender.

George Leonard points out in his latest book **The End of Sex** that "sex" has dominated our lives since Roman times. The word "sex" originated from the Roman word "sex us," and this was borrowed from the latin "secare," meaning "to cut or sever." Leonard states that in earlier times human sexuality did not exist. Sex was not separated, isolated or compartmentalized from other functions in life. Male and female sex differences originally came from the Biblical translation which describes two sexes of animals that Noah took aboard the ark. This belief, this sexual division, has been ingrained in society's teachings and has been passed on through the ages. Our misunderstanding of sex originated from the distinguishing between animals on the ark. This reveals how deeply our views and practices of sex have been distorted.

As we bring our fictional time-machine back to the present, after exploring the stored memories of our historical consciousness, we witness another period of upheaval, a renaissance movement greater than any known before. It is a time when the identity on all levels of human existence are being questioned and expressed in a number of alternate ways. The beginning tides of the hippie, anti-war, womens' movement and other forces of change have set the pattern for a growing expression around the world.

This social activism has cleared its way, and has opened the doors of the ages to free the other half of the life essence once misused or not utilized at all. That quality has been reborn again, proclaiming the essence of being fully alive which is to be whole, human, balanced between internal and external energies. The ghosts of the ages have come to speak through new people, in new ways.

One of the modes of this expression is through the arts. Authors, musicians and actors many others are challenging the old beliefs and norms through experimentation with exciting new ways of cheating.

Dustin Hoffman, in his award winning role as Ms. Michaels in "Tootsie," shocked and delighted audiences everywhere. For the first time a man wearing women's clothing was seen beyond the label of drag queen. Audiences were able to identify with the movie's message. Hoffman plays an actor who cannot get work because he is a male. A deeper meaning unfolds when he pretends to be a woman and becomes a raving television success. The androgyny theme rings loud and clear. Dustin plays a woman who has strong qualitites that not only make him/her acceptable to his/her crew and audience, he/she becomes a model of balanced energies. The role exemplifies the forcefulness and outspokeness of the masculine, softened by the tenderness and humanity of the feminine. In a candid interview with "People" magazine, Hoffman stated that he gained a great deal in doing the movie. He discovered a part of himself that he was unfamiliar with which helped mellow him. The blending of his masculinity and his character role as a woman gave him an evenness, a balance that lessened his stress in playing the role.

Another expression of the new social-sexual experiment can be found in the eccentric character of Boy George, of the group Culture Club. In just a few years this young English performer, lyricist, has marvelled and confused patrons with his unique style of relating. His songs speak of sensitivity and tenderness; a truly feminine portrayal of musical artistry. Boy George dresses and looks expressively feminized and proclaims his bisexuality. He desires to marry and raise a family and in a very traditional motif.

Michael Jackson, like Boy George, has introduced a very feminine style to his music. He sounds more female than male and his form is moving, spiritual and tender. The mood, sound, lyrics and the style are much more in keeping with the feminine quality in males speaking through an art form. This is far removed from the loud, aggressive and extreme sound of heavy metal, or hard rock which is the overly accentuated sound of the masculine.

The re-emergence of part of our humanity in our lives to give balance, is still being explored as men and women search for the keys to open the doors of history. The need is to familiarize themselves, once again, with the natural kinship their ancestors held and practiced.

We have much to learn from our primitive ancestors, often more than we would like to admit. Their way of harmonious living was reflected in their abilities to create the kinds of societies that were cooperative with nature. This attunement and awareness was evident in their male/female relationships based upon an androgynous connection with the inherent qualitities of life existing within the human body and soul. The inner life energies both male and female were balanced with the outer realms of living. The complementary relationships between the two energies and their kindredness gave balance and growth to social evolvement.

It will take time, focus and a deeper understanding of ourselves and what we are, to reach a goal of being the best we can be. Our goal should not be to understand how we lost our abilities or to attain perfection.

Androgyny is not a goal per se. Androgyny is a statement, a blueprint of possibility that can help move us into deeper contact with our human powers, love and wisdom as we evolve into a new type of human race. We must learn to transcend labels when they stagnate or fix us into a certain place. Even androgyny will lose its meaning as we cross over into the next stage of evolution -which is the culmination of centuries of growth and development of the human soul. Until we are ready to make that evolutionary leap, we can use the concept of androgyny as an aide in deepening our understanding of ourselves, and healing male/female wounds to manifest healthier, more loving relationships with one another.

> "Someday, someday, men and women will rise, they will reach the mountain peak, they will meet big and strong and free, ready to receive, to partake, to bask in the golden rays of love, what fancy, what imagination, what poetic genius can foresee even approximately the potentialities of such a force in the life of men and women.
>
> "If the world is ever to give birth to true companionship and oneness, not marriage, but love will be the parent."
>
> — Emma Goldman

ARCHETYPES: THE HIDDEN THEATER OF SELVES

Everyone has more than once had the unpleasant experience of meeting someone for the first time and receiving signals that they don't feel good about you or like you. These meetings are not always negative and painful. Sometimes they are extremely positive. Due to the content of deeper recesses of our minds which consist of memories, images and illuminating and colorful events of our lives, our behavior and personality is affected and regulated. This content existing within our inner worlds is the archetype. This unconscious, material is a record of our individual lives. The largest area of mind is composed of associated sense impressions and all past experience memories. It is this subconscious realm that influences both negatively and positively our self-understanding and our abilities to relate to others. The more we are able to use and appreciate this realm, the more it becomes a power resource in our lives. Lack of use, abuse, or denial of this realm can cause harm, imbalance, dilemma and misery.

Freud, one of the first Western world pioneers to investigate the unconscious world, found fame and acknowledgement for his theories. He only tapped a portion of the unconscious world. He was limited by his own Victorian upbringing and his strong feelings about religion and other spiritual systems. His pioneering work helped society deepen its unconscious attunement and move beyond obsolete, stifling beliefs and attitudes. For such work he must be acknowledged. Another, who once was Freud's right hand-man and closest friend, finally left the Freudian camp.

Carl Gustav Jung's own ideas and beliefs were conflicting extensively with the master scholar, Freud. Jung's work, now being recognized in most every field from science to metaphysics, was first rejected and ignored by his academic colleagues. They viewed him as a mystic and his theories were not widely accepted in the scientific or medical field. Jung attempted to present his theories in the traditional and rational form calling his system of belief and knowledge "analytic psychology." His contribution was not recognized until now. He had a handful of followers, but the quality of his genius was not really seen and appreciated.

The most striking quality of Jung's theories is that he derived much of his information from the beliefs and practices of other cultures. The resultant beliefs were seen as primitive, and certainly not anything more than "superstitious nonsense" by the scholars of the scientific community. Nevertheless, Jung's in-depth investigations of other systems of seeing and understanding the world, beyond the rationalistic style of the scientific, helped collect invaluable information. Although his theories were not fully understood in his time, in this day and age they are not only considered as worthwhile, but as tools for our survival and growth.

One of Jung's greatest contributions was the theory of the collective unconscious. He believed that the hidden, unconscious world of our psyche contained the records of events, emotions, attitudes and the instinctual and social blueprints of humankind's evolution. It was this collective memory that acted as the content inherited from generation to generation, from age to age, and so on. Jung believed that this history material was present in dreams, images and fantasies of living persons and cultures. This theory was supported by the many people who came to visit him from around the world. This collective content was seen as being part of the biological make-up of an individual while simultaneously being reflected in the spiritual practices of any tribe or culture. His study of North American Indians, the Chinese, African and East Indian culture revealed this collective theme. Although the beliefs and practices were labelled differently a typical thread was interwoven within all systems that seems to indicate a common bond with earlier ancestors. Jung found this to be true in Western society as well. He was able to see how East and West complemented each other.

With a background in Jung's understanding of the collective relationships among members of the human race, we can focus on a thread of the collective unconscious system. The archetype would be considered as the living forms within the unconscious domain that speak to us and through us. Jung wrote:

"...that were essential to our near and remote ancestors will also be essential to us, for they are embedded in the inherited organic system".

Very little of our growth and accomplishments as people and a society is new for we live and breath patterns of behavior that have been passed down through the ages. Those beliefs, customs and practices of cultures which still hold their ancestoral roots in high esteem would support this theory. Inheritance of social and family practices through generations shows we still refer to a past blueprint of "this is the way things are done."

A good metaphor for how archetypes function is a stage play. Picture the audience, sitting in rows, waiting to be entertained and they have no idea what to expect. The audience represents the conscious realm, an attempt to satisfy the needs of their senses. They utilize their five senses to experience the event — from listening to dialogue to tasting the refreshments of inter-mission. The curtain is down and the performers are busily preparing for their performance. They are preparing to act out the lives and events of fictional and real human beings. The stage, lighting, makeup and wardrobe people all play a part in bringing the performance to the audience. Meta-phorically, that which is behind the curtain is the hidden domain of the unconscious. The players, the stage crew and others connected to the pro-duction are the living characters of the unconscious system. They give order, representing the substance and structure of the play behind the play that the audience does not see. They do not focus beyond the curtain. Each of the production staff has specific duties to perform to guarantee a success-ful performance. Each has a certain personality that fits his or her function. Often the production staff is composed of people of different races, beliefs and personal lifestyles. However with regard to the show production, they share a common goal to ensure that when that curtain goes up the stage will be ready for the players and their acting out of the play's script.

The stage play is a very good metaphor for showing how the archetype works in our lives. All of the personalities behind the curtain are the archetype representatives. The stage crew and production team could be considered the secondary achetypes, and assemble the unconscious human life system of organization that helps us grow, act, and change in order to survive. The performers could be seen as the primary archetypes with each having specific lines to say, and each performing in a prescribed way. Their roles could also symbolize the living portrayal of human existence, its many events and collected memories that make up the evolution of the human - species. The play itself, could represent a common everyday happening whether it be in a family, group, couple or in one person's life. This play represents a re-play of other events, historically based, which could have been similar in content and purpose even though the characters were different and the time was different. Indeed, we are players upon the stage of life, and the play that we are all part of is the continuous saga of life itself. We borrow lines and props from other times to act out our perceptions and needs now.

This content that we borrow from is, and always has been, stored in our unconscious play libraries. We continue to bring it out and re-play it again. In daily living we act out the behavior, the beliefs, the emotions, etc. of those before us, as if they were incarnated in our souls. If we are lucky, we can tap the source of purity wherein lies the creation of original thought. Mostly we repeat past, even ancient behaviors, thoughts, and feelings without even knowing why or how. It is this hidden world that remains such a mystery to us as we have lost touch with it. It still influences our lives, behavior and attitudes towards self and others.

The world of images, the symbolic pictures of humankinds' existence, the playground or the battleground of the archetype members of the unconscious cast, continue to prepare for the stage production for the conscious. The curtain is down and we lack the ability to know or see what is going on behind that curtain. The curtain goes up, and the spotlight hits the stage only to find the players not on stage, but sitting in the laps of the audience. For in reality, the players, the play, and the audience are not separate. We, the audience, have only learned to believe that they are separate. We must wake up and realize that we are part of the cast, part of the play, and representatives of the archetypical realm in every day life. This is an illumination of the conscious experience where conscious and unconscious are merged in human contact and reality. We must be aware that all is within us.

Finally, we must consider that our living actions, our external reality, is not separate from our internal reality. Externally, we act out the traits of our inner characteristics, or archetypes, expressing these in our conscious lives, usually without awareness. We choose to believe what has been taught; that we live separate lives, in separate worlds. Much of our difficulty comes from the denial of the other. By turning one against the other, that which we have denied has become a stronger force to handle. Until we learn to befriend both sides of our worlds, so that our inner is not separate from our outer we are condemned to live in two separate realities and to believe in our fragmented perspectives. The archetypes, history's ghosts are our best allies come to teach us how to merge and unify ourselves internally and externally.

> "For the anima and animus are the invisible partners in every human relationship, and in every persons search for individual wholeness."

> — J. A. Sanford

ANIMA/ANIMUS

A contrasexual system of male/female relationships in our traditional male-oriented society is based on economic security and has dictated male and female identities and roles. The male role was to be the bread winner and the protector and the female role to be the nurturer, caretaker.

Past attitudes are changing. Through the wave of the women's movement, the sexual revolution and technology, the roles of men and women have been drastically altered. In some situations, roles have reversed or have disappeared with duties and responsibilities becoming a shared venture. Many of the traditional beliefs and practices about marriage, child care, and relationships have been turned inside out. Both men and women have been forced to look at themselves and their relationships with new eyes and from different viewpoints. The fabric of the traditional sex role system has been torn and a new way of looking at 'pairing' has come into perspective.

The task, as many are discovering, is to create new ways or re-create some of the old; to fully understand our world, ourselves and others. We must still preserve some of the foundations we have always depended upon for survival and growth. We must be cautious while we're casting out unhealthy, obsolete patterns of living and not throw away that which has value.

We are now in a time of renewal and reconstruction. Both men and women are searching for a deeper understanding of themselves and their relationships to one another. Both are recognizing that they still need one another in their lives; they desire contact and sharing yet they do not want to repeat old patterns. What draws men and women towards one another? What causes them to be attracted to one another or repelled? These questions need to be considered as we struggle during these times of transitions in plotting a new course for our personal, social, and collective evolution. Paths of understanding and function that are more humane, balanced and wholistic are being bridged. Jung, as we have already seen, provides us with some very important guideposts that can assist us in seeing the effects of our psyche system, and how this understanding is pertinent to our utilization of his offerings. By examining, in depth, his theories of the anima and animus we can expand our focus of these archetypal figures and how they function in our relationships within our conscious and unconscious lives.

Jung thought that these archetypes were the building blocks of all life's function and relationships. Through the positive and natural function of these archetypes, our lives are provided with balance and symmetry. He found in studying the content of dreams that it manifested in males and females in varied ways. A statement from one of his studies shows how this was obvious:

> "Every man carries within him the eternal image of the woman, not the images of this or that women, but a definite feminine image. This image is fundamentally unconscious, an hereditary factor of primordial origin engraved in the living organic system of the man, an imprint or archetype of all the ancestral experiences of the female, a deposit, as it were, of all the impressions ever made by women. . . Since this image is unconscious, it is always unconsciously projected upon the person of the beloved, and is one of the chief reasons for passionate attraction or aversion."

Jung taught that women possess within themselves a masculine image that has the primordial traits of all male experiences and these are also projected on to males in their lives. In his studies, he found that the mother of the male and the father of the female were the persons with whom this attraction begins. As these experiences began with the opposite sex, this primary relationship governs the healthy development of both the male and female. He called this relationship contrasexual, the traits existing within the father or mother, their archetypes, influenced the development of the opposite sexed child.

He saw that this contrasexual relationship as necessary in the beginning life of the child in order for the child to actualize natural characteristics. Babies are primarily sexless in traits and character. They need to identify with their parents' physical attributes and psyche. To develop their sexuality, young boys need a bonding with their mothers to be grounded in the feminine principle (soul). This necessary first connection can be the beginning of a healthy bonding to the young male's biological self as long as the feminine archetype is allowed to become the background of his character while he is also being supported in balancing his character with flexibility, and feeling. Young girls need the bonding to their fathers for the awareness of masculine principle (spirit), to enable them to express their individuality, and reach beyond their biological feminine roots. The young female needs the background support of her masculine connection so she can express herself in a more balanced way to the external world. The importance of a mutual relationship between the anima and animus in male or female cannot be overlooked. Too much of one aspect can create tilted personalities such as, masculinized females, who are overly aggressive and desensitized or males who are passive, overly emotional and have difficulty in expressing assertiveness or his intellectual side in a coherent manner. These examples of imbalanced archetype functioning are only a part of the dynamics that go on in shaping the human being. The social, genetic and other factors that also influence the characteristics must also be considered. A further description of contrasexual relationships is given in John Sanford's book **The Invisible Partners.** He replies:

"In the case of the anima, it is she who lies behind a man's moods. When a man is possessed by the anima he is drawn into a dark mood, and tends to become sulky, overly sensitive, and withdrawn. A poisonous atmosphere surrounds him, and it is as though he is immersed in a kind of psychological fog. He ceases to be objective or related and his masculine stance is eroded by peevishness."

As for the women experiencing the effects of her anumus side, he remarks:

"If the anima is the master of moods in a man, the animus is the master of opinions in a woman. He (animus) typically expresses himself in judgments, generalizations, critical statements, and apodictic assertions that do not come from a women's own process of thinking and feeling, but have been picked up from various authoritative sources, mother or father, books, or articles, or some other collective organization. It is the animus who is behind the autonomous, critical, and opinionated thoughts that intrude into a women's consciousness."

Sanford goes on to distinguish the two characteristics of these unconscious effects in male and females:

"He (animus) thus represents inferior masculine logic, just as the anima represents inferior feminine emotionality."

Let us stop for a minute and discuss the ramifications of Sanford's information. Some of my own experiences exemplify this. I can remember many times when my attempts to express myself, which is now becoming easier, were disasterous when I felt deeply emotional about an issue. I usually ended up seeming like and sounding like an idiot, unable to put across my feelings and ideas in a comprehensive or organized form. During these times I felt totally out of touch, imbalanced and vulnerable beyond what the sitution dictated, but mostly I felt frightened and speechless. While spending hundreds of hours in seclusion writing this book, there were times that I fell into these dark moods and found myself being depressed, overly critical and enraged. I moped, felt sorry for myself and often had the desire to stop writing, abandoning this project entirely. During those times I had learned to use them as teaching experiences and to integrate these feelings into my writing as a deeper awareness and understanding of my self grew. I've seen this with other men, friends and while working in therapy sessions.

The other extreme of this situation for men I've seen going through these moods, is that it can put them on the brink of suicide. I can remember times in my earlier growing phases when thoughts of suicide plagued my thinking, especially during crisis and difficult periods. However I did not understand then as I do now the effects of my invisible anima self. Certain women and some men can affect me this way negatively, while others have a comforting and nuturing presence. Like anyone, my unconscious buttons can be pushed and I can fall prey to the whims of the power of my undeveloped anima.

Likewise, I have seen women friend's unconscious animus kick in during heated discussions. They begin to quote sources of books, become opinionated to distraction and their common sense simply gone. I try to understand and extract a perspective from their comments which has a sound basis for their opinionated, stubborn stance. I've learned to stand back and give some room so they can find the balance which can occur if I am patient. Sometimes we can see clearer but at other times, both of our unconscious aspects take over and we remain, totally paralyzed and overwhelmed by these invisible forces working through us. I've lost friendships, or decided not to begin them with women that affect me in this way. I've experienced a different situation with men who are overly anima-ted in their opinions. Some project their animus on to me, in a sense making me more powerful than I really am, while others bring out more of my feminine traits, when they are overly masculinized. The powerful, unconscious forces in the characters of the anima and animus can result in a positive exchange or a painful and destructive one. Any exchange has the potential to be an unconscious connection or a battle.

All the literature that I've read about Jung's theories and practices in addition to other information gained through the study of various systems of belief in regard to the masculine and feminine archetypes, bears out that these exist deeply in the unconscious part of our being and can be used in either negative or positive ways. The feminine aspect once denied and cast into the shadows can bring untold misery and pain into our individual lives. The masculine counterparts, left unbridled, can also bring havoc and defensive postures into daily affairs. If left to its own bidding, the masculine aspect, can manifest a psychopathic social personality. Aloofness, lack of sensitivity, self-righteousness and manipulation through power are some societal results of an imbalanced expression of human form. Jung also taught that denial of either creates a shadow effect: that which is denied in male or female, in society results in separation and imbalance which creates a force of negativism and decay of the spirit of the whole of the life force. This imbalance causes a devaluation of the unconscious properties which limits our capacity and awareness of our creative gifts of life as well as how we communicate in our interpersonal relationships and in our relationships with countries and nations. Losing sight of the importance of this balance creates a build up of barriers towards one another; males to females, males to males, females to females, young and old. We also find ourselves ready to engage in battle with our invisible selves in anger, misunderstanding and judgment.

Relearning to befriend our unconscious parts, building bridges to join, rather than separate ourselves, increases the hope for a more unified world. The use of these powerful potential allies, will help us grow together, and become the whole that nature intended.

THE ANCHORS AND BRIDGE BETWEEN SOUL AND SPIRIT

If the anima and animus are considered the building blocks of the collective unconscious, the instincts are the source from which building blocks come. Jung called the anima and animus the soul and spirit members of the collective family of the race. Primitive tribes often refer to these archetypes as their "ancestors." Chinese often make pledges on the "grave of their ancestors" and in the Indian tradition one "sees" the spirits of the grandmothers and grandfathers who serve as guides for direction, support and council. Metaphorically speaking, it is the instincts that guide and govern the characterizations, or living expressions of the archetypes. They are the bridge between soul and spirit; the anchors and the interwoven threads of the collective unconscious inherited from the beginning of all life. They hold the key to the beginning of creative form. Do we really know what we mean when we use the word instincts?

Do we believe that instincts affect our lives to a significant degree, or are they merely behavioral aspects of lower animals? Joseph Campbell, a leading scholar of Jung's ideas, believes that instincts are much more prevalent in human beings than previously understood. Our strict adherence to rational thinking since the Renaissance has limited us to our mental fortresses. He explains:

"We are in a far better position to observe instincts in animals or in primitives than ourselves. This is due to the fact that we have grown accustomed to scrutinizing our own actions and to seeking rational explanations for them".

We need a working definition of "instincts." Kant, called instincts; "that which is felt as the inner necessity." William James said, "a mere excite-motor impulse, due to pre-existence of a certain 'reflex-arx' in the nerve centres." Perhaps a more simple definition of instincts is as follows: "typical modes of action that occur regularly without conscious motive or intent." In a nutshell, instincts represent the spontaneity of the unconscious. Instincts together with archetypes within the collective unconscious is a good combination.

Jung wrote a long time ago about the collective unconscious, the instincts and the archetypes. Roger Sperry, nobel prize winning Biologist, shows us that the brain is split, composed of two separate parts called hemispheres. One hemisphere regulates mechanical abstract functions and logic such as mathematics, chemistry, and the other hemisphere governs creativity, intuition and artistic forms. The left hemisphere regulates outward or conscious expression and the right, more inward, unconscious expression. These functions and characteristics support what Jung wrote about a half century ago when he described the anima and animus.

Over the years since Sperry's discovery, the split brain theory has influenced every field of human philosophy and science. The theory has become as commonplace as Freud's ideas, which were in their beginnings, suspect. Workshops have been given to educate lay and professionals and books have been written to strengthen the validity of the split brain, hemisphere functions. For the first time in decades, the fields of science and learning have begun to move beyond the rigidity of the masculine dominance of logic that has been so characteristic of the focus of education until now. Sperry's discovery has contributed to an awakening of parts of human consciousness well hidden from our use and understanding.

Theorist, neuroscientist Paul MacLean has gone one more step beyond Sperry's discovery of the split brain, to suggest that the brain has three parts. MacLean states that each part possesses separate functions, not related to the other two. In his theory the human brain contains an ancient reptilian brain, that functions by instinct and is void of any kind of emotion. This is the oldest brain and least developed of the three. The second brain is referred to as the paleo-mammalian brain, also called the mid brain. The mid brain regulates partial instinctive responses, yet is more sophisticated than the reptilian brain and seeks to balance basic hormonal drives and basic needs such as hunger, thirst, sex, sleep, etc. Conscious awareness is more prevalent in this brain portion, but it is still prone to follow unconscious direction. The third brain, says MacLean, is the neo-mammalian brain. This brain is the most evolved of the three and regulates perceptual processes.

Science contributes to broadening the understanding of our complex natures and functions by separating the whole of our consciousness into individual parts. This rule of scientific method turns our human processes into mechanical functions. Science still refuses to recognize the wholistic relationship that exists in our integral natures, attempting to reduce personal vitality and essence to fitting a rational prescribed scientific mode. This reductionistic, logic-dominated approach still guides the western world's thinking and action. In the name of progress we are torn away from our kinship with nature.

In western society, the separate "I" rules and dominates the greater aspect of the creation. This tradition and practice divides man, family, nature and the potential planetary collective relationship. Since the Descartian era, man has chosen to live divided and estranged from his creatureness, being guided by his logic, rather than working in connection with functions and processes of nature. When man re-unites with his deeper nature, he rediscovers his true self. This point is exemplified by a story that I was told about a former university trained accountant who discovered himself after living several months in the mountains of British Columbia.

I was never given the name of our mountain man so, I'll call him Buck. Buck completed all of his pre-university studies in central British Columbia and entered the University of British Columbia where he received his degree in Accounting after his fourth year. His father, a company vice president, was happy about Buck's career choice and had always encouraged him to enter the business world. After becoming a certified accountant, he married and settled down in a suburb outside of Vancouver. For the next five years he worked for an oil drilling parts company and adjusted to the routine of being a father and husband. During this five year period his life seemed normal by society's standards.

In the early 70's Buck's life changed dramatically. He was divorced and as a result began drinking. He finally left the oil company before they asked him to leave. His drinking increased and he started to take drugs as well. His wife remarried and a short time later was awarded custody of the two children. His parents were saddened by the divorce and Buck's abusive behavior. Buck avoided them as much as possible and when he did connect with them, he would plead for money. Buck ended up in jail and was given a choice to enter either a treatment center for his alcohol and drug problem or do time for his drug conviction. Buck completed his treatment and though he made some changes and benefited from the program, his life was still empty. He could neither face his parents nor his two children.

Buck moved around for the next two years doing odd jobs gardening and working construction. He later settled in the interior of British Columbia. Buck, was a loner without any friends. No one was close to him. He spent days by himself in the woods camping which seemed to revive his spirits. He felt at home amongst the trees and wildlife, in ways he could not in the community in which he lived.

One day Buck disappeared from sight. He did not show up for his landscaping job and never returned to his single room flat over the general store. No one knew of his whereabouts. Months passed, then one day Buck walked into the local pub and told a story about his five month life as a hermit in the woods. Those who knew Buck could see something different about him. He looked healthy, his eyes sparkled; a big change from his haunted appearance before. Whether his story was true or not, it was obvious that Buck had been through an experience that had brought his spirit back to life. People were amazed by Buck's spontaneity.

Buck told a friend of mine that during his last stay in the woods he had climbed to the top of a very large peak that overlooked a valley and had set up camp near the peak, staying for several days. He would rise in the morning with the sun and sit all day until it set. He began to feel a part of the mountains, the freshness of the air was akin to his own breath and the sounds of birds were like music. For hours he would sit, while thoughts of his childhood and adolescence filled his mind. He thought about his life as an accountant, a father and as a divorced person. He remembered his mistakes and his subsequent escape into alcohol and drugs. Those days on top of that mountain made him realize how he spent so much time and energy doing what he thought he was supposed to do. He had followed the socialized script; he went to University, got married, had a family and had a respectable career. Yet he always felt something was missing from his life. He felt trapped but was unaware of how to free himself. In the woods he felt free, at home, in touch with his life and himself.

He said that he was put to the ultimate test on the morning before he had planned to leave the woods and go back to town. He woke up later than usual after a restless night sleeping. He felt depressed and the thought of leaving the woods scared him. He did not want to go back to the people, his job, his emptiness. The more frightened he became, the more depressed he became. Suicidal thoughts flashed through his mind, similar to those that occured when he began drinking years earlier. He walked to the edge of the ledge and as he looked out over the valley, he had a sudden urge to rip off his clothes and jump. The urge became stronger as he began to strip. It felt good to be free of the garments that confined his body. He unzipped his jeans, until all that was left were his boxer shorts. These were peeled away and he stood naked on top of the mountain peak. His breathing was rapid and full and he could feel the blood flowing through his veins. A rush of electricity shot through his body. He felt higher than he had ever been on drugs. The thoughts of suicide were gone and so was his depression. He felt fresh and reborn. The experience was spiritual in a way beyond what he had ever known in going to mass.

While living in the woods, he was able to find plants that he could eat. He had taken courses in Herbology. He taught himself to make snares for trapping rabbits, squirrels and other small animals. He drank from the pure mountain streams. Much of the time he wore as little clothing as the weather permitted. Each day was re-learning experience, not only how to survive in the wilderness, but to know a deep part of himself that had been hidden since childhood. His curiosity about other living things was insatiable. He found himself viewing the trees, the land and the animals as relatives. He began to understand the affinity that Indians once held with the land and creatures.

One thing was clear about Buck, the withdrawn, haunted, lost soul that people knew before was gone. In his place was a man who seemed confident, full of life and hope. Buck was an apprentice and Mother Nature was his mentor. After all those years of torment and self-abuse he had finally found in nature what was missing from his life; his essence, his soul.

This story serves as a reminder for those of us who are looking for a truer meaning of our existence. Perhaps, if more scientists learned how to **learn** from nature, rather than merely studying it, they might find more of what they need. Perhaps, if businessmen, politicians, military generals, and land developers were willing to go into the wilderness and touch what Bly calls the wildman part of themselves, they would regain the sacred bond with nature once known and necessary for survival.

The North American Indians and other primitive tribes knew the importance of the journey into the wilderness, and touching base with the mentors of this realm — this was the reason for their vision quests. They knew the significance of becoming anchored in the primordial path of the life; the stream of life. They realized that if a human being is to develop his whole soul and spirit, he must create a bridge between the instinct and creative essence, like the story told in the veins of a leaf or the rings of a tree. To become a whole human creature one must learn to live in respectful harmony with the wild part of the self, inside and out.

Our instincts are the godfathers and godmothers of our existence. We must listen to their urges. Gurdjieff reminds us:

"Begin by loving plants and animals, then perhaps you will learn to love people."

CONCLUSION

WHOLENESS AND INTEGRATION — Dissolving the 'duel'-ality of masculine/feminine principles.

Since the millenium we have lived and died through the conflict dance of the masculine and feminine energies which compose the evolutionary consciousness of this planet. We have created legends and told of the great fall from grace or atonement with creation. At first legends were collected in the volumes of great books the Koran, the Talmud, the Bible, each with it's own interpretation of our separation from the "essence." These great books became the sacred scrolls and records of historical and spiritual events. Each religion had in its own perspective. Other legends tell of great masters and prophets who came to our planet to teach us the meanings of these great books and to help us understand and apply them in our everyday lives. Throughout the world the different races and cultures have used these great books as guides to their growth and awakening. Other learned scholars have studied these books and have helped show us the validity of their teachings. They have helped us to understand primarily that within us lies the secrets to our beginning, to the great fall, that which the great masters and prophets taught long ago.

Scholars like Jung, Freud, Reich and others resurrected bits and pieces of these legends which have lain hidden in the depths of our souls. They erected new systems to bring these ancestrial beginnings back into our lives, and to give us a renewed direction. They can be credited with lessening the complexity of our history, and clearing away the debris which resulted from decaying practices and beliefs, inherited from centuries of imbalance through generations of our life's journey. Each contributor had his time to influence the direction of society. Freud gave us his version of a system that helped integrate some of the missing historical pieces. Reich gave us the depth and a pathway to our essence. Jung gave us a system that linked the continuous life process, records of events, from primitive to modern day. The spirit of Jung's far-reaching knowledge and understanding is timely and can be used as an integrated tool for the awakening of all of our lifetimes as a human species.

As noted, the archetypes Jung described carry the records and messages stored within the collective unconscious of our existence. Jung's findings tell us that the two main representatives of this historical archive, the anima and animus, act as the collective grandmother/grandfather of our species, reflecting the seeds of the masculine/feminine principles of existence. These principles govern the function of the human family, and the evolutionary journey of our consciousness. Each new generation brings a renewed piece of this consciousness into being, as we continue on in our journey towards wholeness. The missing hidden piece of our history also exist here and can be illuminated. The more that we can learn about this process which is alive within us, the more we can reclaim and assimilate those disparate parts from this, and other lifetimes, and integrate these parts into our daily lives.

Jung called the new form created by integrating anima and animus, the masterpiece. The masterpiece is a fully balanced system, consisting of both masculine/feminine qualities and functions manifest consciously in the human being, whether male or female. It is, at this point, all remaining aspects of human existence and creation itself that reveal themselves in our lives.Thus, we begin to see the threads of the unified whole existing in all beliefs, all systems primitive or modern, scientific or spiritual. Everyday becomes a chance to experience newness and freshness; "each day becomes the beginning of the rest of our life." Everyday, every exchange with self, others and environment, is a constant mirroring and rediscovery of hidden memories of our lives and history in the making. Every moment we can see the magic of our shared journey, not only with our fellows and sisters, but with the rest of our total environment.

EVOLUTION UNFOLDS INTO PRACTICE

The days of classifying people into male/female gender categories; by beliefs, cultures, and nations; of seeing the individual as separate from society, family, nation, world, universe and creation are gone. Today we are face to face with all of our reflections of lifetimes on this planet; a vast network of patterns and historical events of our psyche. We must come of age, releasing our immaturity and the limited awareness of our historical roots. It is time for the God spirit of Narcissus, to look beyond his own image and recognize other archetype family members, who have remained in the shadows since the early days of Greek civilization when the balance and rhythm of the creative forces of anima/animus prevailed.

Today we are witnessing globally, the resurrection of our spiritual relative of time — father/mother, brother/sister, daughter/son, grandfather/-grandmother, who are coming alive within us, lending us a fuller sense of being human.

The planetary family archetypes are emerging from the corners of our unconscious, penetrating through habits of falsehood and denial, despite the discord of our modern era renaissance. The challenge for us is to hear their message and to receive their gifts. The unconscious is opening its doors and the prisoners of time, fear, hate and misdeed are being freed. We are asked to heed these urges, these prehistoric and renaissance stirrings.

We are being asked to be more fully who we truly are and what we can be.

To see ourselves as the possible human, what international transpersonal teacher Jean Huston calls the "planetary person."

"To be a planetary person means to be part of a wholly different modality of knowing and being, which involves a profound consciousness of the earth, a potentiating recovery of one's historical self, and an actual learning from the genius of other cultures. This person is both the consummation of where we have been and the next stage of the spiral. As such, he is our hope, our dreams, our beckoning evolutionary vision, a point of contact with that which never was but is always happening."

It will take time to transform outdated beliefs, values and social practices, which have kept us from our birthright kinship to the whole of the world community. As we embark on our transformation, time is moving us ever so swiftly increasing the urgency of dealing with the changing conditions of our time. We need models and processes that can help us direct our energies, internally and externally, to facilitate the necessary growth, healing and awakening needed to dissolve the fixed images of our perceptions of self and others. We need models to show how our relationships are governed by not only social and learned imprints, but also on intra-psychic levels, for which we are channels and catalysts to one another. We can help each other transform and re-direct historical habits, patterns and events into broader, more collective resources that are planetarily focused, applied and shared. Beneath the fabrication, dullness and the blockages lie our passion for human greatness. This heartbeat of the creation is in every pulse - rhythm of all living creatures, from dinosaur to the etheric.

The teaching/learning models and processes that are needed today must contain flexibility, strength and must enliven, as well as transform. They need to be androgynous in spirit, blending both masculine and feminine energies that speak of the ancient ages as well as modern images. They need the blending of the trinity; father, son and holy ghost, and balanced with mother, daughter, and holy spirit. Together, these form a Grand Trinity. It is neither male nor female, it is both; neither is dominant, but each serves the functions of the other in a complementary and rhythmic dance. Each symbolizes the context of life's historic journey, manifesting this in a different flavor and color. Together these trinities symbolize unity, connection and the human relationship at the soul's depth.

We need a tool to ignite the fires of the depths of our beginnings, to illuminate and balance the soaring of our spirit. It will rekindle our integrative powers and serve as a key to open many closed doors to our inner domain. We need a source for transformation and integration of the old with the new. This serves to remind us that relationships are a reflection of what is missing from our wholeness, and provides the opportunity for us to fill in these gaps with understanding, memory, forgiveness and the reclamation of lost parts of ourselves and our life's journey.

We need to connect with the roots of our creatureness, our selves, as the dynamic other in our life's journey.

We all carry inside of us the memories and experiences with others. These can be reclaimed as a missing link with our past or at least, brought into the emergence of our thinking and feeling process.

We have multitudes of experience stored in the libraries of our unconscious. The more we can use this experience as a resource, the more we can grow and become fuller in our lives. Our unconscious can aid us in bringing the past into our lives through a commitment to grow, to learn through honesty, integrity, and most of all willingness to share with others. It is only a symbol of what our possibilities are as fuller, resourceful persons in our relationships with others and the planetary family of earth.

The New Society

Men & Women, Young and Old:
Living, Building, Working and Learning Together

Nothing belongs to you of what there is, of what you take you must share.

— Chief Dan George
British Columbia, Canada

The new world will be more human and humane. It will explore and develop the richness and capacities of the human mind and spirit. It will produce individuals who are more integrated and whole. It will be a world that prizes the individual person — the greatest of our resources.

It will be a more natural world, with a renewed love and respect for nature. It will develop a more human science, based on new and less rigid concepts. Its technology will be aimed at the enhancing rather than the exploitation of persons and nature. It will release creativity as individuals sense their power, their capacities, their freedom.

— Carl Rogers,
A Way of Being

Most of this book has focused on the male journey. I have attempted to deal with the crisis we men are experiencing today and to provide some information that would be useful in understanding the crisis. I have shared many of my personal experiences. I see a new kind of relationship evolving among men. I'm grateful to see more books and articles available addressing

267

areas of male concern. This is only the beginning as the more men are able to reclaim lost parts of our male spirit and reshape our perceptions and attitudes towards ourselves and others the more our relationships improve.

Now we need to look beyond the focus of the male journey and begin to look at ourselves as men within the context of a societal blueprint; to see the male journey as a part of a greater planetary journey in which women, youth, seniors, professional and lay persons are travelling members. While this chapter moves us closer to the end and/or the completion of this book, it serves as only a beginning for planetary citizens.

Today we live in an extremely volatile and distressing time. The nuclear clock ticks away and the two super powers engage in a battle of ideological wits while crime, rape, child abuse, and other forms of social decay consume our lives. In major cities across the nation, in the most affluent country in the world, a new street people survival subculture emerges beneath the noses of the affluent. Young people are increasing their abuse of drugs and alcohol. Many are scared, angry and feel ripped off in not having a secure future. There is an increase in suicide. The U.S. Government manipulates the public's conscience to escalate the war in Central America, while playing "fox and goose" with Congress to get more money for nuclear weapons.

In relationships, men and women are farther apart than they have ever been, each fearing they will get trapped in the negative need and image patterns that suffocate relationships and self-esteem. Each is still awkward in trying alternative ways of being with one another. Each attempts to reach out to the other; each desiring to touch, without wounding or being wounded, but confused as how to do it differently than before. Each tries to balance the real and the ideal; often not able to distinguish one from the other.

Some religious groups believe that our days are numbered on this planet and that the day of judgment is near. They wait, hands clasped in prayer seeking forgiveness for sinful living. Many try to spread this message, hoping to capture the public's attention and loyalty with their vision.

Others believe that we are embarking on a New Age, the Age of Aquarius. An age when people will live in harmony and as the lyrics to the song express "peace will guide the planets and love will steer the stars." In order for this Aquarian Age to be born, it is necessary to go through the death of the preceeding age of Pisces; releasing materialism and moving towards a brotherhood of all peoples and races. Marilyn Ferguson suggests that we are living in the "change of change." Toffler speaks of a "quantum leap forward, a creative restructuring." John Nesbitt, author of **Megatrends**, refers to these times as the "parenthesis." We are experiencing the death of the old society while the new one is being born.

I'm an optimist, more than a bit of an idealist and I'm also a realist. It would be easy to grab onto one belief, one path and one solution to our planetary dilemma. It would be great to have someone wave a magic wand and dissolve all of our problems, or to wake up from our numbed sleep to discover that we have only been having a nightmare. It would be easy to accept simplistic answers to complex situations.

Today, we are being forced to come of age; to accept responsibility for our actions. It is time to look squarely and deeply into, not only our souls, but the souls of everyone around us. We must learn to see a part of ourselves in everyone and everything — young and old, human and creature, black, white, red or yellow, Buddhist, Jew, Christian, Capitalist and Socialist. We must be aware that we can learn from one another and gain from the experience of knowing one another.

Across the globe people are joining together in a multitude of ways to recognize our new roles for these changing times. We are the architects for the new world. We are collectively responsible as planetary citizens to create and discover ways to prevent the destruction of ourselves and our earthly home. Today we are challenged to travel into the deep pit of fear and despair and reclaim the buried faith and courage we are seeking. We can choose to do nothing or we can choose to try. We all have to choose - to move towards the light or stay locked in the dark dungeons of our fear and limitedness. To be born is not easy. To reach out to one another is a risk we have to take to survive. We must examine ourselves both internally and externally to facilitate the necessary growth, healing and awakening to dissolve the fixed images of our perceptions of self and others.

BUILDING THE PLANETARY BRIDGE

While billions are being spent on the production of nuclear weapons in both the U.S. and its allies and the Soviet bloc countries, millions of people around the globe are active in building a strong and viable movement for peace. Recently, 100,000 Europeans demonstrated at bases which stock cruise and Pershing missiles. The government receives 400 letters from children daily speaking of the fear of a nuclear war. Various adult and youth groups have launched letter writing projects to bring peace between the U.S. and the U.S.S.R. and to end famine in the world. In the Soviet Union, youth and adults express their concerns about a nuclear confrontation with the U.S. Conferences, throughout the world, are held to discuss survival of this planet and to discover ways of preventing nuclear war. The movement towards peace is growing in strength and influence as young, old, lay persons, professionals, scientists, clergy and others from every field of learning are joining together in speaking out against war as a viable alternative for handling conflict and differences between nations.

Throughout the world, people are participating in building planetary bridges. These bridges of connection symbolize, trust, respect and commonality. These are bridges of hope composed of the combined creative ingenuity of all those involved. People have banned together, putting aside differences and are seeking wholeness and unity. This can be our only course of action.

During President Jimmy Carter's administration, when Sadat and Begin met at Camp David to discuss the peace accord, the beginning of a new way of dealing with the scars and hatred of two proud countries was initiated. Recognizing wounds they shared and inflicted on one another was the beginning of the healing of relations between two nations. This courageous attempt by three great statesmen was a model for other nations to follow.

Canada's former Prime Minister Pierre Elliot Trudeau, travelled the world speaking with leaders of western nations and the Soviet Union regarding the banning of nuclear weapons and a joint effort on the part of all nations to get the two super powers to the bargaining table. This was a courageous step for humankind.

In 1983, a young girl of ten from the midwestern U.S., sent a letter to the leader of the Russian people, Uri Andropov, asking him if he wanted a nuclear war to happen between the Russians and the U.S. He not only sent a letter back, but invited her and her parents to be guests of the Soviet government.

A few years ago the Esalen Institute and the Association for Humanistic Psychology sponsored an American-Soviet Exchange program. The purpose was to learn more about the Soviet people and their systems and for the Soviet and American to find ways of sharing skills and resources. As a result, several delegations have gone to the Soviet Union and have met with Soviet professionals and lay people and have shared methods and approaches in humanistic psychology education and family therapy. Other projects and visits are being planned for the future. Those who participated have gained a greater understanding and appreciation of the Soviet people and have found many similarities between themselves and the Soviets. This project has opened many doors once closed to communication and understanding of Russian people, their beliefs and culture. It has also helped the Russians to see the American people like themselves have strong feelings and concerns about their government's actions and they want peace, not war. I am to be one of the delegates in the next Soviet-American Exchange. Through the efforts of so many of the individuals and groups in many countries around the world we can strengthen our hope and optimism for a society and world of peace. We can build bridges to one another with visions of co-existence and contact once we dissolve the enemy context that hovers over us like a deathly shadow. We can no longer live in paranoid isolation wrought with

ignore-ance. The responsibility is upon us to awaken, educate, and participate with our human brother and sister citizens of planet earth in averting
nuclear war, and preparing ourselves for a new world and planetary
consciousness.

RENEWED KINSHIP WITH NATURE

It is obvious that we have lost much of our respect and rapport with
nature. How often do we experience the kindredness of a tree or an insect
without having our minds flooded with images and concepts of what a tree
or insect 'is', left over from high school biology? When we go into the
wilderness on a campout or retreat, we take battery powered generators to
hook up razors, electric skillets, hair dryers, televisions, etc. We have such a
tight hold on our manmade world that we have lost sight of our co-
habitation with nature and our creatureness, which are important parts
of our humanness.

Otto Rank, one of history's great psychological scholars, believed that our
concept of nature has been merely anthropormorphic; making everything,
including nature, conform to our own comfortable image of ourself. Robert
Young, a Cambridge University professor, supports this and has stated:

> "When we penetrate to the core of our scientific beliefs, we find
> that they are as much influenced by the culture as all our other
> belief systems".

Many scientists would argue to the death regarding the purity of their
system and would separate themselves from such a social theory, as it has
not withstood the examination and proofing of rigid scientific theory.

It is not my intention in this brief discussion to launch an attack on
science, which would only feed the archaic flame of rational form, seeking to
argue it's objective side only. My purpose is only to highlight certain points
that are germane in helping augment the building of a new and more
positive attitude between humans and nature.

To re-learn how to live in harmony and affinity and regain a respect for
nature we will need to release our desire to control and dominate. We had
this affinity as children until we were taught otherwise. Our attitudes which
view nature as something to fear if not kept controlled, need to be changed.
An example of this attitude is reflected in a true story that was passed on to
me about a young western Canadian farmer who was having difficulty with
his crop yield, and decided to visit a professor of agriculture at a nearby
university in the hope that an expert would know how to assist him with his
ordeal. "Mother Nature's a bitch," proclaimed the professor after listening to

the young farmer's problem. He further stated that nature is not on our side and has to be controlled in order to do our bidding.

I find this story of particular interest as this professor's attitude is indicative of the macho, tough guy image attitude toward nature which also is reflected in attitudes and interactions with people. Arrogance, sexism and macho attitudes are still flourishing in the 20th century.

When we are estranged, alienated from nature, our recourse will be to befriend nature and join with her in a cooperative venture of coexistence to re-establish our kindredness. No longer can we rape the earth and continue the imbalance of taking without putting anything back. This imbalance affects the ecological system and the human psyche as well. Each time we strip a mine of its mineral resources and rip out tree's roots to make way for a condominium complex, we are essentially tearing out part of the human soul. Unless we can begin to see ourselves as part of the whole life soul; as a part of the water, sky, ground, and so forth, and acknowledge our place in this life system, we will continue to lose more of our bonding with not only the earth, but ourselves.

During my "Brothers" workshops, I take the men through a ritual of reconnection with mother earth. We go out into the wilderness and look for a gift that mother nature has left just for each one of us. It is easy to discover what this is as the rock, twig, leaf or flower that attracts us most in that gift. Then we do some singing as we build a sculpture from all the pieces that we brought in from the wilderness. The ritual is to help us to become acquainted once again with the feminine part of our nature and to begin developing a respectful and trusting relationship with this.

The more attune we are with nature, the more aware we will become of ourselves as people which will surely improve our relationships as well.

Now our task and responsibility is to change our toxic relationship with the mother part of our natures — to begin seeing a tree as a tree and not merely as an object or concept; to smell the true fragrance of a flower and to join with our integral creatureness and to experience this in our environment.

To live in a new society, is to share the burden of healing what has been dis-eased. Our ignorance, mindlessness and insensitivity has to change. Men and women, as caretakers of the planet, will guide the young and others in creating a healthy relationship with nature. Our relationships with one another will be a model of what we see in nature. Our values and attitudes will spring from a more harmonious belief system. Our technology will be less exploitive in bringing about integration between mankind and nature.

In Scotland, the Findhorn community has gained world recognition for growing vegetables in unfertile, sandy soil. The community functions in accordance with natural laws and works cooperatively with the spirit beings of the plant kingdom. Whether these beings exist or not, the crops that grow in Findhorn exemplify a miracle of the coexistence with nature. The North American Indians and other cultures have spoken of the many kinds of spirit entities existing in different domains of the life kingdom. It's time we re-examined some of our own narrow fixed beliefs that have excluded other possibilities from us.

In June 1984, in Western Canada, four Indian medicine men conducted a traditional medicine wheel ceremony of healing mother earth. Two of these men were Red Cloud and Rolling Thunder who are internationally known for their command of native healing rituals. This event marked the beginning of a comeback to our earthly roots. Our native brothers and sisters, who originally lived in harmony with nature, have come forward to share their wisdom with the world and to help us get back in touch with our true home in nature.

We can renew our place with nature and reclaim a missing part of the essence of our humanity. When we develop this resource, we will come home again in our hearts, in our minds and our bodies and be connected with the earth, the universe.

"One touch of nature makes the whole world kin"

— Shakespeare

MEN AND WOMEN AS ALLIES

Walking hand in hand, mind to mind, heart to heart: A duo-commentary.

For men and women to bridge their differences, it is vital that they combine their resources, talents and find the means necessary to not only learn to live together, but to learn from one another.

While completing this book I often shared my feelings and ideas with a good friend, Ellen Finlan Wallace, a special education teacher and social activist. We would agree and disagree on certain subjects surrounding male and female issues, however each discussion seemed to illuminate and add spice to my original ideas and beliefs.

One day while Ellen and I were having coffee, we had an idea that we felt would foster the beginnings of male/female dialogue. We drew up several questions which we felt provided a balanced perspective on the changes that have occured since the women's movement's first stirrings. These questions offered a past, present and future perspective of the changes in male/female relationships while simultaneously providing an opportunity for both male and female opinions to be expressed. For the purpose of this unique dialogue, each of us responded to these questions by talking into a tape recorder, though these responses have been edited for easier reading the original content, as much as possible is presented. The questions we chose for our comments are reflective as we focused on men and womens relationships to date. These are the questions regarding **Men and Women's Relationships:**

1. Where have **we** been?

2. Where are **we** now?

3. Where are **we** going?

4. What has the women's movement contributed?

5. What is missing from Femininsim?

6. Men and women as allies - Is it possible?

7. What do men and women separately and together, need to do to become allies?

Ellen's comments:

Where have we been:

Traditionally men have always been the hunters, the providers, those who would seek work outside the home in order to provide for the family. Women, on the other hand, were the childbearers, those who would care for the home and essentially, the major child care person. Therefore, we have been living in a chiefly male-oriented, male-dominated society where the major decision makers have been men.

The pattern of men being the decision makers has continued for thousands of years. This changed when in the 60's both sexes demonstrated against the war in Vietnam and the injustice of society in general. As a result of this effect, women began to see that change could come about through demonstrations and educating the masses. In this way they could make their concerns known.

The cry of the women's movement was heard as women demanded the freedom men had in the work force and to be accepted for their mental ability as well.

In the 60's, women began to explore their world in new ways. They began to seek self-fulfillment, self-realization and to become more in touch with their inner selves and what they wanted. They began to work and put children into day care centers. As a result of these new goals for women many marriages split up and women sought freedom for themselves and a desire to change their roles.

Where are we now?

As a result of women's desire and moving to change their traditional roles. The relationships of men and women have been polarized. A distance factor is evident. Male and female relationships are different than before. Both sexes tend to be cautious of one another as both are licking their wounds resulting from the war between the sexes and now both are standing back and looking at what they have become.

During the onslaught of women's role transition many entered the work force and today many have moved into middle management positions. Rather than looking at the unhealthiness of the existing situation in the world of management and implementing new changes, new thoughts, new attitudes and possible better ways to operate businesses, they have tended to copy the same sort of rules and methodologies that men have. I believe this will change as women realize that there are better ways to operate a business than the typical "dog eat dog."

Additionally, a lot of men have had their masculine ego's shattered as they have had to give up some of their power and realize that women had something to say that was worthwhile. Many men are beginning to question many aspects about the work world and are starting to appreciate the finer gifts in life that exist externally, apart from the working world.

The war between the sexes has left scars within men and women presently, and in the past. Both are confused about what kinds of relationships they want with one another. Women, do not want to go back to their old roles, and they do not want to relinquish the sort of status they have now. A battle still goes on for some women who want to maintain a child care role and still have what they have worked and struggled to get.

Where are we going?

In spite of the many changes that women have made and the many that have joined the work world in middle management positions, it is still largely a male-dominated world. This will have to change. Most important here, is a birth of a new attitude that accepts people, male or female, for their human potentials, their gifts and talents that go beyond the usual societal labelling which keeps our potentials hidden and unrealized. It is not so important who does the job, but that the job gets done. If we can realize that we all have strengths and weaknesses, and that we are human, we can, together, achieve many goals. We need to remove ourselves from defining who is more dominant. It is possible for each of us, male or female, to achieve more of our potential. As long as we remain alienated from one another, there will also be alienation between cities, nations and the unity that is needed for world survival will never be possible.

It is time for men and women to recognize our differences and celebrate these differences instead of trying to be the same as the other. It is more important that we find ways needed to live in harmony and coexistence — to find the ways to understand one another on a deeper level so that this depth becomes the practice of interpersonal relationships.

What has the Women's Movement contributed?

I believe the women's movement has contributed more than just liberating women. It has brought about liberation for all people, especially minority groups. It has shown that both men and women have the same potentials, the same needs and desires when we look at things from more of a humanistic perspective.

Another thing the women's movement has contributed, though I don't see this as completely positive, is the militaristic ways they began expressing themselves. I think it was necessary to stand up and scream in order to be heard, however, this turned some people off. In the end it was worth it as women continued to stand up and express their concerns about the injustice in society.

What is missing from feminism?

The feminist outlook was entirely centered on females and they never offered any alternatives for coexistence with men. This created an anti-male feeling which was largely unfair to men.

Another area that feminism has not handled very well is their stance and/or attitude about the traditional role of mother and housekeeper. Those women who chose to stay home have been made to feel guilty that they were not contributing to the women's movement.

My personal opinion is that childrearing is one of the most important jobs one could have. Hopefully in the future, we will see this option available to both men and women so that a child care person is at home for at least a few years of the child's early life.

It is ironic that many women have screamed for equality and freedom and now with so many women in the work force and the present state of the economy many women cannot afford to stay home even if they wanted to. Men have always worked out of necessity not choice, perhaps this can change as well.

Men and Women as allies — Is it possible?

Men and women can be friends. It is very important for us to be compatible and companions. As long as we begin to recognize people, male or female, as human beings possessing needs and desires we will be on the road to achieving equality and mutuality.

Our society has become far too satisfied, isolating people in to separate groups that do not allow for necessary and vital communication between people. Our schools need to remove sexist literature that teaches young children prejudice and judgement towards others. Also, the media has to change its sexist, stereotypical attitude towards the sexes. Women are portrayed as being largely glamourous and seen only for their physical attributes and programs often depict only the "beautiful people" images that pressures audiences, outwardly and subliminally to conform to these media images.

Before men and women can become allies, each have to be allowed to grow and develop their potentials to the fullest. People will need to gain back their trust of one another and once again build this love into interpersonal relationships. People have been too alienated which has created further mistrust. To be allies, we have to get rid of the negative feelings that have been created and been locked within. By viewing it and expressing it, we can begin to build bridges between the gaps and learn to live in peaceful harmony.

What do men and women separately and together have to do to become allies?

The first thing that has to be done is recognize that the male-dominated world has perpetuated a lot of fear in people. The competition spirit has destroyed the sense of community which is possible only through cooperation.

Both sexes need to be more vocal about their concerns. Both need to recognize that we have been spoiled by our material world and that "things" have not brought us the happiness we seek.

The key to raising society's consciousness is educating people through group talks, community programs, support groups, workshops and other forms for consciousness raising. We also have to maintain a positive attitude, practicing in our lives, that which will carry over in our interactions with other people. We need to become models and leaders. People will have to take risks. We have to give without expecting anything in return or having hidden motives.

As an educator I would like to see more human relations type courses being offered to our young people. Already many are cynical as they believe that the world is going to blow up anyway, so why should they care. We need to instill a hope in our children and other people so they do not fear the future, and can believe they can create positive change.

I suspect things are going to get worse before they get better. With this we will need more support systems for people. Without these, people will go crazy. Both men and women will need to become more self-aware and more in touch with their inner self and resources, allowing those to direct and guide their path. Once we do this we will become happier as persons and when people begin to help others this will spread, affecting our lives and futures for the better.

Now I will offer my response to the six questions just as Ellen has done.

Where have we been?

Before the onset of the Industrial Revolution, men served as the protectors, providers for their families, as well as teachers and guides for their sons. Mother was the main caretaker for the children and a role model for the daughters.

Prior to the Industrial Revolution men were farmers, craftsman, and fisherman. The sons often followed in their father's footsteps tilling the land or working their craft. Men's role was to be a contributing member of the community and to carry on the family name which was passed onto their sons. Mothers took part in helping prepare the young boys for their apprenticeship with their fathers and for growing into men.

Following industrialization, the father's role still remained as the protector, the guide for his son and the caretaker for his daughter's choice of marriage partner. However, this role began to lessen as fathers became removed from the home and isolated from their sons and family. Mother's role expanded beyond caretakers to other duties once practiced by fathers.

During the industrialization period, education became a major priority in affluent western societies, as the growing industrial empire needed more competent, educated people to fill specialized positions. Education was also a means of shaping young people to the molds that society had set before them.

As the rise of technology took hold the family role became more intertwined with the dictates of the industrialized society. Parents became more like representatives or social parents, and their role was to prepare their offspring to play a part in the industrial dream. Women continued to function in child care roles. If they chose careers these were dictated by the norms of society which set the following allowable professions for women; teaching, nursing and secretarial etc.

As industrialization reigned, the more separate the roles and relationships between mothers and fathers, men and women became. Men became entrenched in their work duties and found themselves living two separate lives; the working man and the family man. Often the demands of his work overshadowed the family experience. Despite the father becoming more and more estranged from his family because of his commitment to the work world, this world provided the substance for the father provider role. The "company man" was born out of this situation as men gave more of themselves to the company, at a cost of their family relationships.

World War II saw a change in women's functions. While men were away at war, women filled the factories that were supplying the military needs of war. Women still cared for the children and served as dual parent roles in their husband's absence. Following the war and with the beginning of reconstruction and the baby boom, mothers once again became the main child care person as fathers went to work and or school. Again, absent fathers became strangers to their families. This pattern of family living persisted until the Vietnam War era. Again, men were required to fight their country's political skirmishes and because of the draft, the country's armed forces doubled. At the same time, the hippie and anti-war culture was growing, causing a national tailspin questioning and challenging socialized value systems. Parallel to this growing movement was the advent of the sexual revolution. The Pill provided sexual freedom for women to explore their inner purpose and to discover pleasure in their relationships with men without the fear of unwanted pregnancy.

During the 60's and 70's, the cry of women was heard around the world. Women were no longer playing second fiddle to men and demanded equality and a voice regarding society's function as well as certain rights they felt should be guaranteed them, such as; equal pay for equal work and the right to compete in the marketplace. The womens movement shook the very foundation of society as the feminine spirit told humanity it had created a dangerous imbalance and it was time to get back on track. Many women joined together under the banner of sisterhood and Kate Millet, Germaine Greer, Betty Freidan and Gloria Steinem became the high priestesses of the movement, providing the necessary intellectual arm of the movement to enable the voice to be heard by a predominantly masculinized society.

For a period of twenty to thirty years the women's movement, under the varied philosophical extractions of feminism, started to transform the male-dominated world. The women's movement has opened doors, not only from the social perspective but also of the human psyche. Some of the actions and attitudes of a few of the feminine groups have added to the problem, as their negative messages speak of men as enemies of women. This perspective has compounded many men's fears and feelings of inadequacies who are not yet ready to listen or look within themselves let alone, change themselves dramatically.

The women's movement has turned society upside down and has made men look at the denied parts of their humanness and it has provided an opportunity for women to explore other parts of themselves.

A lot more has to be done to manifest a more humane and balanced society. The women's movement has provided the initial major step for this to occur. Now it is up to men to begin our transcendence and as women continue theirs we can both move closer to a balanced perspective.

Where are we now?

Since the beginning of the women's movement the voice of women has been heard. More has to be done to bring about true equality but the change process has begun. Women's rights must be acknowledged on an equal parallel with men. In almost every work situation once predominantly male, women now fill positions, some at high executive levels. Women have become competitors and ambitious ones. The language has been somewhat altered to prevent the use and growth of sexist language. Any jobs that were male-oriented, even in a physical manner, such as telephone repair, plumbing, carpentry and construction, all have become infiltrated by women. On the other front, men have become secretaries, telephone operators, clerks of every description and are working in other positions once dominated by women. The pay scale is changing in some places and women can now make equal salaries as men. More and more women are becoming judges, senators, congresswomen and other legal and political representatives. For the first time, the U.S. has a woman in the Supreme Court and on the last voyage of the Space Shuttle Columbia, a woman was on the astronaut team. Members in every major city are continuing their fight for women's rights. Recently, the E.R.A. was almost passed as an amendment to the consitution. Eventually, it will become part of the Constitution.

Women have made giant steps in bringing about change in a male-dominated society. They have threatened social scripts and male egos which has resulted in men being more defensive. There is a fear that the radicalism of the women's movement will destroy the family. Women have found means to tap into their male side launching an assertive campaign to equalize their footing in society.

For the last several years women have expressed independence. Divorce is on the rise. It is common for youngsters these days to be raised by single parent mothers, and the reality of single parent fathers is also on the rise. Day care centers have become the surrogate parents for the many working single parents.

During the 70's, the period of "me-ism," the singles' scene was enjoyed by many males and females alike. Lately some people are finding one night stands and meat markets boring, insensitive and empty. For others, the noncommital lifestyle befits their levels of irresponsibility and immaturity.

In the last twenty years the war between the sexes has raged on. However, in recent years the smoke has cleared, and men and women stand fixed at the edge of transition, each cautious, wounded and confused. To survive we must join forces and use our resources and move forward as partners and allies, burying the hatchets of blame and abuse. We have both been hurt and it is unnecessary to put salt in these wounds.

This is a time to set realistic priorities. We are creating the future now, at every minute, and our goals need to be focused on the common concerns for these times.

What has the woman's movement contributed?

Primarily, I see the women's movement bringing to focus the need for balance. Masculine energy needs to be balanced with feminine power; aggression and action to be balanced with sensitivity and compassion. The women's movement has brought about a deeper awareness and concern for the potential and possibilities existing within people. The movement has helped men see through the unhealthy rigidity of the masculine super image. It has given society back its human soul.

What is lacking in feminism?

What is often characteristic of revolution is the tendency to "throw the baby out with the bathwater." In this case, the women's movement under the banner of feminism, forced many women to become isolated from males and even from some of their sisters. In their fight for equal rights, women are being forced to examine their souls beyond ideological forms and fixed habitual attitudes.

Romance has returned and the 80's can be seen as a period of settling. Marriage is on the rise and courtship and ritual is replacing the promiscuous affair.

Men and women in transition is the theme for the 80's. How we weather the storm is yet to be seen. However I have faith and optimism that men and women will find the methods necessary to cross the bridge to one another.

Where are we going?

The crises existing in the world today as the two nuclear powers, the U.S. and Russia, prepare themselves for a nuclear showdown, has created a shift in direction and goals for both men and women. Ardent feminists are finding themselves questioning many of their original stands on feminism and are taking responsibility for the anger they have stored within themselves and projected onto men. Men are having to accept women as whole persons and realize that behind the structure of feminist ideology lies the other half of his humanity.

This is a dangerous period in history. All peoples, in every nation, are beginning to recognize the sense of urgency and the need for collective concern and action to avert the nuclear threat. Men and women are having to put aside their individual battle swords and come to terms with the existing limitations. To be an equalized society will require time, unfortunately time is not what we have a great deal of. Women opened some wounds concerning their relations with men and anger, hatred, mistrust became a style of expression. Some of this was healthy as it forced men to get in touch with their own wounds and to learn how to listen again to their inner selves. It also alienated and placed men, generally, on the defensive. Women seemed to be throwing an emotional tantrum and all men, regardless, became the enemy and bore the brunt of their anger and hostility. As women learned to depend upon one another in a healthy supportive manner, they also widened the gap between themselves and men. Men were viewed as bad boys needing to be taught a lesson and to fend for themselves. It was now their turn to enjoy the so-called freedoms and powers for which men have always had the opportunity. Also, women who desired a more traditional homemaker/wife role were ostricized by many of their career-minded sisters.

The women's movement provided an anchor for women's growth and development as capable, competent human beings. Women had nothing to lose and everything to gain, but they lost ground as well. When individuals become locked into a fixed stance or perception, they are bound to lose contact with reality, becoming trapped in their own narrow beliefs of freedom. This one fault of feminism is expressed in the negative images created through its displayed anger and radicalism. The intense drive for power has caught others in the crossfire. The problem existing with radical, extreme beliefs is that the other half of the situation or issue is not seen, which causes unnecessary pain and conflict. Goals must be balanced and tapered with reality. Feminism, in certain ways, lost track of goals and became locked into the image of what it stood for. This is not much different from the men becoming prisoners of their image.

Men and Women as Allies - Is it possible?

I believe that we cannot question the possibility of men and women being allies, anymore — this is our only option. As long as we stand at a distance, fearing and mistrusting one another, the balance so necessary for our survival will not be manifested.

Men and women, everywhere, are striving to find the methods and styles of relating that do not alienate and reject the other. Both are attempting to contact the other. For some, it is a conscious move to build bridges and for others, it is an unconscious urge to heal the wounds and acknowledge similarities and differences.

Any men and women who truly feel love for people and see the survival of the planet as the most important priority for these times, are searching inside and outside themselves for the answers to the many existing dilemmas. This places them in a growth, expansive perspective. Men and women are being drawn to work separately and together, in filling the gaps not only between the opposite sexes, but also within their own sex. We are listening to the pulse of the human heart and moving instinctively towards a partnership with one another.

It is no longer a question of possibility for men and women to be allies. The process has begun.

What do men and women separately and together have to do to become allies?

Initially, men and women have to open themselves to this possibility. Women have already developed such a relationship among themselves. Now men have to do the same with men.

Separately and together, men and women need to create new and redefined ways to contact one another and deepen their communication and understanding. Men still need to know more about the world of women on a much deeper level and women need to expand their understanding about men's processes.

A unified effort to explore similarities and differences and tap the gifts and resources of both is necessary. The fullness, the substance of this combination of talents and energy will benefit both who go beyond the separatists' fragmented idea of male and female and move closer to a recognition of the human being. Once we recognize the human element first, the male or female qualities and differences will spring from this in a more healthy integrated way.

Most of all, both must see the other as they really are instead of trying to fit the other into some type of liberated image. Acceptance that we are only human, still learning and growing and both needing respect, love, support, and an opportunity to dialogue, to expand our ideas and feelings is essential. We are on a **human** journey and philosophical, political or religious ideologies must not have priority.

Concluding Note

What Ellen and I have shared in our duo-commentary, is an illustration on of the possibility of men and women finding the ways to engage in dialogue. Both of us could have said more and responded to the six questions in other ways. Others will have their own opinions and responses. What is important is that we have expressed our feelings about issues that have affected both males and females in society today. The attempt to address these selected questions was our creative effort to respond to some very important issues for both of us. We have respected one another's viewpoints, even though we disagreed with some of the context. We will probably continue to disagree on some of the issues, but we will discover more areas of connection as the dialogue continues.

What we have presented will not win any nobel prizes, however, this commentary symbolizes the beginning of a necessary communication between men and women. It is only a small step but it is a step from which we both can gain.

"I come with no easy blueprints for tomorrows constitution. I mistrust those who think they already have the answers when we are still trying to formulate the questions.

But the time has come for 'US' to imagine 'completely novel alternatives' ...to discuss, dissent, debate, and 'Design From the Ground Up' the democratic architecture of tomorrow.

Not in a spirit of anger and dogmatism, not in a sudden impulsive spasm, but through the widest, consultation and peaceful participation, we need 'To Join Together' to reconstitute America."

— Alvin Toffler

ASK WHAT YOU CAN DO TO BUILD TOMORROW

Two key words which broaden our future horizons for human survival are "service" and "participation." It is necessary for people who want to envision a world that is totally just, humane and equitable, to be part of the construction of that vision. It is time for citizens of this planet, of every continent, of every town and village, young and old to tear themselves away from the security of their status quo existence. Turn off the T.V. sets, stop believing and expecting someone else can solve their problems whether they be at the personal, community, national or global level. People who want change must be the agents of that desire. Every citizen must do more than stand in the voting lines or read about the election results in the newspaper. Citizens must begin to be active in humanizing governments, communities and themselves. They must find a piece of the action that matches their capabilities, and resources and which challenges them to step beyond their secure limitations.

If one is a leader or has talents in this area, then this must become his or her most challenging aspiration. We have just begun to realize and tap into our deepest of resources and these times demand that we go deeper than the tip of the iceberg. We must plunge beneath the layers of despair, fatalism and negativity and open ourselves to the vast intelligience and creative wisdom of our people. The society we create will be based on what we decide to do or not do. Nothing can be created out of nothing. Change and social reconstruction does not take place without citizen participation.

This involvement and service will manifest in the highest altruistic, creative tasks. Our task goes beyond other reconstruction periods of history as we walk this tightrope, on the edge of creation or potential destruction seeking timing, grace and rhythmic balance. These times see us having to stretch our imaginations, our mental and intuitive capacities and our desires to become psychic sculptors and gardeners.

We are all sowers of new seeds of purpose, mission and vision. It is our task to infiltrate our species with the hope of a new day and a new way of bringing forth coexistence. We are the fathers and mothers of a new age vision of human destiny and potential. Our commitment and involvement, on whatever level we choose, will be our most important and challenging choice. The fate of the planet is in our hands. All we need to do is reach out, touch and connect these hands no matter how near or far.

THE GLOBAL FAMILY OF "US" — Integration of masculine/feminine principles, body-mind instinct, the four races, religion and science and the planetary brain-heart.

> "WE ARRIVE UPON THIS EARTH ALONE, WE DEPART ALONE,
> THIS TIME CALLED LIFE WAS MEANT TO SHARE."

> — Rinder

Jesus, Mohammed, Buddah, Ghandi, Jung, the North American Indians, Albert Schweitzer, Mother Teresa and many other great human beings, have left libraries of wisdom which have taught and continue to teach us how to find the roots of our humanity and our purpose on this planet.

We are living in a time when the essence of their spirit is coming through in writings, events and actions to assist us in our final liberation. It is now up to US to pass these teachings on to others, to live the principles of these teachings and to do in the world what must be done to save us from our own demise. To succeed in transforming our destructive, masochistic tendencies and historical patterns, we will need to find the center of all these teachings and recognize and acknowledge the common currents that stream through them. We need to change our limited view of how we see the world, each country, each person, regardless of race, religion and belief system. We must see the oneness dimension in all that exists. We are not separate, isolated and we are not unequal. We possess all the conscious and unconscious recordings of the history of this planet, and all life on this planet. It matters not whether we are male and female. We are both and this principle guides the evolution of our lives. Our bodies are not separate from our minds, our animal natures nor any aspect of nature. The seeds of all life forms exist within us and lives and breathes all around us. Once we awaken to the wholeness, this greatness, this miracle of existence, we will no longer have to ask for it. It will be here, there and everywhere. We have endured ages of turmoil, upheaval, progress and movement in order to find the balance factor that exists and has always existed under the layers of misdirection, fear and uncertainty. Deep within, all the memories of our sojourn on this planet, are inscribed on the walls of the primitive caves of our unconscious. These tools, these artifacts of evolution, now need to be brought into the world and shared with one and all. Through this sharing, this dialogue, we can find the common ground and bonding that brings unity to our lives, and helps us to realize that we really are in this together, pooling our resources, giving and receiving. The mother and fathers of creation, in all aspects of our lives, can touch our minds, soothe our souls and guide us to the center of ourselves; to the heart of love of which we are all children, regardless of our beliefs, sex, age, color or creed. The great teachers throughout time always tried to teach us this or to remind us of it. Now we have to remind ourselves and share this in the reality of a new emerging way to be and to live in the world. This new way of building bridges, of being and living will be the new society.

The journey continues on. . .

BIBLIOGRAPHY

Adams, J.: **Making Good.** (Berkley Books, New York, 1981.)

Bach, G., Deutoch, R.: **Pairing.** (Peter Wyden Publishers, New York, 1979.)

Bandler, R., Grinder, R.: **Frogs Into Princes.** (The Free Press, New York, 1973.)

Becker, E.: **The Denial of Death.** (The Free Press, New York, 1972.)

Bednarik, K.: **The Male Crisis.** (Alfred A. Knopf, New York, 1979.)

Bernhard, Y.: **Self Care.** (Celestial Arts, Millbrae, California, 1975.)

Blythe, P.: **Stress.** (Pan Books, London, 1973.)

Bradley, M., Sanchick, L., Fagan, M., Woletzhi, T.: **Unbecoming Men.** (Times Change Press, Albion, California, 1971.)

Branden, N.: **The Psychology of Self Esteem.** (Nash Publishing, Los Angeles, California, 1969.)

　The Disowned Self. (Nash Publishing, 1972.)

Bridges, W.: **(Transitions.** (Addison Wesley, Reading, Massachusetts, 1980.)

Buscaglia, L.: **Love and Personhood.** (Fawcett Crest, New York, 1972.)

Campbell, J. (ed.): **The Portable Jung.** (Viking Press, New York, 1971.)

Castaneda, C.: **Journey to Ixtalan.** (Simon & Schuster, New York, 1972.)

Chesler, P.: **About Men.** (Simon & Schuster, New York, 1978.)

Conway, J.: **Men in Mid-Life Crisis.** (David C. Cook Publishing, Ilinois, 1978.)

Cousins, N.: **Human Options.** (W.W. Norton, New York, 1981.)

Dyer, W.: **The Sky's The Limit.** (Simon & Schuster, New York, 1980.)

Ehrenrich, B.: **The Heart of Men.** (Anchor Press, Doubleday, Garden City, New York, 1983.)

Ferguson, M.: **The Aquarian Conspiracy.** (J.P. Tarcher, Los Angeles, California, 1980.)

Frenkel, V.: **Man's Search for Meaning.** (Simon & Schuster, New York, 1959.)

Freud, S.: **Civilization and Its Discontent.** (Hogarth Press, Los Angeles, California, 1975.)

Freudenberger, N., Richelson, G.: **Burnout.** (Doubleday, New York, 1980.)

Fromm, E.: **Escape from Freedom.** (Avon Books, New York, 1941.)

　The Art of Loving. (Bantam Books, New York, 1956.)

Gillies, J.: **Friends.** (Harper & Row, New York, 1976.)

Goldberg, H.: **The Hazards of Being Male.** (Nash Publishing, New York, 1976.)

　The New Male (William & Morrow, New York, 1979.)

Golden, N.: **Passing Through Transition.** (The Free Press, New York, 1981.)

Greenwald, J.: **Be the Person You Want To Be.** (Dell Publishing, New York, 1976.)

Halpern, H.: **Cutting Loose.** (Bantam Books, New York, 1976.)

Harris, T.: **I'm Ok, You're Ok.** (Harper & Row, New York, 1967.)

Hayden, T.: **The American Future.** (Washington Square Press, New York, 1980.)

Heibrun, C.: **Towards a Recognition of Androgyny.** (W.W. Norton, New York, 1964.)

Huston, J.: **Life Force.** (Delta Books, New York, 1980.)

Huxley, L.: **You Are Not the Target.** (Wilshire Books, Hollywood, California, 1963.)

Jakins, H.: **The Human Side of Human Beings.** (Rational Island Pub., Seattle, Washington, 1978.)

James M., Jongeward, D.: **Born to Win.**(Addison Wesley, Reading, Massachusetts, 1971.)

Jampolsky, G.: **Love Is Letting Go of Fear.** (Celestial Arts, Milbrae, California, 1979.)

Janov, A.: **The Primal Scream.** (Petrigrel, New York, 1970.)

Johnson, R.: **He.** (Harper & Row, New York, 1974.)

Keen, S.: "War as the Ultimate Therapy," **Psychology Today,** June 1982.: 56 - 58.

Laing, R.: **The Divided Self.** (Penguin Books, New York, 1959.)

Leefeldt, C.: Callenbach, S., **The Art of Friendship.** (Berkley Books, New York, 1981.)

Leonard, G.: **The End of Sex.** (J.P. Tarcher, Los Angeles, California, 1983.)

Levinson, D. (ed.): **The Seasons of a Man's Life.** (Ballantine Books, New York, 1978.(

Lewis, R. (ed.): **Men in Difficult Times.** (Prentice Hall, Englewood Cliffs, New Jersey, 1981.)

May, R.: **The Courage to Create.** (Bantam Books, New York, 1975.)

Nesbitt, J.: **Megatrends.** (Warner Books, New York, 1982).

Newman, M., Berkowitz, B.: **How to Be Your Own Best Friend.** (Ballantine Books, New York, 1971.)

Nichol, J.: **Men's Liberation.** (Penguin Books, New York, 1975.)

Olsen, P.: **Sons and Mothers.** (Fawcett Crest, New York, 1981.)

Pleck, E., Pleck, J.: **The American Male.** (Prentice Hall, Englewood Cliffs, New Jersey, 1980.)

Powell, J.: **Why I Am Afraid To Tell You Who I Am.** (Argus, Illinois, 1969.)

Prather, H.: **Notes to Myself.** (Real People Press, Utah, 1979.)

Reich, W.: **The Murder of Christ.** (Simon & Schuster, New York, 1953.)

Rifkin, J.: **Ageny.** (Viking Press, New York, 1983.)

Robertstiello, R.: **A Man in the Making.** (Richard Mareh Pub., New York, 1979.)

Rogers, C.: **On Personal Power.** (Dell Publishing, New York, 1977.)

Rubin, H.: **Competing.** (Harper & Row, New York, 1980.)

Satir, V.: **People Making.** (Science & Behavior Books, Palo Alto, California, 1972.)
    Making Contact. (Celestial Arts, Millbrae, California, 1976.)

Sanford, J.: **The Invisible Partners.** (Paulist Press, New York, 1980.)

Schaef, A.W.: **Women's Reality.** (Wilston Press, Minnesota, 1981.)

Schell, J.: **The Fate of the Earth.** (Avon, New York, 1982.)

Schmall, M.: **Limits.** (Clarkston & Poltes, New York, 1981.)

Schnier, M. (ed.): **Femininism.** (Vintage Books, New York, 1972.)

Simonton, O., Simonton, S., Creighton, J.: **Getting Well Again.** (J.P. Tarcher, Los Angeles, California, 1978.)

Skjei, E., Rubin, R.: **The Male Ordeal.** (G.P. Putnam, New York, 1981.)

Shostrom, E.: **From Manipulation to Master.** (Bantam Books, New York, 1983.)

Speeth, K.: **The Gurdjieff Work.** (And/Or Press, Berkeley, California, 1976.)

Steiner, C.: **Scripts People Live By.** (Bantam Books, New York, 1974.)

Stevens, A.: **Archetypes.** (Quill, New York, 1983.)

Toffler, A.: **The Third Wave.** (Bantam Books, New York, 1980.)

Traner, P.: "Tootsie Drops His Guard," **People Magazine,** Jan., 1983.: 68 - 73.

Viscott, D.: **How to Live with Another Person.** (Arbor House, New York, 1974.)

Watts, A.: **The Wisdom of Insecurity.** (Random House, New York, 1951.)

Williamson, J.: **The Wisdom of the Subconscious Mind.** (Prentice-Hall, Englewood Cliffs, New Jersey, 1964.)

Woodward, K.: "Thinking the Unthinkable," **Newsweek,** July 1983, :31.

Zilberg, B.: **Male Sexuality.** (Little Brown, Boston, Massachusetts, 1978.)

"Resources for Men in Transition" was compiled in May, 1985 by Shepherd Bliss, Joseph Saah and Stephen Simon. Copies of this guide are available from The Men's Center for Counseling and Psychotherapy, 2925 Shattuck Avenue, Berkeley, CA 94705.

Please enclose $5.00 in currency for postage and handling.

Please write for permission to reproduce this material: Men's Centre for Counseling and Psychotherapy, 2925 Shattuck Avenue, Berkeley, California 94705.

BOOKS

Family and Fatherhood

Anderson, Christopher. *Father: The Figure and the Force.* New York: Warner Books, 1983.

Arcana, Judith. *Every Mother's Son.* New York: Doubleday, 1983.

Benson, Leonard. *Fatherhood: A Sociological Perspective.* New York: Random House, 1967.

Biller, H. and Meredith, D. *FatherPower.* New York: Doubleday, 1975.

Carmichael, C. *Non-sexist Childraising.* Boston: Beacon Press, 1977.

Colman, A. and Colman, L. *Earth Father/Sky Father: The Changing Concept of Fatherhood.* Englewood Cliffs, N.J.: Prentice-Hall, 1981.

Cottle, T.J. *Like Fathers, Like Sons: Portraits of Intimacy and Strain.* New Jersey, Ablex, 1981.

Hanson, S. and Bozett, F., eds. *Dimensions of Fatherhood.* Beverley Hills, CA: Sage Publications, 1985.

Humez, A. and Staely, K.F. *Family Man: What Men Feel About Their Wives, Their Children, Their Parents, and Themselves.* Chicago: Contemporary Books, 1978.

Lamb, M., ed. *The Role of the Father in Child Development.* New York: Wiley, 1976.

Levine, J. *Who Will Care for the Children? New Options for Fathers (and Mothers).* New York, Lippincott, 1975.

McFadden, M. *Bachelor Fatherhood.* New York: McKay, 1974.

Olson, P. *Sons and Mothers: Why Men Behave as They Do.* New York: M. Evans, 1981.

Parke, R.D. *Fathers.* Cambridge, MA: Harvard U. Press, 1981.

Rapaport, R & R. et al. *Fathers, Mothers, and Society: Perspectives on Parenting.* London, UK: Penguin, 1977.

Sayers, Robert. *Fathering: It's Not the Same.* Larkspur, CA: Nurturing Family Press, 1984.

Vitale, A., Neuman, E., Stern, M., Hillman, J., von der Heydt, V. *Fathers and Mothers.* New York: Spring Publications, 1973.

Yablonsky, Lewis, *Fathers and Sons.* New York: Simon and Schuster, 1982.

Gay Men

Clark, Don. *Loving Someone Gay.* New York: New American Library, 1977.

Gay Task Forc. *A Gay Bibliography.* Gay Task Force, Box 2382, Philadelphia, PA 19103: sixth edition, 1980.

Kassler, Jeanne. *Gay Men's Health.* (Available at Changing Men's Bookshelf, Amherst, MA.)

Katz, J. *Gay American History: Lesbian and Gay Men in the U.S.A.* new York: Avon Books, 1976.

Levin, Martin, ed. *Gay Men: The Sociology of Male Homosexuality.* New York: Harper and Row, 1979.

Silverstein, Charles, *Man to Man: Gay Couples in America.* New York: William Morrow. 1981.

Tripp, C.A. *The Homosexual Matrix.* New York: McGraw-Hill, 1975.

Weinberg, M. and Williams, C. *Male Homosexuals: Their Problems and Adaptations.* New York: Penguin, 1974.

Men's Movement

Lewis, Robert, Ed. *Men in Difficult Times.* Englewood Cliffs, N.J.: Prentice-Hall, 1981.

Pleck, J. and Sawyer, J. *Men and Masculinity.* Englewood Cliffs, N.J.: Prentice-Hall, 1974.

Shapiro, E. and Shapiro, B. *The Women Say, The Men Say.* New York: Delta Books, 1979.

Snodgrass, Jon, ed. *For Men Against Sexism.* Times Change Press, 1977.

Psychology and Mental Health

Bednarik, K. *The Male in Crisis.* New York: Knopf, 1971.

Chesler, Phyllis. *About Men.* New York: Simon and Schuster, 1978.

David, D. and Brannon, R. *The Forty-Nine Percent Majority: The Male Sex Role.* Addison-Wesley, 1975.

Hillman, James. *Loose Ends: Primary Papers in Archetypal Psychology.* Dallas: Spring Publications.

Hillman, James, ed. *Puer Papers.* Dallas: Spring Publications. 1979.

Johnson, Robert. *He: Understanding Masculine Psychology.* San Francisco: Harper and Row, 1974.

Kiley, Dan. *The Peter Pan Syndrome.* Dodd-Mead, 1984.

Kiley, Dan. *The Wendy Dilemma.* New York: Arbor House, 1984.

Levinson, Daniel et al. *The Seasons of a Man's Life.* New York: Knopf, 1978.

Miller, Stuart. *Men and Friendship.* Boston: Houghton Mifflin, 1983.

Moses, A. and Hawkins, R. *Counseling Lesbian Women and Gay Men.* St. Louis: C.V. Moseley Co., 1982.

Naifeh, S. and Smith, G.W. *Why Can't Men Open Up?* New York: Warner Books, 1984.

Osherson, Samuel. *Holding On or Letting Go: Men and Career Change at Mid-Life.* New York: The Free Press, 1980.

Pleck, Joseph. *Psychology Constructs the Male: The Rise and Fall of the Male Sex Role Identity Paradigm.* Cambridge: MIT Press, 1981.

Pleck, Joseph. *The Myth of Masculinity.* Cambridge: MIT Press, 1981.

Rubin, L. *Intimate Strangers: Men and Women Together.* New York: Harper and Row, 1983.

Skovholdt, T., Schauble, P. and Davids, R., eds. *Counseling Men.* Belmont, CA: Brooks/Cole, 1980.

Solomon, K. and Levy, N. *Men in Transition.* New York: Plenum, 1982.

Tiger, L. *Men in Groups.* New York: Random House, 1969.

von Franz, Marie-Louise. *Puer Aeternus.* Santa Monica, CA: Sigo Press, 1970-1981.

Sex Roles and Alienation

Brenton, M. *The American Male.* New York: Fawcett, 1966.

Farrell, W. *The Liberated Man: Beyond Masculinity.* New York: Random House, 1974.

Fasteau, Marc. *The Male Machine.* New York: McGraw-Hill, 1975.

Franklin, Clyde. *The Changing Definition of Masculinity.* New York: Plenum Press, 1984.

Goldberg, H. *The Hazards of Being Male: Surviving the Myth of Masculine Privilege.* New York: Sanford Greenburger Assoc., 1976.

Goldberg, H. *The New Male: From Self-destruction to Self-care.* New York: William Morrow, 1979.

Goldberg, H. *The New Male Female Relationship.* New York: William Morrow, 1983.

Nichols, Jack. *Men's Liberation: A New Definition of Masculinity.* New York: Penguin, 1975.

Health and Sexuality

Acacia, A., Maeda, A. and Mosmiller, T. *Men and Birth Control.* Oakland, CA: Center for Men's Health Education, 1983.

Beckstein, Douglas. *Men and Family Planning* (annotated bibliography). Center for Population Opinions, 2031 Florida Ave., N.M., Washington, DC 20009.

Chesterman, J. and Marten M. *Man to Man: Straight Answers to Every Man's Questions* 1980.

Chesterman, J. and Marten,M. *Man to Man: Straight Answers to Egery Man's Questions about Sexuality, Fitness, and Health.* Berkeley, 1978.

Crutcher, R. et al. *The Emerging Male: A Men's Handbook.* Arcata, CA: Emerging Men's Center, 1982.

The Diagram Group. *Man's Body: An Owner's Manual.* New York: Bantam Books, 1976.

Friday, N. *Men In Love: Men's Sexual Fantasies.* New York: Delacorte Press, 1980.

Gillette, P. *Vasectomy: The Male Sterilization Operation.* New York: Paperback Library, 1972.

Hapgood, Fred. *Why Males Exist: An Inquiry into the Evolution of Sex.* New York: William Morrow, 1979.

Hite, S. *The Hite Report on Male Sexuality.* New York: Knopf, 1981.

Julty, Sam. *Male Sexual Performance.* New York: Grosset & Dunlap, 1975.

Julty, Sam. *Men's Bodies, Men's Selves.* New York: Dell Press, 1979.

Kinsey, A., Pomeroy, W. and Martin, C. *Sexual Behavior in the Human Male.* philadelphia: Saunders, 1948.

McGill, M.e. *The McGill Report on Male Intimacy.* New York: Holt, Rinehart and Winston, 1985.

Milsten, R. *Male Sexual Function: Myth, Fantasy, and Reality.* New York: Avon, 1979.

Petras, J.W. *Sex: Male/Gender: Masculine Readings in Male Sexuality.* New York: Alfred Knopf, 1975.

Pietropinto, A. and Simenauer, J. *Beyond the Male Myth: What Women Want to Know About Men's Sexuality.* New York: Quadrangle, 1977.

Roen, Philip. *Male Sexual Health.* New York: Morrow, 1974.

Shanor, K. *The Shanor Study: The Sexual Sensitivity of the American Male.* New York: Ballantine, 1978.

Silber, S. *The male.* New York: Scribner, 1981.

Zilbergeld, Bernie. *Male Sexuality.* Boston: Little Brown, 1978.

History

Dubbert, J. *A Man's Place: Masculinity in Transition.* Englewood Cliffs, NJ: Prentice-Hall, 1979.

Filene, P. *Him/Her/Self: Sex Roles in Modern America.* New York: Simon and Schuster, 1975.

Kirschner, A., ed. *Masculinity in an Historical Perspective.* University Press of America, 1977.

Pleck, E. and Pleck, J. *The American Man.* Englewood Cliffs, NJ: Prentice-Hall, 1980.

Life Cycles and Development

Bowskill, D. and Linane, A. *The Male Menopause.* Los Angeles: Brooke House, 1978.

Farrell, M. and Rosenberg, S. *Men at Midlife.* Boston: Auburn House, 1981.

Filene, Peter. *Men in the Middle.* Englewood Cliffs, N.J.: Prentice-Hall, 1981.

Mayer, N. *The Male Mid-Life Crisis: Fresh Starts After 40.* New York: Doubleday, 1978.

General Interest

Avedon, B. *Ah, Men!* New York: A & W, 1980.
Bucher, Glenn. *Straight/White/Male.* Fortress Press, 1975.
Bush, S. *Men: An Owner's Manual.* New York: Simon and Schuster, 1984.
Daniell, R. *Sleeping With Soldiers: In Search of the Macho Man.* New York: Holt, Rhinehart, Winston, 1985.
Doyle, James. *The Male Experience.* Iowa: William Brown, 1983.
Ehrenreich, Barbara. *The Hearts of Men.* New York: Anchor Press, 1983.
Fishell, Elizabeth. *The Men in Our Lives (Fathers, Lovers, Husbands, Mentors.)* New York: William Morrow, 1985.
Goodman, A. and Walby, P. *A Book About Men.* London: Quartet, 1975.
Kaye, H. *Male Survival.* New York: Grossett & Dunlap, 1974.
Korda, M., *Male Chauvinism!* New York: Random House, 1974.
MSRB Press. *The Men's Survival Resource Book: On Being A Man in Today's World.* Minneapolis: MSRB Press, 1978.
Staples, R., ed. *The Black Family: Essays and Studies.* Belmont, CA: Brooks/Cole, 1971.
Staples, R. *Black Masculinity: The Black Man's Role in American Society.* San Francisco: The Black Scholar Press, 1982.
Wilkinson, L. and Taylor, R., eds. *The Black Male.* Chicago: Nelson-Hall, 1977.

PERIODICALS

Articles

"About Men," regular feature, *New York Times Magazine.*
Biller, H. Father absence and the personality development of the young child, *Developmental Psychology*, 2, 1970: 181-201.
Ehrenreich, B. A Feminist's View of the New Man, *New York Times Magazine*, May 20, 1984.
Pleck, J. and Brannon, R. *Male Roles and the Male Experience, Journal of Social Issues*, 34(1), 1978.
Pyke, Rafford. What Men Like in Men. *Cosmopolitan*, 1902.
Rubin, Zick. Fathers and Sons: The Search for Reunion, *Psychology Today*, June 1982.
Steinem, Gloria. The Myth of Masculine Mystique, *International Education*, 1, 1972: 30-35.
Tarvis, C. Masculinity, *Psychology Today*, 10(8), January 1977.
Thompson, K. On Being a Man: Keith Thompson talks with Robert Bly, *New Age*, May 1982.
Vontress, C. The Black Male Personality, *The Black Scholar*, 2(10), 1971: 10-17.

Magazines, Newsletters and Journals

Achilles Heel: A Magazine of Men's Politics. Men's Free Press, 7 St. Mark's Rise, London E8 2NJ, U.K.
Brother: The News Quarterly of the National Organization for Changing Men. N.O.C.M., Box 93, Charleston, IL 61920.
Canadian M.A.N. Terry Burrows, ed., Suite 506, 43 Eglinton Ave. East, Toronto, Ontario M4P 1A2.
Changing Men: Issues in Gender, Sex, and Politics, (formerly M). P.O. Box 313, 306 N. Brooks St., Madison, WI 3715.
Great Lakes Men's Network Newsletter. Bill LeGrave, ed., 3079 N. Humboldt Blvd., Milwaukee, WI 53212.
Journal of Homosexuality. Binghamton, NY: The Haworth Press.
The Men's Journal. Yevrah Ornstein, ed., P.O. Box 545, Woodacre, CA 94973.
Men's Studies Newsletter. Harry Brod, ed., THH331M, Univ. of Southern California, Los Angeles, CA 90089.
Network News. c/o Raven, P.O. Box 24159, St. Louis, MO 63130.

294

Nurturing News: A Forum for Men in the Lives of Children. c/o David Giveans, 187 Caselli Ave., San Francisco, CA 94114.
Reaching Out. A newsletter of the men's movement in the northeast. 906 S. 49th St., Philadelphia, PA 19143.
Research Report. An occasional publication. Wellesley College Center for Research on Women, Wellesley MA 02181.
Single Dad's Lifestyle. P.O. Box 4842, Scottsdale, Arizona.
Transitions. The Coalition of Free Men, P.O. Box 129, Manhasset, NY 11030.

Special Issues

AHP Newsletter, June 1984: "Men: New Realities." Bud Dickinson, guest ed., Association for Humanistic Psychology, San Francisco, CA 94103.
East West Journal, February 1964: "The Changing Image of Men's Health." Kushi Foundation Inc., Brookline, MA 02147.
Ebony Magazine, August 1983: "The Crisis of the Black Male." Johnson Publishing Co., Chicago, IL.
Medical Self-Care, Spring 1983, 620: "Men's Health." Inverness, CA.
Men: A Journal of the Re-evaluation Counselling Community. Rational Island Publishers, Seattle, WA.
Ms, August 1984, 13(2): "What Men Haven't Said to Women." New York.
Sojourner: A New England Women's Journal of News, Opinion and the Arts, May 1982, 7(9): "Still a Man's World?" Cambridge, MA.
Therapy Now Magazine, Summer 1985 2(2): "Men in Transition." Toronto, Ontario.
Voices: The Art and Science of Psychotherapy, Fall 1984, 20(3): "Emerging Concerns in the Psychotherapy of Males." New York.
Win, April 11, 1974, 10(13): "Men."
Yoga Journal, March/April 1984, 655: "Men in Changing Times." Berkeley, CA.

OTHER WRITTEN RESOURCES

Bibliography and Information Resources

Bibliography of the Men's Studies Collection. 4th edition, January 1980. Human Studies Collection, M.I.T. Humanities Library, Cambridge, MA 02139.
Changing Men's Bookshelf: Food for Thought and Books, 67 N. Pleasant St., Amherst, MA 02102.
The Male Sex Role: A Selected and Annotated Bibliography, K. Grady, R. Brannon and J. Pleck. Superintendent of Documents, U.S. Government Printing Office, Washington, DC 20402.
Men's Studies, Eugene August. University of Dayton, Libraries Unlimited Inc., P.O. Box 263, Littleton, CO 80160. $30.
Men's Studies Syllabi, Sam Femiano. 22 East St., Northampton, MA 01060. Packet cost $10. (Syllabi from 30 courses.)

Literature and Personal Accounts

Bell, Donald. *Being A Man: The Paradox of Masculinity.* Brattleboro, VT: Lewis, 1982.
Benice, T. *Men on Rape: What They Have To Say About Sexual Violence.* New York: St. Martin's Press. 1982.
Brownmiller, S. *Against Our Will: Men, Women and Rape.* New York: Simon and Schuster, 1975.
Diamond, Jed. *Inside Out: Being My Own Man.* San Rafael, CA: Fifth Wave Press, 1983.
Firestone, Ross. *A Book of Men: Visions of the Male Experience.* New York: Stonehill, 1975.

Gerzon, Mark. *A Choice of Heroes: The Changing Face of American Manhood*. Boston: Houghton Mifflin, 1982.

Gittleson, N. *Dominus: A Woman Looks at Men's Lives*. New York: Harcourt, Brace, Jovanovich, 1978.

Kriegel, Leonard, ed. *The Myth of American Manhood*. New York: Dell Publishing, 1978.

Kriegel, Leonard. *On Men and Manhood*. New York: Hawthorne Books, 1979.

Maclean, Norman. *A River Runs Through It and Other Stories*. Chicago: University of Chicago Press, 1976.

Mason, Herbert, *Gilgamesh: A Verse Narrative*. Boston: Houghton Mifflin, 1970.

Michaels, Leonard. *The Men's Club*. New York: Avon Books, 1978.

Rubin, Michael. *Men Without Masks: Writings From the Journals of Modern men*. Reading, MA: Addison-Wesley, 1980.

Manuals and Booklets

Disarmament and Masculinity: On Sexual Violence and War, by John Stoltenberg.

Facilitator's Manual for Men's Consciousness Raising and Support Groups, Metro Center YMCA, Seattle, WA.

Fact Sheets on Institutional Sexism, pamphlet, 1982.

Male Pride and Anti-sexism, c/o California Anti-sexist Men's Political Caucus, 828 Spruce St., Berkeley, CA 94704.

Punt, Pop (A Male Sex Role Manual), Hershel Thornburg. Tucson, AZ: Help Books, 1978.

Men In Art and Film

Mellen, Joan. *Big Bad Wolves: Masculinity in the American Film*. New York: Pantheon, 1978.

Spoto, Donald. *Camerado: Hollywood and the American Man*. New York: New American Library, 1978.

Waltes, Margaret. *The Nude Male: A New Perspective*. New York: Paddington, 1974.

Pending Books

Baunili, F., ed. *Men Freeing Men: An Anthology of Writings About Men's Liberation*. New Jersey: Ed. Stevenson (September, 1985).

Brod, Harry, ed. *Men's Studies: New Perspectives on Masculinity*. Los Angeles, CA: Univ. of Southern California (Spring, 1986).

Egendorf, Arthur. *Healing From the War: Trauma and Transformation After Vietnam*. Boston: Houghton Mifflin (1985).

Greif, G. *Single Fathers*. Lexington Books (1985).

Kaufman, M. *Patriarchy and Power: The Challenge Facing Men*. Toronto: New University (1985-1986).

Lewis, Robert, ed. *Men in Families*. Berkeley, CA: Sage (1985).

Lesis, Robert, *Men's Changing Roles in Families*, Binghampton, NY: Haworth Press (1986).

Kort, C. and Friedland, R. *The Father's Book*. Boston: Hall (1986).

Osherson, S. *Finding Our Fathers: Understanding Men's Struggles with Identity and Intimacy*. New York: The Free Press (Spring 1986).

Poetry

Bly, Robert, *The Man in the Black Coat Turns*. New York: Penguin Books, 1981.

Kass, Jared. *Mantalk: One Man's Healing Journey*. Cambridge, MA: Greenhouse, 1981.

Miller, Sidney. *Play the Melody*. Time Out Press, 1983.

Perlman, Jim, ed. *Brother Songs: A Male Anthology of Poetry*. Minneapolis: Holy Cow! Press, 1979.

Shnider, J., ed. *Divided Light — Father and Son Poems: A 20th Century Anthology.* New York: The Sheep Meadow Press, 1983.

FILMS AND VISUAL MEDIA

A Man, 22 min., b/w. The About Men Workshop, 45-14th Ave., Long Island City, NY 11104.

A Man's Place, 30 min., color. Institute for Research and Development in Occupational Education. C.U.N.Y Graduate Center, 33 42nd Street, New York, NY 10036.

Between Men: Masculinity and the Military. Will Roberts, 59 min., color. United Documentary Film, P.O. Box 315, Franklin, NJ 07417.

Caution: Men Working, 140 slides and 18 min. cassette. C.S. Productions, 400 Sibley St., St. Paul, MN 55101.

Changing Men: A Film About The Men's Movement and the Lives of men, Leonard Kurz. Changing Men Productions, P.O. Box 40025, San Francisco, CA 94140.

Fathers, 23 min. Churchill Film, 662, N. Robertson Blvd., Los Angeles, CA 90069.

Heroes and Strangers, Lorna Rassmussen and Tony Heriza, 29 min. Distributed by New Day Films, 22 Riverview Dr., Wayne, NJ 07470.

Masculinity: Fact or Act? 78 slides and 20 min. cassette. Men's Resource Center, 3534 S.E. Main, Portland, OR 97214.

Men in Early Childhood Education, 24 min. Distributed by David Giveans, Davidson Films, 231 "E" St., Davis, CA 95616.

Men's Lives, Will Roberts and Josh Hanig, 44 min., color. New Day Films, 22 Riverview Dr., Wayne, NJ 07470.

New Relations: A Film About Fathers and Sons, Ben Achtenberg. Plainsong Productions, 47 Halifax, Jamaica Plain, MA 02130.

Positively Men, 25 min. Positigvely Men Films, RFD 119A, Apple Valley Road, Ashfield, MA 01330.

To Have and To Hold: documentary film about men who batter women. New Day Films Co-op Inc., P.O. Box 315, Franklin Lakes, NJ 07417.

MUSICIANS

Peter Alsop, P.O. Box 960, Topanga, CA 90290. Songwriter, musician.

Gary Lapow, 2141 Stuart St., Berkeley, CA 94705. Singer, songwriter.

Geof Morgan, NEXUS, c/o Ellen Lefkowitz, P.O. Box 2527, Berkeley, CA 94702. Singer, guitarist.

Charlie Murphy, Good Fairy Productions, P.O. Box 12188 Broadway Station, Seattle, WA 98102.

Romanovsky and Phillips (Ron and Paul), Fresh Fruit Records, 302-2269 market St., San Francisco, CA 94114. Singers, performers.

Willie Sordill, Folkways, 43 W. 62st St., New York, NY 10023.

"Walls to Roses: Songs for Changing Men." Folkways, 3-20 Highland Ave., Cambridge, MA 02139.

Tom Wilson Weinberg, Aboveground Records, P.O. Box 497, Boston MA 02112. Songwriter, performer.

Winds of the People Songbook: words and guitar chords to over 600 songs of struggle and freedom, including many songs for changing men. Available at Changing Men's Bookshelf, Amherst, MA 02102.

MEN'S TROUPS DIRECTORY

Canada

COLLECTIF MASCULIN CONTRE LE SEXISME, 3945 rue Laval, Montreal, Quebec H2W 2H9.

LE GROUPE D'HOMMES CONTRE LA PORNOGRAPHIE ET L'EXPLOITATION SEXUELLE, 842 Murray, Quebec City, Quebec G1S 3B3.

TORONTO MEN'S CLEARINGHOUSE, Suite 204, 170 St. George St., Toronto, Ontario M5R 2M8. (416) 2230025.

TORONTO MEN'S NETWORK, Suite 204, 170 St. George St., Toronto, Ontario M5R 2M8. (416) 233-0025.

VANCOUVER MEN AGAINST RAPE, Box 65306, Station F, Vancouver, B.C. V5N 5P3.

United States

ABUSERS CHANGING THEMSELVES, Emerson House, 645 N. Wood St., Chicago, IL 60622.

AMEND, c/o YWCA, 9th and Walnut Streets, Cincinnati, OH 45202.

BROTHER TO BROTHER, 903 Broad St., Providence, RI 02907.

BROTHERS IN CHANGE, P.O. Box 24159, St. Louis, MO 63130.

CAL. ANTI-SEXIST MEN'S POLITICAL CAUCUS (CAMP), 828 Spruce St., Berkeley, CA 94704.

CHICAGO MEN'S GATHERING, P.O. Box 11076, Chicago, IL 60611.

COLORADO MEN'S NETWORK, 158 Fillmore St., Suite 408, Denver, CO 80206.

COMMENCE, c/o Women Helping Women, 261 E. 9th St., Cincinnati, OH 45202.

EMERGE (A Men's Counselling Service on Domestic Violence), 25 Huntington Ave., Rm. 324, Boston, MA 02116.

GREAT LAKES MEN'S NETWORK, P.O. Box 1441, Madison, WI 53710.

ITHACA MEN'S NETWORK, c/o Robert Heasley, 301 Maple Ave., E2, Ithaca, NY 14850.

MADISON MEN'S CENTER, c/o 306 N. Brooks St., Madison, WI 53715.

MANREACH, 4561 Woodlark Lane, Charlotte, NC 28211.

MEN AGAINST RAPE IN TUCSON, P.OF. Box 41501, Tucson, AZ 85717.

MEN FOR NONVIOLENCE, INC., 1122 Broadway, Fort Wayne, IN 60611.

MEN, INC. 211 4th St., Room 304, Juneau, AK 88901.

MEN'S ALTERNATIVES TO VIOLENCE, c/o Humboldt Open Door Clinic, P.O. Box 367, Arcata, CA 95521.

MEN'S AWARENESS NETWORK (MAN), 428 N. Farwell Ave., Milwaukee, WI 53202.

THE MEN'S CENTER, 122 W. Franklin Ave., Rm. 100, Minneapolis, MN 55407.

THE MEN'S CENTER FOR COUNSELING AND PSYCHOTHERAPY, 2925 Shattuck Avenue, Berkeley, CA 84706.

MEN'S CENTER OF SOUTH FLORIDA, 3301 NE 5th Ave., Suite 418, Miami, FL 33137.

MEN'S CURRICULUM TASK GROUP, Ohio State Univ. Rape Education and Prevention Program, 498 Ohio Union, 1739 N. High St., Columbus, OH 43210.

MEN'S PROJECT, INC. 102 Westport Allen Center, 706 W. 42nd St., Kansas City, MO 64111.

MEN'S RESOURCE CENTER, Viking Sudent Union, Western Washington University, Bellingham, WA 98221.

MEN'S SUPPORT CENTER, 3C-1900 Fruitvale Ave., Oakland, CA 94601.

MEN'S SUPPORT NETWORK, P.O. Box 101071, Anchorage, AK 99510.

MID-MISSOURI MEN'S RESOURCE GROUP, P.O. Box 94, Columbia, MO 65201.

NATIONAL ORGANIZATION FOR CHANGING MEN, 814 Blackhawk Dr., University Park, IL 60466.

NEW BRUNSWICK/PRINCETON/TRENTON MEN'S GROUP, 311 N. 4th Ave., Highland Park, NJ 08904.

THE NEW YORK CENTER FOR MEN, 251 Central Park West, New York, NY 10024.

NORTHEASTERN MEN'S EMERGING NETWORK, J. Breckenbridge, 75 Sunset Ave., Amherst, MA 01002.

NORTHERN LAMBDA NORD, P.O. Box 990, Caribou, ME 04736.

OASIS (Organized Against Sexism and Institutionalized Stereotpyes), 87 Irving St.,

Sommerville, MA 02144.

PITTSBURGH MEN'S COLLECTIVE, 5512 Bartlett St., Pittsburgh, PA 15217.

ROCHESTER MEN'S NETWORK, Box 10514, Rochester, NY 14610.

SAN FRANCISCO MEN'S NETWORK, P.O. Box 421690, San Francisco, CA 94942.

SEATTLE MEN AGAINST RAPE, 1425 E. Prospect St., No. 1, Seattle, WA 98112.

SEXUAL ASSAULT SERVICE FOR MEN, 1502 Nicollet Ave. S., Suite 25, Minneapolis, MN 55403.

SHORT MOUNTAIN SANCTUARY, Rte. 1, Box 987A, Liberty, TN.

TACOMA MEN COOPERATING TO END SEXUAL VIOLENCE, 811 N.L. St., Tacoma, WA 98403.

TUCSON MEN'S COOPERATIVE, P.O. Box 41501, Tucson, AZ 85717.

VALLEY MEN'S NETWORK, 400 Warren Wright Rd., Belchertown, MA 01007.

Others

MEN'S CONTACT AND RESOURCE CENTER, 109 Young St., Parkside, South Ausralia 5063.

MEN'S STUDIES PROGRAMS AND COURSES

(Originally compiled by Sam Femiano.)

Amherst College, Amherst, MA 01002 (Kim Townsend).

Wellesley College, Wellesley, MA 02181 (Joseph Pleck).

Southern Connecticut State University, New Haven, CT 06515 (Stephen Dworkin).

Rutgers University, New Brunswick, NJ 08903 (Michael Kimmel).

Brooklyn College, Broklyn, NY 11230 (Robert Brannon).

Siena College, Loudonville, NY 12211 (Merle Longwood).

Temple University, Philadelphia, PA 19122 (Neal Cazenave).

Univ. of Delaware, Newark, DE 19711 (Margaret Anderson).

Univ. of North Carolina, Chapel Hill, NC 27514 (Peter Filene).

Univ. of Southern Florida, Tampa, FL 33620 (Joseph Ferrandino).

Univ. of Dayton, Dayton, Ohio 45469 (Eugene August).

Univ. of Detroit, Detroit, MI 48221 (John Staudenmaier).

United Theological Seminary, New Brighton, MN 55112 (James Nelson).

Mankato State University, Mankato, MN 56001 (Denny Braun).

Washington University, St. Louis, MO 63130 (Don Long).

Univ. of Southern California, Los Angeles, CA 90089 (Harry Brod).

Cal. State University, Long Beach, CA 90840 (Marti Fiebert).

Ohlone College, Fremont, CA 94539 (Alan Kirschner).

Cal. State University, Hayward, CA 94542 (Michael Messner).

John F. Kennedy Unviersity, Orinda, CA 94563 (Shepherd Bliss).

Univ. of California, Berkeley, CA 94704 (Robert Blauner).

Sonoma State University, Rohnert Park, CA 94928 (Clarice Stasz).

Univ. of Oregon, Eugene, OR 97403 (Martin Acker).

TO THE READER. . .

Now that you have read the book I would appreciate receiving your comments. As I continue to learn and grow, your response will support this. Additionally, if you or someone you know, are interested in having me give a workshop, talk on mens, men/women relationships or other subjects, please be in touch. Write to me at:

> Dr. Frank Cardelle
> Rainbow Bridge Programs International
> P.O. Box 2039
> Winnipeg, Manitoba
> Canada R3C 3R3

Affections
Frank

AUTHOR:

Frank Cardelle is an international therapist, trainer and author with twenty years in the field of Psychotherapy and Education. He has pioneered in men's and men/women issues and other human development areas, conducting workshops, talks and trainings in twelve countries, i.e.: Eastern and Western Europe, U.S.A., Canada, South America and the U.S.S.R. His approach has greatly been influenced through his work with Canadian Indian and Inuit people.

He is founder/director of Rainbow Bridge Programs International and travels extensively as a trainer and consultant at centers, campuses and conferences throughout the world.

Besides "Journey To Brotherhood" he has authored "Youth and Adult: The Shared Journey Towards Wholeness" (Gardner Press), and "Self-Care for Educators" (Spanish edition only).

Frank is a member of Psychotherapists for Social Responsibility and the International Family Therapy Association. Articles about his work have appeared in Esotera Magazine (Germany), 'The Men's Journal,' (U.S.A.) and other foreign media presentations.